CONJUNCTIONS

Bi-Annual Volumes of New Writing

published by Bard College

CONJUNCTIONS is published in the Spring and Fall of each year by Bard College, Annandale-on-Hudson, NY 12504. This issue is made possible in part with the generous funding of the National Endowment for the Arts, and with public funds from the New York State Council on the Arts, a State Agency.

SUBSCRIPTIONS: Send subscription orders to CONJUNCTIONS, Bard College, Annandale-on-Hudson, NY 12504. Single year (two volumes): $18.00 for individuals; $40.00 for institutions and overseas. Two years (four volumes): $32.00 for individuals; $80.00 for institutions and overseas. Patron subscription (lifetime): $500.00. Overseas subscribers please make payment by International Money Order. For information about subscriptions, back issues, and advertising, call Michael Bergstein at (845) 758-1539 or fax (845) 758-2660.

Editorial communications should be sent to Bradford Morrow, *Conjunctions,* 21 East 10th Street, New York, NY 10003. Unsolicited manuscripts cannot be returned unless accompanied by a stamped, self-addressed envelope. Electronic and simultaneous submissions will not be considered.

Conjunctions is listed and indexed in the American Humanities Index.

Visit the *Conjunctions* Web site at www.conjunctions.com.

Cover design by Jerry Kelly, New York. Cover paintings by Walton Ford. Front: *Morire de Cara al Sol,* 2004, watercolor, gouache, ink, and pencil on paper, 41½ x 29 inches; rear: *Pandit,* 1997, watercolor, gouache, ink, and pencil on paper, 59½ x 40½ inches. Reproduced by kind permission of Paul Kasmin Gallery. Photograph of John Ashbery © 2007 The Richard Avedon Foundation.

Available through D.A.P./Distributed Art Publishers, Inc., 155 Sixth Avenue, New York, NY 10013. Telephone: (212) 627-1999. Fax: (212) 627-9484.

Printers: Edwards Brothers

Typesetter: Bill White, Typeworks

ISSN 0278-2324
ISBN 978-0-941964-65-4

Manufactured in the United States of America.

TABLE OF CONTENTS

A WRITERS' AVIARY

Edited by Bradford Morrow

Birding with Lanioturdus

Peter Orner

> *Learning to identify birds is a long and slow process and it takes years of experience to develop the skills needed to tell obscure species from the "little brown jobs"; herein lies the challenge and fascination . . .*
>
> —*Known Birds of Southwest Africa* (1973)

NORTH OF GOAS FARM, along the eastern edge of the Namib, the scrub reaching out before us, the knobby Erongo Mountains rising like blue elbows in the distance. We roam, Obadiah and I, along Krieger's fence line to our spot. Behold Krieger's fence! So expertly and lovingly barbed, it was as if the mad German had gone out there and braided the wire deadly sharp with his own fat hands. A flesh-shredding great wall that stretched gleamingly across the veld for kilometers. And beyond it—the only standing water east of the C-32 and hence birds, at least in theory, birds. Where were the birds?

I must tell you that when we birded, he wasn't he and I wasn't I. So maybe in this way our failure could be attributed to our alternate selves? He was Lanioturdus, the doyen of field identification, and I—I—was his faithful assistant Dieter though sometimes Lanioturdus called me Chauncey.

We'd been out there a couple of hours looking for a slight tremble in the branches. We with our checklist and nothing checked off. We saw sparrows, lots of sparrows, as if they had collectively decided to taunt our incompetence. Can't you two dopes see anybody but us? We'd finished our second half pint of Zorba. According to Lanioturdus it was disrespectful to sit while birding so we stood and my feet were as catatonic as my brain when I saw, yes, an actual bird. It had a red chest and thick red feathers that crept all the way up beneath its beak. A black head and tiny eyes that didn't blink when it hovered in front of us like a hummingbird. It stared as if it was out there finding us and not the other way around. *Field marks:* Seed-cracking bill. White mustastchial flash down the chin. Rufous-buff underparts. Then it dive-bombed so fast beyond the bush my eyes couldn't follow. It wasn't much bigger than a weaver and I would have thought it was one, but for all that bloodish red.

"What was that?"

"What was what?"

"The bird."

"What bird?"

"Just now. A bird. We just—"

"We?"

"What do you mean, Doyen? Red with a black head. Eyes that didn't blink. Looked like a weaver but red. Seed-cracking bill. White flash down the wings. Rufous-buff underparts. It was right here, right—"

"It wasn't a weaver."

"So you did see it."

Lanioturdus rubbed his beard, squinted. Then he yawned, inwardly, without opening his mouth, and murmured more to himself than to me, "Do visions ever translate? Red? Mayn't it just as likely have been off-white with a brown necklace and slightly glossy plumage? These things are possible."

"A chest-banded plover? I'm telling you it was red. Red with a black head. Come on—what do you call it?" I took out my book and started whipping through birds, all the birds we had yet to see, ever to see: whindrels, phalaropes, scrimpter bills, avocets, helmet-shrikes, fly-catching cuckooshrikes, fork-tailed drongos (*Dicrurus adsimilis*), ant-eating chats, Cape Peninsula tits, short-toed rock thrushes. . . .

"Call it?" Lanioturdus said.

"Why are you withholding on that bird?"

The Doyen sighed, pulled his hands down his long, sad face. Teacher Pohamba said that Teacher Obadiah's face got sadder and longer in winter—but that it was only a storyteller's trick. It's as if, Pohamba said, he sheds leaves not for regeneration, but for effect. Anything so he can bore us to death with his wisdom.

Then Lanioturdus began to hold forth. He orated to a faraway space above my head, to the mountains. "White flash down the wing? Rufous-buff underparts? Impossible. Such a bird does not exist. Call it? Call it? Always call it. And the moment we do? What happens? We are lulled into believing we have reached a sort of détente between the understanding and the dark. You think you can conquer all with call it? There was no bird, Dieter. *There never was any bird.*"

"But you're the one who memorizes, who dreams nightly of Cape Peninsula tits—"

"Tits? Yes. Did I say I wasn't guilty?"

"You just said—"

"Listen—is there anything more useful as a means of control than names? Oh, yes, I'm guilty as sin. Where's the noose? We name our children. Names aren't hopes—they're commands. Listen, God comes to a man named Abram and says I'm changing your name. The man's ninety and for his ninety years he's been called Abram, a good enough name as any. But now God says, Listen, Abram, you're Abraham now. And not only this. Congratulations. You're the father of a people. As long as you snip their foreskins. Understand? So Abram says, Fine, I'm Abraham, and no problem about the foreskins. We'll do it when they're defenseless babies so that they will only have a vague memory of the pain, a memory that will linger, but remain unidentifiable. So then God says, Wonderful, wonderful. And there's something else. You're also going to be a father again—literally a father again. With Sarah? Abram-Abraham says. But she's a barren old biddy! Trust me, God says. All you have to do is name the boy Isaac. Isaac—for laughter. Oh thank God, thank God, Abram-Abraham says. But God says—There's only one last thing. Anything, God, anything!

"And so God says, When the boy's five I want you to take him to the mountain and kill him."

Lanioturdus laughed, a rare outward laugh for a man who usually stifled his laughter down into his beard.

"Take him to the mountain and kill him! That's funny. Isaac for laughter! Hilarious! But, see, we need not reach so far back. I knew a woman at Otjiwarango who adopted children. People came from hundreds of k's away to give her their children. The woman's condition was that she be authorized to rename them. Mandela, Michael Jackson, Oginga Odinga, Zephia Kameeta, Kwame Nkrumah, Einstein, Lubabamba, Bobby Kennedy, Pope Pius XII, Indira Gandhi, Weimar, Muhammad Ali, Angela Davis, Toivo ja Toivo, Martin Luther. . . . How would you like this? One day you wake up and your name is Anwar Sādāt? Don't you see the danger in your calling it? In your giving names?"

I held the last of the Zorba to my lips, but didn't drink. He could take you back is what people said about him. Even the most cynical teachers on the farm said that Obadiah could, when he got going, take you whirling back to your seven-year-old self. You at your desk befuddled. Your little feet swinging. When the world was still a beautiful mystery and the tall, gaunt teacher with the wings of gray hair was the only God who could explain it. Master Obadiah, the Great Unraveler.

That day out by Krieger's fence he was wearing shorts. His old, beautiful legs were like withered trees. On his feet were his best tasseled loafers. The wind dusted our faces.

"Weimar?"

"It used to mean hope."

We took the shortest route back to the farm, along the C-32. On the way we came upon a donkey that had been hit by a lorry but hadn't died yet. He was simply wandering along, bleeding. He'd once been white with brown spots, but the blood had soaked his fur from his hindquarters to his neck. We had no water to give him, only commiseration, which he seemed to want to stomp us for suggesting. Obadiah tried to give him one of his loafers to chew on, but the donkey wouldn't take it.

"I am no use to man or beast," Obadiah said to the crust of the afternoon moon. "Farewell, Bucephalus."

He chucked the shoe in the veld. The donkey zigzagged forward along the road as he bled. About half a kilometer from the farm, he dropped.

Later I find the bird. It's not rare, rather common, but a lurker, always among us, but seldom observed. Tends to skulk in the undergrowth. Common name: crimson-breasted shrike. Scientific name: *Laniarus atrococcineus.*

A Flock Descends Into the Pentagonal Garden

Howard Norman

"YOU DIDN'T RESCUE me. I wasn't about to do any damage to myself."

In Halifax they're filming a movie based on my novel, *A Flock Descends into the Pentagonal Garden,* and I want nothing to do with it. Rights sold for $125,000 Canadian. This allowed me to purchase a cottage here in the village of Port Medway from Philip and Cynthia, who live across the road. In fact, I bought it not quite sight unseen, as I'd studied photographs of the interior and an aerial view of its four wooded acres. The cottage has five rooms. It's built along simple lines. Big windows. The kitchen gets the most, but there's good light throughout. From the bedroom I can see the curve of beach, the cove, the farther Atlantic. I work in the second-floor study, a converted attic, really. Not writing much of late, though. Some sort of *rigor mortis.* Frozen in the moment. It's fine. Familiar impasse. Anyway, the movie's producer is a hideous fellow named B. Kremiker, an Icelander. He was quoted in *The Halifax Herald* as saying, "The progress of this picture is the progress of my soul." Who talks like that? Dunce. Last week Kremiker's assistant, Lily Sventgartot, telephoned to say, "Mr. Kremiker prays you'll soon visit the shoot." I immediately arranged for an unlisted number. The shoot, I'm told, is any location at which cast and crew are working. Prays, does he? I will not go out to the shoot. Eight fifteen p.m.—"unseasonably warm for October," the radio says. Full moon tonight. I wonder if I'll witness our local librarian, Marlais Olivant, dressed again in black rain slicker and black galoshes, line books up on the sand. When I saw her doing this last night, I kept my distance but asked after her well-being, as anyone might. What was it she said? Oh, yes: "You didn't rescue me. I wasn't about to do any damage to myself."

*

In telephone conversations leading up to principal photography, which began on September 23, B. Kremiker frequently used certain phrases whose encoded surfaces obfuscated deep hostility, not only toward me but toward language itself. These were verbal sleights of hand, standard-issue non sequiturs no doubt sponsored by the systemic insidiousness of the movie business—not actual language at all, but annulments of language, erasures of meaning. They conveyed nothing. My favorite example, which I wrote down in a notebook, is: *It's not a yes but it's not a no.* This at various times applied to: 1. a certain actress thinking about whether to accept a role; 2. whether the movie based on my story set in Halifax would be shot *in* Halifax; 3. whether the title of my novel, *A Flock Descends into the Pentagonal Garden,* would be the title of the movie; 4. whether Matsuo Akutagawa would sufficiently recover from electroshock therapy in time to begin directing the movie on schedule; 5. whether I would be granted leave of my contractual obligation to "provide additional dialogue upon request."

*

Birds at night.

*

My wife, Hermione—an old-fashioned name not casually bestowed—coined a term for my insistence on knowing which birds were native to northern California, Wales, British Columbia, Vermont, and a couple of other locales where we rented or bought houses before she died three years ago—"ornitheology." Because not only did bird-watching allow me a kind of spiritual purchase on things, but it fed into a little game we played, called "forgiveness." We were both pretty judgmental about people, I guess, in the sense that we were unforgiving about greed, pain caused on purpose, lies told, and other inclinations and fallibilities among our friends and each other. So in order to feel better, we'd get out a field guide to birds, mark the local species, and whenever we detected a transgression perpetrated by a friend or acquaintance—or ourselves—we'd say, "Oh, well, Stanley is going to become a Siberian plover," or, "Larissa's going to become a saw-whet owl," and so on. We'd verbally wave our godlike wand and reincarnate people like that, their afterlives as birds falling within Hermione's general definition of ornitheology. It wasn't a complicated system really, more playful, with a slightly condescending edge, add a little hopefulness that (like the photographer Robert Frank wrote to me on a postcard) *Next life might be kinder.* Hermione took Latin in high school, I didn't, so she was better at pronouncing the Latin names of birds too. Since childhood I've suffered from a condition commonly called "blackout arrhythmia." Ten or so years ago, they came up with a medication, Rythmol, to keep it in check, and in my case it works all right, not perfectly, but a vast improvement, and I have a lot less anxiety about simple things such as driving a car, or staying alone in a hotel room. Still, it is what it sounds like: the heartbeat accelerates or slows, sometimes both in equal measure within a minute—take deep breaths, try and get calm—yet still on occasion, the anxiety cranks up fast and I black out. After we made love, I'd sometimes press my ear to Hermione's chest; great surges of happiness and envy, as her heartbeat returned to an evenness; whereas I'd feel like I was *mechanically* defective, unable to get it right. I'd say, "You're lucky, you know," and she'd say, "I feel lucky." But we were talking about different things. She died on March 23, 1999, at the Hotel Dumont in Halifax.

*

Next life might be kinder.

*

In Halifax last week I purchased a used pickup truck for $450, automatic transmission, painted red, rusted out. Fifty-two thousand miles on the odometer. It runs like a dream, at least the kind I have. Just entering Port Medway, I stopped to look at dozens of sparrows on three parallel telephone lines near the brick library. A sparrow would shuffle along a line to the left, two sparrows would shuffle to the right, another sparrow following, or eight sparrows slide along in unison or one at a time, a kind of abacus choreography that must be going on all the time across Canada, a country of millions of sparrows and telephone lines—and then they all flew off.

The sparrows here: chipping sparrow, tree sparrow, clay-colored sparrow, field sparrow, vesper sparrow, lark sparrow, Savannah sparrow, Ipswich sparrow, grasshopper sparrow, sharp-tailed sparrow, seaside sparrow, fox sparrow, Lincoln's sparrow, swamp sparrow, white-throated sparrow, white-crowned sparrow, house sparrow.

*

I'm reminded of something David Mamet said: "There are no trustworthy movie producers; some are merely more trustworthy than others." Measured and elliptical; makes perfect sense. Night has fallen; full moon; the beach is spectral. What makes me feel like murdering B. Kremiker is another thing he said in that interview: "I no longer think in sentences." Like he's transcended language to the higher echelon of images. Gulls at night are ghosting the cove, along with the occasional petrel. I don't know the birds here yet, so the gulls I'm looking at out the kitchen window might be any of these: Franklin's gull, little gull, laughing gull, black-headed gull, Bonaparte's gull, mew gull, ring-billed gull, herring gull, Iceland gull, great black-backed gull, glaucous gull, Sabine's gull, ivory gull.

*

Here in Port Medway, nothing's changed, as I continue to experience a succinct form of lethargy due to missing Hermione. Some days I lie in bed, reading, listening to the shortwave, no telephone calls coming in or going out, snippets of conversation arriving with startling immediacy. One morning she said, "I just can't imagine you with anybody who doesn't love coffee like I do." This statement was both erotic and matter-of-fact. Two cups at breakfast, a cappuccino or latte early afternoon (at a café or from the espresso machine I'd bought her), an espresso after dinner. This routine scarcely changed during the four years of our marriage. Right now I'm in bed staring at a drawing, circa 1787, by Mark Catesby of a laughing gull, which really looks to be laughing. "Here, I got you this drawing," Hermione said on my birthday, 1999, "but we're living on soup for the next month, and I just ransacked every pocket of every pair of trousers and shorts we own, plus the lint collector in the washing machine"—we were in California at the time—"to get gas money." We weren't really quite that broke, but this was before my novel sold to the movies and Hermione landed that professorship at Dalhousie University in music history.

*

That afternoon, after the sparrows abandoned their abacus, I parked the pickup in the gravel lot next to the library, got out, and walked up to the front door. A plaque said the library was built in 1924. The hours, posted on a card taped to the glass rectangle of the door, were: Monday: closed. Tuesday: 9 a.m.–noon/2–8 p.m. Wednesday: 9 a.m.–6 p.m. Thursday: closed. Friday: 9 a.m.–7 p.m. Saturday: 10 a.m.–8 p.m. Sunday: noon–6 p.m. I always find that the hours of village libraries, to some extent, reflect the local economy and sociology. You know, the library budget, the availability of volunteers, can the community afford even a part-time professional librarian, and so on. Library hours are always deeply meaningful to me, because the upkeep of a library is an enormous effort in small towns. Plus which, there's the Internet now and Amazon, and all the other forms of expediency and access. In the village of Lunenburg I overheard a fellow say, "The wife and I are going antiquing, then to the library," and it gave me a start, a shock of realization that libraries may soon become a kind of intellectual "antiquing." Anyway, it was Wednesday at 4:35 p.m. and so the library was open. Stepping inside, I saw the library consisted of three rooms: the main room, a children's room, and a room set up with tables, floor lamps, and overstuffed chairs, obviously for reading. Behind the checkout counter there was a woman—later I learned this was Marlais Olivant—sleeping at her desk, using her folded arms as a pillow. Her dark red hair fanned out across—I took a close look—*In a German Pension,* a collection of stories by Katherine Mansfield. She must've been reading; the book was open pages down. Why disturb her? There were no other browsers or readers or anyone in the library. Just me and her. The library was a touch musty; why, I wondered, was she wearing a black rain slicker? An oddity. It was a clear, sunny afternoon. Several windows were propped open. I took the opportunity to tour the stacks, noting that the library's most extensive dedication was to maritime history, especially of Atlantic Canada, and to novels. In the section marked Natural History, I saw the usual field guides but also a number of local pamphlets about birds, as well as some birding "memoirs" of the region, such as *When I Walk out in the Morning: Notes on Birds and Bird-Watching from Childhood to Old Age* by Malcolm Drury, who, according to the author's note, was born and raised in Vogler's Cove, a neighboring outport of Port Medway. In his author's photograph, an elderly Mr. Drury had a pair of binoculars hung around his neck, only half smiling at the camera. After glancing through it, I decided that this was the book for me. The writing was direct and informative, with a pleasant style, not too many autobiographical distractions, and there were hand-drawn maps. I tried to figure out the procedure, in this library, of checking out books. I didn't see a computer, only an Underwood manual typewriter on the librarian's desk. I then noticed a rectangular wooden box on the counter and opened it to discover that it contained three-by-five-inch cards, each with rather spidery cursive notations of a book's title, the lender's name and address (no telephone numbers, which meant, I suspected, that delinquents were notified only by mail), the date the book was withdrawn, and the date it was due back. It all appeared quite efficient and perfectly well matched with local tradition. I saw a legal pad on the counter too, which had, in large printed letters at the top:

REQUEST FOR INTERLIBRARY LOANS
(Please include title of book and author's name)

Note: a book may take upward of a month or even more from Halifax and longer from other libraries in the province.

Is it possible to describe how heartening this was, a library, in the autumn of 2004, with no computer anywhere in sight? I filled out a card, placing it next to *In a German Pension,* and after the words "Due Date," left a question mark. I stopped for some groceries, just the basics to get set up: milk, eggs, coffee, coffee filters, bread, lobster rolls, cans of albacore, a few bottles of wine, a salmon steak, lettuce, tomatoes, scallions. Following the map sent by Philip and Cynthia, I easily found the cottage. They had left flowers and a welcome note on the kitchen table. I put the perishables in the refrigerator. I could hear seagulls out over the cove. I unpacked my two suitcases, neatly placing shirts and underwear and socks in dresser drawers, hanging trousers on hangers in the bedroom closet. Through the window, I saw Cynthia and Philip crossing the road toward the cottage. They looked to be in their late fifties, both quite fit and casually dressed, and, just for the walk from their house, holding hands. Behind them, out over the cove, some gulls were arriving, others setting out.

*

Uncanny how all calculations of memory keep adding up to one image: Hermione spilling down the stairs in the Hotel Dumont, shot by the deranged bellman, Alfonse Padgett. And when this image ambushes me, I've learned to immediately counteract it by closing my eyes and seeing and hearing our first conversation. Hermione, the love of my life. Her room was 519. She was working on her doctoral thesis from McGill University on the composer Toro Takemitsu, particularly a composition he completed in 1977, *A Flock Descends into the Pentagonal Garden.* The Hotel Dumont was on Trollope Street. It faced a small public garden surrounded by a black iron fence with an intricately soldered design of small birds, something like the ones Diego Giacometti sculpted to his tables and chairs. There were hundreds of small iron birds on the fence and the gate had an aviary of great variety too. I was living in Room 455, trying to finish a novel and living on a small advance from the publisher but also a modest inheritance left to me by my uncle Isador, who lived in London. Hermione had managed to get two adjunct courses, Intro to Music History and Musical Composition for Nonmusicians, at Dalhousie, earning just enough to make ends meet. She taught Monday, Tuesday, Wednesday, and Thursday afternoons and worked on her thesis in the library or hotel room mornings, after coffee. We met on March 19, 1996, at about 6 p.m. I'd just wrestled an enormous black trunk into the elevator, full of books. She carried a leather valise and when we both stepped into the elevator to the left of the registration desk and I slid closed the gate and pressed 4 and was about to ask which floor she wanted, she looked at this valise and said, "Usually I prefer to go upstairs unencumbered." "Well, probably you've lived here a while, huh?" I said. "I've been here only two days." "Even when I first got here," she said, "I had the bellman carry up my bags. Have you met Alfonse yet? Quite the character, Mr. Alfonse Padgett. He carries up my groceries too. I'm not a snob about it, mind you, it just makes me feel like I live in a real hotel. From the look of you—I'm on five, by the by, thanks—I can't tell whether or not you can manage to tip the bellman." We'd just met; how did she mean this? Stepping into my room I noticed three pigeons on the windowsill. The pigeons were moving behind glass so dingy they could only be seen as silhouettes. I'd left the door open. Suddenly, I heard Hermione say, "I've got some liquid cleaner for those windows if you want. You don't have much of a view, but you might want to see sunlight. Who knows—maybe you're the type that doesn't." I did borrow the liquid and washed the windows, the pigeons remained unperturbed through it, and, despite my hope against hope, I didn't see Hermione for another week, though I'd asked Alfonse Padgett her name.

Pan, Pan, Pan

Yannick Murphy

WE CAME IN after the crash. We had traveled all night on a ferryboat to arrive. I had slept in a berth with my son, holding him close. When we arrived, there were people staring into the ocean. They were looking down at what was floating there in the brackish water of the Nova Scotia shore.

"Look, a toothbrush," my son said and leaned over the pier and pointed. I looked in and it was a toothbrush floating right next to a piling of the pier. I pulled my son back; he was not a swimmer. I did not want him falling in.

Outside the ferry office there were reporters and people with cameras and overhead were helicopters that hovered so close I had thoughts of our hair being shorn by their blades.

My husband and his brother asked what had happened. It was a plane headed for Geneva. It could have been a fire on board. But no one knew for sure. Everywhere the air was filled with the smell of jet fuel.

Traffic was light. No one was driving away from the site. We traveled inland for our holiday. We drove to an inn on a dark lake. It was the geology here, my husband's brother said, that made the lake smell like sulfur, that made the water black like sludge. We stayed in a cabin. The cabin had two bedrooms that shared a wall. It was a short wall that did not reach up to the ceiling. Our son did not want to sleep with us. He wanted to stay with my husband's brother and sleep with him in his bed. At night I would say goodnight to my son, my voice carrying over the wall.

There was a fireplace and three rocking chairs in the cabin and we sat in them in the evening. My son sat on my husband's brother's lap while my son held his teddy bear and tore out small bits of its fur and rolled them between his fingers. My son's doing this had left the teddy bear's face and belly and back almost bald.

There was talk of the crash in the dining hall. There were no survivors. The scene was still being combed. Clothes were found floating in the water or washed up and spread out on the rocks as if someone had been doing laundry there and left their things to dry. After dinner, my husband and his brother and my son stood in the office of the inn and watched the news on the television bolted up high on a shelf above the front desk.

I went outside to the lawn, where there was a game of croquet being played in the dusk by the other guests. I slapped mosquitoes landing on my arms and legs and listened to the brightly colored balls gently tapping against one another.

During the day, my husband's brother, who had picked out the inn as our vacation destination and had told us months before how lovely it was, insisted on a swim in the dark lake. He walked out to the end of the dock in front of our cabin and lifted one leg in a jackknife and jumped. But when he jumped, he did not land in deep water. The water came up only to the waist of his shorts and it poured off his big chest and shoulders in dark streams like black blood when he stood up. "It's a good thing I didn't take a dive," he said. "Come on in," he then said. "The water's fine." But my husband and I shook our heads. We could smell the sulfur from where we stood on the end of the dock watching him.

In the dark lake there were dead black trees that were still standing and poking up from the surface of the water. The trees had no tops and the limbs on the trees were broken and the trees looked like one-railed ladders with trunks that spiraled out in all directions going up to the sky. During the day crows sat on the broken limbs from time to time.

There was a boat and my husband and his brother took it out one night while I stayed by the window with my son on my lap. I could hear the oars going through the water and I could hear their voices even after they had been gone a long while.

When they came back it was my turn to go in the boat. I did not want to go. I did not want to leave my son. "Come on," my husband said. "It's beautiful," he said and he made me hand over my son to my husband's brother and I climbed into the boat with my husband. My husband rowed us away from the cabin and I could see my husband's brother and my son on his lap sitting by the window. I could see them because there was a light on in the cabin and I could see my husband's brother leaning over my son and burying his head in my son's belly, making my son laugh. I could hear my son laughing all over the dark lake.

"Stop," I said at one point to my husband. So he stopped rowing, so I could listen, making sure it was really the laughter of my son and not him crying, the two sounding almost the same.

The lake was like many lakes that were connected. My husband would have the boat pass through narrow stretches and then the narrow stretches would give way to large pools, rimmed by the trees with no tops and whose limbs were broken. We heard an owl and we looked for it but we could not see it. We only saw its shape when it took flight and sailed across our heads and then I could hear the flapping of its wings so well I thought how it sounded as if the owl were flapping close enough to me to graze my head with its feet or to touch me lightly with the tips of its wings.

It turned out I knew two people who had died on that plane. Really it was just one I knew. I had been to college with her. She had lived in the dorm room next door. The first few years of college she was overweight. Then she decided to eat only grains and vegetables. She once turned her hand over and showed us her fingers. "They are orange from my love affair with carrots," she had said. She became thin and boys who were once just her friends confessed they now wanted more.

The other person was not someone I had once met. It was by chance we bought a house in Vermont that he summered in as a child with his family. When we bought the house we also bought what was left inside it. Inside there were some furniture and dishes and some clothes. On hangers were the coats he wore on chilly days and in closets were the fins and masks he had worn while swimming in the pond. In sweaters were labels the mother must have sewn, his name still there. "Paul Hammond." And, then, from his early days as a doctor there was a white coat hanging on a hanger and in blue thread sewn by machine was the name stitched in cursive—"*Dr. Hammond.*"

Some guests, who had just arrived from the site of the crash, came into the dining hall. They said they thought they could still smell the jet fuel and so they got up and closed the windows. I could not smell it. All I could smell was the dark lake. "Smell," they said and held out their arms so I could sniff their shirtsleeves. "Fuel," they said.

"Why are there so many little pieces?" my son wanted to know about the parts of the plane the recovery crew was bringing up onto the rocky shore. My husband explained to my son how water can be as hard as a sidewalk if you crash into it fast enough. My son sucked his thumb and listened to the news report. Apparently, the crew had radioed the tower. "Pan-pan," they had said, using the international urgency call before it became a full-fledged Mayday.

My son liked saying it. "Pan, pan, pan," he said on a walk in the woods. He did not want to walk with me and hold my hand. He wanted to be on my husband's brother's shoulders where my husband's brother carried him up high and ducked down low when tree branches were in the way.

"Pan, pan, pan," he said, lying on a log, looking down into a stream at leaves he had placed in the water to watch them race, while I worried he might slide off the log and be swept away in the current.

On the walk back to the inn my boy said, "Shh, listen," and we stopped. It was a mockingbird calling, its song repeated three times. "Even he is saying, 'Pan, pan, pan,'" my boy said, pointing at the mockingbird sitting on a branch.

The girl I knew from college was flying to Geneva to meet her fiancé. From there they would fly to France to see her sister. Her sister was about to have a baby, and the girl I knew was going to visit her and help with the baby. The girl and her sister were best friends, I remember because the sister had also gone to my college and the two of them were always together. I would sometimes study with them in a room in our library called the roost because it was a loft built up high on a platform with railings on all sides. It looked like a tree house. We would study and talk and drink Tab and eat Snickers bars sometimes in the roost. This was before my friend became a vegetarian and before her love affair with carrots. But the roost was not the place to really get work done, it was the place to go if you wanted to talk and to laugh and that is what the three of us mostly did there.

At night, over the short wall, we talked to my husband's brother and my son. One night my husband's brother told us about his grown daughter and we listened to how she was interested in cooking now. He described a holiday meal she had made for him. The cranberry sauce was made with tangerine and cherries. The duck was glazed in honey. After a while, everyone was quiet and I could hear them snoring but I was wide awake. It was a hot, still night and I was too hot to sleep. I walked out of the cabin and onto the dock. Maybe my husband's brother was right. Maybe the water was just fine. I took off my clothes and jumped in. The water felt as warm as the air. For a second, when I came up I was not sure I was even out of the water. Then I felt the water rolling off me, off my hair and body and falling back into the water and I knew I was up out of the water and I could breathe.

I was standing there in the water up to my waist when I thought I heard my son yelling, "Pan, pan, pan" again and so I got out of the water and ran back to the house to see why he was awake. Maybe he had dreamt a bad dream. The fire in the fireplace was just embers now and as I walked through the door, the little breeze I made stoked the embers and made them glow a deep red. My husband's brother was already standing in the doorway of their room. He was expecting me. His large body took up the door frame and I could not see around him. I could not see my son. "He's fine," my husband's brother said. "He must have had a bad dream. He's back asleep now," he said. I nodded and then my husband's brother said good night and closed their door. I dried off and climbed into bed next to my husband, who was still sleeping. I could smell the sulfur smell of the dark lake that I had brought into the bed with me. I could not fall asleep for the longest time. The smell was keeping me awake. I tried to listen for the sound of my son breathing, but the sound of my husband and his brother snoring was much too loud. I could not hear him over the wall.

The news we saw on television said that Dr. Paul Hammond was on the plane to go to a meeting in Geneva. The news called him a pioneer in the battle against AIDS. My husband had told my son about pioneers once, about how they had traveled in covered wagons across the country, about how they had eaten hardtack and used their wagons to float across rivers. My son wanted to know why, if this man was a pioneer, he did not use the plane like a covered wagon and float in it across the sea to the safety of shore.

In the dining hall one morning, my husband's brother put his foot down. There would be no more talk of the crash. Not on his vacation. Everyone in the dining hall was talking about it and it wasn't what we had come to this place for. We had not come to stay in an inn with braided rugs on the floors, that had breakfasts of maple syrup and blueberry pancakes, that had rockers on a wide wooden porch, that had trails through tall pines, to talk of wreckage all day. It's not good for your son, my husband's brother said to me, to hear this kind of talk. It gives him nightmares. We were quiet at the table then. We sipped our tea. We looked around the room. A guest at a table next to ours held his hand out like a plane flying over the water, then he nose-dived his hand and had it crash into the daisy-patterned tablecloth that covered the table. It was obvious he was describing the crash to the others who sat at the table with him. "This will all die down soon," my husband said. "People will forget the crash," he said.

That night my husband's brother and my son said they wanted to take a walk. "Maybe," my husband's brother told my son, "we will come upon a bear," and my husband's brother raised his huge shoulders up and held out his hands like claws and growled above my laughing son.

My husband said to me, "While they're on a walk we can take the boat out on the lake."

"Do you think there are bears here?" I asked my husband while he rowed us on the dark lake. I was nervous for my boy.

"Don't be silly," my husband said.

It was a windy night and my husband said that he could smell autumn in the air. I could only smell the dark lake, its smell seeming stronger than ever, as if the wind rippling the surface peeled back a layer of smell that was even stronger than the first layer. "How can you smell anything but the lake?" I said. I wrinkled up my nose.

"It doesn't smell to me," my husband said.

"I cannot sleep because of the smell," I said.

"Oh, come on," my husband said. "This is a beautiful lake," he said. He motioned with his arms at the broken trees surrounding us.

When we got back to shore my husband's brother was running around the house. He was banging open the doors to our rooms. He was looking for our son. "We were on a walk," he said, out of breath. "And then he disappeared. I thought he came back here." We looked too. I called his name. There was no answer. My husband even looked up the chimney and called his name up there. "The lake!" I yelled. I ran outside and I jumped off the dock. I landed in the shallow water that would have been too deep for my son, who was not a swimmer. I could not see. There was no way that I could see. I thrashed my arms through the water. I tried to feel if he was there. On land I could hear my husband and his brother still calling out his name. He had not been found. What had my husband's brother done to my boy?

I ran through the water, but that was hard to do. I slogged through it, really, in my heavy denim jeans. I screamed his name. I kicked beneath me to somehow dredge him up. There were layers to the lake, I already knew. I dove in and dug through the dirt. On the surface, as I was taking a breath of air and looking quickly on the shore for him, something swooped over my head. It was just an owl, but for a moment I thought it was my son. He was all right. He had grown wings. He was safe. Was that how it now was for the families of the victims of the crash? Were they busy too with thoughts of their loved ones taking other forms? Were there some seagulls in the air who were once men and women from the fatal flight? The owl hooted and headed for the tree-lined shore. Then I noticed that the water did not seem to smell of sulfur. The smell had changed. Jet fuel, I thought. The smell so strong the crash could have been right here in this shallow dark lake and not out on the ocean far away. That is when I ran out of the water. I ran dripping, the water from the black lake falling off me as I went all the way across the road past the other cabins and to the lawn where the croquet balls were lying all in the same dark shapes, the bright colors they were in daylight now impossible to see.

He was perched on the front desk. Sitting cross-legged over the sign-in book for the guests, his eyes on the television screen reporting the late news. He did not turn his head to look at me when I called his name. "Oh, Mama," he said. "You've got to see this."

We could not stay. I was dripping the black lake water all over the braided office rug. "It stains," the front-desk person said, asking me to kindly leave. I picked my son up and carried him back to our cabin with my head near his, and I smelled his hair the whole way and I kept smelling it even in bed with him that night and I thought why hadn't I done this all along, just smelled his hair? It would have kept me from smelling the lake.

My son wanted to sleep with me because my husband and his brother were already asleep and he wanted to whisper in my ear. He didn't want to wake them and he didn't want my husband's brother hearing what he had to say about the crash that he had learned on the news. He didn't want my husband's brother to tell him to stop talking about it.

He rattled off facts. Two hundred and twenty-nine people were aboard. The plane shattered into a million pieces. There was a fire on the plane. It could have been from a wire. There are 150 miles of wire inside a plane. There are no smoke alarms inside the ceiling of a plane. If planes were restaurants they would not pass the safety codes, they would not get an occupancy permit. The frame of a plane is called a jig. "Did you know that, Mama?" I did not.

"I bet it looked just like a silver bird on fire," my son said.

My son held his bear in the dark and I knew he was rolling bits of his bear's fur between his fingers while he talked. "What else?" I said to my son. "Tell me more."

"There were no bodies, just parts. A woman had a funeral for her daughter with no body," my son whispered in my ear. I liked hearing what my son had to say. I was thankful for the crash. It drowned out the sound of my husband and his brother snoring. It helped me forget about the smell off the dark lake. It gave me back my son.

A few years after the crash, in our house, in the house Dr. Paul Hammond had summered in as a child, we tried to make room for more things. We put the old clothes that were in the house when we bought the house in boxes. We were planning on a trip to the Goodwill. I lifted the white lab coat with Dr. Hammond's name on it that was hanging on a hanger where it had hung for years. When I lifted it off my son said, "Look, ladybirds," and I looked down and saw that ladybugs had started falling out from inside the sleeves.

"Ladybugs," I said, correcting my son while I lifted the collar of the coat. There were ladybugs in there too. There were ladybugs all over in the coat. Some flew and some landed on the floor when I shook the coat. There must have been close to a hundred. The coat was alive with them.

"Ladybird, ladybird, fly away home, your house is on fire and your children will burn," my son said while looking closely at one that had landed on his finger.

I did not send off the coat with the other clothes for the Goodwill. Instead, I left the coat hanging on its hanger in our house. It's still there now, among our winter clothes.

Tears Streak the Reddest Rouge:

duan zui jin si yan

Anne Waldman

—For Elizabeth Murray 1940–2007
No need to tell my eyes the starry zones.

scribe-angels speak:

"set the trapdoors"

& gather medicinal herbs
that grow among rocks at the edge of the river

& now in possession of solar & lunar days

soak yourself in the "tao"
keep the electricity alive "in charge"

your feathers made of metal now

now: Tao

the crafted magical quality frolics in rice fields
a sign by which not other than itself is measured so

and now? so measured so

in/ fields/ as/ one/ would/ be/ so/ Taoist

as/ one/ a/ composition/ works
against the "so"
the culture to include these animals

lyrical eye but Guandukou as was no more
prelingual sound of bird lore & town no more rather

"relocated"

or arrow bamboo which supported
pandas & the white-furred bear no more

now? & running almost clear

butterflies sip nectar from pink hibiscus flowers

three feet to 131 feet higher now
since the dam what's gone missing in action

overhead congealed clouds form from solidified ether

what know of tao, know of now

on the Hubei-Chongquing trunk road

are you experienced?

[SEEN]

radically

____

will be

____

radically

[UNSEEN]

logging companies secretly use that road

or

terror underneath the territory (displace a people, drown a temple)

call it Styx
records itself under clouds and over rivulets

the "locks" huge-slabs-of-door shut like gates of hell

now?

a code of sympathy for "secularization"

a restless Uighur minority Xianjiang province
Halliburton's meadow will soon arrive
or gear up for Olympic flame

with mirror neurons and a deactivated

swiflet

safely

softly

swiflet

as you might add a suffix to tender energy wrapped tight in avian body
catch in hand

a cathexis hold fast

swift and small

fractal bird presence all around

[what's gone missing in action

will it? if it lifts

and closes a rift there

ownership protecting another

swift monkey: *Rhinopithecus roxelana*

golden ones

(swirling rapids) abound

"set the trapdoors

the nets are open"

"Going out to Tokyo Bay, sir"

"not 'going,' we're in, sir . . ."

minutiae dead or alive

        how bird might be war messenger

"the albatross round a neck, sir"

"mines   dead   ahead"

"left   full   run"

"with Bluefin in back, sir"

"Message to Bluefin:

        follow up to zero"

                                        or else

follow her swoops

        shifts

this way

that dart as magnetic prey

verdant cliff

stalactites

& flowering

no leaves
or shaped rather

rare could say or species added

seeking the tao in a cavern-heaven (*dongtian*)

the Tujia sit calmly by
sing boat songs for tourists

of hungry gorge

the V of them

a chevron
zigzag
again a swoop

the V of them
meander
bilateral
forked tail
lozenge
the V again
circle

in bifurcation

egg or
checkerboard pattern
spiral
hoop
then V
axe

comb
column of them
a bird's claw

just one of them for this to enter in mantra brew
a bird's breast
lunar shape
vegetable shape

dove, cuckoo, hawk
waterbird vulture owl all might be extant if . . .

guardians of this pass
an "if" within swift extinction . . . in warring states
an "if" it takes for gardens in support of the sacred forests of bamboo

single coffin belonging to the Ba people, see?

up there, the ledge?

see?

& on the river cliff up there Swallow Cave 100 meters, 40 meters wide,
8 kilometers, it
goes inside see?

caveat   a cavetto   cavitation   of river

agitates

up there?   [seen]

[unseen]

unusual species of bird (I see! I see!)
Aerodramus brevirostis

or

Anne Waldman

Duan zui jin si yan
short billed   gold   silk   swallow

found here, but also long the coastal areas of southeast Asia
named Himalaya *swiflet*

caves on the Shennong Stream & source mountains the Shennongjia we're
    just now
passing

rare yellow lily clinging to rock walls

limestone cliffs of Three Gorges, see? you see?

tears streak my rouge
it's the song about life on the borders of Mongolia does it
my dear friend she's singing
it's a song about loss
the loss of a friend over the border of Mongolia
and it travels

our river begins in Tibet, she sings
(karaoke DVD is on: a mountain cliff of a yellow crane)
& suffers pollution thousands of miles, she sings
no one reverses this curse
irrevocable, I sing
irreparable course of disaster, someone says, *how will you sing?*
no chill at 6 a.m. like the poem says, she says

but chill all the same and the poem that misses its action that is the chill

muggy
or out

the window a fisherman with magic hoop-net
many waterfalls stretch the mountains
sorrow of the harm we sanction sing it
alarming detritus we sanction sing it
a traveler's mind in the night:
boat at a stable clip
drink the local firewater to ease this contradiction
what will I remember of all this

a concrete sky?
single fishing boat?

women friends are precious & we dance with the postures &
mudras of old China

this is what matters
that we women touch one another's hearts

on the riverbank of the world of Warring States
affection spans along a river

soft and clear: warring states murmur in your own civil war within war

this is what matters: survival in the war within a war within war

lilt of that, a "warring state"
metabolism of sanctions for a warring state

how in river mind it wars it wars and it rivers and then it roads away

metabolism of a river, the way it rivers and roads away

river of golden sands

12 dragons create an horizon

points/ a/ finger/ she/ creates/ thunder flash

what saying *war within war within war*

what creates what

and then roads itself away

a dark and sensory pathology that's what
murmurs the mountain

and incessant *chic chi* of the bird

but a woman becomes a mountain in someone's mind

a body or a bird imagines a body imagining this

prefer a trance
prefer a trace
prefer a place
prefer to place refer to place
& seek the gerund
its place in placing
a creak in tones
is seconds
or syllables in and second tone
Tao is a road renounce it
pounce it a road, a way, renounce it
Tao is what you come to see
renounce it a third tone
announce your "tao"
& renounce it again: tao

what desire do you have?   [in Tao

to trounce in ownership renounce your tao

bare your doomed fate, world, with equanimity so that that is your way in
being free
radical
bare your doomed fate, o activist, in community
be not silenced
Tao
obvious appetite: silence
hot milk for your woe
open secret
question or
curious, citrus night, he said
Qu Yuan
look up
in kind introspection
it is a curious night
where her spirit passes
she who painted like the Taoist Ritual from the Plum in a Golden Vase

or the Dipper Mother
reincarnated as a woman named Lady of Violet Light
or Stellar Mother who holds the inner alchemy (*neidan*)

why?
because the starry strings hang down

in retrospect   in changing

heroes all die and they are women
before the strings hang down
& lute goes mute

out in the wind
Tao of the wind
Tao of no wind
and longer Yangtze

antecedence
folded in rage

uplands divert
uplift and gorge
superimpose a position
series of horizontally bedded rocks
erode
discordant and fold again
dark cave of systems requiring echolocation for this & rare bird

I want to make people feel without resorting to drama

swept back wings resemble a crescent or boomerang

tail is forked

        altitudinal migrant

migrant as sweep and system like a meteor

the threads hang down

Anne Waldman

a click noise will echo

two broadband pulses separated by a slight pause:

three energies three heavens three materials three primes three purities three stars
three teachings three terraces three gorges three female mortals dressed in skirts of leaves
& jackets made of grass divine steel of three rings writ of and complete the thirteen of
August

river valleys

& a tiny cup nest

constructed by the swiflet male of thick saliva and moss

[you might try the soup, my comrade

will survive attached to a vertical rock wall in the cave

aerial insectivore glides due to long primary feathers

& small breast muscles

ranging is done by measuring the time delay between the animal's own sound emission

& echoes return from the environment (Mao's face on all the money)

nothing left but a river floating on the borders agitates heaven

---

SOURCES. *Lu Donbin: Yuan Compendium, the Illustrated Biographies; Taoism and the Arts of China,* Stephen Little, University of California Press; *"Seeking a Mooring,"* Wang Wei (seventeenth century), *Women Poets of China,* Kenneth Rexroth and Ling Chung, New Directions; *Three Gorges of the Yangtze River,* Raynor Shaw, Odyssey Books; "I want to make people feel without resorting to drama," Japanese filmmaker Yasujiro Ozu, 1903–1963.

Vagrant Voices: Some Atlantic Crossings

Tim Dee

> *Sometimes*
> *on fogless days by the Pacific,*
> *there is a cold hard light without break*
>
> *that reveals merely what is—no more*
> *and no less.*
>
> —Thom Gunn
> "Flying above California"

THE FIRST AMERICAN BIRD I saw was a slate-colored junco in the winter of 1974. It was in an orchard of bare apple and pear trees at Haresfield in Gloucestershire, in the west of England. I was thirteen. Word of the bird's discovery a few weeks before had got out to where I lived in Bristol about twenty miles south; specifically it had reached my school "field club" (notionally a general nature society of boys and teachers, but following our growing obsessions almost entirely focused on birds). I had picked up the news and persuaded my father to take me to look for the junco. For a month or so he and I had shared our enthusiasm for birds, but by this time I had already left him far behind. At the age of eight, having discovered myself, as it felt, at home at last, I had signed myself over to birds deeply and forever.

At the weekend we drove up to the little village and quickly spotted a handful of cars pulled onto its grass verges. Nearby there were men in outdoor coats peering through binoculars over a wooden garden fence and down the side of a small semidetached council house. Wood smoke wound from its chimney and hung in the damp February air. Haresfield is in the spreading valley of the River Severn, south of Gloucester; the edge of the Cotswold escarpment rises up behind the village to the north and east, and fields give way to straggles of woodland. I cautiously approached the men and without asking or speaking raised my binoculars to follow the line they were looking along. In a fruit tree at the back of the house, about fifty feet away, was a single bird. My binoculars at that time weren't much use and I had no proper idea what a slate-colored junco looked like. I didn't have an American field guide to birds, and my entire knowledge of the American avifauna came from wan photographs and duotone drawings in Time Life and National Geographic books my father had bought for me by mail order. But there was only one bird in the tree and I could just about see, in the dull light of the English winter afternoon, that it wasn't a chaffinch or a sparrow, though it had something of both, with dark upper parts and slightly paler under parts, a rounded head with a small cage-bird-like bill and a twitchy tail. It wasn't very impressive but a great surge of excited sympathy flooded me. It was here, just in that tree in front of me; it had come all the way from America, as if for me, and I was here with it, seeing a bird from America, a wonderfully rare bird in Britain. For a decade from that moment I was in thrall to rarities. I thought of all the orchard trees of the Severn valley, all the valleys beyond the Severn, the widening land across the whole country, and how this was the only junco here, and how I loved being in its company, feasting on its uniqueness, attending to the same space. As I stood there, attempting to eat the bird with my eyes, I could feel my moments with it being laid down as significant and glittering strata in my life, like wet slate itself, the color of the bird's back. I would always have seen a slate-colored junco in England.

My arms ached from holding my binoculars to my eyes for so long and I had a growing sense behind me of my father's eagerness to do something other than stare at a tiny, cold-looking bird in a bare tree in someone's back garden. I lowered my binoculars, and as if the magic twine I felt between the junco and me had snapped, the bird flew down out of the tree and onto the ground somewhere out of view behind the house. That was enough for me. Neither then nor subsequently, as my obsession deepened still further, did I need any earnest scrutiny of the bird's remiges or tertials or ear coverts, the feather detail much sought by my fellow devotees. I loved our shared time a few feet apart, the intensity of the specific encounter, the brightness it cast over a gray day and a dull bird, and it is this I can retrieve so plastically thirty years on. I feel the excitement still, as a hollowing out of my insides, as a sharp intake of breath, a widening of my eyes.

Writing the word "plastically" reminds me that "a plastic" was what we called an escaped or feral bird when, a year or so after the junco, I became a hardcore birder. The question was, always, could you have it? Could you tick off your list the Chilean flamingo that looked like an abandoned wedding dress on the dreary winter mudflats of the Bridgewater Bay a few dozen miles south of Haresfield?

Almost certainly not—Chile was just too far away to contemplate a natural vagrancy. But what about North American ruddy ducks, escaped or voluntarily released from the waterfowl collection at Slimbridge, a few miles north of Haresfield, and already sculling about various local lake edges with all the air of entitlement they could muster with their stiff tails and Nearctic blue beaks? They were breeding and as a consequence became British birds somehow, though I couldn't look at them without feeling that they were not truly mine.

The ordinary birds of the Cotswolds—its chaffinches, sparrows, and thrushes—were always going to feel more mine than a slate-colored junco. Much as I thrilled to writing "colored" in my notebook, the Cotswolds' residents and predictable visitors, not its accidental blow-ins, were what I ended up needing and seeking. I have long stopped chasing vagrants. Recently I have spent more time reading poetry books than bird guides. The Cotswolds are a dangerously pretty part of England, but in two early twentieth-century poets, Ivor Gurney and Edward Thomas, the hills and combes behind Haresfield are conjured as I still see them today: people have been living and working in them almost forever, but the brakes and hedges and the flint-strewn fields and beech woods can receive and hold wild things too. It is a man-made place but it has always given space to other creatures. As juncos do all across America, the birds in the Cotswolds come close to us while remaining totally themselves. A lovely poem by Edward Thomas—so well known it has virtually created, or at least come to stand for, the landscape it describes—knows and shows this. His "Adlestrop" evokes a single encounter with a resident bird and goes on to unroll a lacy map of the species' occupancy in space and time throughout the gently rolling hills and fields of the Cotswolds. At Adlestrop railway station (like everywhere else, also just a few miles from Haresfield) a train stops,

> And for that minute a blackbird sang
> Close by, and round him, mistier,
> Farther and farther, all the birds
> Of Oxfordshire and Gloucestershire.

The Polish poet Adam Zagajewski once told me how he misses Edward Thomas's European blackbird more than any other bird when he is teaching in Houston. He writes poems there of his memories of them in Kraków, where he lives for the half year he is not in the United States. This is from "Houston, 6 p.m.":

> There are no nightingales or blackbirds here
> with their sad, sweet cantilenas,
> only the mockingbird who imitates
> and mimics every living voice . . .

Perhaps the mockingbird is a little too easy a choice for *the* American bird, but I have another question: is it Eurocentrically fanciful or retroimperialist to feel that America misses *our* blackbirds more generally as well? Even its native humans? That something of the European blackbird's fossil fuel is wanted, its coal black cultural certainty being absent from its North American counterparts? I am wrong-footed every time I hear "blackbird" in America, and have to remind myself that the talk is of an *Icterid,* not a *Turdus.* But the name brings half echoes and broken reflections, and a twinge of sweet sadness—*your* blackbird, with all its shortcomings, was named optimistically out of ornithological homesickness. By the time the bird was known for what it was, the name had stuck. It was a bird and it was black. In the absence of the blackbird our grandparents knew, this will be our blackbird, America decided. Yet Wallace Stevens's "Thirteen Ways of Looking at a Blackbird" feels like a poem that would sooner be about the Old World bird. There is no one American blackbird; there are plenty in its family that are not even black, and their songs are described as being "generally rather harsh, with loud squeaks, whistles, and clarion calls" (Christopher W. Leahy, *The Birdwatcher's Companion to North American Birdlife*). Among American blackbirds sad, sweet cantilenas are rare; maybe that is the American way. Wallace Stevens perhaps hadn't a single species in mind—he liked the euphony of the name and its crisp and suggestive simplicity, and he asserted the birds' ordinary beauty ("O thin man of Haddam, / Why do you imagine golden birds? / Do you not see how the blackbird / Walks around the feet / Of the women about you?"), but that could be said of the European blackbird too (Seamus Heaney's final poem in his most recent collection, *District and Circle,* has the line "It's you blackbird, I love"). I don't know much about Wallace Stevens's ornithology (did he have a pair of binoculars?), but as a poem that talks to ancient Chinese poetry and to Keats (his "Ode on a Grecian Urn" as much as his "Ode to a Nightingale"), "Thirteen Ways" needs the Old World as much as the New, and the poem struggles, to my ears, if it must be about *Agelaius phoeniceus* when it sings if it is really about

Turdus merula. Even if he didn't know the European blackbird, it seems Wallace Stevens has made a poem from it.

I hear a comparable Atlantic crossing when Bob Dylan sings in "High Water" (on *Love and Theft,* 2001), "the cuckoo is a pretty bird, she warbles as she flies." Surely, he is singing about *our* cuckoo, not his. Yet this makes sense in this marvelous flighty song, since he is grabbing at what he can as he runs to escape the rising waters of the world, and what is to hand is half-remembered lines and images from the old stories. The cuckoo line—or variations on it—is in many English ballads and songs. "She" is wrong (only male birds sing *cuckoo*), but since the cuckoo's bigger secret (its parasitizing of other birds' nests) wasn't fully deciphered until less than a hundred years ago, only a purist would quibble over this smaller mistake, and indeed, the "she" gives Dylan's line the patina of age that fits with the rest of the song. Both yellow-billed and black-billed cuckoos in North America call with *cuckoo* calls (though Christopher Leahy describes them as "rather 'woody' clucks" and goes on, "it is only the Common Cuckoo of Eurasia that 'says' CUCK-oo and inhabits clocks") and both occasionally but not habitually parasitize other birds. But American cuckoos cannot yet and perhaps never will carry the cultural weight of *our* cuckoo. They are birds still, just birds.

In the late autumn of 1979, I saw a yellow-billed cuckoo on Portland Bill in Dorset, on the south coast of England. The Bill—its name a further inducement to birders if its location isn't enough—is like an island that has remained joined to the mainland and sticks several miles out into the English Channel. It is a near treeless, wind-bashed peninsula, blanched yellow at this time of year, a crash zone for migrant birds struggling over the sea and desperate for cover and food. In late October there isn't much vegetation, and certainly there are no caterpillars for a cuckoo. Scooped up by winds far away in the Gulf of Mexico and along the southern seaboard of the United States, the cuckoo would have been spun across the Atlantic. I imagine its yellow bill gaping in disbelief as sea gave way to yet more sea, the horizon bringing only more of the same. By the time Portland finally offered landfall for the disoriented bird it was too late. It pitched into the grassy back at the edge of a bare field just a few hundred feet from the sea and stayed. It was still huddling there in a mess of feathers when I hurried up—another new bird for me—the next day. With nothing to perch on, the bird's long wings and tail were awry, its downy breast feathers were puffed up in the morning cold, suggesting that it was only weeks out of the nest. This is probably true;

most autumn vagrants are the lost losers of that year's broods. If you make it through your first migration, you might make it through a few more. This bird wasn't going to; it wasn't moving, there was nothing for it to eat. It looked moribund. Maybe it would just slump forward and die. Looking at it was uncomfortable, I felt like an attendant at a deathbed. To feel happy ticking the cuckoo off my list, even as a teenage rarity chaser, I wanted the bird to be more alive, to be wilder. Then there was an extraordinary coup de théâtre. From nowhere, as it always seems, a sparrow hawk, a large brown female, came over the low bank. Materializing from the earth behind, she flicked her wings once, twice, folded them, leaned forward momentarily, lowered her claws, and knocked the cuckoo over with them. She picked it up for a couple more wing beats before softly settling her cargo and herself a little farther along the bank. Mantling her prey, she plucked and ate; the cuckoo's downy breast feathers now briefly floating into the wind, then settling in the corner of this foreign field. The gang of bird-watchers were elated, there were gasps and laughter, not least because those who were arriving now wouldn't be able to add yellow-billed cuckoo to their lists. I was less happy, though wide eyed to have seen the cuckoo and its end. Something about its sensational theatrical exit made me think of all the other unobserved deaths: the yellow-billed cuckoos that had perhaps kept this bird company in their shared distress all across the blasting ocean but which, wearying more than it, had slipped down lower over the sea and tumbled inconspicuously into the swell just a few miles short of Portland; the vagrants who miraculously cross an ocean but meet a domestic cat, or a car, or starve; the million other birds dying out of sight, ordinarily. My time with rare birds, mistakes, erratics, overshoots, and so on came to seem clouded; the whole thing, every vagrant sought and seen, like a protracted funeral; this birding, coffin chasing, us birders pallbearers.

I didn't stop then but I would soon. There was to be one more Yank. In 1980 I put my bicycle on a train in Bristol and traveled overnight to Cornwall, about 120 miles to the southwest. I had to get out at a station that was still some way from the river at Sladesbridge, where I was going. There was an amazing bird to try to see there, an almost impossible thing in England, a belted kingfisher from America. This was only the fifth ever seen in Europe. I cycled through the dawn, cosseted by steep-banked lanes, in warm drizzle, a scribble of instructions and a half-traced map from a road atlas to hand. Then I walked and pushed my bike for a mile or so alongside the river in a deep wooded valley, on an old trackway, until suddenly ahead of me was the bird laughing loudly. I thought of an actor on the wrong stage but stuck with only one set of lines. Other bird-watchers had found it days before (what must *that* have been like?), but that day I was the first and for a time the only one there. It perched like a clown on a telegraph pole, then flew its buzzing flight along the river, and then—and I had to laugh too—hovered like a Thunderbird model on a string. It was big, metallic blue and bright white, with a colossal bill and a comic crest, like a finned American car. It didn't fit in Cornwall and I couldn't really accept its being there; its noise and shape made me think of a kookaburra, a bird even less imaginable. In that soft, temperate English valley the kingfisher occupied another plane or dimension; it was like trying to watch a 3-D film without the special glasses.

Cycling back to the train I was relieved—it was always a terrifyingly breathless outward journey going for a bird you might not see. But having added a belted kingfisher to my list I was left feeling odd. As I peddled uphill back to the station I couldn't stop thinking that although the bird was in England it wasn't really ours at all, and we were wrong to think that because it was there among us it joined us in any way. I thought of the wind pushing the bird east from America, away from where it had wanted to be, a place it knew, out over the Atlantic and its saltwater, and how the bird—otherwise so obviously its own boss—had to accept that. Thinking this, I nearly fell off my bike as my mind blew, back and forth, across the ocean.

The belted kingfisher was the last American vagrant I twitched in Britain. I have now seen them at home, where they should be, up and down the eastern half of the United States, being themselves and looking totally fitting. I have traveled many times to the US for work and for holidays, though never solely seeking its birds. They have always been there, I have always noticed them (after a certain depth of immersion, it is impossible not to notice birds, even in a foreign country), but being in the United States makes me, despite having seen a handful of its birds blown to Britain, a birding novice once again. I spent a week in Los Angeles at the end of February this year; American birds never seemed stranger, never more beguiling.

At Heathrow Airport on my way to LA, I drop off my rented car just outside the perimeter fence that skirts the runways. A morning of smear and low cloud. Already the day feels dusky and is threatening to finish before it has properly begun. Planes are coming and going in their huge galumphing haze of gasoline energy. They lumber along and vibrate themselves into the air, their stretched and over-pumped musculature growling as it takes them up and trailing an oily slipstream. The din seems continuous and hellish but then, between planes, I hear a skylark singing somewhere above the runways or the grass strips that separate them. It is like *hearing* a needle in a haystack—a fine sharp metal music in the middle of booming muffle and wah. In flight and from a height the bird pours its song out and down onto me and the readying planes: a silvery, thin, twisting and flexing wire of sound that talks to itself, and to any other skylarks, and to us, saying everything that it has to. The song is loud enough for the air, it lives with it, and through it. Its aptness is made apparent by the crass attack of the planes on the same air, as they rattle down the runway hotly gulping it in through their engines then hurrying to expel it, laced with globules of oil. Here is our disease next to nature's ease.

I have a window seat for my flight; I look but can't see the skylarks as we leave. I know skylarks have been introduced on Vancouver Island in Canada—plastics for the Canadians—and some have made it into the US just over the Haro Strait. Thinking about this toward the end of my trip I peer down through the thirty-five thousand feet of sky. I can't see them there either, of course. But the looking brings the birds' song flight back into my mind and I catch a half reflection of myself, smiling jealously out into space and thinking of birds' unthinking occupancy of it and the superb but casual intensity of their artistry in it.

As the plane turns out over the Pacific for a moment and bends on toward LAX, I look down and see Topanga Canyon. Flying over the ice of Canada, I'd been reading about it and had marked it as a possible place to walk and look for birds. I liked the fact that the Byrds had lived there once too and made music down there. I looked into the deep and shadowed clefts and at the sun-blasted ridges. Maybe they still were.

Three days later, I walked the tracks up the spine of the hills and climbed higher for several miles, so that the morning flights of ascending raptors—first red-tailed hawks, then a red-shouldered hawk, and last, at Eagle Rock, a peregrine—were below me and I could watch them from above. You catch yourself feeling like a god in these moments: being higher than these consummate fliers. The red-tails were sailing through the thickening air that rose from the woods on the valley floor; the red-shouldered hawk was bleating and shrieking like a bereft child through a canopy of oaks; the folding wings of the peregrine made an arrowed *plush* as it crested a ridge and dropped into the unexpectant calm air of a scrubby valley.

These flights I can understand. Peregrines storm over my home once or twice a year on their way to freak out the pigeons of Bristol from their nest in the Avon Gorge nearby; red-tailed hawks function, it seems, as buzzards do in Britain. There were other wings beating at Topanga, though. I struggled with the wrentit, a bird whose family was totally new to me, and whose compound name is both help and hindrance in getting any purchase on it, and with the ruby-crowned kinglet, which looks so much like *our* goldcrest but isn't. What flummoxed me most, made me feel most foreign, was realizing at Topanga how my understanding—and love, it seems—of the deeper grammar of flight, it being what birds do and fundamentally are, lies at the heart of my experience of them and the world they make for me. I learned this from the flight of an Anna's hummingbird around the scattered cars and small trees in a car park there. Hummingbirds don't move like birds. Nor really are they like insects, which most people might compare them to. Their flight—its zips and stops and dives—is totally theirs, yet I found it hard to think of as a bird's. I couldn't see it, couldn't follow it, couldn't anticipate it. It was a flying bird and yet its flying was alien to me.

Then there was their singing. Hummingbirds make noises that match their wings in weirdness, but I heard other songs at Topanga and I couldn't place them. I didn't know what sort of bird was making them. It might be just a call, not a song. It could be a bigger bird than I imagine, or smaller. Is it even a bird? Could it be an insect, a frog, an American machine, or an American person? I can't see anything moving in the brush, but it could be singing from the ground, or from the sky. I have never liked tricks and I feel here in the company of magicians, of voice throwers, and it makes me out of sorts. I strain, cock my ears, and turn my head toward the sound, like a thrush—one of *my* birds—listening for worms and noticing a plane flying overhead at the same time. An image comes to my mind of me as a cartoon man looking down an impossibly long telescope that actually runs from me to the bird itself. The bird is there but I can't see it, though it is peering back down the same telescope at me. I feel like an extra in an Oliver Sacks book: the man who mistook their birds for his. Topanga's birds were beyond me.

It takes coming to places like the dusty chaparral of these mountains and not knowing what is singing in them to realize that knowing my birds has always been important to my sense of knowing myself. I am not sure who I am if I don't know how to read the birds around me, their habits, and their habitats. John Clare (the greatest bird poet in any English) recalled how as a child on Emmonsales Heath in early-nineteenth-century Northamptonshire, he'd gone in search of the edge of the horizon and found himself lost, as I felt at Topanga: "I eagerly wandered on and rambled among the furze [gorse on the heath] the whole day till I got out of my knowledge when the very wild flowers and birds seemed to forget me and I imagined they were inhabitants of new countries."

To be forgotten before you are even known is the condition of almost all bird-watching. Birds don't care about us, short of checking out the threat we pose. We birders are constant observers of exits; we are ushers holding open doors to freer spaces. Almost always birds are going away from us, are moving on, are looking elsewhere. They rarely seek us out, which is why pigeons coming close after crumbs seem so mammalian and not birdlike. Though many live alongside us, fostering the illusion we have that they've elected to, we are on our own.

Stumbling with my identifications and cloth-eared over the birds' songs in Topanga Canyon, I realized that I understood more of the human musical idiom of America than its avian one. Up the track away from the disorienting hummingbird and the mystery singers, I spotted and identified my first-ever California thrasher and I thought immediately of Captain Beefheart. The name Ed Thrasher came into my head. To my ears it's a very American name as well as a punky pun. As I stared at the bird preening itself, drab brown all over with a characterful long curved beak, I couldn't quite remember who Ed Thrasher was. Was he a member of the Magic Band along with Winged Eel Fingerling, Drumbo, the Mascara Snake, and others? The name sounded suitably made up. I was sure he had something to do with Beefheart. Later, I discovered that he was a photographer, who did shoot the Captain and company, though also plenty of other bands nowhere near as exciting or important to me. But the thrasher as somehow a Beefheart bird stuck in my mind. Then I got it. The bird is as the band was: mostly ordinary and mulligatawny brown but well schooled in weirdness by some controlling deity and forced to wear an extreme beak.

Music and birds were also in my mind because just before I saw the California thrasher, I'd seen a pair of science fiction birds: western bluebirds. Their color is even more extreme than the belted kingfisher's. Their electric blue marks them as birds from the future, or rather from an old version of the future; they made me think of the color saturation of François Truffaut's *Fahrenheit 451*. Made out of materials unavailable, it seems, in Europe, they are perfect birds to see a mile or so from the dream factories of the world, and seeing them, late Wallace Stevens poems flocked to me, those poems of his that needed copper or golden birds, the blackbirds no longer being enough. They had all the "mere being" he so beautifully put into his late (or even last?) poem ("A gold-feathered bird / Sings in the palm, without human meaning, / without human feeling, a foreign song"). The bluebirds flew around all this mental nonsense of mine, unconcerned, innocently electrifying the scene, and demonstrating a tenderness that belied the shimmer of their backs. They were truly paired and were living as if with a mirror reflection of themselves; each of their departures from and returns to one or another perch felt solicitous and they always managed to be in each other's company. Instantly, they made me lonely. I also remembered how much I disliked the song that, co-opting bluebirds in its way, has helped burnish a myth of British stoicism and resolve: "There'll be bluebirds over the white cliffs of Dover . . ." as famously sung by Vera Lynn, the "forces' sweetheart," during the Second World War. We are still waiting and there haven't been any bluebirds yet; the three species, though migratory and therefore prone to getting lost, haven't been recorded in Europe. The song's ornithological clumsiness has always annoyed me; it doesn't know the birds it is talking about so it cannot begin to bring them into any suggestive orbit of its intentions: she might as well sing about dodos. Maybe I am the only person who minds. Sometimes it feels like that.

Ice Cream for Crow is another matter. Because I loved Captain Beefheart I would forgive him more than Vera Lynn, but even so I would argue that, despite its liberties and departures, his song shows evidence—like Ted Hughes's compulsive and multifarious poems about crows—of having evolved at some point from actual observations and a feeling for the mythopoetic inheritance attendant on the bird. Crows are very good birds to think with and good to sing of too.

It's so hot
looks like you have three beaks crow
the moon's so full
white hat on a pumpkin
you know there's something
the moon was a stone's throw

stop the show
I need to say hello
to the crow
light the fire piano
the moon showed up
and it started to show
tonight there'd be ice cream
ice cream for crow

Long after the skylark was drowned out at Heathrow, I watched a pair of carrion crows prospecting at the edge of the airport; American crows were the first birds I saw in the US, nonchalantly patrolling the asphalt at LAX. I like these parallel species, doing much the same on both sides of the world, with just an accent separating them.

The American crow yaps. It has a call like a twanged wire strung between two metal cans; I think of it as the sort of sound that a steel or pedal guitar might make. To me it sounds irrefutably American. What kind of chthonic sentimentality is it in me that hears earth stuck in the throat of our carrion crow as it coughs itself on its way over the fields of England, but hears a performance—*look at me, listen to me*—in the voice of the American crow? From my hotel room in dreary Burbank, I hear the passing trains hooting their wild music and I cannot but think of the sound as a performance of an American train—*I think I can, I know I can*—barreling its voice across the country. It sounds like Tom Waits. The American crow does, as well.

Part of my sense of a country of performers and performances comes from the difficulty I have in feeling California's texture. Is there any depth? The sky is flat cyan, the city is a flat grid, most roofs are flat, the mountains beyond are flat brown, the Pacific is flat calm. "Abundant sunshine" is forecast and delivered, roads go everywhere, all sorts of airplanes and helicopters stack in the air. Surely Los Angeles has a grain but beneath my Old World fingers I cannot feel it. Where is the soil here? There seems to be hardly any. There is dust, dry concreted riverbeds, a kind of ersatz grass, burned arroyos and gulches, and over all but the steepest parts a coverlet of asphalt. Rather than sinking into the earth, as it does over time on European roads, here this tarmac sits.

Taking a taxi from Burbank to West Third Street is like moving through a perpetual lobby; the hotel and the taxi interior feeling as blanketed as the streets, and seeping through invisible fissures in both building and car comes the inane dribble of the smoothie saxophone of Kenny G like some trapped wind or oracular blowback of the man-made earth. It sounds as far from nature as it is possible to be.

At the moment I feel I am a captive on Baudrillard Boulevard (I know as little about his birding skill as I do about Wallace Stevens's, but suspect he would have things to say about the mockingbird), I see some birds' bones and all that is air becomes solid again. Seeking something old, permanent, and beyond the surface, I visit the museum at the La Brea Tar Pits in the center of the Los Angeles plain; it is perfect. Here in the middle of the paved city is evidence of a true asphalt god, here tar has its own paving plans and still bubbles through its own thickening crust to the surface, regardless of what we might do. Over thousands of years, mostly long before there were any people here, the tar has trapped countless animals and preserved them in pitch. The museum, next to the pits, shows the skeletons of those that have been brought to the surface by excavations and by the upheavals of the tar itself. Here, in this wonderful ossuary, alongside dire wolves, American mastodons, Shasta ground sloths, and antique bison, and from a later time a single murdered and ceremonially buried woman, is a local avifauna as alien to Anna's hummingbirds as they are to me. There are one hundred species of bird here, almost all now extinct: fragile eagle, errant eagle, La Brea stork, occidental vulture, Woodward eagle, Brea condor, La Brea caracara, California turkey, Merriam's giant condor, Grinnell eagle, American neophron, and the ancestral California condor. The angels of another Los Angeles assemble themselves from these bones. One wall-mounted wooden cabinet contains five-hundred-foot bones of five hundred golden eagles that have been taken from the tar. As I walk away from the pits, watching the planes stack on their way into LAX, I imagine a line of five hundred golden eagles on their approach and backing into the distant heights of the clear evening sky.

My drifting revenants were dismissed at an intersection by a knot of starlings gathering on the wing, collecting more of themselves at every junction, and moving toward their evening roost at Santa Monica. Starlings are newcomers here, though not the newest in Los Angeles: as I walk along West Third occasionally a shrieking parrot or gang of parakeets flies over, twisting just above the telephone wires and skirting the rooftops. The parrots are color, noise, gabble, and glitz. They move fast and are hard to identify. On the sidewalk I scrabble in my bag for Sibley. He (*The Sibley Guide to Birds*) lists and illustrates the escaped and introduced parrots of California, without judgment, alongside native species. After the skeleton of the errant eagle at the tar pits, the air in its glass case settling between its bones, a bird that would never have seen a single human being, it is precisely the humanness of the starlings and the parrots that strikes me. These unnaturals, my old plastics, have human hands and clumsy trafficking behind them. They are birds in the wrong town, apt expressions of our botched tenancy of the planet, where we have turned commonplace birds into our familiars and made plastic birds suit plastic places. Yet where some would find these avian opportunists hard to love because they confront us again and again with what we have done, I relish the evidence they embody of our entanglement with them.

As the day ripples raspberry red in the west and the evening rolls over from the east, with a supporting cast of starlings clotting and coagulating into flocks, I see two long-tailed parakeets that I cannot identify for certain and one larger bird that I like to think is a yellow-headed parrot, since Sibley describes its "voice" as "human" and transcribes it as a "long descending yadadadadada." This immediately calls to mind my parents' old LPs of Dory Previn and her Los Angeles songs on *Mythical Kings and Iguanas,* which my sister and I knew by heart as children around the time of the slate-colored junco, with her "yada-yada, yada-yada, yada-yada, daaada," and her songs of human jumpers, long descending, from the Hollywood sign, the same sign I can see on the hills behind my parrot.

We have feral parakeets in Britain too and we gave you our starlings. I can't stop liking these shared mongrel birds that make the places they end up their own. The starling, in this sense, is a hero bird. America, it seems, mostly hates them, though they have done just what Americans did. Arrived, moved west, succeeded. Parrots in LA are brash and garish, a reminder of Mexico and invasion from the south; starlings have more Old World sophistication. They are clever, artistic even (didn't Mozart keep one as a pet?) but in the United States they haven't been cast in that role—it occurs to me that perhaps they have been thought of as Jewish? In 1939 Rachel Carson wrote an article for *Nature Magazine* called "How about Citizenship Papers for the Starling" in the face—look at the date—of malignant hostility. Only fifty years after the first successful introduction, the bird needed rehabilitating. It arrived in the United States thanks to the activities of the eccentric Eugene Schieffelin, a drug manufacturer, who, sensing some cultural deficit in the

American avifauna, conceived of the bizarre idea of introducing to the United States all the bird species mentioned in Shakespeare. He would have caught a phoenix if he could have, but in 1890–91 he acquired eighty pairs of European starlings, which he liberated in Central Park in New York. They bred almost immediately. After that the birds took their time, and spread no more than thirty miles in their first decade. There were other introductions, but these seem to have been unsuccessful. The pilgrim starlings, descendants of the original Central Park birds, eventually crossed the continent, like a parable of colonization and westward expansion. They reached California in 1942. There are millions, perhaps billions, in the US now and it is one of the most numerous birds in North America and is found, says Sibley, in the book in my bag, "in virtually all human-modified habitats." Under the heading "Impact," Christopher Lever has this to say of the starling in North America in *Naturalized Birds of the World,* his inventory of assorted human mishandlings:

> Since at least the 1920s, the European Starling has been recognized as an agricultural pest, and the benefit it conveys by probing the ground for grubs, wireworms, and beetles (in summer up to ninety percent of the species' diet may be composed of invertebrates) is far outweighed by its depredations on commercial fruits, berries, corn (maize), grain, rice, and seeds. In urban areas, the accumulated guano of vast roosting murmurations damages buildings and fosters histoplasmosis. Starlings also transmit other diseases such as avian tuberculosis, toxoplasmosis, psittacosis, cryptococcal meningitis, avian malaria, and Newcastle disease. Several aircraft crashes have been attributed to damage caused by starlings being sucked into jet engines. Millions of dollars have been spent annually in attempts to control the species' numbers but with only limited success.

The starlings are gathering now in the high waving palms along the oceanfront at Santa Monica, just as they might round the buildings and trees of a farm yard in Haresfield, in Gloucestershire, or anywhere else in Britain. I love them: their chatter; their wheezing imitative songs that show how much listening they do to what goes on around them; their sociability; the way they live with themselves all the time, always coming together in bigger numbers to make themselves darker than the dark at night, then spreading out every morning like prospectors; their dull plumage, which sparkles when any light touches it; the way they walk on grass like we do.

The next day I am reading a sign on the path to Dante's Peak at Griffith Park: CAUTION WILDLIFE HABITAT. DANGEROUS ANIMALS MAY BE PRESENT, INCLUDING MOUNTAIN LIONS AND RATTLESNAKES. . . . I turn and look down over the flat miles of south LA, the glistening car tops making a scarab diamanté of its intersections, and I think of its parrots and starlings with their electric colors and iridescence. What I see, though, is a giant McDonald's banner advertising new Aberdeen beef burgers being dragged by a light airplane through the thick, urinous air of the heated, smoggy city. It makes a kind of meaty skywriting, the languorous flaps of the banner making me think of the reluctant peristalsis of a gut fanning beefy chunks through the heavy air. Then all at once, there is real theater. Ravens—another bird we share—arrive from all sides of the sky, upstage and down, to eclipse the city with their black plumage darker than anything, and their croaks, the only commentary necessary, and their flying, still as I imagine them flying on the first day of their creation: exultant and laughing and really pleased with their gift. They are, to steal from Emily Dickinson, inebriates of air. One sails on tightly bowed wings toward the McDonald's plane, then appears to switch off its engine, and surfs for a moment, before neatly folding its wings away and rolling left onto its back. It drifts on; it is flying upside down. The bird throws a single croak to the upper air before following the roll through and righting itself. It has stolen the entire scene. Whatever we do on or above this earth makes only one of its stories; there are others; we should attend.

Perhaps the raven was looking back toward Odin Street, near the Hollywood Bowl, which I'd spotted as I drove past on the way to Griffith Park, and it was remembering the old days at the beginning of the world when ravens were the Norse god's news service. The birds seem the oldest thing for miles and miles. I think of Borges's *Fauna of the United States,* with its species list like no other: "We shouldn't forget the Goofus Bird that builds its nest upside down and flies backward, not caring where it's going, only where it's been."

The sun was falling into the ocean; it was time to go. I began to tot up my Californian bird list. Above the Griffith Observatory I craned out as far as I could after the ravens and looked down, past a wintering pair of golden-crowned sparrows at my feet, feeding like famished men in a desert, hurrying down the sweetest tips of the rare fresh shoots of grass they had found in the thin soil, and I looked out across the city toward the beaches and the sea, looking through *my* binoculars for Claes Oldenburg's gigantic pair that stand outside an advertising firm at Venice Beach, binoculars that I could have done with at the wonderful Museum of Jurassic Technology in Culver City to see its minuscule birds made by Hagop Sandaldjian, so small they perch on a human hair, the tiny bright birds making me think of the painted birds of paradise like flaming carrot-colored comets in the top right-hand corner of Jan Brueghel the Elder's *The Entry of Animals into Noah's Ark* of 1613 in the Getty Center; the neighboring painting there by Vittore Carpaccio, "Hunting on the Lagoon" (1490–5) of trained diving cormorants holding their breath underwater and schooling fish to the surface for men to catch (though the label wrongly says something else); this taking me back to the Museum of Jurassic Technology and its display of "Duck's Breath" in its gallery of overlooked ailments and remedies, where children are cured of thrush and other disorders by taking the bill of a duck or goose in their mouths, whereby "the cold breath of the fowl will be inhaled by the child and the complaint will disappear"; which makes me think of the sallies of the black phoebe to and from a burned black barbecue grill at Topanga Park; which in turn summoned Rahsaan Roland Kirk's "Blacknuss," his jazz number made from only sharps and flats, the black keys on a piano; the mesh and murmur of all of this: the California gulls stalking Muscle Beach for scraps, the chicken Caesar and chicken teriyaki I ate, the reruns of *Roadrunner* I watched in my hotel room through nights dogged by jetlag; my Hotel California, my eagles' aviary with its fragile eagle and errant eagle and kinglets and wrentits, mockingbirds, and towhees, and the birds I couldn't see and couldn't hear, farther and farther, all the byrds of San Fernando and Anaheim.

The spotted hawk swoops by and accuses me, he complains of my gab and my loitering.
I too am not a bit tamed, I too am untranslatable,
I sound my barbaric yawp over the roofs of the world.

The last scud of day holds back for me,
It flings my likeness after the rest and true as any on the shadow'd wilds,
It coaxes me to the vapor and the dusk.

I depart as air . . .

—Walt Whitman
"Song of Myself"

After Completion

Arthur Sze

I.

Mayans charted Venus's motion across the sky,
poured chocolate into jars and interred them
with the dead. A woman dips three bowls into
temmoku glaze, places them in a kiln, anticipates
removing them, red-hot, to a shelf to cool.
When samba melodies have dissipated into air,
when lights wrapped around a willow have vanished,
what pattern of shifting lines leads to Duration?
He encloses a section of garden in wire mesh
so that raccoons cannot strip ears in the dark,
picks cucumbers, moves cantaloupes out of furrows—
the yellow corn tassels before the white.
In this warm room, he slides his tongue along
her nipples; she runs her hair across his face;
they dip in the opaque, iron glaze of the day,
fire each emotion so that it becomes itself;
and, as the locus of the visible shrinks,
waves of red-capped boletes rise beneath conifers.

II.

A sunfish strikes the fly
as soon as
it hits the water;

the time of your life
is the line extending;

when he blinks,
a hairlike floater
shifts in his left eye;

when is joy
kindling to greater joy?

this nylon filament
is transparent in water
yet blue in air;

grasshoppers
rest in the tall grass.

III.

Perched on a bare branch, a great horned owl
moves a wing, brushes an ear in the drizzle;
he can't dispel how it reeks of hunger as he
slams a car door, clicks seat belt, turns
the ignition key. Then he recalls casting
off a stern: he knows a strike, and, reeling in
the green nylon line, the boat turns; and as
a striped bass rises to the surface, he forgets
he is breathing. Once, together, using fifty
irregular yarrow stalks, they generated
a hexagram whose figure was Pushing Upward.
What glimmers as it passes through the sieve
of memory? For a decade they have wandered
in the barrancas and grazed Apache plume.
He weeds so rows of corn may rise in the garden;
he weeds so that when he kisses her eyelids,
when they caress, and she shivers and sighs,
they rivet in their bodies, circumscribe *here.*

IV.

A great blue heron
perched
on a cottonwood branch;

tied
a Trilene knot;

a red dragonfly
nibbles the dangling fly
before he casts;

when he blinks,
he recalls their eyelashes;

casting
and losing sight
of the line;

the sky moves
from black to deep blue.

V.

Ravens snatch fledgling peregrine falcons
out of a cliff side, but when they try to raid
a great horned owl's nest, the owls swoop,

and ravens erupt into balls of black feathers.
At Chichén Itzá, you do not need to stare
at a rack of skulls before you enter the ball

court to know they scrimmaged for their lives;
when the black rubber ball rebounded off
a hip up through the ring tenoned in the wall,

spectators shrieked, threw off their robes,
and fled. The vanquished were tied into balls,
rolled down stone stairs to their deaths.

In one stela, a player lifts a severed head
by the hair, while the decapitated body spurts
six blood snakes. You become a black mirror:

when a woman pulls a barbed cord through
her tongue, when a man mutilates himself
with stingray spines, what vision is earned?

VI.

Lifting a tea bowl with a *temmoku* glaze,
he admires the russet that emerges along the rim;
though tea bowls have been named *dusk,*
shameless woman, thatch hut—this nameless one
was a gift. He considers the brevity of what
they hold: the pond, an empty bowl, brims,
shimmers with what is to come. Their minds brim
when they traverse the narrow length of field
to their renovated pond: they have removed
Russian olives, planted slender cinquefoil,
marsh buttercup, blue iris, marsh aster, water
parsnip, riparian primrose, yellow monkey flower,
big blue lobelia, *yerba manza,* and though it
will be three to five years before the full effect,
several clusters of irises pulled out of mud,
placed on an island, are already in bloom.
A bullfrog dives, a bass darts into deep water
as they approach, while, above, a kingfisher circles.

VII.

They catch glimpses of trout in the depths,
espy two yellow ones flickering at a distance.

He thought a teal had drifted to shore but then
discerned it was a decoy. Venus rising does not

signify the end of this world. In the backyard,
he collects red leaves from a golden rain tree.

Here is a zigzag path to bliss: six trout align
in the water between aquatic grasses; wasps

nuzzle into an apple; cottonwood leaves drift
on the surface; a polar bear leaps off of ice.

He does not need to spot their looping footprints
to recognize they missed several chances before

finding countless chanterelles in a clearing.
If joy, joy; if regret, regret; if ecstasy, ecstasy.

When they die, they vanish into their words;
they vanish and pinpoint flowers unfolding;

they pinpoint flowers and erupt into light;
they erupt and quicken the living to the living.

Three Poems
Sylvia Legris

FLIGHT SONG OF THE OLD WORLD . . .

1.

Respiratory
Tract.
Ascend
the alveolar

ridge where tongue
-tip invokes Song

Sparrow,
chi-
chip
Chipping

2.

Sparrows,
Wood
Warblers

warbling
water.
Aer-

o

-dynamic
swim up

3.
the laryngeal
stream.
Water-
winging-

it flight
of the
dumb un-

founded
sound-
tract.
(Respiratory

4.
intractability.)

5.
Pulmonary
dialysate:
Ante-

diluvian
filtration (out

with the old
    and in
with the older),

lungs in-
filtrated

6.
by House
Sparrows
(saggital-

narrow
passage, O_2
bypass).

7.

Passer
domesticus
–200 million

year old flight-
path of old
soul-dead

air, glottal

8.

stoppage,
glosso-

pharyngeal
ballistics.
Old World air-

9.

balloon, inter-
clavicular

ballast,

feather-
light,
feather

Sylvia Legris

GRUS CANADENSIS

Cranes have eviscerated the sky.
—Miroslav Holub

1.

Long
guttural
clatter.

Coiled
trachea.

Pneumatic
antiphonal
dance.

2.

Lungs

an open marsh,
fenland, quagmire
of low gurgle and iron-
oxidized aspiration.

3.

Sandhill crane.
Spark bird,
bird that

burst

into the broncho-
pulmonary
decibel.

4.

Shallow-
bend
maracas. Ribs

an anatomical
percussion.

Rattling
alveoli (breath

pebbles
the shoreline,
a line of un-

hatchable
eggs).

5.

Hollow

bone

intubation.

6.

Eye
the epiglottis,
then eyeball

the distance
from dry lands
to wetland.

7.

Plosive.

Rust-
stained
vocal

coordination;
dry
rustling

bulrush.
Fray

of stilt-
tarsi
and wind

propulsion.
(Exploding
seed heads.)

8.

Tidal volume
versus air flow.

Spirometric
duet.

Disarticulated
ga-roo-
                    oo-oo
blusters coast-

line to inter
-costal.

9.

Muscular relay
of bronchi
and water-

bugler.

ALMOST MIGRATION . . .

1.

of the Half-
Collapsed
Flight-

Depleted
Lung.

2.

Rib-pleated
concertina,
back and forth

windpipe
ambivalence

*. . . debating oxygen as form . . .**

3.

Order
Strigiformes:

Barrel-chested
disputations.
Single-

*Will Alexander

lobed snowy
Owl opus
(new snow-

4.

soundless).
Pneumo-

5.

thoracically
prone
Burrowing

Owl reverb.
Quickquickquick

False-
winged,
false

6.

vocal cords.
Faulty
pneumatics.

Athene cunicularia:
Lung-squatter,
oxygen-borrower.

Fossorial.

7.

Burrow
into feather-
cortex, context

of fossil-
instinct,
migration

-cumbersome
bone. Lung-

8.
lumbering.

Primordial
air (Jurassic

flight).

Three Essays from the Warbler Road

Merrill Gilfillan

NEAR ROME, GEORGIA

THIS IS A PRETTY MORNING in a strange place, a chilly fall morning in an unfamiliar forest, a dewy, southern oak and hickory forest with a bouquet of old ball glove and missed fruit going possum-soft at the feet of the trees. There are warblers in the oaks—Tennessees and myrtles, a few Blackburnians, and a palm lower down. Blue jays cry out with that tone they save for mid-October. Thrushes feed in the upper limbs, and then a thrasher goes up to join them. Oak leaves fall; hickory nuts show stark against the pale blue sky. And all the strange place needs now is a man or woman to wander through, burn through, name the shrubs and berries and dub one of those restive birds in the poison ivy vines the fire-throated Georgia warbler.

Those mistletoe clusters in the bare treetops remind me of the mistletoe shooters I read of years ago, country boys somewhere in the South who knock the mistletoe clumps out of high trees with a well-placed shotgun blast and later peddle them for the Christmas season in nearby towns—a most fragrant variety of the dying art of classical Forage—and the crested flycatcher calling in the middle distance reminds me of a hundred things: things both near-at-hand familiar and starkly exotic, even regal, as it has ever since I encountered its semitropical cousins, the dusky-capped and the ash-throated flycatchers, near the Mexican border—and now its call hints at distant, Olmec/Toltec, influential kin.

But then there comes a white-eyed vireo, busy feeding in the understory, singing a barely discernible, offhand, off-season song now and again, obviously for the simple purpose of keeping himself company, and with that well-known eccentric mutter on my ear, the place is steadied, translated, I am back on solid navigable ground.

Saigyo and other old-Asian-timers referred to birdsong so frequently in their poems that I eventually bought a field guide to Japanese birds in order to guess in more educated fashion at the songs they invoke—like the oft-mentioned bush warbler calling in various weathers from eighth-century shrubbery.

Birds were a critical point of stabilization for those poets' constant, insistent attention to Placement, in their daily refining and tracking of coordinates and footing in the universe. The insistence is of such an existential magnitude that the bearings it seeks become an Ur-placement and the coordinates-of-moment (season/blossom/bird-in-relation) become continuous framings of questions on the order of "Where, in the Enigma, are we?" and "What, in the Enigma, is our lot?" Questions seeking a proper, as in fully awake, human situs within the whirling seasons: primordial crux, with cuckoo calling.

For many years I thought such insistence, persistence, to be little more than poetic/Buddhist convention in the hands of remote masters. Later I happened across the gestaltists' notions on the perpetual unconscious placement-within-world known as "auditory streaming" (or even "auditory scene analysis"), wherein each creature's nervous system segregates the endless sounds of existence into various "streams," assigns them differentiated sources, pertinences, and planes: the world sorted and weighed via the ears.

And now it seems apparent that those poets of a thousand years ago, when they harked and measured, when they gauged the bush warbler in the bush and the pheasant calling up the hill, were instinctively as artists wooing and cultivating those intuited limbic levels of fundamental Placement. They wielded the archetypal Joy/Need of the process in their poems in the same way troubadours, or any dime-store love song, celebrate the Joy/Need of the sensual/sexual.

When I close my eyes in Georgia, or conjure Georgia, it is the mockingbird that is strongest on the ears. It is the endemic constant of the entire quarter continent. It was singing outside the motel, singing from a flagpole at the Etowah mounds, and above the bongo drums in Grant Park, Atlanta, when we left the Cyclorama of the Battle of Atlanta, and from every magnolia tree, barnyard, and Confederate monument across the South.

The mockers are excellent, honest, in-the-same-boat company. The minor-key contradiction between their legendary mimicking music and their fierce, would-be-roadrunner mien is a critical part of their durability. Connoisseurs of the species report that certain individuals included fifty, even eighty, recognizable riffs in their repertories, sometimes working in the barking of dogs, or neighborhood crickets, or the whistling passing postman. They were, in earlier southern days, kept as cage birds—though they were no doubt restricted to the outer veranda.

And mockingbird song provides stout philosophical accompaniment, as well, so far as bearings and Ur-coordinates go. They would have kept Saigyo very busy. The Carolina wren, another constant of the South and binder of the Streaming, sounds mechanical, almost perfunctory in its vocalizations compared to the mockingbird's supple commentary. The mockers handle the material of the world, digest it and redistribute it, often most generously from semipublic places, in what is both a lovely and a vaudevillian exchange. The good-natured mimicry, daylong, nightlong, reaches well beyond mechanistic reflection and establishes a kind of editorial dialogue at once comical and nourishing, which insists that Song is primal information and Knowledge is a well-turned medley.

Someone passed along the anecdote of a nineteenth-century southern farmstead where a mockingbird sang from the home's chimney top each evening and into the night, and the man and wife, as in a benign Greek myth, fell asleep with that muffled cosmopolitan music floating from their fireplace. . . .

Bearings and tidings: "Not alone here yet again."

MAY DAY, THE SMOKY HILL

Yesterday I stopped at the North Fork of the Smoky Hill River and walked out across the bridge on Highway 40, the old National Road. There had been hard rain earlier to the north and the waters were just out of their banks, spreading around the scattered willows and running a muddy brown. There were numbers of cliff swallows looping above the bridge. The new brown floodwater already carried plastic bottles and Styrofoam junk from God knows where. To the north and south stretched the old familiar Smoky Hill uplands, miles of shadow-decked high plains and the great horizontal poise. But, I was thinking, just the swallows, no other birds. Then I heard a meadowlark sing from a fence post down the road.

A week before I had been browsing through *The Summer Atlas of North American Birds*. Toward the back of the book there are maps of species distribution, showing relative populations in graduating tones of orange. As I looked at the map for warbler breeding densities and saw that the mountains of central West Virginia held among the highest numbers of nesting warbler species, the darkest orange, I said to myself, "That's where I should be living."

A few days later I glanced at it again, as I planned my overnight trip to the Smoky Hill country. Far western Kansas ranked at the lowest tier on the "Overall Species Richness" map. On "Warbler Species Richness" the area was as blank white as the outer Great Lakes waters. A gloss and a generalization, to be sure; I know that from personal experience. But I couldn't help noticing as I readied my camping gear and wiped off the binoculars.

When I walked farther across the bridge and approached the railing at one point, thousands of cliff swallows suddenly erupted from below the span and began circling over me. Agitated, but only in the most civilized manner, *tew*ing and swirling in a great far-from-hysterical cloud. From a single species to thousands of individuals in two seconds flat. As I turned back toward the car I confess that I had the distinct impression that each bird was slightly different from its kin, as in temperament, even personality, and giving me a slightly different sort of glance and evaluation. Then I heard a Say's phoebe crying in the minority from somewhere downriver.

As I drove west I remembered a male black-throated blue warbler that not only wandered far west, but somehow became resident inside one of the Denver International Airport passenger concourses and stayed there many weeks. I saw it once, feeding on the hideous carpeted floor with a gang of house sparrows.

The Smoky Hill River has always been tough to get to know, to get close to. It was a far-flung place in Dog Soldier days and it still is by most standards. Years ago I begged a morning walk at the forks, west of Russell Springs, from a friendly rancher. This year I was kindly given permission to camp a night along an isolated stretch of the main river in Logan County.

I planned the visit to see the full moon rise. Yesterday afternoon I pitched my tent in the yard of a hundred-year-old unoccupied stone ranchhouse, just a few feet from a blossoming lilac, and took a walk down to the river and then upstream to get acquainted. The Smoky

Hill water here was still clear and pleasant; the North Fork runoff was nowhere in sight. I hiked out from the cottonwood grove and followed the stream closely for a mile. There were mixed sparrow flocks in the river brush and a Swainson's hawk overhead. I took off my shoes to wade the cellar-cool river and walk up to a whitish butte on the south side. I stopped to pick a token sprig of new four-inch sage, and two brown thrashers began to sing antiphonally over in the trees. Pretty soon, with the quietest of quiets and the cottonwood leaves fluttering, that open-country "all we ever wanted" feeling rose up from its deep well. I came back to camp on that side of the river, climbing up on rises now and then to check the grasslands tilting and teasing to the south. There were wild turkey tracks everywhere preserved in the dried ceramic mud of the banks.

I could watch the river from a quarter-mile distance as I readied my camp for evening, keep an eye on its silver sliver easing through the cottonwoods. I had agreed not to make a fire, so I ate beans from the can and waited for the full May moon to struggle through light cloud cover, which it eventually did with fine striptease flair. Then a distant poor-will began to call. By the time I got my bedroll arranged and closed my eyes, barn owls were shrieking and hissing in one of the trees near the tent, there was a great horned hooting down by the river, and the moon rolled on.

This morning I am walking the other way, downstream. I cut into the large grove below the house, just where the river curves drastically to the right. It is a heady stand of trees and immediately there is an oriole calling, and a warbling vireo. I get the feeling there must be a hesitant migrant songbird somewhere in its leaves; moments later, a Swainson's thrush flushes up from the ground in mild surprise.

Where the Smoky Hill bends to the south it slows to form a kind of sluggish slough bordered by fallen and twisted cottonwoods that testify to a ripping storm some time ago. Beyond the blue jay group it is a clear, still, very early morning. Then the channel fattens into a backwater pond forty yards in length, with ten teal on it. I walk on downstream another half mile or so, sketch a gnarly, pretzel-bent cottonwood hulk, retrace my steps to the blond bluff above the pond, and climb up on top to sit a while amid the scattered sandstone rocks—they seem to weather off into bright flakes with the appearance of delicate fungus flesh—and patches of wild chives blooming pink and white. Would that I had a one-man omelet pan and a teal egg.

Looking south, I can make out with the binoculars three further substantial bends of the river. So many doves calling in waves beyond the stream mellow the place, render it almost sleepy. It's nice to think of the supple river of dove call meandering from this point east across the Kansas plains. Miles to the west, a rough outbreak of deep orange rocks, an extended dark ochre escarpment, catches the early sun. I watch two Baltimore orioles face each other down at a one-foot distance, bobbing and *twerp*ing in stylized diplomacy.

Twenty hours is hardly a lot of time to get to know a place. At least I've laid thankful eyes on this reach of the river, wet my feet in its sweet water, and, most importantly, slept within owl call of its cottonwoods. The roily North Fork flow still hasn't shown up; ranch dams must be slowing it down.

I'm betting a yellow warbler will find that inviting, greenwood grove upstream where I waded across yesterday. He's just not here yet. That song will add a sharp-edged antimirage note to the valley.

A friend recently told me there are groves along the Arkansas River in western Kansas that yield morel mushrooms this time of year in quantities ranging into many hundreds of pounds.

The wild turkey gobblers start up a noisy chorus back toward the ranch house. They woke me at daybreak this morning, just in time to catch the final quarter hour of the bulging May moon before it slipped with surprising speed below the horizon. It was a moody dark honey orange. Just about the color of those bittersweet-toned rocks off to the west. And now these flashy half-orange orioles.

MIMBRES WARBLERS

Looking for birds in the high mountains often entails stationing oneself at a point overlooking enormous spaces, distant ranges and muted valleys far below, and essentially waiting for a bird to appear, zoom in from afar, light in a pine for a moment, and zoom away. It establishes a mood of passive suspension that smacks of the begging cup.

But it wasn't that way with the olive warbler this morning, near Emory Pass in the New Mexican Black Range. When I got out of the car about eight o'clock at 8,800 feet elevation, the hermit thrushes were singing and in a minute I could spot them here and there, pale puffs high in the spruces across the hillside. Then I hiked out the trail from the east side of the pass.

It is inherited knowledge that Emory Pass is a dependable place to find olive warblers, and it was steadying knowledge as I moved slowly along the trail, steadying after thirty minutes of nothing but chickadees and an occasional Audubon's warbler zooming into a pine from afar. But then, at a convenient point above an intimate, open-pine slope, after a brief survey I saw a bird flutter, just once, in a young ponderosa fifteen yards below the trail and put the glasses on it. Through the needles I caught a glimpse of bright wing bar. A second later, I saw a flash of just-so reddish brown, and I knew I was on the right bird. And then it hopped a few inches farther out the branch and into the wide open.

And the olive warbler is a masterful bird. The field guides seem bound to depict it as somehow rough dimensioned and top-heavy. It doesn't photograph well, comes across as a scruffy sort of creature, an unkempt creeper. But they are all wrong—this is a top-notch warbler.

When the bird moved on, dropped down the mountain, I walked back to a comfortable opening I noticed earlier and sat for a while, taking in the immense vista to the east, off over many leagues of foothill and Chihuahuan desert, off to the Rio Grande itself fifty miles out, and beyond, toward ghostly El Paso.

Two days ago I picked up the Rio Grande near Santo Domingo as I drove down from Colorado, and the river's delicate chartreuse late-April presence was with me for the rest of the day. Lacy, fresh-leaved trees, green and citrine all the way, just off to the right a mile or more, eight hours of it. Even through the trying suburbs of Albuquerque, most trying of suburbs, it lent the conviction that whatever monstrosity any current occupants might devise along its course is utterly comprehensible, even pardonable, so enticing and succulent are the river and its edges. . . . And then, south of Socorro, the scent of greasewood was on the air, plangent and deep, and the human realm and everything around it changed.

Looking back, looking down at the vast system from the Black Range, the entire landscape casts the essence of greasewood. In the way a gingko leaf can summon a Chinese/Confucian light, the greasewood zone has its distinctive mentality, far removed from a high-mountain conifer-perfumed head. It casts a stringent, honey green haze of distance, bouquet, and untethered time and careless past through which the foothills tumble and wash silently into the dry Chihuahuan bottomlands. Greasewood of the five hundred million creatures of nearly identical size, form, spidery elegance, all deployed in perfect equitable spacing, copper/umber/olive green, gracious as uranic stargazer lilies.

It is a teleological view, with time motes dancing lazily across the topography. It incites one to philosophical thoughts with an oddly practical edge to them: I find myself thinking (for the first time, I believe) that a dry-eyed mummification is the most fitting and intelligent means of handling the human postmortem. Far better than fire, the blinding hurry of fire. A civil, cotton-wrapped, safe-cave-dried mummification, of course, in the aromatized Chihuahuan air.

Greasewood
in numbers more lovely
than hair.

I came down from Colorado to spend time with the red-faced warbler, and then the painted redstart, the olive and Grace's warblers. When I stepped from the car at the Iron Creek campground in the mountains east from Silver City, a painted redstart was right there, foraging in a box elder almost overhead. A pair of Grace's warblers worked high in the pines. A quarter hour later, as I wandered and watched the treetops, a red-faced began to sing above the little stream—the song was unfamiliar enough to command immediate full attention—and then flew casually into near-at-hand view, straight to the begging cup. When the bird with its provocative crimson almost brash against its otherwise chickadee tones flew off downstream, there was the distinct feeling that the day would quietly diminish from that point on.

At the bridge over Rio Mimbres the other day, that sampling of the great name, there was an oriole in the willows and a half-moon in the sky, and a worldwise cow in the pasture nearby who watched me as she chewed. She had, from the looks of her, some Santa Gertrudis in her past. The river course is lush beneath its shady canopy. Then, off to the east, a signature quail began to call—that pleasing tilde on the morning air—and soon I saw a pair of them along the berm of the highway and couldn't help thinking: the place bears up, still owns and runs itself. . . .

From my spot up near Emory Pass I can see the Mimbres Mountains and portions of the Mimbres valley below, but cannot pinpoint the river among the rumples and folds of the shadowy outwash. We are not in Line-of-Sight relations at the moment. And that is fitting for that stream and its almost painfully evocative name: it lifts us gently to the realm of memory and the speculative, the realm of art beyond the level of the first-hand visible, where we handle things on the carom, the carom off the clouds, and the quail call from the day before yesterday takes pure form as, naturally, the quail on a Mimbres bowl. The design known as "Pair of Quail with Hatching Eggs," perhaps.

Sitting here above that valley, remembering certain favorite bowl motifs like "Three Long-legged Birds" and "Cat-tailed Antelopes and Human Hands," I can convince myself that a Mimbres potter built a pot, as yet unearthed, carrying the flashy schema of a red-faced warbler, or the irresistible black-and-white patterns of the painted redstart, maybe a singing trio of them, brilliantly entwined and wheeling in everyday sidereal symmetry.

From The Tinajera Notebook

Forrest Gander

                    Through my torso, the smooth
        diffusion of aguas ardientes. Another
shot. Dawn

                    Fan whir covers distant
        rooster crow, dog bark cuts fan whir.

That the world has you in its time? Is that what
                                                  she said? Meaning I too
                  drank from the glass on the night table, swallowing
        the spider before I knew
                                        I'd seen it?

        And so the ache to pass through. But through
what? Two girls in high heels
          and Communion dresses
                                        cross in front of the window, necks
                                                              bent as herons.

                  I turn back to the hechicera, her face whirled
        with lines, ashen. . . .
                    You have the eyes of ________, she
        repeats. *De donde viene?*

Forrest Gander

And the present
hoses out. And with it—
Sitting in the lobby in the brain-
tumor ward, its walls painted
like children's rooms with starfish
and trains and jungle birds

and the children shuttling back and forth, the nurse
saying their name and a few words
in English or Spanish, the children
taking their mother's,
their father's hand
following the nurse behind
the registration desk, down
the hall, a sequence of closed doors,

toward the one door open. Radiance inside. Bald
children wearing hats, and a bald baby in a mother's arms, and
here in the lobby, where I wait for my friend,

one of the fathers whose exhaustion
can't be fathomed, begins to snore. If this is

the world and its time,
when I step out
into sunlit air suffused with sausage smoke and bus exhaust,
with its relentless ads
for underwear and liquor,

where am I then?

The Tzotzil
shepherdess
tells me through
the interpreter
she has
heard of
our lost
bird that was
found

* * *

You have the eyes of ________.
I was speaking to the bird.
De donde viene?

Grace's warbler—he's little
but he pishes-in real well.

Had I just translated *Siento que mi fatiga se fatiga* as
My get-up-and-go done got up and gone?
Something my mother used to say.
Then fell asleep for twenty minutes on a bench
in the zócalo and woke refreshed. As
though there had been a door left open
from last night's sleep
and it was sufficient to return only
long enough to close it.

Came to with a memory of lying
in my mother's lap in pajamas
as she cleaned my ears. Vaguely sexual.

Forrest Gander

Grackle din covers bootblack brush, organ
grinder cuts grackle din.

Although I couldn't
take my distance from it—

the sow asleep at the edge of
the dirt lot, a pariah
dog all but kneeling to suck
the sow's swollen teats.

Sound of TV cartoons
carries through the scrim of jungle
into the pyramid complex.

Through my mother, who was a weaver
and spent the year making two rugs
I thought I had learned patience,
but as I approach slowly
to identify the source,
thinking, I don't know, I'm not sure, we'll see,
the metallic clicking in the piñons—insect? frog? bird?
changes pitch and
stops altogether.

* * *

Revealed always
in situation. In Chiapas, the hechicera had told me,
herons will approach from the left.
A sign of what?

Returning again
to the ever-iterated assertion
of my life. With you. And after
a little slack, pop-up moments of
attunement.
Windblown sand veils the road in front of us.
I can't begin
to track the changes of meaning
that have brought us here. Marriag
is what is
passed through. Then

you park and we get out
to check a beehive box
in the black mangroves. Coasting
down into the swamp
from our left, a bare-necked
tiger heron, ten feet away, midair—
its deep yellow iris
blinks,
taking us in.

Owl Puke

Diane Ackerman

I WOULD BE AN OWL if I could, an *ule,* a creature named after its sound. So, I would be a howl if I could, sweet cheat of the night, who slices open the air with soft serrated wings, so silently it neither warns nor muffles the sound of dozy prey. How far? An owl could read the bottom line on an eye chart from a mile off, or hear a mouse stepping on a twig seventy-five feet away. Tuning and retuning, I would be an owl with ears twin radar dishes, eyes winged binoculars. A screech owl because, though baby screechers screech, the adults make the most enchanting soft whinny-howl. Owl of the stethoscope ears.

I'd swallow meals whole, headfirst, tumbling soft and furry down my throat to a fiery plant that compacts all the inedibles into hard pellets. Twice a day, growing bloated and queasy, I'd stretch my neck up and forward, squeeze my stomach hard, and vomit a hairy bony nugget. Oh, I'd vomit gently, all things considered, not thrash and shake the pellet free for five minutes like some other inversely constipated owls. I'd coax these dainty pukes. Not like the giant sea cucumber that hurls up its whole stomach and tosses it, literally, at the missing feet of a wall-eyed fish, stealing away while the fish feasts, a slimy gutless wonder but alive.

I sing of owl puke, the pellets that pave my days and give refuge to fungi, beetles, and other tramps. Do they sound nicer as "fur balls"? I suppose. But a little cat fur swallowed while grooming can't compare to a stony wadded-up girdle of rodent, shrew, mole, gecko, and snake skeleton, mixed with beetle crackle and songbird wings, as if for a jigsaw puzzle of a chimera part mammal, part bird, part reptile, all tasty.

My friend Philip has a Jewish owl named Fivel who delivers messages for him, says, "*Whoo,* already" in a Yiddish accent, and drinks Owl-ade after tiring flights. But his pal, my messenger owl Percy, is an eastern screech owl like the one I saw in silhouette one evening, sitting in the branches of the magnolia tree just outside my bay window. I knew him by the ear tufts and the bowling-bag body, but it was too dark for me in the closing rounds of dusk to make out his amber eyes. See me? He would have read every line on my face, every eyelash. I don't know if he understood about reflection, or the removable exoskeletons of our cars, or our giant house nests built for us by strangers using tree wood and unidentifiable gubbins.

Yes, all things considered, I would be an *ule,* with a ukulele face, a cowl of gray feathers cupping my feathered jowls, talons sharp and strong as ice picks, parachute wings, a demisuit of down, *ule*-tide duels, and voodoo eyes. I would be possessed of the ultimate head swivel: upside down, around back, and front again over the other shoulder. Hunting among oaks, cottonwoods, and old shady maples, with broad wings outstretched and head tucked in tight, I'd flap hard and fast, feel the wind zinging through my garments, rarely glide or hover, while watching all the while for scuffling prey in the leaf litter and lawns.

I would sing duets with my mate during the day and bask in a male chorus at night, the hours tatted by sound. What a panoply of songs and calls! The territorial flute-and-glass-bell tune, *This is my land;* the chortling duet of *food bringing;* the descending whinnies of courtship; the *Here comes the sun!* and *Night is falling* hoots; the happy *pottering around the nest* hum; the scratchy *Yikes!* alarm call; the faint begging calls of hungry chicks; the explosive *Get off my land!* barks uttered in flight; the throaty trills while gabbing with a mate; the defensive hoots and barks at nest invaders; and the billboard-loud ad song, *Look no further, I'm one hell of an owl!*

When frightened, I'd escape myself by blending in with tree trunk or foliage, stretching my frame long, closing my eyes to slits, tightening my feathers, and standing still as old bark. In winter, I'd scoff hot meals of warm-blooded prey, and in summer cool crisp lizards, snakes, and bugs. And, it goes without saying, I would marry for life, a long life of a score or two, lengthened by living in the suburbs and devouring the rat race.

I would be an owl with wide feather skirts to curtsy with when courted by bowing suitors. Oh, the formal dances of courtship, ceremonial and quaintly Oriental. First a springtime male calls, robust as all get out, and I reply, we hoot messages several times, then I see him flying in, watch him perch nearby, and start head bobbing and bowing deeply, over and over, now and then winking one eye. Ignore him and he'll chase harder. Accept and the bill kissing and mutual preening begins, with the preened one uttering soft whimperings of delight, both fine feathered friends amused and enthused. Yes, all things considered, I would be an *ule,* with owl-bright eyes, creature comforts, wide warm wings, and down furbelow to wrap my chicks in owl love.

Catalog and Brief Comments on the Archive Written and Compiled by the Ministry of Sorrow to Birds

J'Lyn Chapman

OUR EYE IS ON THE sparrow. How do we account for the vertiginous death of winged things? We do not, or you do not. We drove, once, along unkempt highways, and the field doves flew into the beam of our headlight. It could have been a moth the way it flickered white, the way it was made small in the breath of our speed. But we did not stop in that summer night. We might have been crying, the complications of our own sorrow and a machine. And we were alone because no one came when we waited, and no one chased us when we moved. Not when we left nor when we arrived. Someone drove a flatbed truck and half of a house. They did not stop for us.

We are secularists who believe in the charity of attention. We believe that there is no god who knows the number of hairs on our heads. And if we are not watched, neither are the birds. We count the birds in the way we would want to be counted—to remember the way we would want to be remembered:

> He prayeth well, who loveth well
> Both man and bird and beast
> —Samuel Taylor Coleridge

The god Eros personified desire for those whose desire was a violent thing. Abjection means to tear asunder self and self. We cannot be whole because we cannot confront our own solitude. We are on both sides of self and other. One configuration: we are a lonely Narcissus. We do not bend to our face reflection, although our beauty is flocculent and makes the water shudder. Similitude of utterance is what we want, and so we soothe ourselves with soft tongues and are taken by the exactitude of our voice. We do not want harmony. We want our self doubled and one timbre. Another configuration: we don't want ourselves—we want ourselves. We say, "Do not give me love."

The self echoes, from the space behind, "Give me love." We believe in desire and its repulsion.

Thanatos is the other violence, means nothing for the dead, for the rest, mourning. We reason that desire is violent because it is predicated on absence and absence is the only absolute. We believe in science and absence, the subconscious and minor losses. We have proven potentiality of presence, which is to say we have proven absence. We belabor the point: all things shall die, but the rest (potential) remain sentient. Sentience is another name for desire. And so, in the dialectic of life and death, you can neither apprehend death as you cannot apprehend desire. You believe death is repugnant, but we do not or we no longer do. We concede our dynamism in the archive.

It is what enables this ministry. The Romans called her Nenia, the goddess of dying, mourning, lamentation. We do not administer sorrow. It is distinction on the blade of a knife. We serve in a ministry of sorrow. It is altruism, although we admit that the precision of our files produces a *jouissance* of sorts. Our service staves off aphasia, and we are, in turn, satiated by our photographs, our lists, our elegies.

It is an automatic production of pleasure, and we do not refuse it. We are stewards of death and we resist oblivion.

We do not anthropomorphize. We do not dress our agendas in human flesh. We do not find it easier to take notice if we imagine that a bird is peace, soul, imagination. The ancients said that if a man whispered his name into the mouth of a bird, he could obtain immortality. To put one's mouth against a bird's mouth is to risk breaking its wings.

> . . . the extreme response of our bodies
> to the absence of balance in nature
> which blindly makes one experiment after another
> and like a senseless botcher
> undoes the thing it has only just achieved.
>
> —W. G. Sebald

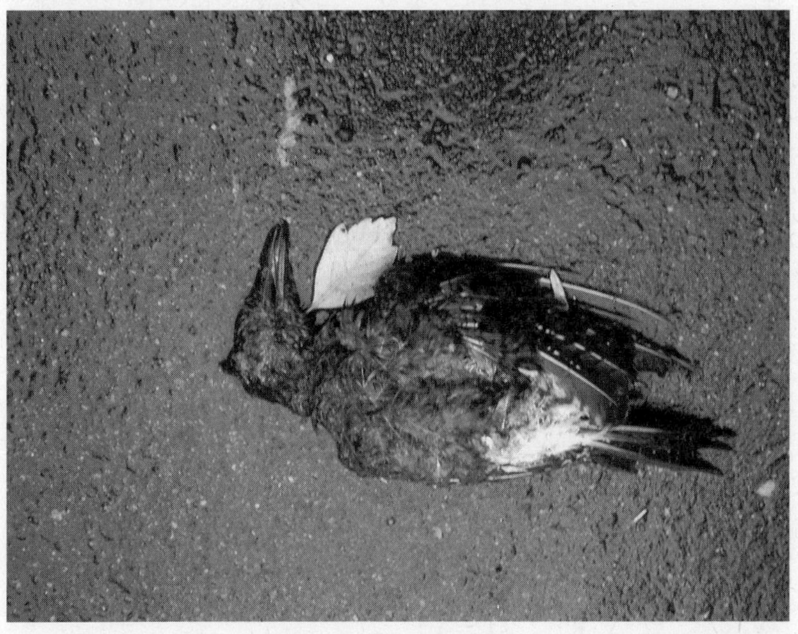

A woman finds a dead sparrow floating in a puddle of water among twigs and the debris from a trash bin the torrents have overturned. An Assisi, she is confronted with the violence of nature, dissension in the cult of tenderness she has tried to initiate and in which she believes nature participates. But she does not allay her disappointment by fashioning a logic of events that begins with man and ends with a dead sparrow.

It is a sparrow flying westward, against rain made dense in the pull of gravity; it is the common occasion of watery bulk against hollow slight. She names herself Drowned Sparrow when she plays cards; she keeps a poker face and clears the table.

A twentieth-century artist had at his disposal any number of texts and textiles with which to make an exotic and striking aviary. But he chose to film mostly pigeons and girls. The girls were pigeons; the pigeons were not girls. He's been charged with nostalgia. He's been charged with overusing birds as motif. Neither charge fits him. If anything, he was a nymphophile, who wanted to steal Diana's lovelies and disguise them as birds for his crippled brother's cages.

Metaphor and symbolism are distinct. The latter constitutes the discourse of nature, made in man's image, functioning as sepia-tinted nostalgia, and does bird and man a mean injustice. Metaphor is a slip not to be avoided. Say, for example, a sparrow flies in one window and out the other of an open room. It is the soul passing through the world briefly. Not like the soul. It is the soul, but not exactly. The house finch is not exactly a house. But it is approximately a small comfort.

A better example is the mockingbird that is not *as* so many birds, but is proximate to all birds. Its every-bird song identifies it.

We fear imprecision, but metaphor cannot be avoided, and even scientists use x and y to mean so many more particular things. And we should not forget the scientific terms "amber mutant," "naked beauty," "body burden," "autopsy," or the symbols ∞ and π.

> Description becomes an act not just of stenography but of philosophically strenuous constatation.
>
> —Martin Swales

We identify birds with photographs, but in the archive, we must offer as many entrances as we can. We identify the bird by its scientific name and its common name, and when destruction has eliminated classifiable characteristics, we use the word probably to mean the bird is somewhere beside itself, either *Spinus tristis* or *Spinus pinus,* for example. The photograph confirms the failure of language and its approximation. See how the feathers are black, but the head with its distinctive markings is missing? Or how all that is left is three clumps of feathers and a bone? (We cannot be certain this bird is even dead.)

In western Texas, a summer storm knocked birds from their nests, telephone poles, and the places where they fed. A farmer reported finding twenty-three dead birds on his property. He burned their bodies in a steel drum. We found eleven dead birds scattered over the span of one neighborhood block. Black swaths of flies drew us to their bodies. Various stages of decomposition. Predators. A wing lay five inches away from the trunk. We photographed a house finch off Highway 83. We bent down low to take its picture. Cattle trucks burst stench behind our backs. There was heat rising from the ground. We retracted at the dim smell, we gagged, there were birds in our mouths and we choked on their wings. And when we photographed the finch with red feathers on its breast and the soft, round head (slightly larger than our thumb), we felt greedy, and that we should make excuses. We called it science, and we came as aesthetes and extravagants, the artifice of our photographs giving us away. Purveyors of blushed-brown feathers. Our shadow in the frame. We were unprofessional, we lacked scientific objectivity, our bulwark and bastion. We came to the body of a bird as if to a lover's. We came with humility. We came for grace. We came on hooves and with the bodies of men. Our cheeks were flushed and our mouths dry. We betrayed ourselves.

Shame on you, shameful dark Orcus,
For gobbling up all the pretty things!
—Catullus

Our lamentation creates equity rather than excess, but it also creates motion. That we might also be known for knowing. We wish to believe that the lover has made a drawer for us when we are gone, lined with a topographical map of our hometown or the paper from a gift we gave. Love letters, photographs, stones smelling of the seashore, porcelain rabbit, book with inscription. It may never be returned to, but it will *be* when we are not. And perhaps the replacement lover will find it, and in some way, we are reintroduced, known by the ephemera we wanted to be known by in the first place. Or perhaps in the guise of keeping them alive, you allow them a descent interval of dim agony. The catalog is mnemonic device and metonym. The catalog gently strokes the tortured body.

The smallest body.

The smallest parts that make up the smallest bodies.

Decomposition shows us something dissection cannot: the perfect v of the lower mandible, monocular eye socket, the beak like a translucent and cleft seed. Exposed machine of metaphor, the sad mechanic exercise: the black feathers of the bird conceal sand and not anatomy, legs like Daphne's hands, Philomela's tongue, opalesque flies crawl out of the feathered shell as if out of calamus-spiked nest.

(What can dissection show us about sorrow? The broken eye, stepled rib, the oracle of entrails. We wore a black sweater and you a plaid shirt. There might have been leaves, maybe snow. Our feet might have crushed these. It might have been our teeth. No one knows how he may end up on some sidewalk in front of some dry cleaner's, or what mysteries are hidden in that other person's closed hand that comes at you out of anger or affection.)

Each dies, and the archive grows. They die eachly, and it is everything. Each being the sound of a breath, and each being the sound of an impact. And when one explodes, each explodes in many deaths, eachly made. Each stays and each goes. Eaches accumulate. Each, each, each, etc. And we are each but must portend the collective, obviate the each—not annul, but make an us, and each and everything made present.

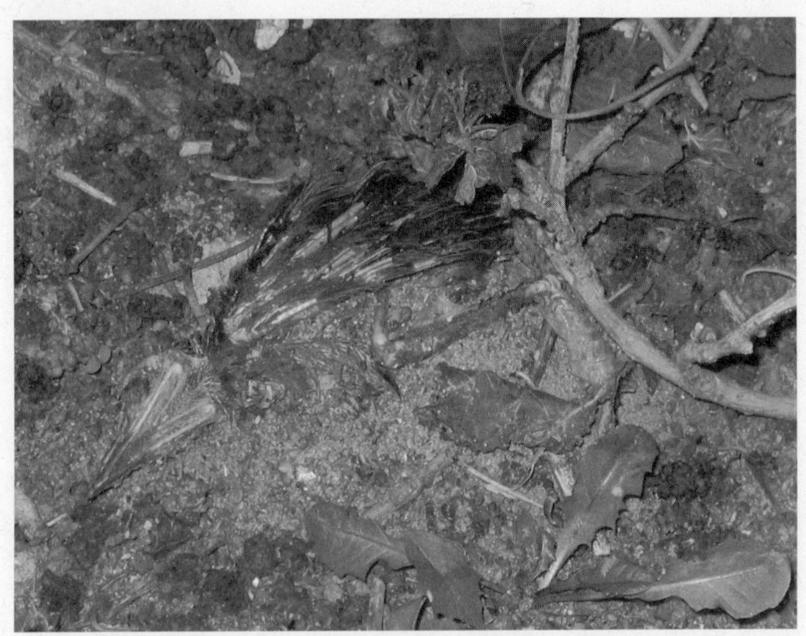

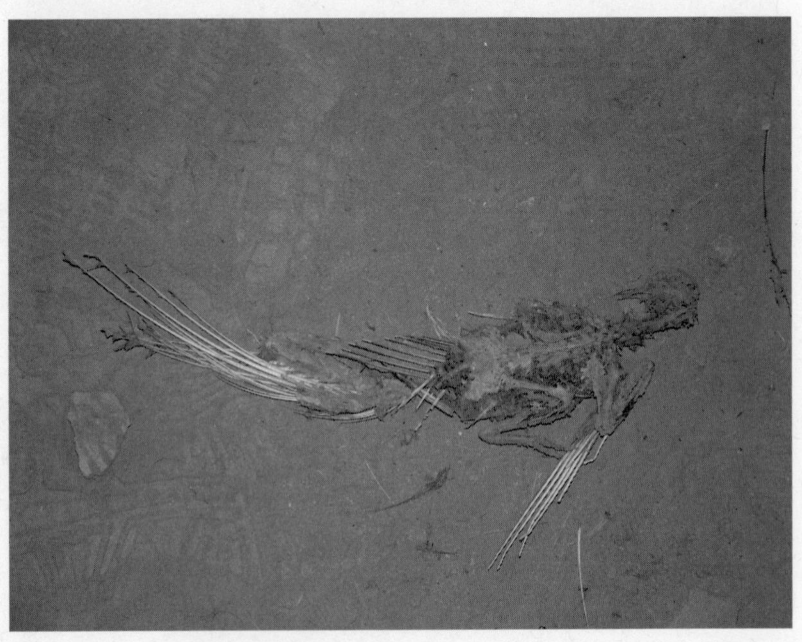

> Our little systems have their day;
> They have their day and cease to be.
> —Alfred, Lord Tennyson

Each a broken light, sparking forth from no sound, no anvil. There is no light more than this: the red-shafted, the ivory-crested, the blue and jet, the yellow-golden, the cardinal, the stormy. And light will burn the branches, if we begin to look. The world is set on fire by attention, and the pyre burns sweetly as weeds and words like weeds.

We were stopped, and looked down, in the walk by the bird, flies, cigarette, glint of coin. We saw the futility in keeping—the ornaments in hydriotaphia and their obsidian speaking something of its keeper. But the detritus we die alongside or do not die alongside, the litter jettisoned from our death and dying bodies or we die too quickly to regard, utter the currency of living things.

And there is this discomfort: the spectacle. Its hard edges. We have bodies too, we say, and we want them wrapped in webby husk, a film, a membrane huddled into self. But our bodies are still overlooked by our own *flânerie,* in which the world, and its subtle schism of that which is alive and that which is dead, becomes our final coup for all we have lost in the leaving.

We are boys on Emmonsales Heath.* We are dangerous for looking. We are peeping idlers "in anxious plundering moods." Our gaze reveals that nests are not safe. The bird and its pink chatter will also shun the chick so young its feathers curl. Nothing is safe from death; look for them.

In a letter, the poet John Clare wrote:

> [N]aturalists and botanists seem to have no taste for this poetical feeling they merely make collections of dryd specimens classing them after Leanius into tribes and familys and there they delight to show them as a sort of ambitious fame . . . with them "a bird in the hand is worth two in the bush" . . . well everyone to his hobby I have none of this curiosity about me.

*The boat on the water, its reflection in the lake, the companion's complexion, the smell of dirt and your mother's cooking. You were a little like a girl, and it made you soft to us as when you killed the bird and left it on the stairs to say, this is my wound and the promise that I will wound for you.

The poet betrays his curiosity, however, in his poems. What is the difference between the dumb bird in a glass box and the word "bird" performed on the space of a page? It is the difference between a crow and a raven, blue dust, stick and dust, dust and the talon still holding the branch, the branch that in three weeks becomes the talon.

What are now called Bird Poems, and what Clare intended to include in a collection titled *Birds Nesting,* bear their name because of the poet's particular attention to detail, the color and shape of freckled eggs, the location and design of birds' nests, and the pitch of "bird music." Poetry animates these birds. Flirting. Rocking. Drilling. "Extacy."

But death harrows the poems—in its absence; in its boys stealing eggs; in its attention to the behavior of birds in defense. The poem is a way to stimulate and protect, to provoke and secure. It flirts by supposing that danger has boundaries, then draws near to softly jerk away. Or, like the partridge protecting its young, it feigns its own death to draw attention away from chicks. It must balance the absence of materiality and the presence of language. Forgetting is a way to remember.

Tom Paulin writes, "Clare was fascinated—and tormented—by

boundaries and enclosures." How different is the stasis of poetry from the scientist whose botanizing feigns the living bird with glass eye and balsam wing?

> The worlds way is a cheating way
> And it would not be long
> Before they met a cloudy day
> And some to do em wrong.
> —John Clare

Several years after the Bird Poems are written, 1837, Clare voluntarily enters High Beach, a Dr. Allen's private asylum in Epping Forest. In July of 1841 he tries to escape. His wife, Patty, finds him improved, but in December of 1841, he is removed to Northampton Asylum, where he lives the rest of his life and writes:

> There is a charm in Solitude that cheers
> A feeling that the world knows nothing of
> A green delight the wounded mind endears
> After the hustling world is broken off
> Whose whole delight was crime at good to scoff
> Green solitude his prison pleasure yields
> The bitch fox heeds him not—birds seem to laugh
> He lives the Crusoe of his lonely fields
> Which dark green oak his noontide leisure shields

We are drawn to boundaries and the danger of boundaries. Flirting a boundary is our resistance to our own death. Not the dissolution of the corporate, but of the corporeal.

Sandhills in Chukotka

D. E. *Steward*

Cape Navarin comes up at dawn in lifting fog, one of the sites of the Pacific

The last headland but one before the Arctic Ocean and the Chukchi Sea

And next, the long passage across the Bay of Andayr toward the last Russian peninsula and the Bering Straits into the Western Hemisphere

On the morning of July 2, we were near 173° West and better than 64° North

With the sun breaking through to leave high subarctic lenticular clouds spread above the fog bank's retreat

As three parasitic jaegers, kleptoparasitism on falconesque wings, flew by over the metallic green sea

Its coruscant sheen like a sheathing of foil

Bering Sea ocean life teems

Darkness arrives and the life of the deep, the smallest worms to the largest squid and whales, swim vertically up into shallow waters to gorge on nutrients before descending before sunrise back into the safer darkness

And first sun out here on July 3 is at exactly 01:33

Bound for Cape Dezhneva

The sun's brilliance hits the pilothouse glass and the air outside in the cockpit warms instantly

Cape Dezhneva is one of the seminal headlands on the planet, with Cape Horn, Cape of Good Hope, Cape Guardafui, Nordkapp, Cape York

Later at nearly 66° deep in the Bering Straits, we're fighting gale-force northerlies slamming us on the nose

With no reasonable anchorage ahead until Wrangel Island at least two days' sail far off to the northwest

Just short of the Arctic Circle at the southern reaches of the Chukchi Sea

Not long after noon far off Ostrova Diomida (the Big and Little Diomedes) in perilous seas, we decide to turn back

Slammed and shuddered as we jive in the strange darkness of wind and spray

Midday but it looked like deep dusk

In the worst weather of the voyage

Imagining how much worse it must get before approaching the line of polar pack ice out ahead somewhere

At one point in June, not yet at 54° off southern Kamchatka, we had schemed to perhaps have the time and weather to sail out into the Arctic Ocean proper

To even get to Wrangel Island

Diablesse, her radar lost in the last three-day storm south of Cape Navarin, remains in sight as we retreat south

Sailing back down along this old-world boreal coast

Its murky and indistinct history, its culture of exotic wilderness tribes

The four Chukchi bird dancers back south of Cape Navarin near the fishing camps on Ozero Pekul'neyskoye, tall, skinny, and graceful

Flat sexy faces

Halting crane-set steps, dipping their strangely concave profiles that you see often here and occasionally in Alaska and the Yukon

In that throughput of Siberian genes dispersed in the Americas

The land bridge is an underlying low-key historical reference to everything up here

With shared languages, indigenous technologies in common, Carabelli cusps, ALDH gene defect, California gray whales, and sandhill cranes nesting in Kamchatka and Chukotka and wintering in New Mexico's Bosque del Apache

Chukchi and Yupik and Inupiaq

Chukchi and Yupik women dance on tundra bluff fishing camps like other lean women pigeon-toe down fashion-house runways

Like paired sandhill cranes dancing

And there are Pacific halibut and arctic char

Whales sounding

Monstrous Kamchatka brown bears scavenging the bouldered strands

The most common land birds on this Arctic Circle tundra are pipits, three kinds of pipits, petchora, red-throated, and water

Anchor off Lorino at 65.29°N, on the way back south to Provideniya

Progranichniki soldiers come out arrogantly and a tracked vehicle with what looks like a standard Soviet fifty-seven-millimeter smooth-bore cannon appears and aims directly at us

Kommando border guards

We're obviously lying off a military zone

A nervous and officious shave-tail lieutenant comes out in an old wooden outboard crewed by two amiable Chukchi enlisted men to tell us imperiously that it's no go

The old Progranichniki mentality still runs things in Lorino

Our skipper offers the lieutenant six *Leonore* ball caps for his huge green Progranichniki hat, the lieutenant says fine, plus two hundred dollars. No deal

And we're left lying at anchor off the beach watching summer life in the village

Three teenage girls come down to wade with pants rolled, then sit on the sand talking in the sun, temperature below ten Celsius and a stiff wind; eventually they climb the steep bluff back into town

Later in the day along the strand a young father skips stones with his little boy and another with his toddling little girl handlines a fish up on the swash

Each tableaux profoundly graceful, the calm that develops that evening, the quarter-mile distance, the absolute unapproachability of the place

From which a narrow single tractor road leaves the settlement over a rise across the tundra

Treeless

The track disappears over esker-moraine tundra hills

It would be very pleasing to walk along it and away over the rise, but it's another far-flung road never to be taken

Hours after midnight watch a lone figure walk out that road with something shiny blue, possibly a berry can, and disappear over the rise

We sail off the anchorage in fresh morning breezes, the mainsail luffing beautifully as a fast flight of long-tailed ducks precedes us down the coast

Down along the wind-polished landscape of the Chukotka coast

Wind and sea

Past the mainmast, against the horizon

The Genoa is flatter, the reacher is larger and fuller

Spectacular day booming south toward Yanrakynnot village

Where we do not land, as interesting as it looks, because sailing comes first for the skipper and it is a perfect sailing afternoon, so we are not here a couple of hundred meters off Yanrakynnot, a village on a steep ridge above the sea

But we are not here because we are sailing

The fiord, Bukhta Penkigngen, is as majestic as anything on the whole voyage, the common eiders cutting across and *nothing* that has not been here forever

Anchor at 173.06.8°W, 64.45.6°N

A yellow-billed loon is vivid diving not far off the stern

Thick-billed murres

A lean red fox trots away on the fiordside

D. E. Steward

Ashore to hike up the Kotlyaren River

Only a kilometer in, come over a bare ridge overlooking the river's green floodplain that finishes in upslope snow all around

At the edge of the ridge's glacial rubble come onto three hunting pits

They could be decades or thousands of years old

Rimmed with piled stones, large enough to hide two or three people lying prone

Hunters lay there probably talking quietly as caribou slowly spread out into the valley from the high fells, until they stood and charged with spears, atlatls, and their long knives

Their tribe, their clan, may have been on their way to cross Beringia

This twenty-first-century day only reindeer sign among the flowers, an abundance of low grasses and tiny flowers

Out on that moss green plain

Not far away a much more recent ring of single stones, probably from a yurt being struck and the stones holding down the bottom left where they fell

Down on the river, sloshing around from hummock to island to boulder to hummock trying to get close to a pair of nesting sandhill cranes that are appearing and disappearing in and out of the river-ine brush

More sandhill cranes on the tundra from the evening's anchorage nearby

Slip slowly, crouched low, step, stop, wait, step, into the lonely intensity of cranes flying in and out, landing, stalking around, bending, bowing, wing-scrape turns

D. E. Steward

Very large, two-meter wingspan, a meter and a half tall

Grus canadensis

The cranes migrating the whole way to eastern Siberia from New Mexico are the largest of their breed

Crawl close, prone into a sphagnum pocket in the fragrant springy cushion thatch with three, at times four or five, dancing nearby, one within a few meters as though courting my form lying there

Two face each other, leap high with wings extended and feet thrown forward, bow to each other, and do it again

Eerie, loud, croaking calls

They break away and run in irregular circles as though protectively with their wings outstretched low

Stop abruptly, pluck and toss grass tufts in the air

Then fly off, circle, and land nearby

Quintessentially of the tundra

Eerie, strong, calls on the wing. Loud, rattling bugling

Then landing, stalking around, swinging heads side to side, a loud vibrancy in their croaking

They continue the dance and short flights in the low midnight light as if they would go on and on interminably

In restless, lonely intensity

Move off from them quietly

Back to the boat, consider trekking across the peninsula to Provideniya, distance only perhaps twenty-five kilometers and apparently quite direct with only one mountain to cross

But the wilderness risk, no map except for a nautical chart, the chance of gale-driven rain or unexpected gorges and ridges, the bears

And if a couple of us had left the boats to hike to Provideniya, we'd have missed the Seklyuk anchorage and Ostrov Arakamdchechen, the whalebone cape

Seklyuk behind Cape Konovak, 172°31.44W x 64°38.7N, was a fine afternoon anchorage, two pairs of tufted puffins mating just thirty meters off, the males flapping like eggbeaters to stay on the females

A male long-tailed duck shooting by very close vividly lit up in direct sun

The hurried energy of the sea ducks so frequent here is what's most immediate, the long-tailed, the harlequins and spectacled eiders, the common eiders

From the dinghy onto the black beach rocks in front of the site, find fresh bear scat, look around carefully back up the draw upslope, walk on toward the bowhead whale ribs that rear up like Carnac's menhirs

They have the graceful, slim Brancusi curve of a whale's torso's shape, tips to the sky pointing at a time-in-zenith infinity

A color photo of Seklyuk on Cape Arakamdchechen—soaring arctic clouds, tundra, windy sea, files of whale ribs and jawbone skulls—clipped five years ago from the *TLS,* October 8, 1999, on my workroom wall almost a hundred degrees of longitude away

Agape and awed at the sacred site, but after thousands of miles sailing up this coast, Seklyuk is what it is, another spectacular Siberian headland

All of which have known ancient rites and mysteries

Whale and walrus skeletons and bones, the tundra-covered volcanic slope down to the glacial gravel strand, the cold, cold Bering Sea

Leaving Cape Arakamdchechen, swing close to Nuneangan, the highest and most populous bird rock of our voyage, a profusion of puffins and black-legged kittiwakes

A large bronze plaque attached to the face at a ledge a third of the way to the crest, unreadable Cyrillic, we're perhaps a hundred and twenty meters off

And high almost at the top of one of the rocks, a lime green beacon that must be one of the dangerous radioisotope thermoelectric generators. Hundreds of these RTGs on the coasts of Russia used as power sources for lighthouses and beacons

Fair game for anyone wanting the strontium 90 in them

Dirty bomb material up for grabs

Turn southwest off Ostrov Nuneangan with the weather dampering down and move up Bukhya Provideniya with radar in near-gale erratic winds, heavy seas and driving rain

A thousand miles north of the Aleutians

Ave Maria

Micaela Morrissette

She herself could once have imitated the notes of any bird.

—James Burnett, Lord Monboddo
Of the Origin and Progress of Language

In summer, in that countryside, there was no dawn, but a sudden sun, that lashed out over the ridge, broke itself upon the sharp peaks, and poured down like rain. The fields swam with wheat, and the wheat bristled and stabbed at the onslaught of the day. On the edge of the fields was a tree, and the sun boomeranged off the glossy leaves and went pinwheeling back to the atmosphere. In the tree was a bird, and the sun sank into its matted hair, and oozed on its scalp. The sun trickled into the bird's eyes, and the bird raised a scabrous claw to wipe it away.

The ridge to the east, then the field, moving westward, then the tree; beyond the tree, a village. The village had not waited for the sun. It had already begun to draw its water, rob its chickens, stir its coals. Its air was greasy with candle smoke and bacon fat.

In the tree, the bird plucked a caterpillar from a nearby branch. With a nail, it split the caterpillar lengthwise; with a gray tongue, it licked the soft open stomach. The bird tucked the body of the caterpillar between its back teeth and its cheek. A breeze blew the smoke from the village into the tree and the bird sampled the smell. Its eyes were hard and beady. It stared at the roofs of the cottages and hunched its shoulders. Its heart beat very fast.

The arrival of this bird had driven away the other birds. They spiraled around the treetop, screaming and hissing. The bird reached out its claws to them. *Tweet, tweet,* said the bird. *Toowit, toowit. Caw, caw.* A parent whose nestlings remained several branches above the head of the bird screeched and veered in to attack. The bird in the tree flapped its wings wildly before its face, but did not ascend.

A boy led his goats along the edge of the field. Approaching the tree, he watched the birds buzzing angrily around the crown and thought of flies on a corpse.

The bells of the village church were swinging. *Bong, bong,* said the bird softly. *Din, dan, don.* The throat of the villagers were throbbing with singing. *Ave Maria,* croaked the bird, *amen.* The goats were ripping at the wheat in a frenzy, and the bird could smell the dust raised by the clogs of the boy as he pelted down the path back to the village. The bird swallowed thickly. The caterpillar had turned sticky and tough in the back of its mouth.

The sun rose in the sky and melted, drenching the field and tree and village. A steady procession swam through the syrupy sun to the tree. The rays slithered off the bird's mangy plumage and plopped in long sebaceous strings from its branch to the ground. Observing several villagers reaching out their hands and handkerchiefs to catch these driblets, the priest issued his reluctant pronouncement: the goatherd had in his exulting innocence erred; this was no angel. The bird shifted on its haunches and splattered droppings onto the ground. A sharp jerk and shuddering twist took place inside it, like a hand wringing a goose's long neck. It teetered dizzily on the branch, and squeezed its claws tighter into the bark. *Ave, ave,* whispered the bird. *Tsstsstssss.*

A gendarme strode majestically into the scene. The bird watched his row of glittering buttons; the gendarme himself was a dark velvety cloth against which the buttons were displayed. A box was placed at the foot of the tree, the gendarme mounted it, hoisted himself to the first limb, and, clinging cautiously to the trunk, batted with his stick at the leaves above his head. With "astonishing speed" and "superhuman agility," the bird let go its branch, plummeted down in a flurry of snapped twigs, powdery lichen, and dead bark, yanked off a button from the gendarme's coat, scratched the gendarme's face, pulled the hair from his head, and clambered back up the tree. Reeling, the gendarme lost his grip and fell to earth.

The bird scraped out the caterpillar where it clung like cotton to the cheek and gums, and tucked the button in its place. The hot metal hissed slightly as it met the flesh, and the bird was rewarded with a small spurt of saliva. The bird swallowed this in clucking gulps. "It's cooing!" cried a child below. *Coo,* whispered the bird. It tucked the hair of the gendarme up safe in its nest, at the Y of the trunk and the limb. There was also a hawk feather, a sheet from an illustrated paper, a dead moth, and bits of a withered funeral wreath, once executed cunningly in the shape of a cross.

Word was sent back to the village that the apparition in the tree was not an angel after all, but a freak escaped from the carnival. Half bird, half human, gender as yet indeterminable, screened modestly by foliage. But tantalizing glimpses had been caught of cruel black talons; hair covering the body, stiff and coarse as quills; teeth pointed and curved like a row of little snapping beaks. As the farmers left their fields and the shopkeepers shuttered their windows for the midday break, the crowd swelled. Some villagers made attempts at capture: a broom was employed, a scythe, several stones. A cat summoned to its duty fled spitting, with its eyes starting out of its head. Seed was scattered on the ground, and everyone moved back a few steps, and waited, but the bird only abandoned its nest and climbed higher in the tree. When the breeze stirred the leaves the bird could be glimpsed, its neck craning, its face turned up toward the sky. The bird observed the passage of the clouds, but saw no pictures there.

The head of the bird was roiling with lice and it sucked hopefully at the ends of its hairs. The edge of a leaf scratched back and forth against its ear. The bark pressed red and white patterns in bas-relief into the legs of the bird and the bird prodded them, watching them swell and flush and fade. The bird's palms were covered with thick calluses and seamed with deep cracks and the bird moved the palms back and forth against its cheeks to feel the scratching. After a time it fell asleep. Whether it dreamed or not proves nothing.

Around the dinner hour, the gendarme reappeared, escorting Mme. J. Many of the watchers had departed by then; mostly children were left. One had speared an apple on a long stick and was poking it among the branches to tempt the bird. The gendarme had a pail in his hand. Shaking her skirts and fanning her face, Mme. J. banished the children and commandeered the pail. She had a jutting shelf of bosom and a wide, gliding stride. Her voice was calm and even. "I'm sure it's the same one," she said. She placed the pail at the base of the tree. It was full of cool water, and inside it swam an eel, dark and sinuous as smoke. "If it's her," said Mme. J., "she'll still have the shift we put on her. Not that she likes to wear it, but she wouldn't know how to take it off. Oh yes," she said, in response to the gendarme's inquiry, "my husband was going to report it to the mayor in the morning. But we only had her the one night. She was killing the rabbits in their hutches, and we were ready for her, and caught her. We got her locked in the shed, and got some clothes on her, and gave her a chicken to mangle—she only wanted meat, and only raw. But the next morning she was gone. She broke the lock on the door and the whole frame was dented and scratched—chewed maybe, even."

Mme. J. and the gendarme settled themselves in the bushes. "But as you know," she murmured, "we live seventeen miles away, and not a stream between here and there, not a puddle even. Poor thing."

In the pail at the foot of the tree, the serpent luxuriated, stretching, stroking its coils against themselves, rolling, and flicking its muddy belly skyward. The bird cocked its head and heard the water sigh as it caressed the eel. It tilted its head the other way, but the faint whistle of Mme. J.'s breath was all one sibilance with the slosh of the water soft against the side of the pail. The bird dropped to a lower limb. Its feet curled and uncurled. The bird hopped quickly. It fluttered to the ground. It huddled very still in the roots of the tree. Its face was in the bucket, and its hands. Its mouth met the mouth of the eel. The eel's tongue flickered. The bird bit down. The eel slithered easily through its gullet and curled itself in the bird's stomach. The bird's face was in the pail, its eyes were shiny and unblinking underwater, then the snick of the noose pulled tight around its feet, and the fluster of wings as the hood slipped over its head.

M'sieu le Docteur ran his fingers over the sharp shoulderblades that jutted from the back of the bird. Solemnly, he counted the vertebrae of the spine. The anklebones were pronounced, like vicious little spurs. He placed his wrist against the bird's wrist, and waited for its pulse to slow to his. He scratched lightly at the horny, twisted black nails that arched from the bird's enormous thumbs. The knees were buried beneath deep, scaly pads. The smell of the body was pungent but surprisingly sweet, like fruit that has fallen and begun to ferment. M'sieu le Docteur probed at the temples of the bird and felt the blood trembling inside its brain. The bird chewed nervously at its foot, but was otherwise docile. Age was difficult to determine; hair was present around the private parts and under the arms, but the entire torso was hirsute. M'sieu le Docteur tapped at the rib cage; the bones tinkled: a brittle, hollow, tinny sound. A flea emerged from the ear of the bird and raced down its chest and stomach, diving into its navel for cover. The bird cupped its hand protectively over it. The lungs were sound. Excretions were normal, considering the raw diet. Ocular and muscular reflexes were satisfactory.

M'sieu le Docteur settled himself at the small table provided for him and observed the bird. As it did nothing but huddle, squatting against the wall, its arms around its knees, its chin pressed into the hollow of its neck, he turned away his eyes, took up his pen, and wrote:

> Upon the apprehension of an apparent specimen of *homo ferus* on the outskirts of the village of S—, I was summoned to evaluate the medical condition of the creature, with a view both to its health and to determining the span of the years it had spent in the wild. With the exception of severe dehydration, the physical examination revealed no disease. Regarding reports made in the last three years of a bird/wolf/ape/devil-like manifestation sighted in the woods and at least twice in the village streets, the physical mutations—presumably adaptations to facilitate a life comprised almost entirely of running, climbing, and hunting—are sufficiently advanced to suggest that the sightings may indeed be assigned to the individual I examined. Whether a child now no more than ten, and at the origination of the sightings only seven years old, could have sustained its own life and defended itself from predators for such an extended period is a question not easily resolved. Yet it is difficult to imagine that this individual spent so much as seven years in civilization, as it has so far betrayed no knowledge of any social convention or means of human communication.
>
> *Human qualities*:
>
> The physical form of the creature is by and large human and female, though some of its parts are of exaggerated size (thumbs, feet, knees), and though it does not put all of its parts to their accustomed uses (scratches head with feet; runs on tiptoe with fingertips stabbing the ground at each pace; approaches unfamiliar objects and spaces mouth first, biting the bed, chamber pot, and my hand gently but firmly, in a spirit of investigation rather than attack). If it is in fact not of an altogether new species, then its peculiarities may be plausibly attributed not only to its savage lifestyle, but potentially to a state of idiocy, arising from its isolation or perhaps the original cause of its abandonment.
>
> While there is no evidence that the creature has ever experienced any meaningful interaction with a human being, neither does anything strongly negate that possibility. If it has no idea of human diet, hygiene, language, tools, or customs, still it does not shy away from people as an animal of a truly undomesticated species might do. I have been able to closely examine the insides of the ears, the bottoms of the feet, the

spaces between the toes, the back of the mouth, the roots of the hair, without opposition. Indeed the creature is perhaps more cooperative than the average human patient of its age. Now that it has resigned itself to its captivity, its stillness when touched is absolute, extending perhaps even to the quieting of its heartbeat. It bears an unnerving resemblance to the quail about to be flushed, more silent than death, but ready at any moment to explode out of invisibility in a hysterical churning of feathers.

General bestial qualities:

The creature's strength and agility are so remarkable as to be perhaps entirely beyond human capabilities, whatever the demands of the human's environment may have been. A gendarme who made the original attempt to communicate with it found, to his disadvantage, that it could race up and down the trunk of the tree in which it was discovered with all the thoughtless ease of an ant scurrying up a wall. The creature was coaxed from the tree and apprehended, but broke away from its captors en route to the jail, racing blindly (hooded) down the street with such speed that several women reported that the wind raised in its wake snatched the caps from their heads. When a mastiff was released to bring down the escapee, the creature bludgeoned the dog so violently with its fists that the animal fell helpless in the dirt, and spectators reported that the prisoner appeared to be attempting to tear open the dog's throat with its teeth, though the hood prevented it from doing so.

The creature has eaten a great quantity of raw meat, and was observed to be greedily sucking the blood from the neck of a rabbit it was given to kill. Offerings of raw root vegetables such as turnips and potatoes have been accepted in a desultory manner. It repudiates all cooked meat, cooked fruits and vegetables, and grains.

Although words were spoken to the creature in several languages, it made no response. Its hearing does not appear to be impaired, however, as the squawking of a chicken outside the window claimed its immediate attention. The creature was spoken to harshly, soothingly, commandingly, imploringly, and in accents of terror, but its expression, or lack of one, underwent no change.

Particular avian qualities:

Tucks head under arm in repose or perhaps fear.

Frenzied attacks against mirror.

Nesting: Interested citizens come to view the creature have brought a number of items for its edification and amusement. Some, such as candy, India rubber balls, and chalk, have been ignored, but others are forming a pile under the washstand, where the creature likes to spend the night. These include: a rag doll, a handkerchief, a rosary, a sack of marbles, a robin's egg, and a small brass bell.

When awake, in constant motion, hopping from bed to floor to corner to door to stool to corner to washstand to bed to floor to door.

Beats hands lightly and repeatedly on window glass.

M'sieu le Docteur sighed wearily. Dusk had fallen while he worked out his report, and he had had to light a candle. He laid down his pen and passed his finger back and forth through the flame. After a while, the bird came up and did the same. M'sieu le Docteur stroked the bird gently along the jawbone and behind the ear, and scratched between its eyebrows. The bird chattered its teeth and made a whistling sound in its nose. M'sieu le Docteur continued to pet the bird until he saw its eyelids closing, at which point with great reluctance he draped the hood over its head, and called for the guard to hold the hood until he had gone, lest the bird discover the means by which he opened the door to gain the night.

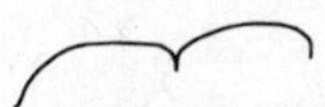

The carriage went hurtling down the long, smooth drive that led to the palace of the Duke, and inside it the bird hooted loudly and preened itself. It ducked its head to snap in its beak the end of the satin ribbon Mme. J. had tied around its neck. The curtains revealed in snatches the leaves on the trees glowing deep gold and brown like brass buttons. Their shining was like the ringing of bells, and the bird jerked against the silken cord that tethered its ankle to the ring set into the floor of the carriage. "Tsk, tsk," said Mme. J., and the bird said, *TtTt* and gently knocked its head against the carriage wall. "Now, now," said Mme. J., and the bird blinked at her rapidly.

The Duke himself, the women with their long smiles and translucent hands, all the scuttling little boys, and the strolling gentlemen flocked around the bird and adored it. Mme. J. and the carriage went rattling back along the drive, farther into the distance, until they were a small black dot disappearing into the orange forest that swelled and thrashed like the sun. The bird watched them shrink and vanish before it veered off the veranda and went swooping to the garden the Duke had created for it.

A giant gazebo was erected, arches woven of twisting twigs crossed at the top and anchored in a generous circle in the ground. These were painted with gold leaf, and a swing was hung inside for the pleasure of the bird. A ladder, too, dangled from the top, woven of thick skeins of silk, and tangled with fuchsia, monkeyflowers, hibiscus, and trumpet vines. Beside the ladder, secured firmly to the roof, was the small canvas tent where the bird roosted for the night. When the breeze picked up, the garden burned with the clashing rays of a hundred small round mirrors that were suspended from the ends of thin silver chains attached to the framework of the gazebo. The bird went mad at these moments, leaping with open mouth to bite at the daggers of light where they stabbed the air. There was a splashing fountain, stocked with green frogs that eventually bred and escaped and were soon to be found in every room of the palace, between bedclothes, under cushions, and on tables.

Now the bird began each morning with a cool draught of water in which grapes or figs had stood. It was bathed in milk infused with lavender, and its eyelids, nostrils, and lips were dabbed with Armagnac until its eyes were wide and bright. A bowl of hot blood was brought to it, in which, on Sundays, snails were placed. The bird's hair was brushed until it crackled and the strands rose up into the air and clung to the fingers of its attendants. The hair was plaited loosely, pinned at the back of the neck, and brought forward over the ridge of the skull, swooping down in a thick curl to tease the bird's forehead. The bird wore a brass bracelet on its leg, and peach-colored hose, and long tunics with sweeping, wide sleeves in shining colors. The bird was ruby breasted, green backed, golden throated, chestnut barred, and flame crested. The little boys made chains of coins and wrapped them around the arms of the bird. When it flapped its wings it rang like a morning chorus of a thousand songs rising out of the wheat.

In the afternoons the bird took lessons in dancing. It learned to spread its skirts and arch its back and hurl itself in a circle. It turned its throat to the sky and lifted its arms behind it. Its neck grew long and active, writhing under its head, and its fingers could spread in a circle until the outside of the thumb and pinky were nearly touching. It could hurtle forward in strenuous crouching bounds, so that its legs seemed to buckle sickeningly beneath it even as it was already ricocheting back into the air. At the end of a performance it could bow to the audience in midleap, its feet kicking out and its knees tucking into its chest. The bird could sink into the ground with the graceful startlement of a gasp. It could tear at its hair and throw back its shoulders until it was two or three times its natural size.

At dinners the bird perched on a tall stool behind the Duke's chair and was fed morsels by the Duke's own hand. When not being fed, it leaned forward to nibble at his ear or curl its toes comfortably against his back. When the musicians came into the hall at the conclusion of the meal, the bird stood on the stool and keened sharply. All the musicians agreed with the Duke that the sound was uncanny, and they always played in the pitch the bird's screaming suggested. As the programs wound on, the bird would quiet, squatting back down on the stool, clucking its tongue against the back of its mouth, and pressing its face into the Duke's hair.

The bird grew pale and weak not long after the sun went down, so once the meal and entertainment had concluded, the bird would climb onto the Duke's back, and the Duke would bear the bird out into the garden, where it would climb the silken ladder to its tent. The little boys would release the rope and the great canopy would fall and slither over the frame of the gazebo, blotting out the moonlight that might play upon the hundred mirrors. The bird nestled into itself; it twitched at the feeble disturbance of its breath struggling against its feathers, and listened to the slug of its heart striking out at the other smothering organs. Its feet were curled so the toenails scratched the arch. When the bird's eyes closed, it felt the brief sting of the rough inner lid scraping against the lens. It watched red throb and cool, tiny black insects skating across the color, until everything was mottled and dull like mud. Cracks traced idly over the mud, portions of it shifted as if something were tunneling beneath, or a foot were pressing from above. Dark blots came, like drops of rain; a green tinge suffused the whole. A smell of slime and plant life. A kind of tilting in the mud, as if the bird had shifted its perspective. A comfortable tilting, a more agreeable angle, the mud oozed over the eyes of the bird and pressed calmly on its brain. The bird suddenly felt slippage, a plummet, groped wildly for its wings. Then there in its lungs was the aftermath of a tremendous sigh, and the canopy came whisking away and the sun was sharp with the smell of Armagnac, and lavender, and frothy blood.

The bird had clung to the finger of the Duke with its teeth, with all the strength in its jaw, but now its mouth was empty and the present the Duke had left on the desk, a nest woven of gold wire and containing two warm goose eggs for sucking, had vanished beneath the hand of the Mother Superior. "You must learn to be good and obedient," said the Mother Superior, "and raw meat and shiny toys are just the things to make you agitated. Here we live simply. The habit you wear will be rough, to scratch the itches before they start, and the food will be smooth and soft, to calm your temper."

The bird did not eat the stews and porridges, the salted biscuits or the sharp red wine, and after a week they twisted it in blankets and fed it through a funnel. At first the bird screamed so that the attending sisters could not even hear the chapel bells tolling for prayers, and an exorcist was summoned. Then its throat grew so raw that the brittle shards of sound twisted and dug at its gullet, and the bird quieted. Thick slicks of blood formed inside it and lurched their way out, stumbling from the mouth of the bird in clumsy belches and then in thundering gallops. During these red effusions the bird made a sound as if it were trying to speak through a gag. It licked at the blood clotting on its cheeks and chin, but the taste was rotten. Once the Duke was in the room, making a loud noise, the nuns spiraling away from him like dry leaves caught in a wind. He had the bleeding haunch of a rabbit, which he held to the face of the bird. Everything within the bird leapt and shrank at once in a terrible convulsion. Something held the bird and shook it for several minutes. It felt itself go upside down, then inside out. Then the meat was taken away and the Duke put the tip of his finger in the bird's mouth and sat like that for a while before he crept away. Not long after, a man came to draw the majority of the blood from the bird's body, and this afforded some relief. The bile of the bird became watery and pale and the bird enjoyed a faintness like the sensation of flying. Then like the sensation of sinking. Its body was covered with bruises; peering down, it saw itself hidden in a rose bush. The bird was molting. The air of the room was crowded with strands of its hair; sometimes the breeze picked these up and carried them out into the sky. The teeth of the bird dropped gently from between its lips and rolled onto its neck like a pearly collar. The sisters collected the teeth and also the nails and kept them in a leather pouch.

A sister was always with the bird. Sister Marie-Therese watched in the early morning when the bird was gray. Behind its veil of shadows, she saw its features released, dissolving and shifting, sweetly and gently. Then the light would come in fragments through the tree outside, picking out the beak, which would grow in response, and the eyelids, which glowed red. The bird was naked and pale in the dawn, and came into existence with the advent of the light, the ruff of its neck golden, its arms green as the leaves through which the sun struggled to meet it. The bird woke when the bells tolled for matins, and Sister Marie-Therese would bend over to hide its plumage under the brown blanket.

Sister Marguerite-Marie was most often there in the formless, endless afternoons. She brought lumps of sugar for the bird, sliding them to the back of its mouth. The bird stayed very still, waiting, and felt the sugar rearrange itself, biting at first at the bird's tongue, then spreading, investigating the pockets of the jaw, and traveling in a long procession of granules deep and down. The bird could feel the sugar burning all the way to the pit in the middle of it. Sister Marguerite-Marie told a story about a girl from China who had a beautiful bird that she loved very much but that one day escaped from its cage. In great distress, the girl resolved to visit a wondrous enchantress and beseech her help finding the bird. On the way, she met various animals in distress. A cat was trapped on an island in the middle of a lake. A rain-dragon was lodged in the arid earth. She helped the animals, and they gratefully came with her to the palace of the enchantress. The enchantress herself was like a bird, a giant blue-black crow. Her palace was of blue and white porcelain, and every inch of it was painted with blue birds. But the girl saw her bird pictured on the wall as well, and she understood that the enchantress had trapped all the birds of the air, and frozen them in the walls of her palace. The enchantress was just reaching out her long claw to snare the girl when the cat leaped up and swallowed the enchantress whole. Then the dragon flew into the sky, and rained down water on the palace, and the birds awoke, and turned from blue and white into every imaginable and unimaginable color, and rioted in the air, and the palace crumbled, and the girl put her bird safely back in its cage and they traveled home.

Sister Marguerite-Marie told the bird a story about a great flood that covered the entire earth. One man built a boat to weather it, and brought a male and female of every animal that existed onto the boat. Giraffes and dogs and unicorns. But there was only one dove in the world, and it could not come alone, so it snuck into the boat under an elephant's ear and stowed away. When the captain discovered it, he was wroth, and threatened to feed the dove to the lions, but the dove begged to be spared. So the captain banished the dove from the ship and said it might only return if it came bearing evidence of land. The dove flew over the formless, endless sea, in which no fish swam, and on which no sun shone, so that it could not even watch its own reflection, and after a time it began to doubt its reason, and to suspect that there had never been a ship, a captain, or an elephant, and that it was and had always been the only living creature in the world. And the dove nearly dashed itself into the void of the waters. But at that moment a giant finger pointed out of the clouds in the form of a beam of light and it lit on a sandy beach on the far horizon, and the dove struggled on, and plucked a twig from a tree on the beach, and without pausing for rest or refreshment, veered back to the ship, over the exulting waves. And the ship landed there, and all the animals were saved, and in gratitude to the dove the captain opened his chest and fed his own heart to the bird. And so the captain lived immortal in the dove, which, being the only one of its kind, could never die, but which, having the captain within it, was no longer alone.

Sister Marguerite-Marie told the bird a story about a hungry jackdaw that, observing how well fed was a family of quail, rolled himself in the dust until he was brown and presented himself as a quail. The quail took him in, and fed him and cared for him, until one day the jackdaw was so happy and comfortable that he burst forth in his chattering song. Immediately the quail recognized that he was a jackdaw, and pecking at him mercilessly, they drove him away. Miserably, the bird crept back to join the other jackdaws, but as he was covered with dirt, they took him for a quail, and attacked him, and bit him until he was dead.

Sister Marguerite-Marie and the bird ate sugar together all through the afternoon, and sometimes she would bring leaves of mint or basil and they would eat those too. Sister Marguerite-Marie would chew her leaves, but, as the bird no longer had any teeth, Marguerite-Marie would roll the herbs between her fingers until the leaf broke and the juice sprang out. She would rub her wet fingers on the bird's lips and nose and behind its ears. The juice would burn like sugar, and the world would be wet and sharp and green.

Sister Marie-Immaculate watched over the bird in the night, telling her rosary. The bird's eyes were open and the dark pressed against them as Sister Marie-Immaculate recited the Apostles' Creed. The bird shifted slightly in the bed and curled its toes around the blanket as Sister Marie-Immaculate recited Our Father. Sister Marie-Immaculate said a Hail Mary for faith, for hope, and for love, and the bird clicked its tongue with the fall of the beads. Sister Marie-Immaculate gave glory to the father, and the bird meditated on the Joyful Mysteries, the Sorrowful Mysteries, and the Glorious Mysteries. Sister Marie-Immaculate offered the Fatima Prayer, and the bird whispered, *Oh, my Jesus.* Sister Marie-Immaculate said, "Hail, Holy Queen, Mother of Mercy, our life, our sweetness, and our hope," and the bird whispered, *Salve Regina.* The bird could hear the hiss of the beads sliding on the string, the scratch of the thumb of Sister Marie-Immaculate rubbing the wood. In the hair of Sister Marie-Immaculate was the ghost of incense; it was not like wood smoke; it was not like the petals of flowers that have fallen. On the breath of Sister Marie-Immaculate was the rough smell of red wine; the cold salve of lard; the thick odor of beans, like a woman's sweat; the powder of the wafer, like ancient dust. Sister Marie-Immaculate could smell the wool of her own underclothes, damp from the steam of the kitchen; the slick of oil on her face had a palpable weight. She could just see, in the bed, the white of the bird's face, a shock against the night, and the black holes of its eyes. She could hear, in its stuttering breath, a wakefulness. She began again. By the time she came to the Agony in the Garden, she could tell from the whistle in its nose that the bird was asleep.

The Queen of Poland came to visit the bird, and they took communion together. The Queen was disappointed that the bird could not hunt with her, for she had heard that it was faster than a falcon, and that it had returned the Duke's prey to his hand; nonetheless, she caressed it extremely. The bird said, *Gracious lady,* and if the Queen could not at first make out the words, when they were repeated to her by the Mother Superior she was greatly pleased, and favored the bird with a handful of gold coins, which the bird offered to the collection plate, excepting one that it kept in its nest. A poet came to see the bird and recited the poem he had composed in its honor and the bird nodded its head.

Mme. H. was engaged in writing a life of the bird. The bird was able to narrow down its origins to Martinique or Canada. The description it gave of its migration over the dark, inchoate seas was not included in the published work. A man with chapped cheeks and flushed, delicate ears founded a new philosophy on the bird. His coat was resplendent with buttons, but he did not offer one to the bird, and it kept its hands close by its side.

A journalist visited twice, each time with a different companion, each selected with a view toward the appetites of the bird. The first companion was a child, with crepe-like skin webbed with blue veins. Even the journalist was tempted to take a bite. The child's eyes were trembling in their sockets with fear, but the bird patted the fragile skull and begged the child not to be afraid. *God has changed me very much,* said the bird, and when Sister Marie-Therese repeated the words intelligibly, the child crowed with delight and crowded onto the lap of the bird to tug curiously at the long, mournful beak. The second companion of the journalist was a soft, sugary woman whose flesh spilled from her like cream from a pitcher, bubbling out of her clothes, overflowing her chair, in a generous profusion of fat. This time the bird shook its arms about itself in agitation, and had to be removed by the sisters. Marie-Therese informed the journalist that the bird had been overcome not by hunger but by nausea, and that it no longer ate meat in any form, preferring seedcake and communion wafers to all other food. Nonetheless, in the journalist's paper there appeared a long article about the vampirism of the bird, with references to pale young novitiates, and the bird was forced to write a letter to the editor.

After the bird was able to understand years and that they were passing, the Mother Superior invited it to join the convent, but the bird with sorrow declined. It was understood to say: *The rosary is circular and its decades therefore infinite. Nonetheless, eternity is not long enough to expunge the sins I committed when I was in the garden, refusing to eat of the tree that would teach me good from evil.* The Mother Superior spoke more plainly, explaining to the bird that since the death of the Duke, the bird's income would not suffice to cover its board as a guest of the convent. The bird took a small flat in the 12ème arrondissement of Paris and placed an advertisement inviting the curious to come and wonder at what the glory of God had wrought in a savage creature.

The bird arranged twenty chairs in its drawing room and invested in a wardrobe of black silks and velvets, profuse with ruffles, and with long draping sleeves. However, many of those old enough to remember the bird's apprehension in S— found the six flights of stairs too difficult to navigate. Children would sometimes arrive in a giggling band, dart forward to capture a black feather from the bonnet of the bird, and scamper away in hysteria, without leaving any coins. Marie-Immaculate, now Christine, who had left the convent, came on Sundays to take the bird to Mass, bringing baskets of biscuits and wine and pickled cornichons.

The bird often rearranged its nest, polishing its buttons and coins, and crumpling its papers tighter into little balls. It sat with its arms on the sill of the window and sang *Je Mets Ma Confiance* and *Frère Jacques.* It kept a canary named Pierrot.

The bird took long naps in the afternoons. It awoke in the slanted light to see the flocks of dust motes swooping and diving in the breeze. It could feel the warmth of the day wriggling against its skin, tucked beneath its feathers. Twisting its neck to look through the window, it could see saints in white robes and angels with interminable wings drifting and sighing against the sky like clouds. Pigeons burbled comfortably in the eaves and the low hoots of the bird as it yawned did not disturb them.

The bird raked away the covers with its toes and drew itself up on its knees. It would not get out of bed that day to pray. Its chin nestled into its breast and it opened and closed its eyes, watching the light tangle in its lashes. It started and hunched at the sounds of steps in the hall, and continued to watch the door long after they had passed, tucking its hands nervously under its arms.

There were fleas in the bed and the bird watched avidly as they flashed into existence on knee or toe or pillow, blinked out, then reappeared on knuckle or elbow or sheet. One had bitten the bird on the shoulder, and it gnawed with satisfaction at the little welt. On the sidewalk below, a cat was crying forlornly. *Miao,* said the bird.

In the air was the smell of smoke, beer, leather, wet cotton on the line, the stinging scent of the soap with which the girl across the alley was washing her hair. Darker, heavier smells: the overripe peaches in the bowl on the bird's kitchen table, the patch of yellow mildew sprinkled across the corner of the ceiling, the odor of the bird's own skin, sweet sharpness stabbing through a musky closeness, like mud slathered on leaves of basil and mint. The bird's stomach growled. The nails of the rats scratched as they bustled around inside the wall. The bird pressed its very hot palms against its very cold face and felt the temperatures exchange. Its fingers were stiff and cold. Its head was alive with fire. The bells of the church rang with a sound like sun shining.

Cardinal in a Forsythia
Rick Moody

LOST: SISTER'S WALLET. Her guitar. Her boyfriend. Eyeglasses. Smoking jacket. Copy of *Flip Your Wig* by Hüsker Dü. Joy about composing these lines. Joy about composing any lines. Joy about reading anything at all. Taste for bourbon. Copies of everything Vargas Llosa ever wrote. And Gombrowicz. Ability to remember passages of poetry and lines from books. Sense of outrage. Names of some people kissed. Addresses of many people loved. Ability to be really rude. Unobstructed view from deck. Morning glories. Sparrows who used to nest in the birdhouse on the side of the shed. Belief in the redemptive power of a transcendental and omnipotent agency. Belief in political change. Several bicycles, some of them stolen. Virginity. First true love. Second true love. Third true love. Faith in true love. Cheap synthesizer bought in New York City and used in band in college. *Sid and Nancy* T-shirt. Ability to be mad about my childhood. Field recordings of people singing love songs in Ecuador. Certain words. Word *nemesis.* Greek and Latinate words that used to seem glamorous. Tolerance for abstraction. Tolerance for solitude. Paperwork. L. L. Bean table bought when there was no money for any other table and kept for ten years. Sister. Innumerable pets. Dial phones. Subway tokens. Strip clubs in *Times Square.* Peas from a can. Evening News. Forty-fives. LPs. Prerecorded cassettes. Whipped cream from a tub. Tortellini. The IBM Selectric II with correcting key. Sweet Tarts. Tom Seaver. Jerry Koosman. Another pair of eyeglasses. A lot of weight. Certain causes, e.g., hunger strikers at Long Kesh; the Sandinistas; the Tibetans; the Cambodians; the East Timorese. Faith, calm, serenity, self-respect, innocence, anything left to lose.

Found: Redemptive power of a transcendental and omnipotent agency. A sense of insignificance. A violent distaste for the political process. The community of other human beings. Good luck. Massive amounts of good luck. Memories: most of them wrong, or massaged into a shape that flatters. An indifference to my personal suffering in certain circumstances. Willingness to change. A desire to listen to the stories of others. Twenty dollars. Ten dollars. Fifty dollars. Sunglasses. Ten pounds. The cellular telephone. The laptop computer. The Internet. Surveillance cameras on street corners. Compact discs. DVDs. MP3 players. Blogs. Vlogs. Things to look forward to. My singing voice. Tenacity. Saggy flesh. Memories of sister laughing, memories of sister dancing; memories of other deceased people, Lucy Grealy, e.g., memories that start to crowd out things happening concurrently. A bad knee. A bad back. A bad ankle. Tonsillitis. Paperwork. Nieces and nephews! Anglo-Saxon words like *guttersnape, giddyhead, cobblestone, nonesuch, fribble,* and *sockdolager.* A taste for the Beats. A taste for beets, olives, capers, mustard, and some varieties of cheese. Violin lessons. Many causes, like the hunger strikers at Long Kesh; the Sandinistas; the Tibetans; the Cambodians; the East Timorese; the rights of gay persons to marry; the rights of animals not to be consumed by humans simply because humans think they're smarter; faith, calm, serenity, self-respect, innocence, more things to lose. A cardinal on the deck. A cardinal on the lawn. A cardinal under the bird feeder. A cardinal and his mate. A cardinal and her mate. A cardinal and a red-winged blackbird. A cardinal and a chickadee. A cardinal and a brace of mourning doves. A cardinal and a pigeon. Two cardinals on different branches of a locust tree. Female above, male below. Cardinals alighting. Cardinals startling up. Cardinals foraging. Cardinals singing. Cardinals and a blue jay driving them off. A cardinal in a forsythia, in April, when the bush is in bloom, and he is attempting to attract the opposite number. A cardinal in a forsythia, certain of the bright perfection of his plumage against a yellow backdrop. Why didn't I stop to notice?

Five Poems
Eric Linsker

IRREVERSIBILITY ODE

I.

I was just outside witnessing in that tree I told you about a
  transaction
the sparrows both sides of their faces
leaves from having to appear
snatches of old laws

leaves slight resurrections in wind dead
veil lost the very idea of a face
unsmoothed contact
this squirrel has smooth decline

of back his eyes closed at me
the irrelevance or whatever I tried
I tried to catch something

and the sparrows sitting
on top of the bush exhausted with difference
also I walked across the grass
it makes life too much I heard a bird I have never

heard before that means there is maybe a new bird
their eyes are OK
"What do you do? Yes"
in the street a girl holding her neck

both sides
now maybe we can stop using the word joy
lost the very idea of seeing
I'm sorry: the leaves are coming into the room

I am looking forward to the birds
it is hard to tell their fronts from their backs
because it is all singing
the tree I cannot see blocking the light I can see I have already

come to the floor squinting in the yellows
arrows in the tree
the sparrows extrinsic
the dream of consent—on the branches' wrists

between what is and what ought to be—dissimulating—the sparrows

II.

I was just outside witnessing in that tree I told you about a transaction
sparrows supplementing leaves from having to appear
and a blue jay who cannot supplement—mattered regalia
sparrow on the branch—deadpan—machéd-up and sitting
on the bush—torpid dream of consent

but one who absorbs or will not absorb flowers because of a deep almost
  shockingly deep respect

I'll walk and feel something pushing on me from the side it is happiness the
  possibility of
                                                                                    the perception of the

world up to now
the sparrow extrinsic
and so extinct
extinction is relative
myself mirrored
is it different to step on in leaves yes partly
because they are many-rooted—holding this cup in my hand

at a slant
—I tried catching the moments when the leaf came off
the birch—the exact point of separation
how to break something

III.

I think I'm going crazy with the beauty
the sparrows—between what is and what ought to be—dissimulating—
and the middle is not even mine is from straw dogs

the squirrel does not need to hunt what is it to hunt an acorn how is that
different—
finding—
one eating the find while the other waits there are animals who wait

each spring they make sacrifices
The wall is holding me
they'll always be now

IV.

erial limning
'ees are all my consciousness allows and branches
ıe compensatory effects of power
again have nothing and am running into such resistance
feel my spirit hit and I surge back there is no way to say this that I know now
I just went
y the river
rat
ıe building is wet

aving lost all motivation except to be touched by the tree

V.

or the girl
de-realization
unsettingly—no modicum of circularity
hitting or up

"lost the very of a 'face'"

I have the wind on my arms and face
dead veil lifting dead veil
unsmoothed

the rabbit's awake
the moth at the red bush
or tree at

VI.

I have opened my window—leaf that falls from
outside the tree—splayed because . . .

mattered regalia—"the irrelevance or
whatever"—her hand near his face
holding the wall—blue excavated, not hearing an alarm
the squirrel his eyes closed
excavated—clutching her hand like pills
lips to it—out from the afterwards

I was just outside witnessing in that tree I told you about a
transaction

VII.

I tried to catch something

it's something about the way the branches part with

each other—a shock to that abstraction

to write and have it come back

the sparrows—between what is and what ought to be—
dissimulating—

I've been trying to catch something but the whole world comes up
spindles of the upshot

grosser intricacies
ethics of extinction

Irreversibility (Morning Bell)
actually fighting it
off

There is no outside outside
fill the window
the sparrow sitting on top of
the bush like an unpassed

vast difference
I'm on my
it is apportioned
it is subversive here—

all time occurring at once I just wish it could

VIII.

was speaking Windhover as I went to get coffee and there was a red bush in the island
wet

the squirrel knows wind in the tail
erasing veils with veils

you think the bird is a leaf it takes the angle of prayer up
the blue jay with its bearing
the enough
into you

language is coming back
the bird sitting on the bush
as it does
the spot over which it
it is different to stand on a bush and a tree
the difference is exhausting

IX.

the escalation of hearing
the bird in
and through the horizontal bush

I really have to be careful
exhausted with difference
also I walked across the grass

something makes it too much

they meet one with the find in the mouth
if it is not too late I heard a bird I have never
heard before that means there is maybe

a new bird
she makes too much life on the side of my tree
and the consciousness of justice
and in London speaking in a cathedral I feel it in the end
of the line irreversible "something which exceeds its meaning
and interpretation"
what is meaning if it's not shared
sensation underaiming the reality
of the blessed I am overcome with sensation and there is wanting to know th
other
wanting the other to know

X.

he jumped the window as verb

no it is Hamletian

I am looking forward to the birds
their eyes are OK both sides of their face
my eyes are not OK if this is about me

then there's that red bush in the island
mutualized by itself
"What do you do? Yes"

ıarm
t's a very good question

There are just now dozens of geese on the river I thought they'd left it looks
 like they're trying
he leaves are still everywhere tore about the air
›eneath him silver air the squirrel eyes closed
ınd eating

XI.

What does it mean to do something wrong if no one else thinks it is
 wrong—not even "god"?—where does it leave
the soul what does it build

the rabbit falls into the water and loves it
not hearing an alarm
one's just slow because he can see very well

the chair totally collapsed

dark trace screen

those eating in the book of j with god

appropriate

control within an environment

the topic of life

when a tree dies it does not go away
they are here but for whom

XII.

Can I be saved
what are we supposed to do with these
leaves slight resurrections in wind

I lean against the window every day trying to get
rid of them or make them here

they are here but for whom
the squirrels? The squirrels have smooth
declines of back

the casements
the pear thrip
the sea behind closed
doors the room empty except for me

get rid of me
at the window
in the dawn I've stayed up for
no one else
I don't see anyone else
eyes on the street no one

the leaves coming into the room
the room empty except for me

the leaves know

someone is laughing on the other of the wall

to ruin it

THE BIRD GOES BEHIND YOU

the bird goes behind you

the half-second delay the
squirrel in leaves
wet casements
"readiness-potential the practice of bare attention"

I do not worry because I am not trying to construct continuous selfhood for
the squirrel I

am not trying to
onstruct anything for the squirrel I do not think maybe shelter
naybe I pull up my sleeves and feel the wind the mind on my wrists

he goldlit hawk underwings crunched shoulders to land on the tower vane and
then
elanding—and their
elinquishing

o not overcompensate for what is not love

ardinality
nfinite sleds
he sparrows at the end of the branches so as to be

OPERATIVE SPRING

ear/gaseous twigs lacking fluency in the chunks of branch ripe
ot centered shade, and the shade of the thrush
stained by the suthering wind, loosens from the
ther, bit-green/brown flap of sound, redstart, touring on its side, a
grass/attempt sticking
ith snow seen by, it brushing/delineated *yellow ashes of human dropped*
rsythia like *thrush,* who handles its world when it looks away, the
owers are marching hitherward it is known before
where they arrive they move
elike some things I know not what/wheatear, cannot hear them, cannot hear
rush now, I think we should slaughter them

NEWS OF THE FOREST

news of the forest
going down the stairs backward

arrows in the trees
that restraint

Eric Linsker

things are to share in this life
I heard a woman say

I find their hands infuriating
there is so much light

it is not too late
the bird flies "behind" the tree

he wanted to splendor it with his legs

someone committed suicide here today
it wasn't me

he survived
because we want to know

the tree I cannot see blocking the light
I can see

the trees are so small when you take away
the leaves
also when you take away hope

in the nape of the valley
a different car now

the common world

I come and I bury the goldfinch in the honeysuckle

then we sat on the box
beneath the tree

that end is reached

Eric Linsker

ODE (DISTRACTED)

Face of God wrapped in cellophane
water poured over so that he hears
his face. I want these eclipses

sleeping in the swan
his cellophane wings the interviewers
something is permanent for a while

crowned with gas
right now Where is God in the bird
going up to the tree

the bird who never waits
The window is cold
so like the sea

ashen leavening
if I could name you there would
no longer be games

the leaves each one
stapling the ground with existence
though things are cut shorter

also the ripeness of his eyes
why doesn't anyone ever speak of his
eyes sending to some retention the ash
on my fingers like a bird

like a bird I'd say I had my eyes again
The fishermen that walk upon the beach

Eric Linsker

Need cannot finally be calculated
His wings the interviewers
made to understand that they in their fluttering

ought to be killed
when the body
becomes increasingly heroic

and I said to perpetua for she was
there look at these perfect roads
I'm not sure how not to lie down

the wall it is like tulips in water
the soaking God Monsieur La Far
what if the head were touched in sleep

the pillow falling I'm looking
I'm looking at the tops of two trees the herd in the tree
blown straight up and the gray-ocean-underside

the white paper on the table
you reach for opening your
eyes a little more there's a part of brick

taken away
the sound of the bird's wings from the brick
like a peach being cut

Ascending Flight, Los Angeles

Nathaniel Tarn

. . . it is characterized by a pale subtle happiness of light and sunshine, a feeling of bird-like freedom, bird-like altitude, bird-like exuberance, and a third thing in which curiosity is united with a tender disdain.

—Friedrich Nietzsche

I.

Seen face to face in domestic converse:
no compassion. Seen in a group of persons
in social converse, none either. Seen solo
waiting, far off and isolate, colorless as
a grounded, wingless, songless passerine,
compassion's ocean rises, flooding chest
chasm, a fraction further, extrudes tears up
and into eyes. Here, vastness of the angels'
heart downtown, close to all arts and music,
sparsely filled up with buildings, their al-
zebras in crazy inundation of Californian
light. Always a few degrees above our own
and riotous with varied flowers and greens.
Airwise, blinding green parrots and such e-
xotica as might seem to belong here crackle.
Little Tokyo, Little Beijing, good rebates on
blouse-grown wings. The tears sink down to
rest in curiosity. Inveterate explorers wake.
Abandoned left-wing veterans rot on streets.
Beyond a world mayhem continues. Crying
sees murder; curiosity: consumption. Through-
in a day, hang out, eat, drink, shop, & consume.

II.

Birds from colorless to color; flowers color
to colorless. To stop life's turn to nightmare
adopt the colorful patience of birds. Flowers
take flight and become birds, add color to
the birds in sky, so high, their colors hit invisible. This is the level we desire to reach:
bird high, plant low—*famose* cosmogony.
Out there in Hollywood, air-breasted women
trying to become birds and failing even, why
at ascent to flowers! To conjugate, lone
mind, all that is beautiful way and above all
human understanding. Planes in their traces
along sky move white from unknown city-
unknown city, and this for no known purpose
you can witness low—but bird is clear in
purpose how much high, as hummer was at
nose the other day while gardening. (Since I
was raising flowers to the power of air.) As
child, remember Mitchell in the movie, eyes
up intently at a lone seagull—and she'll be
loveliest ever to fly, him whispering, and so
she was in metal clad, flying countries alive.

III.

In cities, when the noise by day is overwhelming,
birds have evolved in time to sing by night, thus
to be heard by other birds. That's what we birds
are doing now, that once were poets of the day.
We sing at night, all hope on standby, but we *are*
heard by our own kindred. Meantime (deliberate)
people may rot into sweet Angeleños. We crummy-
nals! dropping them there while shopping! O! O!
Wait! Wait! For ages now I shall read selfsame,
very same book over and over, not skipping book-
book, place-place, or landscape-into-landscape.
I'll persevere presentially with one enlightened
me, ago when we could climb not even castles,
lifted my darkness, and, suddenly made mirror, I

sent back simple verbs to one scale of our time.
Emotions are dead leaves, yet some may carry
to sing as if a world were morning, as if light,
still tinted by the birds, were truth and possible.
After the night, after angelesque dreams, a great
light sphere rolling into the room, a rubber cage
with convict bird inside—clothed in all colors
the despised can dream. World granted. Novel day.

Crow & Robin

Elizabeth Robinson

I.

Nearby, I hear the sound of wood planks clunking against each other, and through the trees comes the clack of hammers, sometimes a buzz saw.

The man laughs, then says, "Have you ever murdered a man?"

His co-worker makes no reply.

The man begins to sing a song, but stops, interrupting himself with his own laughter.

II.

At home, I sit at the kitchen table and look out through the window at the neighbor's garden. I think about you. Rather, I imagine that I am you. What would you make of the ragged peonies, and why hasn't the neighbor cut them back as they die?

From inside your body, how do peonies smell? I am embarrassed by the limits of imagination. That is, how my desire fails as empathy and settles into voyeurism. Have you ever deadheaded a peony? I want to know not how the old felted, browning petals feel, but how they feel to your fingertips.

I wonder if I'd ask a stranger, as you would ultimately be, a question arising out of genuine curiosity. I wonder if I'd dare to trespass into my neighbor's flower bed and cut down her ugly, used-up flowers.

III.

Across the street, Griffin is three and a half. He walks to the edge of the driveway holding a bouncy ball. He aims carefully and then sets the ball down to roll it.

The ball rolls evenly. Griffin's one-year-old sister totters carefully toward her brother on her new walking legs. The ball connects with her shins, bringing her to her knees. Her face bounces down and then off the ball.

Griffin retrieves the ball and walks to the edge of the driveway, starting again.

"Griffin, honey," calls the babysitter, "Griffin."

IV.

Outside my window, on the second floor, two birds squabble. One is a robin and the other looks to be a crow, big and aggressive. The robin is getting beat up, but stands its ground. A huge gust of wind causes the bough to move from due north to due east. The birds rotate before my eyes, parallel with me.

The wind carries the package of itself on the arguing bird voices until a pedestrian walks by and the crow, startled, slides off the bough and goes away.

I wanted the crow to be ashamed, to leave the branch ashamed that it had forced itself on another bird's home. Then I realize that I am the crow and you are the robin and a sense of adoration and admiration spreads through me like a new version of the weather.

The crow comes back again and again and I hear the raised voices of the birds commingled in the bigger, agitated voice of the wind.

V.

Is it really wrong to look for evidence that will prove what you want to believe anyway? I often find what I'm looking for on the chain of continuity, the leading to or following from. Here, on the chain of reason, proof that things may be connected off-kilter, without our realizing the connection.

This morning, as I was listening to the radio, I heard this story:

A semi truck is pulling out of a gas station driveway. Just as it rolls out onto the street, a man in a wheelchair rolls in front of it and gets stuck in the grille of the truck. The truck driver drives four miles at speeds of up to fifty miles per hour, completely unaware of his front-loaded passenger. When the truck finally stops, the wheelchair is detached from the truck and its occupant is unharmed. He describes the experience as "quite a ride."

VI.

Could there be more to the crow than its obnoxiousness? Doesn't it too have a right to be hungry, to need shelter? I watch it trying to get its glossy head into the bird feeder meant for finches and sparrows. Very smart. If I were the stand-in for the crow, then could I convince someone to love me? I imagine watching you watch the crow, your good humor, but your sense ultimately that this bird is not subtle. A pest, you think it should blow away on a summery gust.

Coming home from work, I see my young neighbor Griffin running up the empty sidewalk looking back over his shoulder. As though, I think with amusement, there was someone following him.

VII.

I am raking up the fallen mess of leaves and sticks in our yard when I notice that the woman next door is carrying sticks and branches out to the curb. We both continue without acknowledging each other. After a while, I see that the man across the street is sawing off a half-broken branch from a tree, and then that another neighbor is silently raking debris from the storm.

Far down the street, some day laborers are talking animatedly in Spanish. Otherwise, there are no human voices.

VIII.

In the middle of the night, I wake up to terrified screaming. One creature preys upon another. And after the screams, quite near, the wounded animal takes up a desperate, snoring breathing. I turn on the porch light, and the breathing stops. Then starts again, more irregular.

I can't see what is out there, even though the sound of it is so sharp that it's in my nostrils and on my tongue. I wish you were here, to comfort me. But I make my fear correct itself: *I* would be *you,* the self at a loss. The invisible hand that rests on the shoulder of its own body, guiding it. We do not know what comfort is.

I turn off the porch light, close all windows, and make my way, deliberate, back to bed. I imagine the ragged breath. I half dream you, getting up, making coffee, looking out at daylight. About half an hour later, three final screams just barely cut through my sleep.

IX.

I go away to a wedding, though you do not know that I am gone, and I don't want to forsake you by any admission, carrying with me what I do carry of you. A memento tucked illicit into a pocket.

I walk around the lake that adjoins my hotel. The sidewalk is covered with blots of goose shit that have baked, slick, into tar. The lake is surrounded on one curve by highway and on the other with a strip mall. A red-winged blackbird poses on a long shrub stalk and trills at me. I fake-smile at the construction workers who say hi with fake friendliness when I walk by.

Red plastic letters in block capitals stand out from a stucco wall: PHYSICIANS' MUTUAL. A nest sits neatly in the upper niche of the "H." You see what I mean, don't you? I mean, that is to say, I see what you mean. The bridge from one upright line to the next. I could have told you after all that I was going to a wedding.

X.

Adoration and admiration for whom?

From inside your mouth, how fine to feel the tongue move against the palate and to say:

"Nothing in this world is random. Design proves its own divinity."

If I dared, your voice would sing.

Instead, I initiate the gesture forward, the bending toward. The shrub sits before you, waiting to be pruned.

Time Bends

Maureen Howard

WE HAD BEEN BEST of friends. A possible way to begin? I am writing this down. My profession, such as it is, does not lend itself easily to words. Numbers are my game. At times I do explain as I chalk the blackboard. For any given point X and any line L, what is the closest point on L to X? Simple stuff, but this is about Bertram Boyce, his confounding story. Bertie, chairman and CEO of Skylark, a telecommunications empire, so his enterprise is called in the business section of the *Times.* Bertie is charged with conspiracy to commit fraud. I am waiting to take the stand as a character witness, have been waiting for two days as you well know since I deliver Cyril to school while you stay home with Maisy, our congested girl, yet again a prisoner of the nebulizer. But this is not a family story. I leave Cyril at school and head down to the federal courthouse, which we have often seen on cop shows. The echoing hallways are dismal, unfamiliar offscreen. I have been called to testify that Bertie is an upright player in the financial games of this republic, in sum, a good old boy, has been since I first knew him, eighth grade. He is charged with fraud, backdating his options, tinkering with the books of his corporation so that gain became loss, or vice versa, good tricks that would please my students, many of them preparing for the business world.

I am writing in the small green notebook in which you record our sightings of northeastern birds. It has been years since I scribbled more than a quick note with pen on paper. Attorney Thaddeus Sylvan informed me that Security might not look kindly on my laptop, though my life and times are easily accessed, from the incompleteness of my Yale degree to my credit rating to the theorem I am attempting to work to its probable conclusion. Your notebook slipped easily into the pocket of a gray flannel suit worn to Wall Street by my grandfather. I now know why I rescued it along with his pocket watch, so that I might wear it when called to testify on behalf of Bertram Boyce, who's between a rock and a hard place, but silenced as I am, sequestered in a small room with unforgiving metal chairs and a behemoth of a scarred wood table, I may resort to the shorthand of clichés. I further note the suit might well have been tailored for me. It seems, as I look over the page, that I write in a retro voice much like my grandfather's. Cyril O'Connor was a gent who was formal at breakfast, who muted his affection at bedtime, and contained his exuberance when our Yankees won the game. It is a shame you never knew him.

Bear with me, Lou. I will ease up. I'm attempting to describe the occasion when I reattached to Bertie, who I will claim as my good friend. You were along for the ride. I believe it is best to turn back to that day on which Bert and Artie found each other again, embraced in a Judas moment, though who betrays, who saves the day, was yet to be determined. Should anyone other than you audit this memory bank or question its possible inventions, they must know you cannot testify against me insofar as you are my loving wife.

BIRDING

October 10, 2005
US Weather Station, Central Park, 65°–70° (I'm guessing), possible afternoon shower.

A volley of shots in the distance. A thrasher fluttered into the bulrushes. I faked a pistol with my hand. *Backfire,* I said.

A great egret flew to the island in Turtle Pond. Displaying his annoyance, he chose not to perform his strut. In something of a huff, you lowered your binoculars. We'd come for songbirds stopping off on their migration to pleasant winter climes. The day was unseasonably warm as though the years flipped fast forward and phoebes had long abandoned the sheltering grasses that surround the pond.

There was nothing to fear on a Monday afternoon in Central Park. Above—swift-sailing puff clouds; below—the still water glazed in sunlight.

A second volley. *Backfire.*

I know it's backfire, you said, as though to convince yourself no sharpshooter crawled the swampy undergrowth. Took me a week to get you to come with me birding, never my great thrill, yours. I wanted to see your pleasure at the green-gold of the warblers, to observe your full attention sketching their pinstriped tails. I wanted you to breathe easy, Lou, for a few hours of the day. Our Sylvie, more than friend, who often looks after the children, had gone off to California, a visit to her stepdaughter who has a deal of oceanographic info about autumn days too warm for New York. You checked your watch, opened this small spiral notebook that I write in now to record our sighting of the egret and the single thrasher in the reeds repeating his mockingbird cry. This outing was going as well as could be expected given that we had abandoned our children to a student of mine with no training in kid care other than a brood of small brothers and sisters back home.

Turtle Pond lies directly below Belvedere Castle, once a stone shell, a hollow stage set built to enchant the eye. All such notes, Lou, come by way of my grandfather, a would-be historian if life had not ordained his career on Wall Street, allowing only an occasional Sunday walk in the park to instruct a boy. So, if I include the Delacorte Theater with its seats facing an empty pit that day, we might have been a couple of lost groundlings from a pageant of heroic legends. Tourists and a busload of schoolchildren were on the viewing terrace above, looking down from the battlements to the little body of water and the island both, as their guide made clear through a megaphone: ENTIRELY MAN-MADE. A disappointment to his audience surely, but there we were by way of entertainment, Louise Moffet and Arthur Freeman, playing our observation of the birds for all to see. With the next volley of earsplitting pops, you mimed fright. If these outlanders had simply turned from us, looked down at the roadway on the other side of the castle, they would have seen men in their conservatory jackets attempting to deal with a disabled tractor or truck backfiring at the utility shed. I enclosed you in the rough body hold of a protective embrace. How long had such childish fun been in short supply? Shrugging free of me, your cap tumbled down the embankment. Artie to the rescue. In a princely gesture I set it atilt on your head. Worry lines not permanently etched into your forehead were hidden by the shadow of its bill, but your cheeks were ghostly pale in the bright light of day. You tucked in the ponytail. That day plays in my head like a PowerPoint show: here's the moody egret, here a lone phoebe seeking shelter in the reeds from the guide blasting Vista Rock with misinformation, here's my wife, both gorgeous and plain. Mind if I put that down? You insist you are a throwback to household mom as in black-and-white reruns. I might say a fading American rose. Upon occasion I still call you Miss

Wisconsin. Cheese, say cheese.

Pen poised above this very notebook, the stern set of your mouth would not give way to a smile as you estimated the great egret's height. I brushed the wet grit of the embankment off my khakis. Then, as though to amuse in a game of I Spy, I trained my binoculars on the audience above. The schoolchildren, you may recall, waved little flags—red, white, and green—but the tourists seemed puzzled or plain embarrassed by their bird's-eye view of us horsing around. Yet what had they seen? A private moment. There are always lovers in the park, though not often caught in an act of observation. Adjusting my lens, I dictated notes to you on the enemy's shaggy plumage, their slack mandibles, and splintered beaks.

They could not hear me describe them as goosey gander, common tern, but no doubt heard your cry, *Oh, Artie.* The high chirp of your laughter reached up to include them as they watched our tussle, your love punch to my ribs and my gentlemanly gesture, taking your arm as we climbed toward the Great Lawn, where soccer practice was in progress, boys in the blue jerseys of Trinity School. I knew the route. Next the Pinetum, where you hoped for a red-crested kinglet, then the Reservoir, expecting the arrival of grebes basking in the sun. Again you checked the time. Our Maisy had the first cold of that peculiar season, which did not deliver crisp fall days. I'm uncertain how much to recall of our encounter with Bertram Boyce, who had not yet been charged with backdating his options of Skylark shares, and several counts of fraud, but I am certain I lured you away from the apartment with Maisy's congestion, with Cyril's trembling tower of Lincoln Logs. I offered you the consuming delight of birds in their citified migration.

In the park that day you hurried ahead, past dog walkers, babies in slings, past the elderly taking the air, dodging skateboarders—illegal on the walkway. The pretzel salesman had resumed his summer post. A fat boy in a red shako and white satin cape, much gold braid on his breast and belly, began a melancholy "Taps" on his bugle. Day is done, gone the sun—broke to drain the spittle out of his mouthpiece.

Checking your watch, four fifteen, you were not amused by this touch of Fellini.

Columbus Day, I said. *The parade long over.*

I wish they would stop fooling around with the calendar.

Yes, our Cyril had wanted to go to school that morning, but the holiday was stuck on to the weekend. He always wants to go to school, where he cannot help but outwit his classmates less endowed. His cleverness is a cross he will have to bear. It is only now that I recall Bert Boyce and Artie Freeman breaking through the Fifth Avenue crowd when Columbus Day was kept in its proper place, the disruptive twelfth. Snotty nerds lusting for the drum majorettes and their flock of twirlers from the outer boroughs, those high-stepping girls far beyond our reach.

In the Pinetum we did a swift look-see searching for the red crest of the kinglet but there was only the resident clown in a battered derby prompting his flea-bitten parrot—*Hlo there! Hlo there!* In your impatience you took the Reservoir track counterclockwise the long way round. Not a merganser in sight as we headed to the crosstown bus to go home to the children. We'd come to the park at my insistence. Our pretense of pleasure now seemed a failed duty until you caught the noiseless swivel of an owl's head, flick of tufted ears.

The long-eared, napping till end of day, did not deign to acknowledge our ogling eyes trained on him. Drowsy creature, yet I believe he knew we were below on the track, heard every step of our approach, listened to each soft breath of our silence, a comfort compared to the panting of joggers. We had discovered him on his perch, fully disclosed. If he'd been in a story he'd be wiser or at least crafty, the role he's too often assigned. You wrote in this very notebook, making sure the turn of the page was noiseless. Flipping back, I see with what care you drew the eye stripe, cutting a perfect V to the owl's beak. In any case, I had my prize for the day in your extended moment of pure delight, which swept aside Maisy's catarrh, the terrifying pops of an old combustion engine, and the fear, never mentioned, that my work was not going well, that I might not find my way through the knots of higher mathematics to the solution of one small problem. In clear sight of the owl, the troubling world dropped away from you. If I were to ask, Louise, you will confess once again that you have this thing about owls, starting with barn owls on the farm in Wisconsin. The first prize you ever won was for the sketch of an owl perched on a downspout. How often you have told the grizzly story, every night watching that bird from your bedroom window until the dive for its prey, the death shriek of its victim.

Our binoculars captured the Halloween mask of the owl's flat face. I should not, must not deprive the bird of his owlness, see him as pompous and befuddled like Owl in the book our son loves. An uncertain shuffle brought the prolonged silence to a halt. Do you remember the old woman huffing and puffing her way round the track and that you signaled her to stop? With a flip of the hand you ordered: *Look, look up.* We were enclosed, a party of three sharing this vigil, waiting for the bird to make his move. In a contest of wills it seemed this urban owl might outlast us. Finally, the shabby old girl broke the spell, shuffled toward the tennis courts, her breathing audible—heavy, uneven. The sky had darkened, leaves rustled underfoot. The long-eared was surely gloating as we walked toward Fifth Avenue, his unblinking eyes on us. Fair to say I preened a bit. I'd coaxed a laugh from you at Turtle Pond and for some time, long minutes of owl time, you'd been lost to the world.

Now the guard has come in to this waiting room, which reminds me that this is Bud's story, Bertie's. I was the only kid allowed to call him Bertie and will use that boyhood moniker when I speak of our friendship, which was rekindled that very day, the day of our birding in the park. My *guard* is a uniformed court attendant, Tim McBride, gabby Irish, *been in the job since . . .* what follows is the real dope on Jimmy Hoffa disappearing into a cement grave or the void, same year as bilingual signs in the restrooms, here in the courthouse, that is. My case has not been called, will most likely not be called today. The parties are still in judges' chambers. McBride releases me till after lunch. *My case,* an odd way to refer to the troubles of Bertram Boyce, which are far from mine. His are unfortunately dated. Bert took liberties with time. My problem was clocked—will the scholar in training triumph over the odds or fail to make the grade given time? It is a question that troubled you, Lou, though I believe the solution was solely mine.

Released into the city at high noon, I could head up or downtown. History lies in both directions. Downtown is Wall Street, where my grandfather went to the office every working day. He invested, bought and sold, made money. We are living off him now, Louise, though he's gone these six years if I reckon correctly, which I should be able to do since he has willed me the luxury of going back to school to pick up my love affair with mathematics. So I had the choice of walking down the blocks to look at the stock exchange, which rang the market to my grandfather's attention each day, not going as far as the Trade Center wound, or taking the route up to Soho where we lived our first years together, in a loft, your loft with the materials of your trade all around us—paints, charcoal smudges in progress, canvases stacked against the wall. I was in that empty room at my request, the privilege granted by the machinations of Bertie's lawyer, who believed I was fiddling with statistics and correlations for my class in applied mathematics. Furthermore, I did not want to spend time under the surveillance of attorney Sylvan, famous for finding loopholes in the law, costly to the nth degree. I had been coached by him, his every slick word put in my mouth, thinking that when the time comes I will say what I have to say truly about my schoolboy adventures with Bertie, about my larky jobs at Skylark, which were more play than employment.

My choice was not to travel downtown for recess, Lou, not to recall the dutiful life of Cyril O'Connor, and not to walk up to Lower Broadway, where we were so gone on each other our nights of love consumed us. You see I have loosened up, though consumed is too heady a word, or too visceral. My tongue freed by a hot dog with the works on Canal Street as I perused the discount junk in the shops, odd lots of T-shirts with goth symbols of the Reich, dog beds, doll heads, faucets, copper wire, cruets labeled OIL AND VINEYGAR, framed posters of Che and the Eiffel Tower. These products lay in their mass graves guarded by their keepers, who seemed to be doing business of sorts, perhaps as subject to investigation as Bertram Boyce's deals at Skylark. Troubling.

You were well acquainted with troubles that day in Central Park, naturally. Or not so naturally, your fears crossing the line from daily concern to manic organic. Alar in the apple juice, bacteria flourishing in plastic bottles, E. coli, tuna with its dose of mercury—all loomed large as the national debt. A whiff of the super's stogie in the hallway, Asian flu, Teflon, and faulty seat belts—right up there with toxic waste. Nothing to fear but fear itself, attempting the shopworn line, I failed to amuse even myself. Along with your catalog of horrors there was Maisy's persistent congestion, and the uncertain course of my career. Love, in one of its many distortions, allowed you never to speak of my possible failure though I was working harder than I ever had in my life. Lou, there is the one unspeakable word—talent, if in fact the gift of numbers was ever mine to squander. I may not be nimble, an old dancer one step behind the beat. Better to record the owl's composure on a warm October day.

That night when Cyril and Maisy were safely stashed in their bunk bed, I discovered you were keeping an account of the current war's fatalities, though only *our boys* were admitted to your file. You had copied each soldier's name, age, rank, and hometown into a baby book, a present from your mother intended for Maisy's vital statistics—first tooth, inoculations, first word. On the cover a stork carts a swaddled newborn in its beak. I suggested the death toll of Operation Iraqi Freedom is online—www.iraqbodycount.net. *Oh, that's only information,* you said, transferring a private first class, twenty, Linden, New Jersey, and staff sergeant, thirty-four, Shreveport, Louisiana, from *The Times* to your register, inscribing each name with a pen dipped in India ink. Kind of crazy, the record made personal, and then Louise Moffet, once an artist on the cutting edge, now invested in the role you have embraced as housewife and mother, costumed in apron and sensible shoes, closed the baby book, took up a mystery, British. Potboilers, you call these murders set in the manse or vicarage. The gardener did it or the village doctor you thought so kind. The night of our birding you challenged the sly smile of my bewilderment.

You know the satisfaction, Artie. Puzzles, solutions.

Our pleasant ongoing argument in which I point out that a problem chalked on the blackboard is without motive—no adultery, sibling rivalry, not even greed to provoke a crime.

Ambition?

You win.

And fell asleep with the murder unsolved. I scanned my preparation for class—harmless proofs completed, then lay your book aside, turning down the page not to lose the place in that story. Even in sleep you looked troubled, gone from me, but earlier that day I had you back. As we headed along the sidewalk to Eighty-sixth Street, I was hopeful till worry surfaced in tightness around your mouth, an audible sigh as you looked across Fifth Avenue at the apartment house where I lived with my grandparents when I was a boy, an orphan in fact. You will not go there, a slippery expression you would never use, though you take care to avoid the wounds of my childhood, which I believe long healed. I have hoped more recently that Bertie with his troubles, all too real, might release you from conjuring up the demons of my past, and from the free-floating angst that pursues you. OK, pursues us all, but we get Cheerios in the bowl before reading the morning paper.

Some of us do. Some do not.

I imagine how easily you might cut me off with a gentle correction. Backdating to that day of owl and egret, your ponytail slapping air, for no reason at all, gave me hope. That night, the night of our birding in the park, while you slept, I turned on the tube, muted it to indulge in our nightcap addiction to the comic turns on the dysfunctional state of our nation, timely funnies attempting to heal. The pantomime without clever words and background laughter seemed as inadequate, to wing a metaphor, as a Band-Aid on a suppurating sore. Or merely electronic—a fleeting message held in our hand . . . pick up juice, healthy snacks at the market. We'd lost track of the sand castle blown away in Desert Storm. So it's ever been while Rome burned, though have you noticed there's no tune for this war? *Where have all the flowers gone?* My mother strumming, *Long time passing. Long time ago.*

I am writing in a new notebook with unlined pages, bought at Pearl Paint, where you ordered your supplies when, my Lou-Lou, you were still invested in your art. The little green notebook is, after all, for the birds. When I returned to the courthouse, Tim McBride presented me with a sealed envelope. The lawyer for the defense—that is, Thad Sylvan—asked me to consider in my testimony the charities of Bertram Boyce Jr. and the corporate goodwill of Skylark. And what, in our past connection, did I remember of the Boyce family holidays, the religion of their choice? I remember the mother (divorced) went to Aspen for Christmas, Bermuda at Easter. She took Bert along until he was old enough to be abandoned to the Park Avenue apartment or sent to visit his father, a mysterious tinkerer in Bethesda, Maryland, who held patents on medical apparatuses that saved lives, paid the bills. I did not share these memories with Sylvan, who should do his homework. Why had he not asked poor Heather Boyce, who, in *Newsweek,* walked up the courthouse steps with Bertie arm in arm, a couple properly suited for good works. Their names are printed for all to see in programs of the symphony, the opera—Bertram and Heather Boyce, right up there with the heavy donors. The black tie at the Modern and the Met, which drives you crazy, Lou, their attention to couture, never art. And Project Hope, the llamas with big soulful eyes, Heather supplying indigenous folk with herds of the beasts yielding alpaca for her costly sweaters. Shearing, carding, spinning for a week's handout of rice and beans.

There's this. I had a few beers during recess. Observe, dearly beloved, that I was ever so slightly greased. Up for the self-portrait, not the idealized Artie Freeman you once sketched, boyish with a thatch of hair gone early gray. You got my smile that comes too quick, my air of bemusement. Forever looking on, not part of the show, the squint of my eyes at every sleight of hand, moral or monetary. *Jimmy Stewart,* you suggested, one of those innocent heartthrobs.

Clark Kent without glasses.

A wimp?

In disguise.

Back to Bertie, back to business. I have written more of me, more of you than the subject of my deposition. *Not deposition,* I am corrected by Tim McBride, when I attempt the legal lingo. I put the two of us on the stand while Bertie awaited his day in court. My recall of birding in the park, the day we met up again, I now understand, is a confession. The only one I ever knew who confessed was my grandmother, Mae O'Connor, the least sinful of women. She was shriven, strange word, at Ignatius Loyola a few blocks from the apartment. I waited on the church steps facing Park Avenue expecting a glow, a hum of holy, about her when she emerged from the blessed darkness, but it was only Mae fumbling in her purse for the list of groceries we must pick up at Gristede's. A shame you never knew her. Now I see this memory business, this getting it down, might be a simple image that I use for my class. You can't, Louise, fill up a circle with circles that do not overlap, but if you allow the overlap, then there can be many if not infinite circles that will allow Mae O'Connor to take her place in my story.

Circles within circles as on that day heading out of the park. Past five, you repeated, in case I missed the urgency in your voice. Across Fifth Avenue, the apartment house where I lived as a boy was encased in scaffolding to update its limestone facade. The window where my mother stood with her *love child* (my grandmother's version of the tale) was draped in netting, misty as the occasion of my birth. As a boy I wanted to be born on Krypton, where by some improbable chance my father lived, but where was the dynamic logo, my soaring flight over Metropolis? Two lapdogs nipping and nosing each other blocked our way. I took your hand to stop you crossing as a siren cleared the way for an ambulance racing down Fifth Avenue from Mount Sinai, lights flashing. A cab jumped the curb, an ordinary mishap in the city. As we made our way across to the bus stop, the pedestrian, trapped in the stoplight, raised his electronic arm in a friendly salute. Safe, safely across. Chill coming on, cloudy sky, if memory serves. You checked your watch again. *Five fifteen.*

Day is done, gone the sun. Now why? Why did I sing that funereal tune?

From the hills, from the lake . . .

To get the laugh. *Oh, Artie.*

Speaking of the old woman in the floppy black coat, bleach-stained jeans shredded at the cuffs, I said, *Wasn't she a funny duck?*

Wasn't she ever!

We recalled her look of slight offense when you ordered her to silence the dragging pit pat of her tread. With some relief from our cares of Maisy and mathematics we reconstructed the scene of the intruder joining us in observation until she broke the spell. You suggested the heavy gasp of her breathing put the owl off its kill.

Though she got into the bird . . . and the two of us.

I question the two of us. In the past our eyes and ears were in accord when birding, specially in the city, my admiration for you always on display, the milkmaid walking with a proprietary air through the whole spread of Central Park as though tracking the back acres in Wisconsin. That day we were not in sync. Our argument—could it even be called that?—had little to do with sighting.

Kind of a washout, you said, *birdwise.*

You're missing Sylvie.

That must have been it. No need to recall the untidy woman squinting up at the owl, coat stretched across her bum. The same age as Sylvie, give or take a few years, yet she was in no way like our friend, who is slim and stylish, the cap of white hair carefully sculpted to her head, *Like an angel,* you've often said, *ageless, one of Fra Angelico's darlings.* And if our Sylvia had been home to take care of the children, you would have been free to enjoy a few hours of the fall migration in Central Park. I hustled you by the apartment where I lived with my grandparents, a motherless, fatherless boy. Why are you scared of him?

McBride believed the case, mine and Bertie's, might be deferred. Have I made it clear that Tim only came around now and again for a chat with the professor doing his maths? I hadn't the heart to correct him. He admitted me to the empty room then went off on his assignments, slapping at his hip, searching for some lost authority, the black holster of Security. I am not dangerous, so left on my own. Or dangerous only to myself, writing not one word in defense of my old friend, but these many words of self-incrimination, backdating my limited options to the incident of birding, recording only personal discoveries of that Columbus Day, still avoiding our chance meeting with the accused.

At the bus stop: nurses from Mount Sinai. Teenagers comparing test scores in shrill, competitive voices. I cannot forget one sad striver with a mini tattoo on her wrist, silver stud in her nose, concave chest weighted with schoolbooks. You stepped off the curb to see if the bus was coming while I took measure of the distance I ran from my grandparents' apartment to the museum. Take measure is a Cyril O'Connor phrase, reasonable, prudent, unlike these pages written for you. I stood at the corner judging the distance I crossed to the Temple of Dendur, ran up the front steps of the museum, in through the massive door, cut right to the Egyptians. So familiar to the guards they never stopped me for my pass, sharp kid eager to show them my ill-drawn barges to the underworld circa 2 BC. Not so strange after all, my obsession with the pharaohs and their vast company of underlings to serve them in their tombs. Even Bertie, conspiring with me in all plots against the popular faction at school, was not let in on my devotion to Isis. My fix on the goddess was a reasonable accommodation to my mother's death when I was eleven, a way to believe in the afterlife, not as my grandmother believed in the apparatus of heaven with angels surfing the clouds, saints in cumbersome robes. Reviewing my route to the tombs fitted out for the long run of afterlife with the comforts of home, I maintain it was not the worst idea, writing to my mother in hen-scratch hieroglyphics, so why does it trouble you when my clever tactics for survival are long packed away? True, I wasted time searching for the phantom father, now only the loose end of a story. Never fear, Lou-Lou Belle, the grief of my childhood is not a genetic disease.

The crosstown bus came toward us from Madison Avenue. I stepped free of the students, drawn into a circle of noisy flirtation. You called to me, frantic as though calling for help, waving your cap, hair flying. You stood by the open door of a limousine, its extravagant length blocking the bus stop. Passengers decamped in the middle of the street. Slowly, yet grandly, an emaciated version of Bertram Boyce stepped out of the long black car that established his importance. In my self-imposed solitude, I should have been figuring what to envision for the classroom, the next problem built on the last, but the business of writing without chalk or computer is rewind, back go back with only Tim McBride stopping by, hand automatically patting his missing piece as though at any moment he might draw. I replay the scene—Bertie helping a woman with babe in arms to collapse a stroller. He steers her up into the bus. The private-school kids observe Mr. Wonderful with teen irony, then the boss, once my boss in one of his roles, takes me in hand, settles me in the beige leather comfort of his limo. The old authority of his order to the driver: *Downtown.*

You said, *A ride across the park will do us.* Something like that, cryptic.

Bert did not introduce us to the girl with a cell plugged into her ear, a spill of mahogany hair veiling her face. We spoke softly, not to interfere with her compelling business.

Bertram Boyce, dry as a pod with a terminal tan. He seemed an endangered species in a fringed—serape? poncho? We watched Bert stroke the girl's leg up to the black leather skirt that ended far above her knee.

He said, *Long time no see. Better part of a year?*

Christmas, my line. Yes, the holiday visit with Bert's wife and kids in their suburban splendor. You will not forget the extravagant gifts under the professionally decorated tree. Bert, dispensing goodwill of the season, offered a priceless claret, Lafite Rothschild: *Some prefer '85, '86 more than OK.* A fete out of the nostalgia manual—Dickensian goose, Bud with the girth of old St. Nick. Better part of a year for that rotundity to scale down to skin and bones.

You surely remember Heather Boyce flashing a watch ringed with diamonds, a trifle Santa brought down the Tudor chimney. Boyce children, bored with our kids, were dismissed to their Game Boys.

Heather, can you hear her? *So what can you do? The holidays.* Something like that, putting words in her mouth as I've put them in yours. Isn't that the idea of writing it down? Call back the day, things said in passing or by intent, translation from the foreign film of memory into the subtitles of here and now.

Hear her? See her? Heather, who has never shed the yearbook smile of savvy innocence, the pleasant efficiency with which she packed away your offerings to Fern and Bertram III? Sketch pads, Chinese brushes quickly discarded, might have been from ye olde curiosity shop with a bell over the door. The Christmas invite, an awkward duty for both parties.

Court dismissed for the day. My keeper, McBride: *See you tomorrow.*

Same time? Same cubby?

Cubby brought on a scolding. I did not value the privilege I enjoyed, attorney Sylvan having procured this cell so I could prepare my assignments. Had Thad slipped McBride a gratuity?

This room, conspiratorial whisper, Tim ran his hands over the digs and stains of the table, *interrogation room, used to be.*

Did money change hands so that I might sit among the ghosts of the guilty? Released for the day, I drew circles within a circle on the

Broadway Line. It's not possible to limit overlapping circles, to determine how many are possible. Students will guess a scribbled infinity at one glance, though this simple visual has nothing to do with their progress in Math for Business Dummies, everything to do with my notebooks and the spill of words written in ballpoint on paper, circles within circles. I could not run word count on the inked page, *that's only information,* closed shop on the Broadway Line listening to the muffled beat of my neighbor's music, having written not one word in defense of my friend.

I am reminded of Einstein's letter to someone famous in which he confessed that images ran in his head long before the difficult search for language. The notebooks stored in my backpack with their weight of words seemed, well, wordplay, skirting some image central to the story that is mine as much as Bertie's, as though we are still competing as we did back then, first day in the schoolyard. Let the image be the soccer ball with its patchwork of pentagons he shot my way, and my penalty kick these many years later, roughing him up in my version of our story. But then we were tough on each other, always outside the varsity game in progress played by our classmates.

Gina, that was her name, as though I could forget the fourth party in the limo. Gina's commanding presence, uncomfortable at best. She swept back the red hair. Upon second glance, not a girl.

You're Freeman, the boyhood chum.

Backdating, Bert filled her in on the apartment where I lived with my grandparents. *Right there where we picked them up, a block from the old homestead. Grandpa was Wall Street, last of the ticker-tape honchos.*

Gina stayed in the present. *You're the guy working on knots.*

Your Ghostly Honor, I may have actually joined the prosecution in my estimate of that leathery woman, she of the great legs, who tossed off what might, or might not, be the subject of my dissertation when she apparently hadn't a clue that we, the Freemans, had moved uptown. Why get into it, Lou? She seemed well aware that I was a Boy Scout tangled in a small stubborn knot of string theory. This Gina sneaking up on the site in which my theorem depended upon the work of others. She would see at once the problem was not mine alone. And know we broadcast our progress with a sense of camaraderie, as though latecomers low on the ladder settle into a

Viennese café, spelling our answers out on linen napkins as in the old days, though the acrobatics of a rung up while scribbling through cigarette haze may not work, not at all. You see how precarious it was, yet how available my various routes to solvation.

Perhaps that Gina is even aware that Ernst Gottschalk, our leader in the quaint Hall of Mathematics, is the man I dodge even when he's gone a-conferencing, not settled in his endowed chair, elegantly tailored beyond the three dimensions of the world we inhabit in our out-at-elbow Gaps, worn student jeans. The door to his office flung open, no appointment needed, as though we play in time gone by—kindly teacher welcoming a confab with befuddled adjunct in need, though mostly unavailable as he publishes the next and the next paper, the only one that counted back in '78, the dark age of a quivering quantum past. Gott, who still holds with No. 2 pencils, red erasers, an ancient's belief in the contemplated mark on the page, the rubber crumbs of correction. Still, I slouch by his door each day. Idle fear, Louise, as though his sharp eye might catch me out in a miscalculation. Tut-tut shake of the ponderous head with its unruly ruff of white hair. For now I will call it more than a touch of paranoia connecting that Gina, Bert's Munster mom, to Gott, a legendary figure of fun and fear you have never, may never see. Our leader does not frolic at math parties, partake of our pizza sweating in the cardboard delivery box, sip our tepid beer.

Gina multitasks, Bert said. *Nanos, surveillance. Gina, this is the professor.*

Recall her bangled arm raised in greeting.

In the past Bert claimed the title entrepreneur—telecommunications in Africa, oil in Belarus, gold in Peru—seemed multi enough. At his emporium the door was always open, a job arranged for old Artie when in need, so I'd run the books on the screen always this side of the law, or play PixArt, imaging whatever the boss imagined in his climb to the heights. I trust you will never forget Skylark's shot at a weather channel, Bertram Boyce controlling the elements. *Make it rain, Freeman. Give us a blustery day.* More often than not reality echoed my cloud cover or the mist of a spring morning. Snow fell softly on the tristate area credit of Arthur Freeman. We marketed the sun, the rain. The atmosphere in the limo that day when we met once more was heavy, a climate of restraint, with a forecast of possible grief.

*

Heading across the Eighty-sixth Street transverse there was hardly time for me to tell my sorry tale. I would not—and, as you feared, may never—gain the dimension of professor. Through the dark glass of the limo the park glowered above its stone walls, trees and sky dimmed, blur of a dirty white cloud. Bert scrolled one window down to admit a wave of fossil fumes then, skeletal hand on your thigh, made his move in the old one-on-one maneuver.

How's the art business?

I'm not in business. You sweetened your answer with a smile. Let it play out, the uncomfortable silence enclosing us at the stoplight in the park.

Then Gina on the phone, canceling out the old friends of Bud Boyce. *I'm on the board,* she said to whom it may concern on the other side of the wireless, *so I'd go in that direction.*

Direction of feathering her nest?

October 18, 2006

On that morning I saw Bert ushered up the courthouse steps. He looked spiffy with a silk handkerchief in his blazer pocket, Heather tottering behind on perilous heels, forced smile playing to the audience. Cameras that day of judgment. I was ordered to keep my distance by the defense, T. Sylvan, Esquire, who does not deserve his arboreal name. I am well aware of the unkind view I'd taken as the case presented itself at the distance of judge's chambers. If I had my day in court I would have said the nice things, believe me. Bert, the devoted father and husband, simply lost his way in the prevalent culture of greed. Why not skim off the cream? My grandmother, Mae O'Connor, taught me about top o' the milk when milk came in a bottle, when children were instructed not to skim or backdate though everyone was doing it. *Mea culpa,* another of her lessons came to mind as I opened the new notebook once again, took my place in the punishing chair. McBride had brought me a mug of coffee, a friendly gesture. He sat with me for a moment, took the weight off his legs. Phlebitis goes with the job. Forty years he's been at his post, forty! Knows how they swing, the scales of justice. Tim feared there would be a motion to dismiss. He looked with a trained eye for hanky-panky at the words covering this page as though to ask—*Where, professor, are the numbers?*

Topology, that's a crowded field, Gina said.

Later you would remark upon the jangle of her bracelets, her superior assessment of your canvas jacket stained with Maisy's spit-up on the shoulder and your fly-away cap. In the gathering gloom of the limo you rapped your binoculars for attention: *We don't have much time away from the children.* Protecting me, not yet a post doc, much less a professor, from this woman with a superior smile, and, as you noted, too much eyeliner and a smart mouth, this Gina with tasks insufficient to keep her from surveillance of Artie, the boyhood chum. So you rattled on, abundance of species here in the park. *A long-eared today. Owl, that is.* You attempted the great egret's mournful cry though he had been out of sorts, silently strutting on his pipe-stem legs.

When the limo pulled up to the bus stop on Central Park West, Bud offered door-to-door service. You said, *Just drop us, we need the walk.* That's how I remember it, strange need of a walk when you'd been counting the minutes till we'd get home to the kids. There was something desperate about Bert's air kiss aimed at you upon parting, corner of CPW, the programmed ring of Gina's wireless ordering him back to business in the limo. Tapping me with a skeletal hand, chairman of Skylark said: *Don't be a stranger.* Not an offhand remark, a plea. We then faked one of those embarrassing male embraces. Bert, transformed to dry skin and bones. What was left of my friend's solid state? There's your problem for topology. And why that woman?

Many questions, though on our way home in a taxi, I may have simply asked, *Can you believe it?*

I believe it. Poor Heather.

Why the peasant costume?

Not peasant. Turista. It hides his wasted body.

You wondered about that—poncho? About the design woven into the gray wool, a pattern circling in on itself, the fringe of dangling strings with the weaver's knots you thought might be read, knots forming words, and the alarming sight of Bert's bony feet, his manicured toes peeking out of rough sandals. You never liked Boyce. Till that day I did not know he once suggested that the two of you *get it on,* the boss and my wife riding downtown in the old Boycemobile fitted out with a screen tracking the commodities market. And yes, I was pissed or at least affronted, but you awarded the incident a girlish disbelief you can still call upon in honesty. The current floating palace is less office, more lounge of a first-class hotel. Smoked glass of the windows mutes the city. Did Gina get it on with Bert? He seemed too frail, flesh fallen away, what you could see of it under the floppy gray garment.

Such a find, you said, *in the chili bean market, unwearable when you get it home.*

Bud had looked a sad clown at our parting. You carried on about that Gina, then disapproved of yourself as a prude. That woman intimate with the small problem I worked on, suggesting I'll never find my place in a crowded field. You haven't much of a clue about topology, only that my superiors are attempting to map the world, beginning to end, without landmass or bodies of water. Though you have given it a try, you remain a tourist in this geography of abstraction.

Remember the logo? I called to mind the wingspread on the Web site and stationery of Skylark, on the annual report, and the same simplified wings of my design that were woven into the corporate carpet. *Bird that never was.*

Bird thou never wert, correcting your husband, humanities dropout, a comic relief man chirping *wert, wert.*

Oh, Artie, checking your watch again. How long had we waited for the crosstown bus, then malingered in the stretch while Cyril and Maisy were abandoned to that student, a strange girl they had never seen?

Gone the sun from the river, from Riverside Park. Darkness falling as I sorted through bills to pay the cabbie.

All is well, safely rest, God is nigh.

Now why? Why did I sing that? To beg a smile.

If I relied on the memory of my laptop with its stellar capacity, I'd not have the full story that day of our birding, even less of the present. Could I have imagined Tim McBride's educated guess as he let me into the abandoned interrogation room? That the Boyce case might never go to trial. So why was I absent from my classroom duties, simmering on a back burner? Why reconstructing, as though with imaginary numbers, the events of a day on which we sighted the long-eared who, as noted by you in our communal notebook, would not ruffle *his speckled cascade of feathers?* I had come in good faith to speak my piece about Bertie and found that for the most part, I was defending myself, still telling the story of the castle in Central Park that now harbors the official weather station, Your Honor, and the timeline of that day as in: It was well after six when my student really could not, Professor Freeman, consider the money pressed on her, and besides it was fun helping Cyril with his homework. Cyril, who was then five, does not have homework. And Maisy, she was sorry to report, had been coughing, perhaps running a fever. She's a stunner, that student, or just a well-brought-up girl, sweetly rejecting my offer to walk her home in the dark.

It's only 6:27, said Cyril, flashing his digital watch, grown-up gift from our Sylvie. With high fives for the children, the student was gone, a last promise of the day.

That night I couldn't get near the extra dimensions that might, in a very long run, anoint me a professor. *Don't be a stranger.* Bert's look searching me out seemed desperate, but we were exactly that, strangers. He knew it, yet he sent that woman, whatever part she played in his life, to ferret out my small problem. That Gina who seemed to know I was sulking in a corner of string theory appropriately called *flop transition* as though the tilted rubber ball of space was named for, or after, the failure of Artie Freeman.

It was no go when I attempted to work on while my family slept, that is how I think of it now, my family safely tucked away for the night. I logged off, took up the bird-watching diary, which lay by your chair along with the discarded mystery. I have now violated the green notebook with an account of my courthouse days, flipping past the pages on which you recorded Columbus Day, 2005. *Great egret (Casmerodius albus) 4:30 Turtle Pond, should be soon on its way south,* your lovely sketch of our owl (*Asio otus*) *5:10 Reservoir Track,* with your drawing, but without your usual observation as to sex or probable age, though you had noted: *Boyce, a molting goshawk, predator, Eighty-six & Fifth Avenue. He wears a gray tunic to hide his wasted body. The fringe is patterned with knots that must mean something if you can read them. Is he sick or even dying?* The book left open, I believe I was meant to answer. I carried it to my grandfather's desk, took a pen from its secret drawer, and wrote: *Dying or trashing his life. Lou, it's numbers in those knots that dangle from Bert's gone-native garment, not letters that tell a story. Numbers, an accounting or tracking of days tied in by a woman in the Andes, a bit of pre-Columbian string theory I might at best master, at least understand.*

It occurred to me that night of our birding, not for the first time, that our family life in these rooms was inauthentic, no need for our children to be stacked in a bunk bed, Maisy below nestled in her plush menagerie, Cyril above clutching his tyrannosaurus rex. No need for us to fear toppling his tower of Lincoln Logs. Just behind me the hamster tumbled incessantly in its cage. A cluster of shrinking balloons hovered on the ceiling. There was no need for this pretense of student life. We should look to our own migration, a refuge sustainable for more than a season of uncertainty. I sold Cyril O'Connor's apartment on Fifth Avenue, glad of the take. You said we must move from the loft downtown, the first of all your fears the contaminated air of our injured city. So here we still are in cramped quarters, a little late for growing pains self-inflicted. Is that what Bud, costumed as a starving peon, was up to? He had stroked the leg of the all-knowing Gina as though under a spell.

I opened the baby book with the stork on the cover. It was the first day you had not noted each verified death in the war. The blank page was marked with a postcard from Sylvie Neisswonger, who is more than our friend. The Oceanographic Institute in La Jolla, California, sat firmly on its hill. *Waters rising! Love to all, natürlicht.* Sylvie's handwriting is schoolgirl perfect, *natürlicht.* What's more, you did not read a mystery that night, no body in the library, no clueless inspector from Scotland Yard. Then, as I finally attempted to set the course for the next encounter with my students, more pedagogical tricks than math, you stood beside me, Maisy in your arms. You had affixed a nebulizer over our daughter's face. Mucus sucked in little blips from her nose and mouth.

I said: *Now this is the scariest thing.*

You shifted Maisy from left shoulder to right: *Not really.*

Her temperature would be brought down by pink sugary drops, nothing magic. As you replaced the disfiguring apparatus over her face, I understood the pleasure of your control. You hummed in your soft lullaby voice. Do you remember that the only thing that mattered was to wait in silence for the even draw of her breath, for the moment when Maisy pushed the plastic tube away? Then we waited for the sleepy smile on her flushed rosebud face. Together we put her down with the bear and the lion, the tortoise and speckled snake. *All that's missing is an owl,* I said in an attempt to keep our vigil light.

When Maisy breathed easy, I noted that you wore the nightgown, the one I like, though it buttons to your neck with difficult pearl buttons, the blue nightgown now dimmed in the wash. And I saw, not the first time, streaks in your pale hair, dark as dull bronze.

A full year of delays. Like that Gina, I opted for the present waiting for a judgment to be handed down, that's the feel of those courthouse days. Skylark in ruins unlike the midscale Buick that shares its name, much like the frail body of my equations towed to the scrap heap of rusted ambition. When it finally came, the reprieve, McBride was proven right, proud of himself, predicting Bertie would not be charged with backdating. The case was too flimsy, he says, but the plaintiff is not off the hook. Boyce must pay back, then be a good lad, ante up with a slap on the wrist, a year's public service. Skylark may never soar again, spread its wings over the dusty pits of Peruvian gold, or peck at the infinitesimal grains of nanotechnology. In the first flush of their victory, Bertie and Heather losing their cool, embraced me, but I was never sworn in, never took the stand. I had not testified that my friend discovered Freeman, the new boy at school inscribing hieroglyphics in my algebra text, that he had a slim chance of beating me at chess, that the neighborhood was ours, every alley, shop, embassy, and elegant doorway between Fifth and the Boyce apartment on Park, where we played games of my invention on a primitive DOS system free of interference from Bert's socialite mom. Play, we had played hard and long, which kept me from diving for salvage in my mother's watery grave. Back, back then when Bert finally psyched out my trips to the Egyptian collection, but the *Opening of the Mouth* was never revealed. Only now comes to mind, Louise, the ritual I enacted in the back bedroom of the apartment you dread, King Tut mumbo jumbo that might bring the goddess to life so she could breathe, speak to her boy, play a song on the lute. That was private, middle-of-the-night stuff. Still, never-call-him-Bert was my buddy and the alliance began in which I was to play office boy as he rose to corporate power.

On the courthouse steps we lingered in a light drizzle, Bert, the payback kid, almost fully restored, as though that desiccated version of himself reflected only the misdemeanors of the backdated past. My lines as a walk-on had been written out of the script, though where, may I ask, is that Gina now feathering her nest? Bertie and loyal wife are escorted to a modest black livery by their lawyer who looked like he swallowed the canary, brittle bones and all. They turned back, inviting me to join in the triumphal lunch.

A rain check? Can't bring to mind how I begged off. Work, I suppose, heavy duties of my professorial life.

Justice was deferred, which brings to mind my grandmother, who said something like that about our sins, most particularly sins of omission, that we would face them come Judgment Day. McBride in his various roles—prosecutor, defendant, judge, jury—will go on to his next case. At least I was free of the privileged room.

Tonight as I stood at the window looking through the leafless trees to the Hudson, I saw a familiar boat not yet stowed away for the season. It will sail downstream toward the Seventy-ninth Street boat basin, I'd guess. A ship with a single mast, and it is only now that I remembered skylarking. When we were in high school we came across the term in a computer game we played too often, an early version of MYST. No knights defending a phony castle, only the crew of a pirate ship. Apparently Bert did not forget the perilous game played by these black-hearted sailors. Climb the mainmast, latch onto the rigging, swing out far over the sea. City boys making our mark in the classroom, we never had the occasion to skylark beyond the virtual, but we climbed too high, Bertram Boyce and Arthur Freeman.

That first day, postcourthouse, I returned to campus, a homecoming of sorts. Our leader, Gottschalk, caught me out, called me into his office, something of a stage set this proper old-fashioned realm with wooden bookshelves to the ceiling, an oak desk of modest proportions on which the sole computer looks a prop, dizzy double helix spinning on the screen saver. We all know in Mathematics Hall that this room with its arched windows looks on the livelier courtyard of the business school endowed with incorruptible steel, sheathed in glass. But it is here in Gott's office we confer under the water-stained ceiling, the dim overhead light, and take our course assignments from our chair. Gott, attempting a youthful look that day, had gelled his white hair (cockatoo in breeding plumage), a double-breasted blazer overdosed with brass buttons, the stud of some prestigious award in the lapel. Tap, tapping a printout in hand. Tilted dumbbells of extra dimensions floated to a decorative purpose atop the title page. He turns to a back page. Under *Also Noted* noted:

Fellow at MIT, Gott said, *an elegant paper.*

Squared it away, so to speak, the very problem I had been working on. Fellow at MIT beat me to it. We had stalked each other. Had I not been at the courthouse I would have known of his triumph without our leader's old news. So, it's a slice of humble pie, happens all the time, Lou, fellow edged me out in the crowded field. It was then suggested, in Gottschalk's no-nonsense words, that I am *a live wire* in the classroom, perhaps not a perfect fit with the theoretical, as though I were a pinched shoe. Then again, statistics have taken an energetic turn in the genome race, not to mention the tech market with nanos come into play. At the end of the day, end of the story, I have been advised to limp on to new fields.

You have computational skills, Freeman.

Like Cyril, that's our bright boy. Now why did I say that?

Not to get the laugh, though it was all quite pleasant after the tight shoe dropped, Gottschalk suggesting how I might recoup. Move on? Einstein tells us that to move on, to take the next step beyond the signs and images of numbers, *conventional words must be sought for.* It is no consolation to know that he never figured everything, though he sure tried. Every last thing, how the universe got it together in this our long allotted space time. Well, I'm no Alf, i.e., apparently not much of a mathematician at all. But there is an endgame to the mystery that may give you some pleasure. Why had I not known that the problem was solved? Up there in Cambridge, fellow at MIT looking beyond his successful calculations to a bright autumn day on the Charles. Because I had not accessed the information that a boy's quest for an answer had been, in fact, answered. In those courthouse days, I became devoted to words written down, addicted to news of the past, which suddenly seemed more pressing than the tabloid headline: FREEMAN FLOPS TRANSITION. Early on I had failed with King Tut tricks invoking my mother, and in our time lost the scavenger hunt for my phantom father. Perhaps, after all, this is just a family story. I see that these pages did not come easy at first, then too easy—spilling off the backlog of our birding, the meager discoveries of a day in Central Park. How I mocked your catalog of fears, my possible failure right up there with habitat loss, thermal inversion.

Conventional words, Louise: I am sorry.

*

One night not long ago, precourthouse, when your mystery was neatly solved, we laughed as usual at the festering state of the nation unhealed by comic turns on TV. We looked forward to the midterm election that might salvage what is left of our honor. For a moment all was right with our little world. I attempted to join in the fun, deliver my layman's praise of your recent work. The homey vision of your art, mind if I use the word, which you have all but abandoned. You'd been working ahead on what Cyril calls Mom's project—it's cool.

I said: *A turn on the kids' refrigerator art, Lou.* Cyril's precise launchpads and rockets, Maisy's scribbles freehand. I believe, post-courthouse, care must be taken honoring your vision, so let me correct and revise.

Moffet's paper memorial to our soldiers dead in this war decorates the glass shelf over the stove in our kitchen. The names of the dead are not memorialized in black marble, just written in ink on fragile paper scraps stapled one to another, one to two, two to three, three to four, and so on. They were first recorded in a book meant to track the weight, height, amusing words, and fevers of our sickly child, but that record is long gone. Moffet's memorial is now inscribed on brown butcher paper that winds between the measuring cups and the copper stockpot that was my grandmother's prize, then circles back on itself and sweeps round the broken coffee grinder. Where have all the young men gone?

Bonifacio, Jerry L. Jr., 28, Staff Sgt., Army National Guard; Vacaville, Calif.; First Battalion, 184th Infantry

Escobar, Sergio H., 18, Lance Cpl., Marines; Pasadena, Calif.; First Marine Division

Hodge, Susan M., 20, Specialist, Army National Guard; Ridgeway, Ohio; 612th Engineer Battalion

Johnson, Leon M., 28, Sgt., Army; Jacksonville, Fla.; Third Infantry Division

Kimmell, Matthew A., 30, Staff Sgt., Army; Paxton, Ind.; Third Battalion, Fifth Special Forces Group

Sneed, Brandon K., 33, Sgt. First Class, Army; Norman, Okla.; Third Infantry Division

Though each link holds steady, as the months pass, Moffet's work is in need of repair. Gone to graveyards every one, sadly forgettable names weep in the steam, which I believe is what the artist has in mind. Looping down dangerously close to the flame, it is eerily festive, her Möbius strip with no inside, no outside, no end.

In our cottage industries of art and science, we do move on, discovering the last stale breath in the shrunken bladders of this year's birthday balloons, the hamster replacement spinning in his cage, Bert's sentence called off pending our further interrogation. Again, I place my notebook updated by your chair. You will remember the owl, the cold eye of that Gina, our Maisy's congestion, your impatience one day in the park, the ten-dollar bill pressed on my pretty student who couldn't possibly, Professor, a girl with no fear of the city dark, though big readable numbers on Cyril's watch told us 6:27, *gone the sun, from the hills, from the lake, safely rest. . . .* That is the trouble with memory—it sorts through the chaos, brings images to mind, watchtower of a phony castle, Bert sniffing his claret, the rough stuff of his poncho, rigging and mainmast, a gold doubloon for the scoundrel who takes a death-defying chance.

Louise, notebooks in hand, stands before her husband, the plaintiff's side of his desk.

"Our Sylvie," she says, no need to say more. The children are safe at home. She has seldom been to Freeman's office, a bleak room top of the curious little temple, Mathematics Hall, a cast-off aerie he shares with his aspiring pals—an acknowledged genius, boasting his baby fat, who brings cookies to the children when invited to supper, devours them before the kids get a chance; an Indian woman who affects biker gear to counter her astonishing beauty, great reserve. Artie is alone as Louise knew he would be, his schedule posted on their home page titled: *Works and Days.*

"Your version of our birding? What you wrote, down there in the courthouse?"

She begins her case against him, then turns to the blackboard, of course, of course there must be a blackboard in an old wooden frame screwed to the wall. An elaborate problem covers most of its surface. Underneath, some joker, or serious student, has written PYTHAGORAS SUCKS.

"You left these for me to read as though we can no longer talk."

"Lou-Lou."

"Don't Lou-Lou me."

"Easy way out, writing it down."

Artie comes round the desk, turns his wife to the window. It is a spectacular autumn day, the sky wiped new blue. Students denying the chill in flip-flops and shorts litter the steps leading down to the broad campus from Low. The view from this height trumps that from Gottschalk's office. Homer, Plato, Socrates, the usual suspects inscribed in the limestone cornice of Butler Library catch the late sun.

"Computation?" she says. "He's got to be kidding."

"Gott doesn't kid. Demographics, genomes, whatever . . ."

"Not what you wanted, not ever."

"Just different. I will not *contribute.* Love that terminal squeak? The big bang, first or the last, will blast off without me. Fellow's paper beating me out by a mile may be published too early, pie in the sky, amount to nothing at all."

"Then why is it elegant?"

"You hear me talk solutions—beautiful, stunning. Some friend of Einstein's said elegance ought to be left to the tailor, the cobbler. Take Gott, for instance, the proof of his pudding may amount to nothing more than his elegant labels—Gucci, Armani—or so we students suppose."

But she wasn't listening as she had so often to the tolerable lectures attempting to make his work real to her, bringing it home. When they lived downtown in the loft she had followed his every word, or tried to. At the turn of the millennium Louise understood perfectly why the world would not end in a slippage of time, Y2K snuff the soul out of our computers. With reparation we would move on. Artie had called his return to mathematics the makeup class in whatever the world might be made of, that his little lineup of symbols and numbers were the merest foot soldiers to a general theory of everything, don't you know? At times he would attempt to draw strings coupling, or make visible the loop-de-loop of quantum frenzy. She never quite got it, but took the pencil from his hand, shaded in, crosshatched to get the depth of possible dimensions. Her own work had given way to house and children as though, much like old Gottschalk, she wiped away the rubber crumbs of her art, leaving the smudge of line and perspective unsolved.

On the grass median below, a card table flaps its antiwar poster. No comers to read the leaflets, sign the petition. It is too brisk, too bright a day, the message worn, ineffectual. *Long time ago,* 1968, that war. The students stormed the president's office. That siege doesn't come to mind, just she wished he'd not used that gentle folk song in his account of her work. She must tear down her kitchen art—the private notice of her mourning seems foolish today, art speak to no listener other than Artie. Once she had drawn the arrow of time for Freeman, a birthday card, and once exhibited a cloudy solution in a bottle, half empty, half full. It was a show playing with uncertainty, but just the assault of time on the body, that's all. Time passing as we know it day by day. *Not mere numbers,* he had said of the evaporating fluid in a hand-blown bottle—his judgment kindly, self-effacing. Now when she listened to his babble of knots and loops, she did not try to understand, not this time. Perhaps she was never meant to. From the rising pitch of his voice, she guessed he was going on about proof, what matter whether the conjecture was true or false. Something absurd, how he fell into the swamp of the excluded middle, laughing, still foolin' around.

He said: "Oh, Artie," imitating the caress of her incalculable scolds.

"Don't," she said, "don't go there." She held the notebooks to her breast, his new one from Pearl Paint and the old greenie with her bird notations.

"There may be ninety thousand genomes," he said, "more as they map it down."

She heard the shuffling of papers into his backpack and the familiar snap of his laptop as he prepared to walk Cyril to school every morning. Closing up shop, but she did not think so, not now, perhaps never. He couldn't give up playing the numbers. On the way home they would speak, a few words with a bitter edge to be glossed over. Then they would talk for how many years? They would move, though never from a classroom, and she would again have a studio. Change of direction might not suit them, not again. They would honor the yearly trip to the farm in Wisconsin. Just outside of the city, a garden perhaps, doghouse, sandbox, but never a red plastic feeder to fake out the hummingbirds with sugar in a bowl. She would plant red flowers, though she could not yet name them. Our Sylvie would find them still within range of their starting line, Lower Broadway. He would make light of her fears. She would endure his mixed metaphors, his puns, the dated phrases of his grandfather, Cyril O'Connor. The difficult pearl buttons at the top of every nightgown would be snipped off for the hope of easy access to nights reclaiming their eager bodies in the loft skin to skin. Nightclothes came with the children. She wished he had not used that song. It belonged to his mother, to her mother too. Or perhaps he did not remember the appropriate line: *Where have all the young girls gone? Taken husbands every one.* Though that was not true, not true of his mother, who left him by accident to an orphan-boy life. He switched off the buzzing fluorescent light, the room behind her in semidarkness now. She thought, how unfair: Artie lost, Bertie won. Would they still go to Connecticut for the Christmas goose, the tasteful Boyce glitter, snubs from their spoiled children? She would not speak, the anger was still there, a clutch in her throat that he'd never said, just written his failure out in so many words as though it were no more than a story. Put words in her mouth. On the way home, she would relent, hand over the notebooks—say good job to his account of their day in the park entirely man-made, their birding, her fears. But that would not do, for that's what she said to the kids, good job, when they showed her their brave efforts with Play-Doh, Legos, with Magic Markers in their refrigerator art.

The sun at the window was still bright, almost blinding. Squinting, Louise could see a Frisbee fly over the patch of lawn on the campus designated for play, and a tour guide leading prospective students and their parents up the steps into Low where they would be awed by the dome of the rotunda, for sure a temple of learning. She could hear Artie scrape back the chair from his old desk, funky like Gottschalk's. As though there for a show at the end of this day, birds flitted from tree to tree on Campus Walk. She would not call them city pigeons. Pale mourning doves, she named them in a coo. *Coluuumbidae.* When she turned, her husband was erasing the intricate problem on the blackboard. Chalk dust fell in a haze. Not to steal his words, she waited for him to say it.

"Clean slate."

Bird Cantos

John Kinsella

CANTO OF ALL BIRDS CELESTIAL

All birds celestial, moving through purgatorial
vapors, ascending from trees glowing gold,
bands of color in their wings, arising from earth

itself, interlopers calling the surveyed area
of flyover "our property"—cutting across cornices,
levels, layers, circles, rings—the list is held

by a magnet to the fridge, "birds seen on our . . .":
black-faced cuckoo shrike, pink and gray galah,
ring-necked parrot, kookaburra, azure kingfisher,

sacred kingfisher, rainbow honeyeater, crow,
willy wagtail, black-shouldered kite, nankeen
kestrel, wedge-tailed eagle, peregrine falcon

(telegraph lines on front road), mountain duck,
white-faced heron, black cockatoo, little corella,
senegal dove, silver eye, rufous song lark,

Jackie Winter, pardalote, goshawk, swift,
golden whistler, pallid cuckoo, magpie lark,
red wattle bird, New Holland honey eater,

crested tit shrike, white-breasted robin, gray
fantail, weebill, yellow-rumped thornbill, painted
quail, red-capped robin, magpie, zebra finch,

white-faced heron, egret, butcher bird . . . flying
from seven trees of gold on the crest, shedding
seven bands of color, perched on star pickets,

twists of barbed wire, alighting wild oats,
severing fruit, scratching gravel, shaking down
jam trees, earthing the aerial, infusing undergrowth.

CANTO OF THE UNCANNY

When three times the white-faced heron
appeared over a downed obelisk patch
of pasture, three times in the space

of ten minutes, I knew the uncanny
had come back to irritate and frustrate,
to unpick the homely walk-through

the stand of York gums and jam trees
on the rise of the block. Unheimlich
possessing home comforts weirdly

rocked back on its heels, stop-motion
animation, white-faced heron anima
so bursting with action

in staid go-nowhere repetition.
The Scots side of the family
is not tracked back, though "canny"

is a nursery rhyme in home
etymologies; this doubling
familiar, mirrored in my glasses

for Tim to laugh at—it circles?
Or is it stuck there, he asks, unflying? Unifying.
Such repetition is involuntary?

Tim's recycling of songs is obsessive.
His need to play CDs, match
numbers with tunes. He likes

double CDs with at least sixty-two tracks,
he can count to one thousand. Freud's patient
with his "omnipotence of thought"

lives silently in the community—
about five clicks away, in town
where smoke hangs like river mist.

It is an animist town, obsessed
with settler images, the hidden
revealed on anniversaries,

hood ornaments on cars
leaping to life, exotic wagon wheels
with hoops bashed out by wheelwrights,

mantelpiece bric-a-brac picked up
on the way through via South Africa.
Tim says he can remember

being in Mum's tummy, or likes
to be told . . . to be shown the soundings
taken of him in the world of liquid.

He suppresses nothing. And we
answer what he asks. There's something
familiar about this white-faced heron,

stuck over the downed obelisk patch
of pasture. The tales told me by my
grandmother whose mother's mother

was Scots held no birds. Later,
she filled in the blanks with crows
and cockatoos—not quite generic,

but a loose amalgam of species
seen out and about, as if something
familiar had been stirred up,
stuck up there in the sky.

John Kinsella

CANTO OF WINGS

Locust wings ignite at sunrise,
rippling like cellophane through stubble,
on roadways, on tenuous surfaces

of shallow farm-dams steaming already.
Birds of many species are at them, gorging light,
night too short for digestion. Some of the birds

are seed eaters caught up in the frenzy.
As the sun moves, the locusts stream
with it. They flow westwards,

mirroring the flash of meteors
against the sun-blind skin of atmosphere.
Meteors come out of the constellations

of fixed belief. We pray to ward off the plagues.
Ants carry fragments of carapace into clotted
tunnels. They dissect the finery of wings

with brutal finesse. Abundance. The wings
of single-engined planes move through damaged air:
it is too late for them to shadow the locusts:

on the wing, they are too hard to hit.
The pilot is growing older, his wings aging
faster than flesh. All being well, he'll outfly

the pests, will see out the cycle of locusts.
All being well, he'll fly further than the egret
weighed down with locusts picked from surfaces:

he dreams of growing wings, but tells no one.
Of sound body and mind, past his best flying years.
He flies into the sun, contraire to the locusts.
        Sunglasses wrapped like a fallen angel's.

John Kinsella

CANTO OF LISTENING TO BIRDS IN THE TREE

Calls can't be identified in lexicons
of neo-Jindy-ism, though templates
clatter from broader spaces of sky:

as narrow as a terrace might be, there is room
for ground below, the tree, a burgeoning
zodiac above telling time like the universe

isn't altering further; who discourses here?
The chatter of urban chic that's rural,
versus shaman country urbanized?

I listen, basking in air's starvation,
appetite of birds in foliage designed
to hold moisture, bark thickened to hold

out fire; I listen with politically sensitive ears,
wondering why my ironies go to waste: between
squawk and chirrup, shades of forest cogitate

and the damned flutter like food. Doused in sunblock,
there's no seeing through new narrators,
climbing higher with new growth,

getting closer to sun increasing their factor.
They annotate: on the beach, *they* show
nipples, but more importantly,

who *really* runs the supermarket? A letter to the editor:
how dare *they* not trust *my* family,
when other families are turned blind eye?!

They move faster than we can pray,
ask them for something—kickback, solid
return on aural investment.

Like Something Christenberry Pictured

C. D. Wright

If this were not a marked beginning, but an end or more severely, *the end,* and you were ready to make peace with your major failures and hidden contradictions, and you were about to start the countdown on your own long-lived-in body (and so,

a little flyover in remembrance);

you would seem alert enough to attend this imminent loss sensing your own twirl in the void accelerating toward its outermost ring while your sputtering mind starts its rewind of the crud-and-gem-encrusted strata through which poetry has taken you as if some kook might jump out of the holly at any moment and extinguish you with one stroke;

hit pause before contact is made between your phantom assailant and your individual quote unquote soul and you are physically hied to a ramshackle building risen in full sun from uncut grass, the walls stripped of canned and dried goods and a single stick insect sticking to a tatter of color on a post struggling to support a torn roof

(like something Christenberry pictured)

fast-forward to glimpse last-year's-tired-of-sitting self in a coarse concrete hall, anemic palette and dais of drowsy party officials; a withered wand of a woman facing the audience, the foreigners, holding her granddaughter's hand reciting the *Manas* by the hundreds of lines, and the expressionless girl picking up when her infallible hand is squeezed; thus transmitting to her infallible memory the epic of her people,

mesmerizing until it's unbearable when you hit forward again to edge your rental car off the shoulder so you can photograph with your cell phone an alligator snapper crossing the road so poky the sixteen-wheeler that barrels over it blows the moss from its back and it freezes in position to recover from the sudden ventilation, then picks up tempo just enough to clear the truck bearing down in the opposite direction,

it tips over the edge of blacktop

under the unfinished garage of sky toward a section of river where nothing much is moving in a stand of cypress making a final stand against the final clearing of an exhausted land and you half expect to be chosen, to be the one to glimpse the trailing feathers of the bird no one has been able to vouch for which is why you chose the tertiary route through empty corduroy fields the instant you stopped

at the crossroads, as they say, which was the very instant you stopped looking for meaning and began rifling among the folds of feeling instead where things were to be made new again; where and when the benighted and unresponsive have begun to lose their grip even on and unto the benighted and unresponsive

It is like waking up
to the old-fashioned smell of roses
it's like finding a few words
collected on the eyes
of visiting moths; like giving of your blood, generously
to live and die
as if the same occasion
having never owned a catamaran
but having cooled off in Bright Angel Creek
danced slow-mo at the Night Spot
sped through the hot air
past the second-story wedding dress stores

C. D. Wright

of San Luis Potosi
having stayed up to watch the cereus open
the last time it bloomed twelve years ago
when the boy was still a boy when
the elevator doors opened on
a once-elegant man
playing Rhapsody in Blue
on the mezzanine of a once-elegant hotel
having cruised alongside
the Big Woods at 12 mph
straining to glimpse
an apparition of a wing

Ah, the flesh flashes and passes
so simple and satisfying as drinking milk
out of the carton or going from
maddeningly boring stretches (in front of a monitor)
to eating clouds (faintly lit within)
burning pages of bad poetry
stepping out of the story
(ineluctably over, fellow travelers)
here just long enough to testify
to a blinding intensity
under the big dry socket of God
the camera mounted to capture
ordinary traffic violations
fixes instead on your final face
a single frame of unadulterated
urgency is what you see, urgency it is

The Imaginary Dead Baby Seagull

David Shields

"SCRATCH ME," NINA SAID, so I scratched, like an alley cat I scratched. She turned over, lay facedown in the sand, and untied the back of her swimsuit top. She folded her arms into a cradle and rested her head, shut her eyes. I was sitting on top of her and she was stretched out in front of me. With my ragged nails I scratched until the muscles in the tips of my fingers ached, until her skin became red and splotched and free of itches. I would have scratched until I had stripped away all of her skin, peeled off layer after layer of dermis and epidermis and sebaceous glands, picked away at the backbone and spine, I would have played around with the vertebrae had Nina not said, "Softer, you're hurting me."

I lay down next to her in the clammy sand and softly kneaded her, stroked her back, and rubbed the tension out of her rigid neck muscles and shoulder blades. With the edge of my fingernail I drew lines straight as razors, sharp as knives down her side. Softly, though, nothing if not softly. I scratched her scalp. I planted salty wet kisses in the middle of her spine. I massaged her horizontally, vertically, diagonally. Her ear was a conch and my voice was the Pacific Ocean, my tongue was the waves, and I whispered into her ear and told her the secrets of the sea. But Nina didn't answer. She didn't respond. She felt good all over and breathed little sighs of exhaustion and began to sleep.

It was dawn. Nina was asleep and oblivious to the clear crystal morning and uninterested, simply not interested, she would have said if she were awake, because she'd established a sleep cycle as an important aspect of her life, which I'd rudely disrupted the night before and which she was now in the process of restoring. She liked to dream and explain the unconscious to me when she awoke, but now it was morning. She was asleep and I was awake, watching the morning rise.

I cupped sand in my palms and sprinkled thin streams of granules up and down her back as if from an hourglass. I was Time and her back was tabula rasa, but nothing happened: she didn't budge. She dozed and dreamed and corrected her sleep cycle. I blew hot breath into the pores of her skin, gathered her hair—covered her back nearly to her waist with her locks—and got under her swimsuit bottom by grabbing the folds of her gooseflesh, but Nina was nothing if not a sound sleeper. Once her eyes were shut she was dead to the world and so she napped.

We were alone on this dismal beach; there wasn't a soul in sight, only Nina, and she was snoring and wanted no part of me for the moment. I took a comb from her canvas bag and drew pictures in the sand. I erased the sketches, leveling the area, then lifted my white polo shirt over my head and spread it on the flush surface of the sand in front of me.

"Nina," I whispered, but she continued to dream. I emptied the contents of her bag onto my shirt. "Nina," I said once more and made sure she was still asleep, which she was, out like a light. I ransacked her stuff, her hairbrush with a handle made of cracked green glass and tufts of knotted hair wrapped around the bristles and her black comb wedged into the middle of the brush; pins of all sorts, broken bobby pins and safety pins and hairpins; enough Kleenex in every color of the rainbow to kill her ceaseless colds; her fountain pen; her white diaphragm case. I jingled her keys, none of which opened doors or locks easily anymore because Nina had so badly mangled them in various fits of anger, and I counted her change, mostly pennies.

I wanted to know more. I wanted to know everything. I opened her wallet. I shuffled through the cards in the pockets and plastic flaps: discount cards to theaters that no longer existed, calendars of holidays she didn't know and didn't care to know and never celebrated, her expired driver's license, her library card on which her name was misspelled. And no color snapshots of herself or her friends or former lovers, only black-and-white photographs of my face, scowling into infinity, ugly as sin. I flipped through the pages of her date book (page after private page of weekly appointments with her shrink and the number of hours she slept each night) and the pages of her red address book (the addresses and telephone numbers of people whom she considered special but who really had very little use for her). And I read her lists—endless, unhappy catalogs of things she should do and chores to occupy her time, which, when done, were blackened until unreadable, scratched out with a felt-tip pen until the entire page of duties was slightly indented, at which point she'd conjure up a new list of things to do.

Seagulls were walking on the shore as if they owned it and I shooed them away, told those web-footed bastards to scat. They did: they spread their pearl gray wings and soared up into the air toward those hulking sand dunes down at the other end of the beach and off the shore a ways. I turned my eyes from the sun, which was brighter now and blazing equidistant between the sea and the top of the sky. Waves came surging from somewhere out in the middle of the ocean, pushed the shoreline back, and deposited algae and splintered driftwood on the beach.

"Nina," I said. Still sound asleep. I knelt down in the sand, picked up her journal, held it in my hands, and riffled through its pages—thin, translucent sheets of white onionskin that were unnumbered, unlettered, and tied together at the top and bottom and to the back cover in a tight knot with twine. The front and back covers were made of thick cardboard. The front was painted white and had her name printed in Gothic letters in greasepaint in the top right-hand corner, and the back was chrome yellow. She wrote in splotched ink from a fountain pen. The ink had a pure, diluted quality to it, a kind of grainy black that intimated unequivocal truth, and her handwriting, uniform and flowing, promised more of the same: closed-off loops and swirls occurred at exactly the right moments, crossed t's flew across the page, and actual periods rather than dashes ended sentences. Nina was under the impression that everything mine was hers, everything hers was mine, and I folded back the cardboard front cover of her journal. Nina thought no act, even murder, she said, could be malicious in her eyes, if I had committed it. She loved me that much, and I focused my eyes on the first word of the first sentence on the first page of her journal.

His Body. We were walking down an alley late at night. There were only dark houses and bushes on either side of us and the promise of dogs. I admit it—I was scared—and Walter, poor Walter, must pretend he's never scared. I wanted him to take my hand or hold my shoulder or do something nice and reassuring like whistle, but instead he tripped over a fallen tree twig and landed on the gravel, quite bruised and horribly embarrassed. His hands were cut. His hands are like claws. He squeezes so hard and I tell him to stop, but he squeezes harder and says he's letting me know he's still there. He's always still right there, pawing away at me. He invited me to a movie and we sat way in back. I can't see the screen very well that far away, but Walter insisted we sit in the last row. It was quite dark and the cushions were ripped out of the seats, so we were practically sitting on steel springs. He kept knocking knees with me, and I kept sliding over on the torn seat until I was leaning halfway into the aisle. In the movie, bodies were falling here and there, colliding, going through contortions of all kinds. Extremely attractive male and female bodies were unclothed and in color, and Walter was laughing. I wanted to watch the movie—I'd never imagined half the positions—but Walter was knocking his knobby left knee against my thigh and his right leg was draped over the broken back of the chair in front of him and he was laughing. Laughing at lust! Poor Walter.

I thought about the movie and laughed again, causing Nina to stir. I closed the journal, put it back in her beach bag along with the rest of her things. Laying the bag down where it had been, right near her, next to her feet, I tickled her toes, especially the middle toe of her left foot, stubby, deformed, bereft of toenail, and without any real sensation since very early one morning when she was seven years old and stepped right on a rusted nail while trying to pick up speed in a homemade go-cart called El Fuego. In order to save her whole foot from being amputated, half the toe was severed. I tickled what was left of it and moved on to her other toes, her big toes and her pinkies and the scrunched-up arches of nail and flesh in between.

"What were you laughing about?" she asked.

"A baby seagull nose-dived into the water. Its wings just stopped flapping."

"The poor thing. Is it all right?" she asked.

"No," I said. "It drowned. It didn't know how to swim."

"Why didn't you save it?" she asked.

"It was halfway out at sea. I would have saved it if I could."

She cried.

"Don't cry," I said.

With my fingernails I picked away at the calluses on her heel until the hard, thickened skin gave way. I peeled it off and rubbed the tan backs of her legs, the tough muscles and tendons and the bony crevices behind her knees. I moved up her body toward the back of her thighs and hams and explored the area around her loins, but when I so much as touched her back she squealed and slapped my hand away.

"My back's on fire," Nina said.

I tied and knotted the back of her swimsuit top and hitched her swimsuit bottom up higher on her hips. Nina turned around and brushed the sand out of her face and the sleep out of her eyes. She sat up and caught her first glimpse of the sun. It was high noon, and the sun, directly over us, glanced down and off the surface of the sea. We walked to the water's edge, stood in mud and slosh, then walked further into the ocean. Waves splashed about our lower legs. I let go of her hand and belly flopped into the sea. I did the Australian crawl, the breaststroke, the butterfly. I did the sidestroke. I floated on my back. I treaded water. I swam out to where the imaginary dead baby seagull would have drowned, and I swam back underwater and snapped up Nina's legs.

"No, don't," she said as she splashed into the Pacific and I dragged her out toward deeper water. "I don't like to swim." Nina blew bubbles, slapped at the surf with her hands, turned her body this way and that, paddled her feet occasionally. She swam fine. I flipped her onto her back and told her to float.

"Walter, I told you, I don't—"

"Everybody likes to float," I said.

She puffed out her breasts and made rotating circles in the water with her arms, even called upon a frog kick to propel herself slowly away from shore. "The water's not bad at all," she said. "This is fun." She was a natural floater and she shut her eyes, sang pop melodies almost in key, let herself drift.

I called from the shore, "Looking good," but she didn't hear me—she was already nearly rounding the corner of our little cove—so I hurriedly dried myself off with a towel, sank down in the sand, and opened up her beach bag again to read her journal.

BYOG. Walter takes me to the strangest places. We went to a rundown bar with a door you could hardly open, splintered and without a handle. No one was dancing, least of all us, because I don't dance in public. My body's a private thing; it doesn't belong to the world at large. It was such a cheap place you actually had to bring your own glasses, and Walter pulled a couple of dirty glasses out of his coat pocket. "Let's go, Walter, let's go somewhere else that's quieter," I said, but he put the glasses on the counter and ordered a double bourbon for himself, asking me what I wanted until I finally said, "The same," because he was getting impatient and I couldn't decide. We sat at a caved-in table in the back of the bar. Walter got up every so often to get himself more liquor. I have never seen anyone drink so much so fast in my life. Everyone in the bar was shouting their lungs out and the band was playing so loud that I couldn't hear Walter, who was carrying on about some aspect of the music. I kept drinking whiskeys right along with him in order to stay sane. Walter leaned over and asked if I wanted to dance and I said, "No, Walter, not here," and he stood up and tugged on my arm and I said, "Goddamn it, not now, not here." The jazz was loud and noisy and shitty and the drummer had only one arm. On his left side was just a sleeve that flapped against his shoulder. Interestingly, he was better than anyone else in the band. We were the only ones dancing and Walter did the mambo wildly and spun into the wall and collapsed, poor Walter. . . . We stumbled up the hill to my apartment.

Nina pounded her arms and paddled her legs, floating ashore. She stood up when her feet hit bottom, took the towel from around my neck, and dried herself off as we walked back up the beach to our hideaway. Nina was nothing if not determined to restore her sleep cycle by the end of the day, so she sat up against the rocks with the towel rolled up behind her head, her feet crossed, and her arms folded under her white swimsuit top, and slept some more.

The tide was higher than it had been all day and rising. There wasn't much shore left for the gulls to prowl, so they were out at sea, perched on rocks or skimming the surface of the ocean, hunting for late-afternoon snacks. It was colder too. A light wind was coming in off the water. I shook Nina awake. She changed into her jeans and picked up her backpack, and I picked up mine. I carried our sleeping bags, walking ahead of her along the back shore toward the sand dunes. I wanted a final view of the Pacific from the top of the dunes.

We couldn't leave the same way we'd come—the tide blocked off access to the path through the cliff in back of us—and we were able to get off the beach and onto land only by crossing a river that once had fed the ocean but was dry now and the source only of gutted rowboats, then scrambling up a spiral staircase, which emptied out onto the pier overlooking the beach. Nina had her troubles; she nearly lost her balance standing up in one of those damn rowboats, and she all but lost her breath for good climbing the rickety steps. I took her backpack for her and so I was weighted down—two sleeping bags and both our backpacks and shoes filled with sand.

Nina was tired and hungry. She wanted to leave behind the beach, the sand, the dunes altogether, but I dragged her along through the dry grass and the weeds toward the hills. I ran toward a sand dune that was high enough to provide a good view, and steep, but not too steep to climb. Nina preferred to stay down at the bottom and rest. "You can tell me about it," she said, but I shoved her up the slope. It took us a while, but we made it to the top. She would lose her footing and fall to her knees in the sand, sliding downhill until I could grasp her by the arm or leg and boost her back up.

"Lie down," I whispered for some reason. "I'll make you a bed."

I would have built up the sand around her and covered her body, heaped sand upon her from top to bottom, and pinned her shoulders had not Nina said no. "No," she said, "I'm not tired." She'd straightened out her sleep cycle. She faced the sea, watched the sun sit on the water out at the horizon and the full tide flood the empty beach and chip away at rock near us, right below the dunes, and then she sat down and took the fountain pen and journal out of her bag, removed the top from the pen, turned her journal to an empty page in the middle of the book, and wrote, then handed it to me when she was finished.

The Seagull. Walter, will you please take a quick swim out to sea to check if the seagull is still alive? Maybe it is—maybe it made it onto a rock out there and didn't drown. I don't want to feel responsible for its death. I don't want to leave the beach with a guilty conscience. Please, Walter, please check. If it did drown, shouldn't we bury it or at least report it to someone in charge of the beach, the game warden or whoever? What I don't understand is how you could have simply watched it drown. Why didn't you try to save it? I would have, and I don't swim half as well as you do. I just don't think I understand you, Walter. When will you stop laughing at misery? I'm so sick and tired of your pseudo-strength. All I want you to do is laugh at what is funny and cry at what isn't, but you won't do that, will you? Please, Walter, see if it's still alive.

I held her fountain pen in my hand and thought about leaving Nina stranded on top of the sand dune, diving headfirst into high tide, and swimming against the current to see if the bird was still alive; plunging down to the bottom of the ocean and scrounging around for a dead seagull; telling Nina that the baby seagull had no chance of survival because it had never existed, that I'd read the first two entries in her journal and would make it my business to skip the rest—all these things I thought about and shook my head. I gave her capped pen, her closed journal back to her.

A Song Unbroken

Melanie Rae *Thon*

FIVE CROWS PERCH IN a single tree, weirdly silent. *What is there to say?* The drowned dog rises and sinks with the pull of the water. She's trapped between ice and stone—snagged but not saved by a coil of wire. *Is it wrong to love her?* She's beautiful still, silky blue in the shadows. Arlo Dean crouches at the river's edge. *Everything dies.* The bank's too steep for him to reach her. One crow swoops low, and the choir starts squallering.

The clever birds could free Talia, tug and twist the barbs of wire. One day Arlo watched a crow pull a pin from a gate to chase nine rottweilers across a field. The dogs yelped, and the crow shrieked, wild with laughter. Later, a whole congregation appeared to feast on dog food. Such joyful noise, their blistering racket.

These five squawk and crackle, waiting for Arlo to understand, to drag Talia out and open her. *Life for Life—isn't hunger the blessing?* Arlo watched crows rise as he left work that morning, fifty or a hundred then, flapping hard, yammering. The sky glowed between their wings. *But you didn't believe. You didn't trust us.*

Eight years out of prison, and Arlo Dean is still amazed he's free to follow birds, or go home and crash in his mother's basement. He stopped for coffee—extra large, extra dark, six packets of raw brown sugar.

For small gifts, he's grateful: every morning of his life Arlo Dean can choose to do this. He's free to work alone, in peace, night shift at the bakery—no one watching his skinny back, nothing to hear but bread rising.

He figures he drank 2,088 tepid cups of pale coffee down in Deer Lodge. Hot water was dangerous—tempting, it's true: Arlo wanted to blind the ones who peered into his cell or gawked in the shower. He was never not seen, never not visible.

He received one teaspoon of white sugar each day, which he could use to sweeten the pitiful coffee or sprinkle on his glob of oatmeal. Exchanges were possible. If he managed to hoard or steal six aspirin, if he cleaned another man's cell, or knelt on the floor to cut that man's gnarled toenails with contraband clippers, Arlo might score an extra teaspoon for Easter.

If he'd had the patience to count the white grains, that number would equal his humiliations exactly. When his mother said, *Do you need anything?,* the only word in his mind was *sugar.*

She bleached her hair blonde after his father died, and here she was, so strangely radiant. *Beautiful,* he said, *like Marilyn.* She laughed in her lovely rippling way, three rising notes, and then a soft falling flutter. The other men in the visiting room turned to see her. Beautiful, yes: it was almost true, true enough from a distance—Marilyn Monroe grown thin and tired, lipstick glossy pink, bright hair a halo. Light from high windows caught the fine strands and sizzled.

He was allowed to hold his mother's hand, but not allowed to let his knees touch hers under the table. She bought them each a bag of popcorn, and he tried to eat, to please her, but his throat hurt, and he couldn't swallow.

One night they killed a man in the single-wide trailer just outside the prison wire—lethal, legal, injection for murder. His fingers curled for the last time—*Sleep now, Little One*—twelve witnesses watching—*Life for Life*—so close they smelled each other's heat, breath and skin, damp leaves burning.

Do you need anything?

She was permitted to kiss his cheek, to leave a shimmering pink imprint, to hold her son in her arms while the guard's watch ticked away thirty seconds.

Ten seconds more. Touch me.

Arlo was the prison gardener, trusted with a tiny spade, a trowel, a metal claw for digging. He wanted to tell his mother how perfect the tulips were, how much he loved them. He'd done nothing to deserve this: the tulips bloomed because they bloomed—they couldn't stop themselves from opening. They were soft rose or deep violet—scarlet, orange, peach, ruby—white inside or streaked with yellow. *Do you know my voice?* He felt them listening.

They had magical names: Queen of the Night, Blushing Beauty. They were Golden Surprise and Pale Fire. One morning it snowed, and he thought they'd die, but he knelt to scoop the ice from each blossom, murmuring as he touched, *Be well, be healed,* and the sun pierced the clouds, and the rays of light saved them.

Why all this talk of God? The dog shattered ice, and the boy leaped after her. *You might have saved them both—if only you'd come faster.* The crows couldn't wait for Arlo this morning, but he found these five again, hungry at the river—and the sun rose, and the coffee was sweet and hot and bitter—every day, every breath, these miracles. Where water flowed free of ice, light slanting through trees streaked the river gold and silver.

No wonder the crows mock him now. They can mourn like doves, but prefer this jackling. Six hours gone. Two crows swoop so close he thinks they'll take him.

He sees Iris McKenna on the opposite shore. He'd recognize her any day of her life, from any distance, *Iris,* forever his since the day she stashed her pink tricycle in his garage and vanished. *As if you knew, as if you chose me.* Eight years since that day—perfect, he was, four months out of prison, a weird pale man living in his mother's basement: *Arlo Dean, Person of Interest.*

The police questioned him for two hours. *Help us,* they said. *We just want to find her.* Iris McKenna, five years old and so small—*thirty-nine pounds*—a hundred pounds lighter than he was—blonde, sunburned, *Iris,* blue shorts with white stars: *I'm sure you remember.* The officers showed him pictures of the little girl lost until he wanted to confess, until he loved her.

Rip out his spine.

He's still afraid of her father, those words, Roy McKenna's long fingers, the way he can't stop feeling them, imagining himself, a silvery fish sliced down its back, still alive, all his bones in one clean pull lightly lifted out of him.

If he passes Roy McKenna in the parking lot, if they move toward each other down the long aisle of a grocery store, they pretend not to see, not to know, not to remember that night, the words, the rain, the terrible sorrow—they look up and nod at the last possible moment, so polite, almost shy, like boys, both embarrassed, two men who met once upon a time long ago in prison.

He thought he'd die if she died. He lay on his bed in his basement room, watching the news at midnight. *Now, tell me.* He tried not to look for the little girl because he didn't want to be the first to see—wherever she was, whatever had happened. But the rain came, and a cold wind blew through the open window, and his skin hurt, *Iris,* and he walked out in the rain, and came home in the rain without her.

Is this love?

She didn't die. She spared him.

Today, her cousin is the child lost, and Iris hopes to find him. Hundreds have come to search. In the beginning, they sang the boy's name, full of hope, voices brilliant. Now, their footsteps are their prayers, the wind their breath, a word inside them. They've scattered far along the river's edge, each one alone, borne by faith or fear, finding a path moment by moment.

Do the crows understand love? He's heard them laugh with loons and churr to vireos. One sweet day when he was small and quiet, he found a family of crows lying in a field, wings spread wide, eyes half closed as if they'd all swallowed poison. But it was only the sun, warm grass, the bliss of being crows after so much clamoring. They spoke in secret trills and warbling whistles. Later, they chased a hawk into the woods, their cries harsh as his, clear and cruel.

He could call to Iris, but he lets her go, lets her believe in Kai and Talia. She's following a boy in tattered camouflage, skittery and quick, moving in and out of shadow. He's one of the starved children who waits for Arlo at the back door of the bakery, hoping for misshapen loaves and day-old pastries. The crows come too, day after day, hungry angels. *You think it's easy eating half your weight in garbage?* Sometimes Arlo slips the kids warm cinnamon rolls straight from the oven, a plastic knife, a slab of butter. He gives them five dollars for milk, and they laugh. *As if,* Neville says. They never thank him.

One dark December morning, Rikki said, *You can have me—a dollar a minute.* She's twelve years old. *Almost a virgin.* Crows count crimes generation to generation. If your grandfather blasted birds, their children's children find you.

He's passed a dozen homeless kids today—*Trina, No, Neville, Rikki*—and he wants to tell them all to go home—*if it's not too late, if it's still possible.*

Ridiculous now, the fights with his father. *You can't argue with the dead. They besiege you with memory.* There was the day Vernon Dean threatened to burn his black jeans and ripped T-shirt. *No need,* Arlo said, and did the job for him—stuffed his own clothes with straw, set his bad self on fire. He left the earth scorched, for this he was sorry.

Another day, not so long after, Arlo found Mother in his basement room, feeling inside his shoes, shaking his pillows. *Oh, sweet Lucie*—so sad to see her, the one he loved, the one who didn't scare him—Mother crawling under his bed, Mother in his closet weeping.

She confiscated four knives and a carton of Kools, a precious blue bottle full of Darvocet and Oxycontin, discovered one lucky day in Darla Fiori's dresser. That patient girl had stolen the pills one by one from her suffering parents. Arlo's mother snatched the nasty speed he'd scored from Jackson Toller—ten fat black capsules, a vile high, cut with baby laxative and strychnine. Arlo dropped three hits one night and shit himself silly, muscles frozen hard, little heart shrinking. But he kept the stuff stashed—*in case of emergency.*

Lucie Dean repossessed thirteen cans of cat food, meaning she didn't want him to feed raccoons at his windowsill. She left the razor blades because she didn't know how he opened the skin of his arms and legs in her bathtub, carving a jagged heart in his thigh, etching a stick man in his belly.

Grounded, his father said, *three months, no privileges.* He demanded the keys to Arlo's truck, white with a blue door and green fender, the beautiful battered truck he'd salvaged from the junkyard.

Crazy now to think of it, choosing between his mother and the truck, his bed and the car seat. Sometimes sweet-skinned Emily Boone let him shower at her house, and he took whatever he found, whatever he needed: her father's flannel shirt, the gun from her mother's nightstand.

Once, just once, sweet Emily stepped into the shower with him, and they kissed until the water ran so cold it pierced them.

He was proud of himself, living in the truck, not flunking high school. He worked three nights a week at 7-Eleven, and those nights he got dinner—a burrito or corn dog—barely chewed, quickly swallowed. Emily said, *I'd fall for you if you weren't so skinny.*

The little gun was his best friend, small enough to tuck down his pants, heavy enough to cock him off balance. He needed the pistol at work because you never knew when some hopped-up kid low on cash might take you down for a liter of Coke or an ice cream sandwich.

Then it was Christmas, reindeer leaping over roofs, lights everywhere twinkling. In the park, deep snow crusted hard on benches, melted and froze—*yes, here, lost children buried.* A thousand crows flocked together, their bodies becoming one for the night—this body warm, this voice silent. He saw seven drunken Santas leaving a bar together, red suits stuffed fat, fat cheeks all rosy. They tugged each other's beards and punched each other's bellies. One fell down, and the others howled, piling on top of him.

The day after was worse, and the day after that, his birthday. The merry lights blinked on and on, but everything was over.

A clear night, stars splintering, terrible and cold, so the birthday boy tucked his little friend down his pants and went out walking. Bare trees cracked, and Arlo Dean, seventeen years old that very night, heard his bones answering.

He didn't want to go home, but there he was, and his father blocked the doorway, talking and talking, trying to make Arlo agree, asking him to promise something.

The little Christmas tree in the corner flashed red and green and blue and yellow—and his mother's face looked flushed and hot, and he just wanted to get inside and smell her. The cold little gun burned his hand, and he waved it in the air before he heard it popping.

Daddy?

Superficial, the doctor said, *flesh wounds, lucky.*

Arlo was lucky too: six years to serve—assault, not murder.

But Vernon Dean died all the same, ten months after Arlo shot him. So beautiful: *blue sky and high clouds—not cold, but almost.* Lucie Dean found her husband on his back in a pile of yellow leaves. *Peaceful,* she said. *He'd just finished raking.*

Arlo couldn't escape his father in prison: the weary guard slumped in a shaft of light, the big naked man in the shower. That one had grown old and withered, muttering to himself, face gray with stubble. The man stared and spit. *Do I know you?*

One night his father slipped between the bars of his cell. Arlo felt his weight in the room, the shape of him, the pressure of air on skin shifting. This father seemed sad and sorry. He couldn't touch his only son. He didn't have that kind of body.

Arlo tried to wake, to speak, but the dream inside a dream pinned him down until he remembered a long night long ago when he knew this father and loved him perfectly—when the father was kind, and not afraid, and not angry.

The boy must have been four or five, slight for his age, strapped in a car seat. He drifted to the edge of sleep. They could have been driving for days or hours. Time was strange then, a crevasse, narrow at the top, but so deep, so far to the bottom.

Every night was the end of time, the last time he would see his mother. He had two night-lights at home so his clothes wouldn't rise from the floor and float out the window without him. His blue elephant was home too, *safe,* his mother said, but he didn't believe her. Billy Bear was safe—here, on the back seat beside him.

He thought he remembered when the bear was bigger than he was, but that wasn't true now, and it made him sad to see Billy looking so small and tattered, one eye gone, left leg leaking.

He whimpered in his miserable half sleep, and his mother turned and lightly touched him. *Shush, it's OK, almost home now.* Almost, forever and forever, such a tender lie, but it was better, a little—the dark moved over the earth, very kind and quiet—and his parents whispered, and the breath between words made the words holy. His father laughed from the soft place in his belly, and his mother laughed from her throat, rippling—he loved that sound, those two, their music. Laughter was love—for him, and everything.

The sky glowed purple above the tops of trees, and a single hole in the clouds filled with gold light, deep and clear, the last light ever—so kind, the light, to let him see it.

Trees blurred, their bodies becoming air. *Why are you afraid?* Dark in the dark. *You, too—nothing.* He saw the shapes of birds and the shapes of animals, the owl bigger than the fox, the fox faster than the rabbit. He saw the eyes of a deer, reflecting their headlights. She was his alone because he alone saw her, safe at the side of the road. *Tonight, yours, forever.*

He saw the shape of his little hand and the crumpled shape of Billy Bear who had fallen to the floor on his face, sad and small, half blind, crippled. Arlo wanted to cry for Billy, but he was too tired, gone from the earth, snatched by sleep, pulled down and under. Then suddenly they were home, and sleep released him.

Daddy unhooked the too-tight seat belt, lifted him high, held him close against his warm body. Mother said, *I can,* but Daddy said, *I've got him.* He carried his boy up the stairs as if Arlo weighed no more than a stuffed bear or the shadow of a rabbit. *Little One, Beloved One, you didn't.* Daddy hummed as he climbed, sweet and soft, a song without words, made of breath and vibration, heartbeat and pulse, his own, and his father's.

Daddy must have changed his clothes because Arlo woke into a blue day wearing his blue cloud pajamas. Even now, from this terrible distance of time, the shapes of trees at dusk, the merciful sky, a phrase sung without words can bring back the night, the one night, forever and ever, when love was breath, and breath music.

If he can trust the eyes of a deer, this night is longer and more true than any night that came after. *Now, take me.* If Vernon Dean were here today, alive at the river, he'd whistle through his teeth, and they'd pull Talia out together. Arlo waits for the song to come whole and unbroken.

Ten crows pace the shore. Twelve more from the trees watch them. Beautiful they are—not black at all, but iridescent in this light, shimmering with green and violet. *Please.* They beg him now, voices low and husky. *You might starve in a month, but we could starve tomorrow.* Thin as Talia is, her body could sustain them.

Something touches his shoulder so tenderly he's afraid to turn, to see or not see the shadows of crows, God, his father. *Arlo?* It's Roy McKenna speaking his name, so softly, the big man whispering, so afraid of what it means to find the dog, *Oh Talia,* and not find the missing boy, the one he loves, his nephew. *Help me.* He has a rope and a hook, and together Arlo and Roy, these two bound by love, raise the drowned dog from the river.

Four Birds

Joseph Campana

OWL

It's you, said the tree and
the darkness said nothing.

Summer turned to snow
and still no answer.

It's you, said the sky but
the darkness scarcely blinked.

Eyes opened wider and wider.
So the world began: it showed us

nothing. *It's you,* I said. And then:
I'm waiting. The night was so dark

and still so real. I was tiny and the
trees were tired. All was silence:

so ravenous, so unmoved.

CARDINAL

Spill or be spilled, said the
law and the forest grew

and grew quiet and the quiet
was lasting. *If I had blood*

to spare, said the air, *it*

would already be spilling.

The air stopped short,
the earth trembled.

Had you any nerve you'd
have already stretched forth

to spill me. Then there would
be no one left to be singing

If I had hands I'd have
blood on my hands.

CROW

Crow said, *Murder,* and
then there was one. If

there were two, if
there were myriad:

black wings covering
black winds beating sky.

Sky said, *Malice.* Crow
saw it shining. Glitter

of the needful, glitter
of the wanting ones:

dark hunger dark in
trees. Whither, crow,

now: who will you run to?

Crow said, *Murder.* And
then there were more.

And then there were more.

Joseph Campana

JAY

Don't be blue, said the sky
but the world would not

listen. Each night tasted
like drowning, each day

choked on its own bloom.
There were darker things

than the eye of sky, there
were smaller things too.

Don't be, said the blue
so the light stole away.

As for the twisted leaves?
As for the idols of morning?

Nothing left to be
nothing left to know.

Garden

William H. Gass

IMPATIENS OR TOUCH-ME-NOT, BUSY LIZZIE

PROFESSOR SKIZZEN WAS SITTING sidesaddle on an orange crate he had upended in a dormer nook of his attic. This left-over space had become his office because he could carry on business better from any cranny that refused to accommodate a telephone. Though hidden from almost all eyes, it was lit by a single high window that provided lots of southern sun and a good view of the distant trees. If Joseph heaved up the sash, he could peer directly down upon his mother's garden, upon the tops of hedges and low shrubs, and take in the outlines of her carefully laid-out beds. In the middle stood the great vine-smothered beech, its bench, and a puddle-sized pool where Skizzen would often vainly search his reflected face for a tuneful line. Sometimes he would catch sight of his mother hunched over while wielding a hoe or, trowel in hand, sprawled upon the ground, her legs sticking out from behind a bush, her hat poking up above a forest of fronds. He had discovered to his horror (it had by now become a small disturbance) that Miriam liked to sniff the earth and the low stems of her plants precisely at the point they went into the ground. Where the living and the dead intersect, Joseph had observed, but his mother would have none of it. The earth is as lively as you or I, she said. I smell it but I also listen to it breathe.

Only a brisk walk up a rising street from where he perched, Whittlebauer sat as steady as Stonehenge, and there his students gathered. He heard the college bells divide the academic day into equal and peaceful parts, but never felt the years as they slipped away.

If Joseph's seat was not very luxurious, even precarious, rudimentary, it was appropriate, and would not encourage nodding off, which he was now inclined to do, although his customarily scrappy little lunch should have left him alert as a hunter. Two similar boxes lifted a drafting board to the level of his knees. Many years ago—oh, so many, Joseph thought now—he had come upon this castoff in a salvage shop in Urichville. On the plane of his improvisation, made interesting by ink stains and the tracks of thumbtacks retreating like boxers to neutral corners, he cut out columns of fresh bad news from the daily papers, labeled them as to subject, pasted pictures with their accompanying clips into scrapbooks, and rested a handful of raisins nearby his glass of rewarmed tea.

So much had changed since he and Miriam had moved into the gothic "spookhouse" as he'd heard the kids call it while under the influence of Halloween. The college owned the place as they did many of the old mansions near the campus, and let faculty members live in them rent free, awarding the houses like prizes instead of paying their occupants a decent salary. It was also a way of keeping valued teachers from seeking more monied pastures. Joseph guessed that rich farmers had built these mitigations of their wealth when they retired to town. As homes, they were tall, ornate, whimsical, constructed from timber that was both local and plentiful, and band sawn according to new techniques that made possible the extravagant filigrees of Queen Anne. Every such home was required to have at least one biblical moment pictured in art glass and positioned within a sunstruck landing window: Susanna, clothed as though she were nude and ogled by the elders, Ruth in a swath of rose-colored cloth standing among the alien corn.

Miriam welcomed the large yard with cries of ancient Austrian origin. There was no doubt that she was a different woman from the mousey cottage complainer she had been during their early days in Woodbine when she "sweated over tubs of plastic," and marched rows of unwilling flowers alongside walks and around borders, as if their modest cottage had to be outlined in petunias and forget-me-nots the way a Valentine sported its scallops. Vines had climbed about like too many squirrels, shinnying downspouts and smothering lattice with wild rose and honeysuckle. Others came from the walls of the college—dropouts, Joseph called them—to lie in gutters like sunning snakes, causing rainwater to shower along the eaves into the sodden soil below and filling a declining number of tulips, as though they were goblets, until the petals sprang apart.

As a landlord, the college was as much an absentee as God in the deists' conception of him, and it permitted the property to run down in a manner suitably decorous and stately. Annoying as this was, for Joseph Skizzen it had the considerable advantage of his privacy, for no one was likely to wander unwanted upon his attic masterwork or even raise an eyebrow at his and his mother's living arrangements: neither the potting table in the dining room nor his bedside scissors would cause a snook to be cocked, neither his boxes of flypaper and pots of paste, nor her piles of muddy gloves or empty packages of flower seed, already neatly sleeved over tongue depressors, waiting to mark, as though they were really graves, the place of some plant's birth.

DICENTRA SPECTABILIS OR OLD-FASHIONED BLEEDING HEART, WILL SELF-SOW

Nowadays Miriam wore durable trousers that elastic closed at the ankles; she strapped on padding for her knees; fastened around her waist a carpenter's apron stuffed with tools and little sticks; drew over her coiled and braided hair a floppy broad-brimmed khaki hat; and encircled her neck with a kerchief soaked in insect repellent. Gardening was war, and like a professional soldier she also bore a firm, stern face into battle, uttering hoarse cries ("Whoa!" or "Woe to you," Joseph wasn't sure which) when, for instance, she removed an invasive violet from her carefully calibrated pools of grass. She would howl and slap her thighs whenever a stray cat came to poach, for she generally thought of the birds as her friends unless, like hawks or crows, they were predators or lazy sneaks who laid their eggs in nests not of their own contriving the way the cowardly turn-color cowbirds did. She claimed the trees needed the visits of the birds to remind them of how much they were desired.

Sometimes, momentarily defeated, she would burst into Joseph's breakfast kitchen. Ah, calamity! Where is my red currant jelly? I shall cook *hasenbraten . . . hasenbraten mit rahmsauce* . . . how would you like that? I'm sure I would love it, Mother. Well, we shall have a year's worth. Joey, I suffer from an overrun of rabbit. They are eating all my petunias; they decapitate my zinnias. It is massacre for my marigolds. Poor baby bloomers. Malignant *hassen! Ich hasse hassen!* They sit in the grass like city folk visiting a park, and chew my clover. They fornicate in the nighttime and give birth by dawn's break. A root of ginger, I need, and some spoonfuls of jelly. I shall *braten* them for a year—ev er so slo ly. I shall tear out their hearts and feed them to the earth. Joey, their big eyes shall become my buttons. I hope their howls shall not disturb the music in your ear.

Miriam tolerated lightning bugs, dragonflies because of their beauty, bees because of their service. She granted butterflies a pardon even though the charming worms of the swallowtail were insatiable (she'd plant extra parsley the way she once would have set a dinner plate for a visitor), but hornets received no such reprieve because they tried to bite off frayed edges of her chicken leg when she enjoyed one for lunch.

Do not disturb the dew. Some nights the world weeps. Late morning light, before the sun grew uncomfortable, was therefore deemed the best time for gardening, and Miriam would, as she said, work hard on behalf of her friends, moving her ministrations from shade to shade. No longer were her enemies droning noisily through the night air, or—in her lost husband's language of fear—were they vaguely whispered to exist behind bushes, royal beards, or government bureaus. And she had allies: ladybugs to eat aphids, lacewings to go after white flies. Some of these good damenbugs carry parasites into the garden, she'd say—I have to watch out for that—but mostly they fatten on potato beetles and similar bad behavers. But you aren't growing potatoes, Joseph would protest on behalf of the gorgeous black-and-gold insect as much as the welfare of the tuber (or, choosing whatever the argument seemed to require, in defense of the onion's thrips or spinach's leafminers, the squash's modestly gray bugs, cabbage's maggots, or the carrot's weevils). Ya, but our neighbors are. Better the nasty things should die here. The poor potato (or corn ear or bean pod), Joseph joshed, it's born only to be eaten by somebody. God saw to that, Miriam said with satisfaction. God made aphids too, and . . . and . . . Joey might chant, trying to continue his indictment with a spaceholder—but Miriam would break in anyway—so that damenbugs would have something nice to dine on! interrupting with redoubled pleasure because she had scored a goal in her game. God designed loopers too, codling moths, and cutworms, Joey was then left to finish lamely. With her face, his mother brought close to him a serious smile: each of us eats, and each of us is edible. Envy eats us. The church teaches us that. Anger, also, an eater. Miriam made her pronouncements as if they were pronouncements. This impressed Joey but irritated Joseph, who thought the tone only suitable to speakers with a certain status.

Upon her plants she loosed a vociferous stream of advice. Pointing to the bleeding heart that was prospering in its place across the yard, she would address a flower in front of her that was flimsy, and order it to do as Marlene was doing: look at that raceme of red hearts—like fat fish.

When Joseph wasn't meeting a class, he and his mother would sometimes exchange shouts about their business, pro and con and up and down. Joseph called his "reports from the ruins of reason." Miriam merely bellowed, as routinely victorious as any Caesar. She took her midday meal resting on an overturned pail and looking wan as a beaten soldier, sore footed and weary, while Joseph munched his sandwich—lettuce and liverwurst—searching the columns for a story, and flinging bread crusts from his window. More reports from the ruins of reason. This, he would cackle, is for the birds.

Today not a single baby had been made into marmalade. Normally the Inhumanity Museum ate up agonies no one could bear to dwell on. Professor Skizzen was of two minds about the admission of such reports. An infant would be found with its neck broken. The mother had been visiting relatives who lived only so far away as the next street, and had left the child in the care of her boyfriend, a fellow of seventeen, not the father of anything yet, but formerly a backfield star. The real father had left some dim length of famishment ago, and to nowhere had reported in. The kid wouldn't stop crying and had been shaken until his lungs collapsed and his neck snapped. What to do about classifying that? Botanists always had an answer. Lucky them!

DIGITALIS, OR FOXGLOVE, IMPOSSIBLE TO DUPLICATE

Sometimes, when a gentle breeze made the blooms bob, and a cardinal sat at the top of their holly tree like a Christmas decoration, performing its territorial song, its tail pulsing with the effort as if it were pumping each note though some designated distance, perhaps as far as Joseph's even loftier perch, then the professor would be tempted to descend and walk about in the garden, in the cool of the shade, though Miriam thought he did so like a health inspector, his hands clasped behind his back, promising not to touch, but bending slightly to be nearer the fragrance of a flower or the wrinkled leaf that spelled fungus.

It was just that he worried over their welfare, Joseph insisted. Miriam maintained that her son didn't believe she could do anything really well except cook, and expected the garden to fall over dead of black spot, larval infestation, or webworm, at any moment. That wasn't true, Joseph felt, but he knew that it was Miriam's habit to pick black spotted leaves off her rose bushes one by one, or routinely to rake them up from the ground around the plant if they had fallen, and then to burn her collection at a safe distance from all things as if they were the bedclothes of plague victims.

Train the beetles to munch the black spots, Joseph suggested, whet their Japanese appetites, redefine their Asian tastes, but his mother was never in the mood to humor him when the garden was involved. Let them make nice lace of the leaves, was his advice. Do you notice how they never eat the hard parts but leave the veins. Remarks of this kind would rile her, because what she got from her garden was not only reprieve and renewal, but romantic transportation to the old days—by wagon as in the old days . . . plodding horses back then . . . sing-alongs of the old songs . . . cider made of apples fallen to the ground . . . the redolent hay—when Rudi Skizzen had begun his love affair with her round, wet eyes, and when, as Nita Rouse, she had barely recovered from her childhood. They eat everything but the skeleton, Joseph said, and he was not alone in his opinions. They go clean to the bone, the way you eat a chicken's thigh. That's what, according to Mother Nature, they're supposed to do. Silent, frowning, Miriam threw up dirty hands as if to ward off his words. Am I, then, evil too? Because I chew? Professor Skizzen received a scornful look instead of an answer that might have been "maybe."

I'd rather think about the good people, not the wicked ones, Miriam could be counted on to say. Look how that primula lies on the earth like a kiss on a loved one's cheek. She would smile because she knew such sentiments embarrassed him, at the same time reaching out with her arms in tribute to the flower's intense yet tender blue, its velveteen allure. They are as pure and innocent as I was before I became a washerwoman, when we lived in the low hills on the farm, *ach,* how the day would break, as clear as birdsong. Whereupon Joey would point to the shrill green leaves the primrose possessed, almost prehistorically indented. Miriam would agree that the plant was medieval and had been sewn into tapestries in order to stay in bloom forever.

Yet it was Joey who was the tenderhearted observer of the scene, worrying about everyone's health, and suggesting remedies he had seen in old books for this or that perceived ailment. It was Miriam who ruthlessly rid herself of anyone weak, ripping the plant from the earth, not hearing, as Joey did, its pathetic outcries. It is not individuals we are growing here, but families, she insisted. I worry about the clan they come from, the kind of plant they are, not about this Hans or that Kurt or my Heinrich. Still, she named them all and lectured them all, and threatened them with failure and removal very much as the professor was forced to hector and chide his students by the system in favor with his college.

Joseph, who had cultivated snobbery as an essential professional weapon, was always surprised by Miriam's eagerness to learn the Latin names for the plants she grew, and to insist upon their use, so that when Joey spoke about the "primroses" she would correct him with "prim yew-luh," emphatically broken into its pronounceable parts. If he complimented her "Jacob's ladder," she would respond with "Po-lee-mow nee-um." When he admired her patch of lilies, she told him what he loved was called "Lil ee-um" and that they were the belles of summer. Then it was Joey's turn to complain that there were too many "ums." It's a Latin ending, she would say with a pleased growl of disgust, because she loved to correct her professor. As they crossed the garden on a grassy lane dotted here and there with the projecting ends of quite white rocks, Miriam recited the labels she had learned, halting by the beds where the named were flourishing: Hettie Hem-er-oh-kal is, Rudy Rud-bek ee-uh, Hortense Hos tuh, Gail Gay-lar dee-uh. Connie Ko lee-us.

This new learning was both gratifying and disturbing. Everyone ought to have a proficiency, about which they could claim the honor due anyone skilled, the respect appropriate to every form of learning. For Miriam, as these proficiencies grew, the garden grew and as the garden grew, she flourished. She became active in the Friends of Woodbine's Gardens, a group of ladies who met once a month to exchange enthusiasms, information, and neighborhood gossip—quite a lot of gossip if Joseph's ears were any measure. Nonetheless, he had to be happy his mother was finally a member of the community, had friends, as well as a familiar, much approved, ongoing enterprise.

Yet Skizzen had no such friends, his connection with the college had become purely formal, he was close to no one, and, if anything, moved further away every day like the sun in winter. Was he improving his mind as she was? were his fingers more agile today than they had been a year ago? did he glow with pride when his students excelled, or when one of his observations was published? no and no and no the answer came. Only his madness progressed along with the museum that was its most persuasive evidence, and it was advancement that came through accumulation not selection, repetition not interconnection, or—he feared—any deeper understanding.

He had once thought that the many terrible deeds of men might be understood by positing some underlying evil working away in the dirt of each life like the sod-web worm. Perhaps there was an unrequited urge at the center of the species, a seed or genetic quirk, an impulse, knack for destruction, a type of trichinosis, or a malignant imbecility that was forever ravenous. Maybe our wars worked to keep our numbers in check. But that hope turned out to be Heinrich Schenker's doing, who had put the idea in Skizzen's head by insisting that for every harmonic composition there ought to be such a generating center—a musical idea from which the notes that would be heard emerged, and were thereby governed, the way words issue from a mouth, and the mouth moves on account of a consciousness that is formed, at least in part, by a nature as obdurate as an underground god who hammers, at his forge, the white-hot blades of his weapons.

NICOTIANA OR THE TOBACCO FLOWER, BEST IN C+ SOIL

Joseph enjoyed the progress of the seasons, especially that period in earliest spring when the trees showed the tiniest tip of the red that was going to swell and turn into a furl of green around the end of every twig. The color was like a tentative chirp from inside an egg until you turned your head a moment, perhaps to confront invaders—cabbage whites like tossed confetti, or dandelions as orange and unacceptable as yolks where they disgraced the grass—only to find that while your attention had been withdrawn, the entire tree had burst into an applause of bloom.

Music, above all, is what drew Joseph Skizzen to the garden, particularly on those days, as crisp as radish, when the birds were establishing their territories. The air seemed to sense the seeds and the seeds to grow toward the songs of the birds, and he thought he knew the plants that had sought out the twitterers, and those that had risen for the wren, or a fern that turned, not to the sun, but to the chatter of the chickadee, so quick were the petals of their song, so sharp so plentiful so light, so showy in their symmetry, so suddenly in shade. Astilbe, a name that could be played—uh-stil bee—a plant that could be sung.

But the robins wanted worms and the white-throats wanted grain; he had read of a hunting season specifically designed for doves; the honeysuckle was rapacious, one stalk of bamboo was soon twelve, and violets choked grass while looking cute. Miriam yanked weak plants from the earth and thinned the strong as if they were Jews, but Joseph could not tease her in those terms, not an Austrian. So he suggested that perhaps a little food . . . no, not worth the bother, she'd reply while troweling a plant that had prospered in its present position for removal to a place where it would look better. I need to force these to flower, she would say while wielding a pair of snapping clippers. Deformities were dispatched without remorse, as readily as the infected or those that reverted to their prehybridized days or whose blooms surprised her by being magenta. Creams and pinks that had been together several years were ripped asunder because they were no longer thought to complement one another, and poisons were planted in otherwise wholesome specimens to kill whoever might later eat a leaf.

Miriam wanted a dog who would catch rabbits until Joseph pointed out how dogs were copiously indiscriminate poopers and dug in beds of bulbs while pretending to bury bones when it was really just for the hell of it. She then proposed acquiring a cat until he observed their tastes regarding birds and reminded her of how they yowled at night. She begged him to dispatch a garter snake that wore a streak of gold like a zipper down its back, because the snake surprised her hands when they uncovered its concealing leaves, but Joseph demurred, defending the reptile's reputation as harmless and beneficial, though she said this Eden needn't be a haven for snakes just because the first one was.

You can't improve on God, observed the professor.

He worked before hybridization, responded the faithful.

I'm not a Saint Patrick for hire either.

It's all *scheiss* about him and the snakes. Anyway, I wasn't about to pay for a saint who ain't.

Instead she released throngs of ladybugs from mail-order boxes. She also had to be persuaded about the virtues of spiders and praying mantises. Webs she abhorred, although she knew the results of their operations were desirable. These loud lemon-colored garden spiders think they own the plants they hang their webs from, and pretend to be flowers themselves, suspended from sunlight and air, feeding on gossamer.

In the alleged state of nature, Joseph would begin, it is said to be a war of all against all. I know you are teasing, Joey. No one can go against gardens. So let me be with my beauties, at peace with nature and all this world's tossing and yearning. Joseph couldn't help himself and therefore reminded his mother how unnatural gardens were, how human-handed every rose was, how thoroughly the irises were trained, how the prizes plants won in their competitions were like those awarded after a proud parade of poodles, each clipped like a hedge. She should not ignore the size of the industry whose profits depended upon fashions in flowers encouraged by the press or those ubiquitous catalogs, both of whom provoked fears of diseases, worms, and insects that could only be controlled by the poisons, hormones, and fertilizers they recommended. Nor should she make light of the myths extolling the harmless healthiness of gardening, even alleging its psychological superiority to every other avocation. She should notice how the seed companies' bankrolls grew more rapidly than their marigolds, despite extensive artificial breeding; she should also admit the plants' reputations were puffed and as pretentious as their adopted stage names—Moonglow, for instance. Had she ever laughed at the names for paints? The garden, he felt compelled to suggest, was like a fascist state: ruled like an orchestra, ordered as an army, eugenically ruthless and hateful to the handicapped, relentless in the pursuit of its enemies, jealous of its borders, favoring obedient masses in which every stem is inclined to appease its leader.

Once he had aroused his mother's ire, Joey would repent his meanness and attempt to calm her by repeating what the great Voltaire had advised. . . . Ya ya ya, she would hurry to complete the notorious sentence, I know, I know, I should fertilize . . . cultivate . . . weed my garden. Well, widen your eyes. So I do. So you do not. What do you do? but stir me like a *gulasch* with your smarts for a spoon. Play the day till it's through with paste and snippers. As in the kinder's . . . *ya, dass ist* . . . the kinder's garten. You used to play the piano in the afternoon. Day zee . . . day zee . . . the plants liked listening to her answer true. Like a cloud cooling the sun.

Sometimes her scorn, only partly assumed, stung him a bit, but he had hidden his ego so far beneath the layers of his cultivated public selves that even the hardest blow was diverted, softly absorbed, or fended off. The truth was that he was proud of his mother's garden now. She had achieved a renewed life through her interest in it, and her mind had prospered as much as her emotions had, something rarely true, he understood, of love affairs. She would literally disappear into its shrubbery, hidden on her hands and knees, planting and weeding, folding her fingers in a more fundamental form of prayer.

The garden had but one bench but there Joseph would sometimes sit to enjoy a brisk breeze because it discouraged the mosquitoes that flew in from every point on the globe, he felt, to intrude upon his peace and spoil its brief serenities. The swifts swirled about like bats, presumably stuffing themselves with pests, but there were always bugs and always would be bugs—leafminers, fire ants, flea beetles, earworms, borers—his mother had taught him that—aphids, white flies, thrips, and spider mites—the way there would always be weeds—crabgrass, foxtail, purslane, pigweed, nematodes—it was a wonder, she said, that anything worthwhile remained alive—as well as murderous diseases—leaf spot and brown patch, bean blight and root rot—*mein Gott!*—but he made these things too, to bore and spoil and chew, she would say, cursing them in her childhood German—the loopers, maggots, weevils of her flower beds and borders.

So her world and his were not so dissimilar after all.

ILEX OR WINTERBERRY, RED SPRITE SEEKS JIM DANDY FOR COMPANIONSHIP AND POLLINATION

From his attic window Professor Skizzen gazed down upon snowy ground. In a patch near the kitchen door, where Miriam had spread seed, numerous quarter notes swayed across a hidden score. What were the birds playing when their heads bobbed? three quick pecks, a pause, three quick pecks, a backward bound that Skizzen decided to call a stiff-legged scratch, then another pause quite brief before the series was performed again, a dance peculiar to the white-throated sparrow if his mother's identification was correct, because the oval-headed doves rattled off eighth notes like a rifle and then rested, the cardinals cocked their crests and bounded forward like balls, while grackles clacked on nearby wires. Suddenly a branch would sway, a shadow slice across the crust, or a jay caw; then the flock would flee as if blown into limbs and bushes, leaving the dove, like a lone hoot from a horn, placidly putting its beak to the ground—tip tip tip tip—making the most of the moment's lack of competition.

A few withered rose hips, a few bent dry fronds with enough substance for a shadow, a few brittle sticks pierced the snow's sturdy surface to lead the eye over one stretch of death to another, and encouraged the rabbits to bound across it, and the squirrels to race up a tree, snippily flashing their tails. Elsewhere, beneath the now solid sod, where there remained but little warmth from a sun a month old, moles in dark runnels rarely moved, and bulbs, that would later bloom so raucously, kept counsel to themselves as if indifferent to entreaties from their nature. Skizzen, always perverse on Tuesdays, let his thoughts offer praise to those buried blades that were so eager to push through the first wet earth offered them and flaunt their true colors. In the buried bulb. That's where growing went to winter. That was elsewhere's elsewhere.

Spring's final frost would bite those bulbs for their boasting, and bring their beauty, so fragilely composed, to a rude and cruel close, the way wily sovereigns tempt the tongues of their subjects in order to learn who might be bold enough to wag them, and thus nip oppositions, as we customarily say, in the bud. Human warmth might draw you out and leave you exposed, Skizzen concluded, and considered it a thought worth noting down for use when he spoke to his class of music's lulling little openings, childishly gleeful sometimes—carefree was the word . . . yes . . . sunny their disposition—strings of notes that did not pull a toy train clattering behind them as they seemed to promise, but drew open suddenly the very door of war.

Most of them used to fly away in winter—the birds—performing feats of navigation while on their varied ways that made the magi seem novices at geography, since they, at least, had a star; but now so many simply stayed, and toughed it out, counting on the sentiments of humans who had for centuries protected those they couldn't eat, and even kept some cozy in cages most artfully fashioned for them, or prized them for their plumage, or pitted them in fights, or said they sang at night when lovers . . . well . . . so it was rumored . . . did whatever they did.

HYDRANGEA OR LEMON DADDY, THE FICKLE BUSH

Joseph tried to encourage the escape of the heat that built up in the house during the summer months by keeping the attic windows open, even if he risked, through one of his rusted screens, the entry of some unfriendly flying things, especially bats, which could hang as handily upside down as his news clippings on their flypaper chains. He remembered a recent exchange with his mother, who had exclaimed: Joey, you read newspapers all day but you don't know what's happening! He had replied then that he hadn't a garden club to keep him current. Still, he paid her heed, and soon saw what he had been missing. Now his new group, strung near the opening of a dormer, featured pederasts and their victims, a bunch he had with reluctance begun collecting despite his mother's prodding because he had realized that the absence of sex crimes and criminals—

rapes, brises, and other genital deformations—was possibly suspicious. Homosexuals and other aberrants, exhibitionists, porncones, sodomists, and other mysterious transmixups—were an absence not to be too eagerly filled, but people and practices that nevertheless belonged in any proper inhumanity museum, the nutsyfagans and other detrolleyed toonervilles—mother molesters, aliens, weirdos, those were the words—the unlike and therefore unliked, whose unnatural acts promoted inhumane behavior in the species. It gave Joseph no pleasure at all to pursue these topics, in fact they made him queasy, but he felt it a duty to his dream to include them. And because of his mother.

Stir reet stir reet, he thought the wrens said, and then stir reet stir reet again. Not music, he suspected. Not conversation. Only pronouncement. Cheater, the cardinals insisted. Cheater cheater cheater.

CALAMINT, TILL FROST, DAINTY OF BLOOM AND TART OF ODOR

A stinging wind brought tears to Joey's eyes when Joseph looked down on Miriam's garden filled with captured leaves. They flew just above the mums to be caught in hedges that had lost theirs and whose briars were now eager to seize any debris the wind blew in. I still have mine, my leaves and vines, Professor Skizzen thought, flystuck and fluttery, though I'm not evergreen. Angered by his blurred vision, Skizzen brought his fist down on his right thigh. The blow couldn't reach through the cloth to cause a bruise.

The Secret Conversing of Birds

Martine Bellen

metimes it starts with a murder of ten crows congregating on an echoing
field
Persian onions in bloom, wild leeks, crimson poppy.
w, caw, the crow circles its cry, never returning
the taking-place, the spin-off point, as if Doctor Maximus, of theosophical
eculation, donned in body's negative dervish frock, swims
e earth's solid breath (*ku? ku?, where? where?*). Is he listening to melodic
mmering at the goldsmith's smithy? Dancing for hours, never
rning twice, as if the good doctor were exiled in the flesh
Rumi where illuminations join at an interior and anterior edge, where
everything
he same, only somehow something is not—, his feminine tears
omerge the bolted landscape as they mutually dissolve. With loss
motion goes memory, with collapsed space our dervish halts,
erly alone, uttering to strings of light—*ku? ku?,* he says—*ku ku,* they reply
o his shelter of thought that forms a hapless desire for
leep divine homelessness, as if homelessing amounts to attaining or being
tiated into the inspirited spiritualis, as if buildings abruptly refuse
conceal their exhausting dance, as if we follow our homes
roughout our lives, as if our lives
pend on our seeking or seeing
ying tears where poeming commences.
if the ancient dances of homing and whirling were distinct.
we circle our cries to call ourselves home)

Rumi knows the kitchen and weaving places, hemstitching
Fraying seams after the tangerine moon
Has risen, the indivisible sun sets
Behind grenadine syrup—willful, reviled,
There are great mirrors around him,
Bolts of blinding shine reveal
Sunlight swords (sun's words),
Dawn whispers, "Are they coming or going?"
The purple light of reason. What is Great Purple? A season passing.

Dancing above amethyst sand, camels carry souls across the desert—transporting
You and me to our next bodies.
I'm a language cashier at a pet shop
Where more dialects are spoken than words in the megadictionary.
We carry birds—young parrots with green plumage, a rooster
Who heralds in the Morning Prayer that each species
Diligently attends, as they tend to do. We have *the* dog of the seven sleepers who sits
Vigilantly protecting their dreams, awaiting their awakening
When they'll feed him the sweet kernel, which contains our most precious c
He'll taste the world in it.

I sell temporary kitties in the form of reconstituted sponges.
Place one in a tank of water filled with fresh thoughts
And she'll implode into nuclear color. Down a sliding pond. Licking
Her paws and the eyes of her kitty-cat pals, preening toes and assholes,
Batting around more reconstituted sponges (other temporary kitties).

ring winter, peach-faced lovebirds disappear
the mirror game. They can play forever without striking
eir reflection—the winged body, our technology body
at utters the absolute, resolute, like a figure
ich is uttered into existence.
ter does not issue (rush) out the mouth of a stone bird
t what isn't animated? Even grief, even sleep.
nountain of skulls.
ıat isn't animal!

ctor Magnanimous spinning counterclockwise in a black dervish coat,
tombstone headdress a reminder that an essential remainder
ats the earth with who we've been before.
ing the sky, cackling, careening, dragon bones melting, leopard
ots fading feathers floating
Into snow crystals / icicles / starlight stalactites /
faithful dog
ally fed his desserts justly—ebullient, turbulent, sighing winds shifting
and turning
Into whirling birds.

Two Intimacy Poems

Catherine Imbriglio

RESUMPTION INTIMACY

I.

A sandpiper flits ahead of her along the shore until a gull
swoops and scares it away, recasting bird boundaries,
air sea earth patterns a walker
steps into, voluntary associations with colorful
seashore implements, sand sculptures. Underfoot
the high tide closing in motions up her memorybird impulses.
She has a seabrained disposition—small sand dollar, white stone,
orange stone, three larger stones with black, green, orange flecks—
in hand. See in me as you wish, my night nest name, the dead
resuming in a bird, metempsychosis,
mother to daughter to daughter
passages, day handy in footprints, bird over human, human
on top of bird, wet sand, dry sand, particles, waves ratcheting up
for impending low-tide convergences.
Some think blank slate models ideal for entertaining
"not me" practices, but she thinks damaging information,
sea swipe, salt scrub, perpetual in and out ID rituals.
What of the convicted killer in her family on her paternal side,
no one she knows, but of course people can google it.
She was trailing the bird as an intimate walk companion,
exclusive, like a good in itself, sound shapes willed, unwilled,
sex, affection, housework, health care, advice, conversation,
companionship. Really, she was stalking the bird, just as in dreams
she dreams her bird sicknesses. Trust and risk are involved,
the body of the mother in the sandpiper asking for it.

II.

The landing gull may have been white with a gray back.
Whenever a bird comes near she startles before the bird,
as if mother, daughter had summoned one another's hidden
personhoods. Who goes there.
A bird is then twinned, a private public object
you can't isolate from the predatory biological world
where it might become a value-will issue, mixing allowances,
pecking orders, remittances. No household lasts long
without extensive economic interaction among its bird members.
And what is the media used to represent bird value in these bird
systems. Fees, bribes, tips, donations of eggs, blood, organs
come up regularly, noticeable in genetic transmission
boundaries, time-outs undercutting sin sentiment,
any stones in hand, vindication, birth children:
surely by now you have googled my name,
seeking out the criminal's. Whither
shall I watch for you. She is tied like that to the bird,
the way water brings out color in beach stones,
choice management, instrumentality, undercover
stoning impulses. Or is she preying on you
in the form of a bird, distributing and consuming your goods
as hers, extending ties across boundaries into other settings,
pairing swimmer, water rat, lifeguard, turkey vulture.
How old are your dreams. Who are you in that far from land
petrel: Wind-blasted. Sea-skimming. Whither
shall I watch for you. "You" not easily containable
when pulled together inside a bird.

III.

Lying awake in the dead of night she wonders
which is the bird that first starts all the others' a.m. singing.
I am going to market for possessed glass, buying me
a pitcher to hold schools, armies, churches, sometimes
their termination. Can you damage a bird's social standing
when all these flocking relations generate
their own forms of wacky transfers and trust is asymmetrical.
How old are your dreams. One morning in a steamed-up mirror,
thick white circles around widening brown eyes no nose
barely a mouth: gray waterlogged face, goggle/halo eyes
in owl head, a monster daughter image.
Flash back to memory acquisition, pulse, shared secrets,
interspecies meanings: rules, body information, body services,
resumption rituals. Look, under terms of endearment, a precarious
cohabiting: trash, shame, sloppy habits, tedium. Away
from voyeuristic third parties, one first bird does too
start all the others singing.
In spheres you seek to expand and contract, everyday graphics,
my daughter hand where you rubbed it, no black or blue
bruisings, fewer age spots, on which intimacy could prosper.
Is this a more authentic feathering. What am I supposed
to. Lower your voice. Calm down
to a feigning focus no more than necessary.
Bird in the mouth, mouth in the bird: scavenger, token,
parent, visitor: yes no: integral choice more choice than in mirror-
looking: who are you anyway: question to mark, mark as to bird:
how old in your dreams, your halo-eyed flights, birds, beach
stones, whither will I watch for you, your out and out
shift-shapes, your sandpiper my owl head pulling together
light tides dark tides, as in any bird, any human.

NOTE. Some of the language in this poem (with varying degrees of modification) has been borrowed from Viviana A. Zelizer's *The Purchase of Intimacy.*

Catherine Imbriglio

WING INTIMACY

—For Bradford Robinson

here is a pier extending into the channel and docks with shacks along the boardwalk.

Ve pick one shack we sit in front of it.

his is just a value sketch for bestowing fishing-village objects, out-of-wind fortitude, winter watercolor.

ne person sits on the ladder/ramp to the door of the shack.

he other sits on a plastic gasoline carrier near the dock's pilings.

he ladder/ramp has strips of wood nailed onto it for foot gripping.

ope, barrels, chains, lobster pots, spars, hoses, anchors, wire, gaff, pails: seasonal workspace absent strangers bequeath to occupying strangers: bright day lit up, as on the bias; emotional coding, there, without intending.

ome touch to come go, local value space to wind value space, dispersal narratives bracketed from refurbishing technique, caress, graze, caress, solid dock over ephemeral dock, blue-green water color under brush-stroke, brushstroke over empathy.

ou can hear availability error in the bells, gulls, the rubbing of the boats against their fenders.

ome of the shacks along the dock have broken windows.

has been a mild December so far, many days in the fifties.

wo scoop nets on the far side of the shack we have inherited.

ll the sides of this one are simply sheets of board, not shingles.

sh tails and fins also, nailed to the anterior of the shack we are in front of.

Some of the fins look like wings, but he says no no, they are just fins, probably.

You can see dried blood, oily black film, ragged flesh where the tails and fins were hacked by the fisherman.

Imagine: A me first: off with their heads. A me next: off with their bodies. A me after: post hoc justification, a series of boastings.

Real wings, these have to be wings, on the other side of the shack, not visible to him.

Shall I title my sketch "Menemsha: Bird, Anger at" or "Sample Americana Empathy."

You can count the shafts of the feathers, but they are disintegrating feathers, some already missing, others becoming matted. Start over.

Bird wings, fish tails, fins, display of: me leaning on the shack wall, counting body parts and then sunning.

I was there but can't mount for you a motor-valued summary.

My wildlife anatomy: bookish; my vision memory: sketchy.

The channel markers bend hard against the incoming tide: red right return see, that I remember.

I who am nearly always jumping out of my skin: serenity.

We were there, he planned it, one more time, together at this place, unexpectedly.

All of us into us: fishing industry: boats, dock, shack, tools: red point of re return: value stretch caught in neural machinery: moral grammar into throat halyard, mouth gag: prefrontal cortex times amygdala, fight or flight fidelity.

The tide is strong, it pulls the brown-gray cormorants swimming up the channel backward.

'e is at the edge of the dock, quiet, looking at the opposite side of the channel, the boats and the hill cottages, not quiet, full of motion, in his sketching.

'ow hear this: somatic internal organization a function of fixation, intimacy like height of fashion, laughter, endurance, plausibility; retaliation scale raising or lowering actor-observer bias; recency effect: one person's outrage another's idyll.

he sun, I am standing in the sun, probably red-faced, sea-coated.

he day is cold but not bone-chilling.

t Menemsha, relative worth to hue, saturation, lightness; revenge trophy as breath of fresh air under a troubled wingspan: air enough to come touch the go of it.

Zvirbulis
Sven Birkerts

FOR THE FIRST TWENTY YEARS of my life I believed that we were the only Birkertses in the world, our little family of four (only much later, five)—no relatives, no outliers, just us. But then one day when I was already on my own, only home on a visit, my father passed a photograph across the table to me. It was a casual gesture, offered in the spirit of "Here, look what we saw." He and my mother were just back from a trip to Europe. They had been in Germany, in Stuttgart, where my father had gone to school after the war. The photo showed a storefront: simple, no frills, with the lettered sign BIRKERTS prominently over the door. It took me a moment to get what I was looking at, but all at once I felt a nervous tweak in my deepest core. That there were other people moving through the world with my name, signing documents, maybe answering classroom roll calls, unsettled me. So much for my longstanding myth of singularity. Not that I needed to think of myself as unique, one of a kind. But I always had. There were just the four of us all that time. Identity crystallizes subtly around just such assumptions. But no more. What did they sell in that store? Did locals says things like, "If you go past Birkerts' . . ." I thought about this for a time, and then I forgot, and the old assumptions more or less settled back into place.

Birkerts is a German name, but both sides of my family are Latvian all the way back. For a good part of its history, though, and presumably at the time of what I used to imagine was the great conferring of names, Latvia was ruled over by German land barons, and some of us were tagged by the local powers that be. Who knows how it worked, why this name or that. Birkerts. I was always told that it meant "of the birch," and from childhood on I've considered that stippled white-barked tree one of my two totems. When I see birches, anywhere, at any time—it's automatic now—a small signal travels out. I feel a reaffirming sort of vibration.

My other totem, as I'll explain, is the sparrow. This one has to do with Latvians and their ancient pagan culture, and what was finally an animistic/pantheistic tendency to assign people surnames according to creaturely resemblance. A great many of my people carry these original identifiers, surnames like Balodis (pigeon) or Vilks (wolf) or—on my mother's side of the family—Zvirbulis, meaning sparrow. My mother was Sylvia Zvirbulis, and to look at her, or at any photograph of my grandfather, is to understand the logic of bestowal. Even now, when he is in the mood to prod her a bit, my father will address her as "*spitsa nase,*" meaning "sharp" or "pointy" nose. To which she responds as she has for years—with what I think of as a funny little sparrowish movement, shaking her head and making quick beaky stabs at the air in front of her.

Literal physical association is one thing, fairly quickly exhausted as a quirk, but what I wonder about is the deeper business. For I don't believe that such coinages were undertaken in a spirit of pure whimsy—these are family names after all. Nor do I think any attribution would stick if there weren't some genuine felt congruence—just like I don't believe that the words of any language were created by simple fiat. I want it to be that they survived, entered the repertoire, because of their essential poetic fitness. Emerson wrote somewhere to the effect that every word is at root a poem, by which he meant an incarnation of some deeply felt reality into a sound. Language mysticism, yes—but I do subscribe. Still I have to wonder not only whether there was something beyond a conspicuous pointyness of nose captured by that first assigning of the name, but also, more interesting to me, if the deeper family soul didn't in the subtlest and most complicated ways keep faith, aligning itself, unconsciously of course, to some essential sparrowness.

You would think that if I were so intrigued by this I would have long since done some research on my namesake bird, but I haven't, not a bit. This is evidence of my laziness, to be sure. But it's also part of a larger self-consistency, for I have always for some reason been unwilling to seek information if it is not in my natural path of action to seek it. I resist researching even the things that interest me—at least if that research requires a deliberated step to the side of whatever I think I'm doing. So I have no real facts about sparrows to conjure with, nothing beyond what I have observed, which is, I'll concede, not much. Still, if I had to make a list based just on my incidental observations I would propose as follows: sparrows are small, brownish and grayish, winged, built for short fluttery flights, watchful, on the lookout for seeds and crumbs, bits of things; they like to perch, singly or with one or two others of their kind; their heartbeats or pulses—or whatever it is that birds have—are on a permanent high-speed setting. Possibly they burn whatever they consume quickly.

Outwardly it's obvious that I don't share all that much with the sparrow. I am large, for starters. Brownish and grayish, OK, that fits. But I don't have wings—and generally think of myself as a distance man, a long-hauler (long swims, long walks); I do fancy myself as watchful—vigilant—but only in certain respects (about shifts in people's moods, about words, spoken and written or printed), while remaining famously oblivious ("obtuse" is an adjective that has been used more than once) about appearances, niceties, the value of things. . . . Crumbs and seeds don't often pique me, not if there are sides or slabs of anything to be had. But yes, I do enjoy perching, fixing myself in places so that I can watch. For example, I don't mind waiting for flights or buses or events to begin, provided I can occupy myself by studying whatever is around me. This is not to be confused with research—in fact, it's the opposite: a kind of relenting to circumstance that allows a study otherwise not available to me. But my perching has to be solo. I don't like others, even if they are of my kind, anywhere near my place of watching. I'm a solitary creature. And my pulse and heartbeat are not at all on high—quite the reverse. I can only dream of burning off what I consume. I am very little like a sparrow then, at least in these ways, but I would be lying if I said there was not a sweet, almost secret-seeming bond I feel with the little creatures whenever they cross my path. And they cross my path almost every day.

I see them when I go out walking, which I do every morning, pretty much without exception. Either I go in the direction of town, in which case they are up there on the wires, or flustering around in hedges and bushes, or else I make my way through the little preserve area down the street, where they always find themselves outnumbered and outgunned by the redwing blackbirds. These flashier birds are a direct circuit back to my Michigan childhood—the swamps that were my stalking grounds—and I never tire of following their flights. In fact, I get so distracted by those wing flares of bright red that if I want to see my namesakes I have to forcibly redirect my attention. This is not what attention is about—it's like telling yourself to be impulsive—but it works well enough to give me that intimate flicker of connection. It's true. I see them and I actually feel linked—such is the power of projective identification.

My picture of Latvia—my postcard—is a place of lakes and fields and birches, another of the no doubt distorted figments by which I live. But I got that impression somewhere—early on and very clearly. Certainly the Latvian landscape paintings I've seen—including those done by my grandfather, who was himself a landscape painter—convey that basic essence. I love the world depicted in these paintings with a sentimental force, stronger, maybe, than anything I feel from having been there. Though I've visited Latvia three times in my life, I was always in the city, in Riga; I have spent almost no time out in the countryside. If that countryside seems more vivid to me, it's partly from staring at these paintings, but also because my father used to speak so fondly of the summers when he was growing up and large gangs of young people were sent out to work on the farms. I must have been at just the right susceptible age when he told me his stories, for I've taken the feeling of that life all the way in. Never underestimate the power of a child's fantasies, or, from the parent's side, the impact—what was said, and how it was said, the tone of voice. I'm back to the words and the sounds again, the nouns: *upe* (river), *mezhi* (forests), *lauki* (fields) . . . I listened with my entire listening self, taking them in. So much so that even now when I say those words, and a small handful of others, some gate inside the language swings open. Remember, every word was once a poem. Maybe this is why my childhood language holds a thick, textured density that I hardly ever get with English, though my English overran my Latvian fifty years ago. The first spell is the strongest.

The last time I traveled to Latvia I went alone. It was before the collapse of communism, so my whole experience had a more than slightly nervous-glance-over-the-shoulder feeling about it. Walking out of the hotel a visitor would be followed—this was confirmed a dozen times. It seems so long ago now. I am forever being told that I wouldn't believe what Riga is like now—so alive and stylish, nothing like the old place I remember. But appealing as those descriptions are, I have no real desire to update my Soviet-era images. Nor do I really believe that such replacement would change much for me. Riga was for me long ago plucked from time and sprayed over with some kind of metaphysical fixative. It is, and will remain, an utterly illogical jumble of medieval cobblestones and German baroque detailing and the worst Khrushchev-era prefab dreck, with a beautiful park of bridges, flowers, and rolling green dropped into the very center, nothing following as it should on a mere map because every important corner and stretch of sidewalk has been tagged with one or another of my mother's or father's reminiscences, to the point where my walking segues were finally more about time than space, and the little embankment where someone and someone once sat together abutted directly—almost overlapping—the coffee and cake shop where my grandmother met with her friends.

I do have one sparrow-related anecdote, which I hope can be fitted here like a keystone to join the American and Latvian sides of the story, if "story" is not too grand a term for this extraterritorial meandering.

The last time I traveled, wanting to save money, I signed up to fly with a charter group composed of American Latvians going to visit relatives. I was in my thirties, married, and I remember how unnerved I was to have to share a hotel room. I'd been paired up with a man named Viesturs, though he insisted I call him "Vic." How disorienting: to be in a small hotel room speaking my intimate, private language—the language that I have pretty much only ever spoken with my family—with a person calling himself "Vic" who seemed at first handshake entirely alien. Once we arrived in Riga, though, I hardly even saw him, except silhouetted in the bathroom doorway late at night as I woke to the sounds of his returning from his latest round of visiting.

I was there to spend some time with my grandmother, who was old and ailing, mainly bedridden. I would visit her for several hours every afternoon during the week of my stay. She received me in her bedroom in her ancient-seeming, cluttered, high-ceilinged apartment (where my father had grown up). I let myself in and called out to her. I would usually find her lying in her bed with her eyes closed—she had bad cataracts—opening them only to greet me or to look at notes she had made. She had an agenda of things she wanted me to know about. I would watch as she brought her scrap of paper so close it almost touched her nose. She had stories about my father as a boy, and herself as a girl or in her courtship days (there was an ill-starred romance at the core of her life), and there were things she'd remembered that she wanted to tell me about writers she had known. Mostly she talked calmly, sequentially, very much the schoolteacher she had been for more than fifty years, but when she got on the subject of Peter, my grandfather (and namesake—my middle name is Peter), she would always ask me to hold her hand. Talking about him, her manner changed completely, and her voice became emotional, wavery.

My grandmother could only see me for a few hours a day, but she had arranged for me to have a companion for my visit, the daughter of one of her old students, Ieva (Eve). I had met her many years before when I had visited with my sister, but I was now shocked to see that she had become an attractive young woman. She was—I realized this before anything else—completely familiar to me. Not so much personally, though we had met many years before, but . . . genetically. This is very hard for me to pin down, because it has to do with Latvianness, with the myriad elusive aspects of appearance—skin color, hair, a certain softness in the features—and how these somehow carry over into voice tones, mannerisms, everything. Ieva had a tuned-up shyness that could flare into impetuousness without warning, and even this seemed Latvian to me. She was fresh faced, with a creamy complexion, and very slightly plump in specific places—the neck, the wrists. What else? She was as witty and conversationally responsive in that moment-to-moment way as anyone I'd met. She had recognized, probably instantly, that she could humor me, and as my Latvian was rough to say the least, she didn't hesitate with the swiftly lifted eyebrow, the wry corrective interventions, the mini-lectures she conducted with mock seriousness. Within minutes of our meeting up again, Ieva had set herself up as my tour guide—for a week she instructed me in her world.

We traversed the beautiful city of Riga in every direction. She pointed, lectured ironically, and flirted. And of course I flirted back. I hadn't had so much fun in years, such a sense of walking a tightrope while looking down on the safety net of origins. How can I explain this? I was playing the old delightful game, but in translation. But also not, because in another way it wasn't translation at all but the original human business. We were touring all the places I'd heard about from my parents, the sites of their growing up. She seemed to know all about them, their story. The sense of knowing and being known was very intense. Combined with the fact that we were getting on so well—I felt the needle moving into the red zone, the red zone within a Red Zone, a condition that the twin factors of shyness and impossibility steadily intensified as my visit went on. We were out together every day. We walked everywhere, talked, told our stories. There was a sense of permission about doing this: I would be going away in a few days, a day. Oddly, but maybe also understandably, I had never confided anything to anyone in Latvian and had no developed language for the things I really thought and felt. Maybe for that reason everything I said felt fresh, itself a new sensation for me.

We had a joke between us. Upon my arrival, playing off my mother's maiden name, she had presented me with a children's book—*Sarezgitais Zvirbulens,* which could be translated to mean "mixed-up little sparrow"—and this became her joke. The cover showed a cartoon rendering of a mussed-up-looking bird. Me. We took our extended tours of the city, and as we went on with our stories she wove that *zvirbulens* theme into everything. Finally it became the binding thread of my visit. The mixed-up sparrow on the street corner, dazed in front of the store display, wide eyed on the trolley. Absolutely nothing happened to ground the electricity of those hours except a lone goodbye kiss when it was time for me to leave, a kiss that did sustain itself a bit longer than a friend's kiss might have.

My last visit to Riga remains a beautiful contained memory that has faded to near indistinctness—though as I wrote about it just now, putting words to it for the very first time, I caught a hint of that old sensation. But only a hint. I was like someone touched on the shoulder, almost waking, but then falling back into his dream, though the analogy works better the other way, this being the wakened state, and that, with its aura of old traces and residues, the dream. As such, of course, it is best left alone—not to mention that I am no great believer in dream analyses and interpretations. Except that just this once I feel moved—compelled—to reflect, though I would proceed not in the Viennese mode, but the Argentinian, à la Borges. I can't help it. The whole memory comes back to me now with such a strong metaphysical saturation. And I find myself considering the theme of alternate lives and destinies, playing with the Borgesian idea that as the two of us pursued our tour—through the Old City (itself a kind of dream protruding into our Soviet present), out along the white sands of the Jurmala shore, crossing this way and that through the park—I was somehow being granted a glimpse of the conjectural life, a picture of how things might have been if the coin had landed tails, not heads: if this and this and this turn had not been taken by my father, my mother, if I had gotten myself born as who I am, but in what they had grown up believing was the intended place. The bird is in there too, the spirit bird, watchful and hovering, ministering to the grains and seeds, moving about in the tangle of all those roots—*sarezgitais zvirbulens* indeed, dazed not just by beauty and connection, but by the idea of all the fate that was traded away when those other turns were taken.

JOHN ASHBERY TRIBUTE

Reginald Shepherd
Eileen Myles
Peter Straub
Jed Perl
Charles Bernstein
Ben Lerner
Brian Evenson
Cole Swensen
Marjorie Welish
Marcella Durand
Ron Silliman
Christian Hawkey
David Shapiro
Anselm Berrigan
Susan Stewart
Joan Retallack
Brenda Hillman
Richard Deming
Kevin Killian
Geoffrey O'Brien
Ann Lauterbach
Robert Kelly
Rae Armantrout
James Longenbach
Graham Foust
Susan Wheeler
Rosangela Briscese and David Kermani

Edited by Peter Gizzi and Bradford Morrow

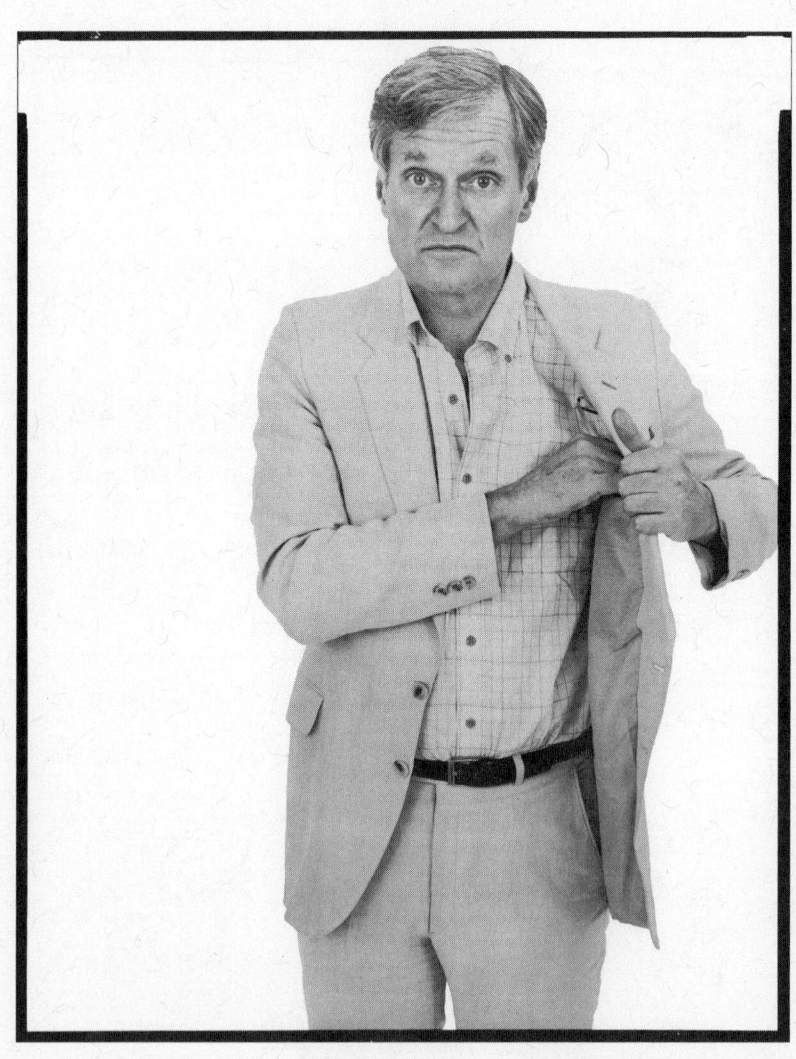

John Ashbery, poet, New York, September 27, 1983.
Photograph Richard Avedon.

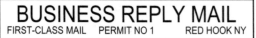

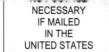

NECESSARY
IF MAILED
IN THE
UNITED STATES

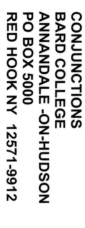

EDITORS' NOTE

LAST WINTER DURING one of our frequent and free-ranging conversations, we found ourselves talking about one of our mutual favorite writers, John Ashbery, and wondered—given the great acts of generosity he'd shown us, all of us, over the years, through his brilliant poetry and criticism—how we might best honor him in his eightieth year.

Our idea was to solicit personal essays from a group of distinguished fellow writers at various stages of their own writing lives, inviting them each to engage one of John's major books published over his half-century-plus of literary achievement. Our wish was to gather in this collective of personal responses to the Ashbery canon—from *Some Trees,* published back in 1956, right up through *A Worldly Country,* which came out earlier this year—a Festschrift portfolio that would constitute an enduring document, illuminating the ongoing significance of this great poet's work.

Happily, as readers will see, these creative essays took many forms: meditations, critical and historical discussions, notebooks, poetic reengagements, memoirs, and often an innovative mix of all of the above. The result is a contemporary negotiation with John's remarkable poetry, prose, and plays and a birthday salute to one of our most beloved poets.

In addition, John has allowed us to include several remarkable early works, "The Poems" and "Song for a Play," both out of print for over fifty years, and the wonderful *Three Madrigals,* which heretofore has been only available in this original holograph version illustrated by Ashbery himself in a scarce limited edition of 162 copies published by Poet's Press on May 2, 1968. We want to thank John as well as David Kermani for allowing us to republish these splendid Ashbery treasures.

—Peter Gizzi & Bradford Morrow
October 2007
Holyoke & New York City

Three Early Works

John Ashbery

With an Afterword by Rosangela Briscese and David Kermani

SONG FROM A PLAY

Roses stood among the pans
As the sick ejected bitter humors;
Lilies came and went like passions
On faceless private errands;
Somebody sent me an amorous
Skeleton clothed in geraniums
With a card signed "Compliments of Jerry."

What could we reply, with the green
Ripeness falling across us, and lovers
In vicious pursuit even through dreams
Unless death were a vital sac hidden
Under every leaf and erotic gesture,
Allowing excursions into peace, beyond
The locked joy of the moment?

But the yellow foliage that now
Is running to cover the planet's face
Is dead motion that goes on awhile
After the genital force has stopped.
And the departure of love does not
Happen on this planet, it is a kind of action
Not permitted by the imagination.

—1947

John Ashbery

THE POEMS

1. Animals of All Countries

The tiger returns to his own, and the beaver;
The others return to their own.
The bride returns to her own, the beech returns to her own.

And I, on this blue night of yellow stars,
Where should I turn?

"Return to the passing cars,
The dark, mysterious, speeding cars."

2. Heidi

In front of the house stands a little garden.
Six flowers are in it.
In front of the house, a car.
Is there a bunch of flowers on the seat of the car?
That I cannot tell you.

What songs do you sing to us, Heidi?
What other flowers do you bring us?

3. The Conquest of the Sky

I was sad when our brothers had entered the country.

4. The Circus

And is it not . . . enough?
To borrow tragically one's skin?
To live like the painter Michelangelo,
"All bottled up inside, a burden to oneself, a mystic burden?"

5. Mountain Flowers

What joy and order in these poems!
It does not matter that some are without heads,
That others have two bodies, and some neither bodies nor heads;
That some are green, some red white and blue, and others red
white and black!
I dreamed that I saw my window from below:
Somebody was throwing all my belongings down into the street,

Including all my poems! Purple and orange, white, green with flowers
or white polka dots,
All escaped my grasping hands, save one,
A black one, which floated quite naturally into my hands.
The title: "L'Invitation au Voyage."

6. Tropical Butterflies

Dawn breaks thousands of windows in the city,
As though a tear fell
From the eye of a smiling person.
The bathers are ready
On their platform;
The soldiers are parading
In furs, for it is a cold morning.
At this moment, butterflies fly over the city.
No one notices them,
Or that the lights are on, as though it were not day.

7. Flowers on Your Way

I placed flowers on your path
Because I wanted to be near you.

Do not punish me.

8. Animals of All Countries, II

If you would talk well, be a good listener.
If you would listen well, do not listen to the song of Heidi,
Or that of her friends, the lions.

9. Robinson Crusoe

Though I call you dear,
Though we do that in bed together,
Still I do not see you.
My eyes are wandering in distant countries.

10. Heidi, II

She said, "It is different in my country.
In winter the flies do not die.
It is not cold enough for the people to die, or the flies."

She opened a door, and sunlight came pouring in, reflected from
 the street five stories below.
"Shall I tell you the real pain it is to die?"

The Song of Heidi:
"My land is an asylum, but cold."

The song of Heidi to the married couples:
"My radio speaks many languages,
Yet I speak but one:
The song of the flowers,
The song of the flea of Naples, of the brilliant Icelandic night,
The song of my feet."

11. Orchids

From the land of the samovar
The orchids are traveling!
They crush the grain to the ground, they sweep all before them.
They mutilate the shepherd, his flocks are dispersed.
They know no human feeling, they know only that they are all one color,
Which is pink, or yellow.

12. Animals of All Countries, III

I have come to repair the damage of the orchids.
Look, in my hand I have a healing snake.
Bear witness, Scotland, to what I am about to do.

13. Birds of Paradise and Hummingbirds

Walk with me to the end of the road.
There is a little house there, with a garden behind a moldy old wall.
The old people will see us, they will come out and ask us in.
If not, there is my car several miles further on.
We will be good there. It will be perhaps enough.
In the morning the light will be kind to us.
You will never know my exact age, nor I yours.
Like two birds of paradise, we will kiss in the rising wind
And a great giant will come down from the mountains to help us.

—1955–1956

John Ashbery

THREE MADRIGALS

THREE MADRIGALS

1

THREE MADRIGALS

First Madrigal

Temperature now that farms project
weed promise
abnormally kiln weed I praise the citadel
sitting down to table moorish hygrometer
measured Dust. A dust table, the dim-clad men
you pry the empyrean: plaid from the
rocks. The hen... hand
igloo-mortuary staff dribble wet hand promise. A thin ball

2

reed hand

we sitting up

for twos them are frightened . . . :*. piano slobbered surface

black violets

ball of hairs advanced from the hut rigid ool

rack. weed-dandelions placed on.... to wrinkle on...]

there]

where the helmet gets very strict we churn frightened East]

Anglia gopher manhunt on]

the half-grown river and trees stables sharks tables sables the]

hunt for perdition]

the rabbit sigh bell and the gopher osprey cadmium]

zephyr bag zoology]

Joy

black, crumbly violets

those afternoons on the Bosporus

"The Bluebells of Scotland!"

3

I know not when I shall see you again

My father, disapproving of our inti-

would wean me from you

I start tomorrow morning for Athens, Georgia

think of me, who

although many miles removed

is ever near you in her

thoughts;

whose constant love

neither time

nor distance can efface.

A love ....deeper than friendship

4

Second Madrigal

Calling
the acolyte in
O the were promised
done short

Weedspray over the governed
island thing
you carved nor effaced missile

The pan
of earth

Come then
opening the
not even insect shell allow
and all pass
into the curve !!!!!!!!!

and the reeds
glory to clasp hands

raving because it could not be otherwise: because
the pulp, shorn from
the fruit, stands alone on the table. The books,
laboratories, the

5

bells (O arduous for the lifting! the mangled days]
of month]

of June

careless boats moulted high procession of fathers famished
the sad news

elephantiasis gizzard spittoon

and although I know
how cold all words of comfort are
to a heart crushed by sorrow
yet if the loving sympathy

of a dear friend feelings grow from the smooth]
stone]
the forest kisses

6

Would you lend me the use of

passion that seeped from
box
fortifies the lake.
"Your foot is hidden by the lake."

A loving card
from kindness grew
the
old age swiftly

on gray feet comes stealing
under the shadow of the mountains and the black rocks
the incantations

and his old man is
beside the car.
"The cherry trees are in bloom."

7

Third Madrigal

Not even time shall efface
The bent disk
And the wicked shores snore
Far from the divining knell!

On his lived perch
Let not the master be cast
Back on the petitioner
To wise limits of the secret

That hurt the whole city.
The ever prospering shepherds
Are that, who have tasted lament
The shell splashed bitter darkness on the shore

Near the intruder's arch.
The last party to be seized
at twilight, and time was cold
To the lovers. And seized their praise

8

Wild that to the room
With brother and sister came.
That passions are a fence
Draw the vines out of the earth

And listen to new
Memory falls on your olive hands,
The undying luck
Of the dying million ageless

Pushed to hands for approval.
Along the level bay
A dim blaze of diamond
Walking to you: what you had

Carnival – *** _ ** fish
* **** _ * * * * ___ However
accompany / ***** * * .:* Reply. shareholder
Baseball furniture store

favorable ; ______ **''' _* of 2

9

oblige ----------
(;) the semicolon

received   Otherwise, your own
8th   and one Glaucon
rent store fish   study of them
laugh pain
----- comes   , , , , , , , ,

pecuniary   encyclopedia
and the not   awkward   reservoir
brutish   comprehending the knights," etc.
gas fair   Especially was so
fish store   and encouraged   the dime
even before.......   Please   Manx

weekly   tin   neglect

spanked encouraged
??   :   laburnum
tooth Detroit
manual   blank mnh
or   (----)   limnh

10

mattress

hawk

personality table pregnancy

apron bin ,,,,,,,,,,,))))))))))*****

,,,,,, **** * :: ::::.:;.,:::.,...,./:/.:-*

shoo Amy any analyse amiably accentuate

foregone tide enfant

............./

cooperate building lynx stuffed

board

osprey ostensible Orkney of olfactory ore or orator advantage

John Ashbery
1958

Afterword

Rosangela Briscese and *David* Kermani

EARLY WORK BY WRITERS as prolific as John Ashbery often gets neglected, sometimes to that writer's relief; issues of literary merit and youthful enthusiasms needn't arise. But in Ashbery's case, with preparations now under way for the first volume of a *Collected Poems* from the Library of America, to be edited by Mark Ford, his early texts are resurfacing. The Ashbery Resource Center (ARC), an archival and research facility sponsored by the Flow Chart Foundation on behalf of Bard College, has been asked to assist with the identification and retrieval of these vintage pieces since, as custodian of large portions of the Ashbery archive and collections, it has been working to identify, organize, document, and preserve these materials.

Ashbery's poetry has long had the reputation of being difficult, but at the same time its engagement with the "real world"—including other literature, visual and decorative arts, music, architecture, theater, and film—is one of its most pervasive but subtle characteristics. However, understanding something of the context within which it exists can further illuminate its many dimensions. The Library of America project reminded us of the interesting trajectories that many of Ashbery's early writings have had through the cultural landscape.

It is clear that Ashbery's early work is not insignificant. Two poems written while he was a student at Deerfield were published under a pseudonym in *Poetry* in 1945. "Some Trees," which first appeared in the *Harvard Advocate* in 1949 while he was an undergraduate, was included in his 1953 chapbook *Turandot and Other Poems* (issued in New York by the Tibor de Nagy Gallery, with drawings by Jane Freilicher), and then became the title poem for the manuscript chosen by W. H. Auden for the 1956 volume in the Yale Series of Younger Poets. Perhaps the comment made on the *Harvard Advocate*'s Web site in an essay on the history of that publication is not as audacious as it initially seems: "[In the pages of the *Advocate*,] Wallace Stevens's work—which became so great—begins so slight. John Ashbery's work—which became so great—began so great."

The three pieces published in this special *Conjunctions* tribute were composed during little more than a decade. Although barely known today, they exhibit Ashbery's characteristic fascination with various branches of the arts, and they attracted significant attention at the time from his peers and colleagues—those whose interest in crossing boundaries, breaking barriers, revitalizing traditional forms, and inventing new ones paralleled his own. Their contexts are rich intersections of various influences that have shaped Ashbery's creative world since his childhood and are still present in his life. The following brief descriptions can only hint at the networks of information that may be traced through materials in the ARC collections (some of which is available online at www.flowchartfoundation.org/arc); however, it should be evident that further investigation of these contexts can provide new insight into Ashbery's work.

"Song from a Play" was written while Ashbery was a student at Harvard in 1947; its sole publication was in the *Harvard Advocate* during his third year, in early 1948, along with the announcement that it had won an honorable mention in the "Garrison Competition." Kenneth Koch and Frank O'Hara were at Harvard with Ashbery, and were also involved with the *Advocate,* so the majority of the original group that would eventually be known as the New York School of Poets was already present.

The poem's title reflects the involvement of Ashbery and his colleagues with music and the theater. Music is indeed central to Ashbery's method of writing. He often likens his poetic intent to that of a musical composition and considers the legendary performance by David Tudor of John Cage's *Music of Changes* on New Year's Day 1952, which he attended with O'Hara, to be one of the seminal events of his creative life ("I suddenly saw a potential for writing in a new way"). Ashbery's play for which this "song" was written, *Everyman: A Masque,* has three characters: Columbine, Everyman, and Death. It remains unpublished, but its performance in early 1951 as one of a series of four one-act plays on the inaugural bill of the Poets' Theatre in Cambridge, Massachusetts, survives in a tape recording. A group of JA's Harvard friends collaborated on the production, which featured music for flute and piano composed by Frank O'Hara, and sets and costumes designed by Edward Gorey.

This was a period of intense theatrical and cinematic activity for Ashbery and his friends. Although his play *The Heroes,* written in 1950, would not have its first production until 1952 in New York by the Living Theatre, he had already starred in Rudy Burckhardt's silent short film *Mounting Tension* (1950) with young, then-unknown art-world personalities Jane Freilicher, Larry Rivers, and Elaine de Kooning (the youthful Ashbery had set out to be a painter—specifically, a surrealist!). Ashbery acted in O'Hara's play *Try! Try!*, with sets by Larry Rivers, which was on the bill with *Everyman* at the Poets' Theatre in 1951. O'Hara later returned the favor by playing one of the leads in Ashbery's theatrical parody of silent films, *The Compromise, or Queen of Caribou*, written in 1955 and produced in 1956, again by the Poets' Theatre. (This play also includes a song: "From the Yukon to the Arctic Circle / Everybody's in a whirl. . . .") Like much of Ashbery's poetry, these plays investigate traditional forms and conventions, often with surprising results. Ashbery's involvement with theater and film continues to this day: *The Heroes* was produced recently in New York, and *The Compromise* was done in Paris; he performed the role of the Narrator in Guy Maddin's live multimedia film extravaganza *Brand upon the Brain!* several months ago, and is planning to collaborate with Maddin on a screenplay.

Ashbery wrote "The Poems" in 1955–56, during his first year as a Fulbright student in Montpellier, France. He recalls being inspired by a premium offer found in a bar of chocolate he bought on a train (possibly on his way to Amsterdam); one could send away for pictures and collect sets in different categories—specifically, those used by Ashbery as the section titles in this poetic sequence. And, as occurs elsewhere in his work, the inspiration here is slightly displaced: it is the visual imagery evoked by the titles and descriptions of those images, rather than by the specific visual images themselves, that is the source of the poetry. (He has also used titles of films he hasn't seen as titles for poems.)

First published in *Evergreen Review* in early 1959 and reissued later that year in Daisy Aldan's anthology *A New Folder* (the successor to her magazine *Folder*), "The Poems" became the title sequence for a lavishly produced fine-art edition with silkscreen prints by Joan Mitchell, published by Floriano Vecchi and Richard Miller at their Tiber Press, one of four volumes issued as a boxed set in 1960–61 (the others were by Kenneth Koch, Frank O'Hara, and James Schuyler, with prints by Alfred Leslie, Michael Goldberg, and Grace Hartigan, respectively). The Ashbery/Mitchell volume was praised by the painter, poet, and critic Fairfield Porter, in his review of the set in *Evergreen Review,* as the most successful "collaboration" of the four because Mitchell related her work both to the nature of Ashbery's text and the format in which it was being presented. A few years earlier, Porter had defended Ashbery's *Some Trees* in a letter to William Arrowsmith following Arrowsmith's negative review of the book in *The Hudson Review,* describing Ashbery's poetry as a new form of music.

Although this was the last publication of "The Poems" until now, most of the other poems in the Tiber Press edition were republished in *The Tennis Court Oath* (Wesleyan, 1962), including the now-classic "'How Much Longer Will I Be Able to Inhabit the Divine Sepulcher . . .'" and "'They Dream Only of America.'" However, the Tiber Press volume itself has figured in several important museum exhibitions, including *The Stamp of Impulse: The Abstract Expressionist Print* (2001), which redefined the important role that printmaking played in the careers of those artists, the period of her collaboration with Ashbery having been one of great transformation for Mitchell. The catalog of that show includes David Lehman's essay "Poetry and the Abstract Revolution"—indeed, for many years Ashbery made his living by writing about art, and throughout his career has collaborated with artists of all kinds, including offbeat projects with painters Jane Hammond and Archie Rand in recent years.

"Three Madrigals" was written in 1958, around the same time as many of the poems in Ashbery's controversial *The Tennis Court Oath;* it makes use of collage techniques that Ashbery also used in "Europe" and other works of that period (according to Ashbery, the end of the "First Madrigal," starting with the line "I know not when I shall see you again," came from a nineteenth-century manual on the art of letter writing). However, "Three Madrigals" remained unpublished until 1968, when it appeared first in *Angel Hair* (edited by Anne Waldman and Lewis Warsh), then as a chapbook issued as a fundraising venture by Diane DiPrima's Poet's Press; in the latter the entire work, including the cover design and colophon, was produced as a facsimile holograph in Ashbery's hand, as it is reproduced here.

Ashbery's bold, quirky cover design reflects his enduring interest in the visual arts. As inexpensive photocopying technology became available, he designed flyers announcing his own readings and collaborated with Joe Brainard on *C Comics.* He also made numerous collages, sometimes working alongside Brainard, who would occasionally send him envelopes full of clippings and postcards to use as raw material. One of Ashbery's early collages, a collaborative venture with classmate Fred Amory, was used on the cover of the November 1948 issue of the *Harvard Advocate;* a painting and several collages by Ashbery are included in a current traveling exhibition, and he is working on more collages for a possible gallery show in New York.

The DiPrima edition of *Three Madrigals* is conceived of as both a visual and literary work of art. The text itself becomes an object that evolves toward the end to resemble musical notation, reinforcing the acoustic and even theatrical implications conveyed by its title. And the musical life of this piece continues most impressively through the composer and musicologist Eric Salzman, whom Ashbery had met in Europe as a fellow Fulbright student. In 1967 Salzman set most of Ashbery's poem "Europe" to music in *Foxes and Hedgehogs: Verses and Cantos* (premiered in New York under the auspices of the Juilliard School of Music, conducted by Dennis Russell Davies, and then in London, conducted by Pierre Boulez); Salzman then used "Three Madrigals" as one of two texts for *Nude Paper Sermon* (1969), his seminal prototype for a new audio art form. That same year, John Cage selected the score of *Nude Paper Sermon* for inclusion in his book *Notations,* which presented musical scores as visual artwork.

So, we're back to John Cage, whose *Music of Changes* so radically affected Ashbery's writing. That piece resulted from Cage's involvement with operational methods of chance derived from the *I Ching,* to which Cage had been reintroduced by his student Christian Wolff, whose parents, the famous literary publishers Helen and Kurt Wolff, had just brought out a new edition of it. And, coming full circle, the most recent musical composition based on Ashbery's work (of the dozens written during the past half century) was premiered this past spring: Christian Wolff's setting of Ashbery's "37 Haiku."

Only in the Light of Lost Words Can We Imagine Our Rewards

Some Trees (1956)

Reginald Shepherd

SOME TREES, JOHN ASHBERY'S first regularly published collection, contains numerous poems that explore how the artistic consciousness relates to the world in which it finds itself and what that consciousness makes of the world it is given. In his examinations of how it feels to think, and of how thought and feeling interact with the world to make art, Ashbery is an heir of Wallace Stevens, whom he has called, along with early Auden and Laura Riding, one of "the writers who most formed my language as a poet."

As I reread the book's title poem, it seems to me in many ways a response to Wallace Stevens's "The Snow Man." In both poems, an object or group of objects in the material world, arbitrarily chosen and yet significant because of that choice, is the occasion for a meditation on how to live in that world, how to make one's way through a world not of one's making. In Stevens's poem, one "must" have a winter's mind, the mind of a man made of snow (which is to say, a man who is not a man at all), to look out on the winter landscape and perceive no misery there, in the sound of the wind and the leaves in the wind. But what does "must" mean? That one should have such a mind, that one should turn such a colder eye upon the world, declining to invest it with feeling and meaning? Or that only an actual snow man, "nothing himself," at one with his wintry landscape (indeed, a feature of that landscape), could so see the world, perceiving "Nothing that is not there and the nothing that is." Given how much of something the poem presents us (nothing is nothing to see), asks us to behold, I would settle on the latter point of view.

"Some Trees" presents a friendlier landscape, although an equally contingent one. These are, after all, only "some" trees: there is no guarantee that any other trees will offer such muted epiphanies, or even that these trees would do so on a different morning. "These are amazing." These and no other trees? Or would any group of trees so amaze, if looked at properly? (I am reminded that for William Carlos

Williams, poetry was a mode of attention, and anything could become a poem if paid the right sort of attention.) These trees are amazing in part because they are in relation, "each / Joining a neighbor." As Nietzsche wrote, before there can be one, there must be two: that everything connects is a never-ceasing source of wonder. And these mute trees speak, their "still performance" a silent analogue of speech. In his sonnet "Correspondences," another poem about relation, Baudelaire wrote that nature is a living temple from whose pillars confused words issue forth. Are not these trees, some trees at least, such pillars in nature's temple?

And we have arranged to meet by accident (a throw of the dice will never abolish chance, as Mallarmé has reminded us) far from the world and yet wholly within it, agreeing with its speaking picture, its silent discourse. As far from the world as agreeing with it is very close indeed, though never fully there (can we ever be fully there, fully present?), on this morning that seems full of possibility, as beginnings always seem to be. And suddenly we are "what the trees try // to tell us we are," though the poem never tells us what that is (to do so might shut down possibility), or even who "we" are. The poem is intimate (every reader is invited to be part of this "we," like these trees, each joining its neighbor) and yet distant, from the world, from any reader (who is this we of whom we are not only invited but assumed to be part?). The trees, after all, are together yet apart: rooted in place, they cannot move any closer to one another or, for that matter, any further apart.

But these trees mean something, or so that is what they try to tell us, whoever we are. But how do we know what they are trying to tell us, or that they are trying to tell us anything? It is in this way that the poem responds to "The Snow Man": it is, after all, "a winter morning," and the days are "Placed in a puzzling light" not unlike Stevens's "distant glitter // Of the January sun," cold light in which one sees "the junipers shagged with ice, / The spruces rough" in that distant glitter. More trees seen in winter light, some trees and not other trees (pine trees, junipers, spruces). The trees in Ashbery's winter morning are probably bare too, perhaps also crusted with snow, shagged with ice. And maybe it is morning in Stevens's poem, the sun not rising far above the horizon all day.

We behold some trees and they mean to us, we hear some wind and it means to us. We are not snow men. In Stevens's poem, what we see is the burden the bare trees bear, but also the beauty of that burden: cold pastoral. What we hear in the wind's sound, in the sound of the leaves the wind carries and drops, carries and drops, is misery. One must have a mind of winter not to hear it, and who has such a mind? Not the speaker of this poem. In Ashbery's, we see those trees and somehow hear them too. They mean, but what they mean is the possibility of joy: "soon / We may touch, love, explain." Not now, and not certainly, but we may, and we may soon. (This seems a bright and sunny winter morning, cold but invigorating.) The words that issue from nature's pillars are after all confused, but that's to be expected when speech has become a still performance, or rather, when it is as though a still performance were speech, as though speech had become such a tableau vivant.

We have not invented such loveliness (the loveliness of hope, the beauty of potential), and we are glad not to have. It is something beyond us, an outside that confirms and consoles us. It surrounds us, a comfort but also a constraint: contra Schopenhauer, the world is not all will and idea. As Stevens writes in his "Adagia," "All of our ideas come from the natural world: Trees = umbrellas." Or at least some trees do, a shelter from the rain or even from the snow.

The silence is already filled with noises (the noise of the wind, perhaps, of a few leaves in the wind, some leaves). The world around us, this little piece of it, this place in which we have arranged to find ourselves, to meet one another and our world by chance, is "A canvas on which emerges / A chorus of smiles" (the synesthesia is, I think, deliberate, the speech of a still performance, some trees' soundless urgings). It is "a winter morning, / Placed in puzzling light": we can experience but never wholly understand the world; the light discloses but does not explain. And it is moving: we are moved, whoever we are this morning, but the world is moving too, life is all motion. "Minute by minute they change," writes Yeats; and Stevens reminds us that the blackbird whirling in the autumn winds (so close to winter, yet so far) is just a small part of the pantomime. The days are reticent, at least our days are reticent—or rather, our days have put on such reticence (the reticence that tells us so much once we choose to really listen, so much we have not invented but we have definitely interpreted). We may soon touch, love, explain (all these things that trees can't do, not some trees, not any trees), but when we don't know, or even if these things will happen at all. Right here, right now, these implications, innuendos, inflections of morning light seem sufficient: "These accents seem their own defense." What else can be expected of the world but hints? That the world should speak at all, however reticently, in however puzzling a winter morning light, is enough, is amazing indeed.

Poems call to poems. The sestina "A Painter" takes up the imagery, tone, and themes of "The Idea of Order at Key West," presenting us with a male painter (or rather, a painter manqué) as distinct from a female singer, but also with the same question that Stevens addresses in a letter, "whether a poem about a natural object is roused by the natural object or whether the natural object is clothed with its poetic characteristics by the poet." The two poems appear to arrive at different answers to this perpetual question of poetry, of art itself, but they are not so far apart as they at first appear, both lingering by the seashore as they do.

In Stevens's poem, the unnamed woman sang "beyond the genius of the sea." The water was not fully shaped by her imagination or her voice, but the motion of its waves and tides, pattern calling to pattern (like those trees telling us what we might do, what we might be), "Made constant cry . . . , / That was not ours although we understood," and part of what we understood is that this voice is "Inhuman, of the veritable [that is, true] ocean." "The sea was not a mask," not a projection of human desires and fears, a screen of human meaning. "No more was she." She was a woman walking by the ocean, singing what she heard, which was both the sea and her own voice. "But it was she and not the sea we heard." She was, as Stevens writes, "the maker of the song she sang." The sea was her locale. But still we heard "the dark voices of the sea," and more than that, her voice and more than that, our own voices and more than that. The sounds of water and wind were "meaningless plungings" out of which we made and make meaning. Her song she made out of the sounds she heard, made us see and hear the world more acutely, made a world for us: "And when she sang, the sea . . . became the self that was her song." At least for her: "there never was a world for her / Except the one she sang and, singing, made." And yet she made the world for us as well. When the singing ended, the lights of the anchored fishing boats "Mastered the night and portioned out the sea . . . / Arranging, deepening, enchanting night." Like the pillars of nature's temple, the sea speaks words that the maker orders, words of the sea and words of the sky, "And of ourselves and of our origins, / In ghostlier demarcations, keener sounds."

In Ashbery's "The Painter," a man, unnamed as well, sits "between the sea and the buildings," between nature and culture, painting the sea's portrait. Or rather, waiting for such a portrait to paint itself. The poem's repeating end words indicate its concerns quite clearly: "portrait," "subject," "canvas," "brush," "prayer," and "buildings." We are in the realm of the relations among representation, the making subject, that subject's subject matter, his medium and materials, his hopes, and the concrete manifestations of his cultural context, which both restrain and make possible.

The painter expects the sea, limbless and eyeless though it is, to seize a brush and "Plaster its own portrait on the canvas." Having planted himself between nature and artifice, he expects nature to produce its own art, until those on the other end of the spectrum, the people who live in the buildings, remind him that art is not life. "Try using the brush / As a means to an end." The sea is too vast a subject, too unwilling to subject itself to a painter's moods or prayers. But he wants "nature, not art, [to] usurp the canvas." Attempting to take their advice, he paints his wife, but makes her "vast, like ruined buildings," like the sea, "As if, forgetting itself, the portrait / Had expressed itself without a brush." A good try, at least: there is something on the canvas, however boundless. "Slightly encouraged," he tries again, dipping his brush into the sea as if for a benediction. He no longer expects the sea to paint its own portrait; now his soul will do so, wrecking the canvas (Picasso called his pictures "a sum of destructions," and such a demolition of what is can often be crucial to the creation of what might be). The sea is his subject once again, but it will never subject itself to him. The task is too large; he is crucified by his subject, "Too exhausted even to lift his brush," and mocked by other artists more securely ensconced in the realm of culture, the land of artifice. The sea will never sit for a portrait. His painting is only a self-portrait, or so others declare, and it is blank (he seems to have no self of his own): "Finally all indications of a subject / Began to fade, leaving the canvas / Perfectly white. He put down the brush." Unlike Stevens's singer by the side of the sea, he does not seem to realize that his portrait of the sea must be his own and made by him.

"Le livre est sur la table" is also in dialogue with "The Idea of Order at Key West." Knowing that beauty exists only by reason of absence or oddity, "deprivation or logic / Or strange position," in this poem, "We can only imagine a world in which a woman / Walks and wears her hair and knows / All that she does not know." Which is to say either that in a world in which "beauty, resonance, integrity" are so difficult of access that our only recourse is to imagine this woman who knows what she does not know (itself a notion with a double sense), or that such a world of knowing unknownness can only be imagined, being so far from our own. This woman might well be walking by the sea, singing the sea, before she goes into the house, "from which the wailing starts," a kind of song after all, however mournful and cacophonous. And then there is a young man placing a birdhouse "Against the blue sea": "He walks away and it remains," a token of human presence and also a liminal object between the natural and artificial, man-made but housing natural creatures. Meanwhile, other men appear who live in other kinds of boxes: "The sea protects them like a wall." But a wall against what? A woman appears again, or the representation of a woman, a line drawing worshipped by the gods, "in the shadow of the sea / Which goes on writing." While Stevens's woman sings the sea in singing herself, this sea writes itself. "Did all secrets vanish when / The woman left?" can ask either whether all secrets have disappeared in her absence or whether all secrets have been revealed in that absence. I suspect it asks both at once: there are indeed collisions, of land and water, of mind and world, of art and nature, "communications on the shore." The book is on the table, and we are reading it.

"The Instruction Manual": how mundane, how earthbound, yet how necessary if one is in need of instruction. And when is one not in need of instruction, if not on the uses of a new metal then perhaps on the uses of one's own mettle, new or old, or even where such mettle might be found? One place it might be found is in the imagination, which as Stevens points out discloses but does not invent. Someone is always in need of instruction somewhere, and someone else must provide that instruction, write that manual. But he would rather look out the window at the people walking up and down the streets with an inner peace he knows they possess because they are not him, because they are so far away from him, because they are not tasked with the task of instruction. He begins to dream, he rests his elbows on the desk, and leans a little out the window, and he sees a city indeed, not the unnamed city in which he is busily not writing an instruction manual, but "dim Guadalajara! City of rose-colored flowers! / City I wanted most to see, and most did not see, in Mexico!" But, "under the press of having to write the instruction manual," he sees it now, or fancies he does, the public square with a band playing Rimsky-Korsakov's *Scheherazade* on the elaborate little bandstand, the flower girls in their rose-and-striped dresses, the women in green in little white booths serving green and yellow fruit. In poet and critic Catherine Imbriglio's fine phrase, the speaker is "a sort of voyeur in the land of his own imagination."

Poetry is an art of "as if," a way of "what if," and "The Instruction Manual" presents us with a vivid picture of what has not been seen at all, of what exists only in the imagination of the speaker, who does not (or not yet, not in this poem) write the manual of the title, but does indeed write something, a manual of sorts, this guide to a Guadalajara of the mind, or at least of one mind. It is as if we too have been to Guadalajara in our minds. What if we had been to Guadalajara? Here are some things we might have seen. More broadly, here are some things one might see when one looks with the mind's eye.

The poem is indeed an instruction manual: in those moments of vacant labor, in those moments when the world is too much with us, near or far, we can take refuge in the mind, can travel anywhere in the globe while still chained to our desks. The poem will show us how to imagine this other place in greater detail than we have ever noticed anything more immediately around us, certainly than we have seen or cared to see the office where the instruction manual still waits to be written, its potential author having traveled elsewhere.

Though by the poem's end, his journey's end, he must turn his attention away from the Guadalajara he has written for us and back to the instruction manual that was his motive for imagining this mental Guadalajara in the first place—"What more is there to do, except stay? And that we cannot do"—the speaker (the maker, the poet) has at least earned himself a respite from what is, and has taken us on a trip to a place we have never been and never will go again, since it is not Guadalajara we have visited, but rather "Guadalajara."

The Oath Unbroken

The Tennis Court Oath (1962)

Peter Straub

I WISH THIS COULD BE less personal, but it can't. In 1966, when I was a twenty-three-year-old English teacher at the University School of Milwaukee, I contracted poetry as if it were a localized low-grade fever that demanded constant applications of its own substance. Seen from the outside, it must have looked like a kind of addiction, except that the results were entirely healthy. I felt awakened, nourished, and washed clean by what I was reading. The depth of need and the quality of pleasure in the satisfaction forbade entry to most conventional forms of discrimination—though I would have argued this point strenuously. Among many others, I read—well, more or less devoured—Theodore Roethke, John Berryman, Robert Lowell, Anne Sexton, James Dickie, Robert Francis, Richard Wilbur, Muriel Rukyser, Louise Bogan, Elizabeth Bishop, Robert Bly, James Merrill, Robert Creeley, Robert Olson, William Carlos Williams, Galway Kinnell, W. D. Snodgrass, Mark Strand, Diane Wakoski, d.a. levy, Robin Morgan, Lenore Kandel, Peter Wild, Shirley Kaufman, David Mus, Ron Padgett, Greg Kuzma, St. Giraud/Bill Knott. This list could go on for at least a page. . . . If it was on the poetry shelves at the university bookstore, I was willing to give it a try. For a person with almost no money, I bought a lot of books. On the basis of core samples taken in the poetry aisles, I picked up many titles by poets I knew nothing about.

None of the poetry books I bought and read in 1966 (and 1967, until I finally got around to *Rivers and Mountains*) had the effect on me that *The Tennis Court Oath* did after I got it home and opened it up. That effect was well-nigh galvanic. The book was radically different from anything I had ever read: really, the ruling aesthetic radically differed from any previous conception I'd had of what poetry was or could do, which means that it had next to no contact with everything I had been taught about poetry in university English departments. In fact, *The Tennis Court Oath* very consciously overturned the way I, and many other people, had been taught to read poetry and think about it. This was completely liberating. Once I was able to respond to Ashbery's second book as a collection of particularly adventurous, not to mention tremendously stylish, avant-garde poems and not some kind of natural phenomenon like an earthquake, I realized that nothing I had been taught about literature need necessarily apply, that the concept of "rules" could be seen as irrelevant to the actual process, that no matter what anybody said, a certain randomness was built into works of literature, and that the border between what appears to be sense and what is experienced as nonsense is so porous as to be liminal. *The Tennis Court Oath,* or, more accurately, what happened to me when I read *The Tennis Court Oath,* made it possible for me to write. Some will not see this as an unmixed blessing.

The poems that most touched me were "'They Dream Only of America,'" "Thoughts of a Young Girl," "How Much Longer Will I Be Able to Inhabit the Divine Sepulcher," "Leaving the Atocha Station," "Our Youth," "Faust," "Europe," and "Idaho," especially the last three. "Faust" made the sestina form seem contemporary, lighthearted, and almost offhand ("Business, if you wanted to know, was punk at the opera"), even as its line ends, anything but random, moved it toward total darkness ("On the bare, sunlit stage the hungers could begin"). "Europe" and "Idaho" seemed to me then, and as far as I know actually were, completely unprecedented in American poetry, blithely experimental, disjunctive, rejecting of the ordinary consolations and assurances of language usage, yet filled with self-evident pleasure, even joyousness. (In "Europe," Ashbery keeps quoting phrases, sentences, and paragraphs from William Le Queux's giddy, wildly stiff-upper-lip novel of World War I, *Beryl of the Biplane.*)

Some of "Europe"'s brief sections suggest that the words and phrases within them exist as fragments of a more conventional text from which all the surrounding matter has been lost, such as:

17

I moved up

glove

the field

The ghosts of many possible narratives, several of them about baseball, move through these lines. Other sections, including those from Le Queux, invoke a larger narrative the poem itself has no interest in providing other than by means of the fragment at hand.

32

The snow stopped falling
On the head of the stranger.
In a moment the house would be dark

Lovely, I say. It sounds, at least to me, at once gothic and Japanese, a moment from an exotic but familiar context, except for its refusal to melt into absolutely transparent English by changing the second line to "On the stranger's head." This refusal, a deliberate *retard* inserted into the line, is what makes the fragment speak for a suggested but unnecessary whole.

The primary impression created by "Europe" is of a freewheeling, overwhelmingly generous impulse toward a form of communication in which the possibilities of language are experienced as limitless. "Idaho," which I still find irresistible, locates the same impulse within a comically confined, in fact satirical, format, that of the kind of commercial romantic fiction that existed immediately before the invention of category "romance" novels. That the profligate, swarming inclinations of "Europe" should be channeled into a vessel that Ashbery (one imagines) finds both charming and risible results, inevitably, in detonation. On the occasion of "Cornelia"'s twenty-seventh birthday, long strings of question marks, exclamation points, quotation marks, and pound signs unfurl across the page; the narrative fabric shreds and reconstitutes itself; "Biff" finds himself distractingly aroused by "Carol," a train whistle blows; and the birthday girl herself hastens toward a ripely foreshadowed exit.

nerve-centers
    birthdays

indeed. The entire poem seems to me to anticipate the ending of "Variations, Calypso and Fugue on a Theme of Ella Wheeler Wilcox" in *The Double Dream of Spring,* not solely because of the heated-up, "genre" quality of the prose.

Like the document of 1789 that provided its title, Ashbery's second book was a shot across the bows of the ancien régime. What I see in it now is the record of an extraordinary talent seeking to define itself within the discovery of an inexhaustible fertility. Later on, that inexhaustibility led to "The Skaters," "Self-Portrait in a Convex Mirror," *Three Poems,* and *Flow Chart.* Other aspects of the book opened up ground that would be explored and codified not by Ashbery himself but a generation of poets then mostly still in or just out of college, all of them deeply familiar to readers of *Conjunctions. The Tennis Court Oath* remains an indispensable masterpiece.

Now I also see something that completely escaped me when I was in my early twenties—the disquiet, desperation, and anger underlying the confidence and sense of assurance that informs the brusque refusal to connect. We are not a great distance from "On the secret map the assassins / Cloistered," the first line of the title poem in *Rivers and Mountains,* for these half-submerged feelings, too, helped to propel him forward into that wonderful book.

The Meandering Yangtze

Rivers and Mountains (1966)

Charles Bernstein

IF YOU DIDN'T KNOW what was going to happen next would you live your life any differently?

Now everybody knows that you never can tell what will actually happen next. But for the most part, and barring emerging conditions, it's possible to go on from one day to another as if everything was happening, if not according to plan, then at least as expected.

Then again, you could go on the road or out to sea or just be out to lunch and the surprises might pile up like slices of baloney on the manager's special.

A more promising model might be the weather, unpredictable in its changes, but over time fractal patterns may be discerned.

In the stadium of explanation, each complete thought follows the next under the regime of logic. Explanation abhors weather.

I am writing this sentence on a chugging, uncomfortably musty ship, which is making its way down the Yangtze, China's longest river. The boat glides on a thick ribbon of brown, sometimes garbage-strewn, water, bounded on both sides by tall green mountains.

The river makes its way without making sense.

The mountains seem imperious, as mountains usually do, beholden to nothing and to no one, except perhaps the river at their feet. I am a part of neither, mountain nor river, a foreign visitor to a foreign land, where many of those I meet speak English as a foreign language. They know the words but not what they mean in use: it is an English without cultural context, a machine language version not programmed to recognize figures of speech, social tone, or local inflection.

The distance is as deep as one of the Three Gorges upon which I slide, like a skater dreaming she is a waterfall.

There is a method to his madness but also a madness to his method.

Certain pervasive features in John Ashbery's work make their first appearance, full-blown, in *Rivers and Mountains,* which was published in 1962, four years after *The Tennis Court Oath* and the same number of years before *The Double Dream of Spring.* ("The Meandering Yangtze" is a line from "In the Dusk-Charged Air.") In the poems of this collection, and especially "The Skaters," Ashbery introduces a nonlinear associative logic that averts both exposition and disjunction. Ashbery's aversion (after *The Tennis Court Oath*) to abrupt disjunction gives his collage-like work the feeling of continuously flowing voices, even though few of the features of traditional voice-centered lyrics are present in his work. The connection between any two lines or sentences in Ashbery has a contingent consecutiveness that registers transition but not discontinuity. However, the lack of logical or contingent connections between every other line opens the work to fractal patterning. "The Skaters" brushes against this approach by suggesting that the point of contact between the lines is a kind of "vanishing point." In order to create a "third way" between the hypotaxis of conventional lyric and the parataxis of Pound and Olson (and his own "Europe" in *The Tennis Court Oath*), Ashbery places temporal conjunctions between discrepant collage elements, giving the spatial sensation of overlay and the temporal sensation of meandering thought. Skating is the adequate symbol of this compositional method.

In the meantime, the Yangtze cruise-boat loudspeaker continuously blares a music soundtrack alternating with piercing tour-guide announcements, so that our view of the pristine wilderness of the gorges is overlaid with tour-guide chatter alternating with the Muzak. The loop includes "I'm Never Gonna Dance Again" from *Footloose,* "Auld Lang Syne," and the theme song from *Titanic.*

Not to be too heavy-handed (or ham-fisted or grandiose) about Ashbery's aversion to the heavy hand, but . . . his wry references to system as idiom, incident, overlay operate in a minor key against the major chord of Big Systems and their teleological tyranny.

In *Rivers and Mountains* the primary transition (or hinge) phrases are *but, ever since, and, now, when, which, yet, so, or, so that, and so, and together we, and yet, still, near by, and now, nevertheless, but still, where was I?, sometimes, anyway, somewhere, also, and slowly, outside, only, now, therefore, because, as long as, nearly, in reality of course, that, if, for, in the meantime, outside, above, but to return, and what if,* and, at the heart of it, *meanwhile.*

And yet, one can also find some of these textual pivots in *Some Trees.* Not so *A Worldly Country,* Ashbery's most recent book, where the rough edges of the transitions are smoothed over by a genial colloquiality; or it is like rocks at the beach sanded smooth by time, or old buttons on a cardigan?

I can go anywhere and never leave the page. A river divides me from the other shore. Or I am on the other shore and the river divides me from myself.

"And the voyage? It's on! Listen, everybody, the ship is starting! We have just enough time to make it to the dock."

What if the poem wanders like a river, widens its ken, contracts, is sometimes deep and sometimes shallow, has its periodic rapids yet sometimes the current goes dead?

The symbolic dissolves into the idiomatic.

Consider a brief passage from "The Skaters," first cast into a *conventional lyric voice:*

Sleepless, I dream of my father's farm
and of the pigs in their cages at dawn.
I wake up and go out for a walk
on the street of the Cathedral.
I see so much snow
but I am afraid that soon

it will be littered
with waste and ashes
and my prayers will have no
white sanctuary.

& now deformed into a *disjunctive mode:*
pigs in cages / snow
waste, ashes / towering cathedrals

& now *Ashbery:*

. . . The pigs in their cages //
And so much snow, but it is to be littered with waste and ashes
So that cathedrals may grow.

Suddenly, it must be 7 a.m., a loud alarm sounds, and the cruise boat docks. Once off the ship, we are put into bright orange life jackets and then herded into small boats to go up one of the river's little gorges. A sign warns those over age fifty to be sure to travel with an able-bodied companion. At the end of the passage, we are directed to walk on a narrow floating plank of perhaps five hundred feet at which point we are issued hard hats and sent scurrying up a steep staircase into the mountains. All the while, the tour guides are barking on their portable megaphones and there is a faint whiff of Muzak from speakers lodged deep into the landscape. At the peak, we are directed to look at an acrobat riding a bicycle across a tightrope strung across the river, from mountain to mountain. I think of *La Strada.* The experience is less sublime than outward bound.

Speaking of "leaving out": one thing Ashbery leaves out of his work is the overheated, hyperbolic, charged-up, emotion-laden styles associated with the prophetic, confessional, "beat," "projective," and political poetry of his generation. His deflationary diction provides a powerful counterforce—a negative dialectic—to fighting fire with fire, anger with anger, outrage with outrage, suffering with expressed anguish, self-righteousness with self-righteousness. Moreover, Ashbery's poetry is a (literally) breathtaking swerve away from the bombastic rhetorics of the years of his coming of age, during the Second War, of the apocalyptic thinking associated with the Extermination Process, of the H-bomb, and of the strident anti- and pro-communism/capitalism of the Cold War. In "The Skaters," there is a wry comment about the "professional exile" who is used to taking in the news—this week's revolution—as just one more spectacle in an endless series ("Here, have another—crime or revolution? take your pick"). The passage captures a postwar ennui and disaffection often associated, and sometimes condemned, in Ashbery's dis-*engagé* verse. But the poetic logic of the passage is different: its (dys)engagements are a form of Emersonian aversion: the refusal to be baited by events packaged as commoditized news opens up a space not of confrontation and reaction formation but reflection, interiority, privacy, imagination. A space of freedom (*Freiheit!* as "The Skaters" insists, lapsing into a German too startling to be ironic).

I've always understood David Lehman's title *The Last Avant-Garde,* which focused on Ashbery and his most immediate poetic company, to mean *last* in the sense of *the one before this one.* For avant gardes are always and necessarily displaced floating flotillas, out on a nameless sea that everyone is always naming. Lehman makes the rhetorical mistake of advertising his subjects as apolitical, in the process mortally undermining Ashbery's fundamentally political and ethical engagements and disengagements (his *clinical* value in Deleuze's sense). The politics of Ashbery's poetic form is its cutting edge.

Even the tallest mountains have tops and the deepest rivers bottoms, but we will never know them because we are too much part of them.

We? I hardly know you. Stay for a while.

In "The New Spirit," the first section of *Three Poems,* Ashbery notoriously remarks, "I thought that if I could put it all down, that would be one way. And next the thought came to me to leave all out would be another, and truer, way." A keynote passage from "The Skaters" anticipates this formulation:

> . . . This leaving-out business. On it hinges the very importance
>   of what's novel
> Or autocratic, or dense or silly. It is as well to call attention
> To it by exaggeration, perhaps. But calling attention
> Isn't the same thing as explaining, and as I said I am not ready
> To line phrases with the costly stuff of explanation, and shall
>   not,
> Will not do so for the moment. Except to say that the

carnivorous
Way of these lines is to devour their own nature, leaving
Nothing but a bitter impression of absence, which as we know
involves presence, but still.
Nevertheless these are fundamental absences, struggling to get
up and be off
themselves.

In this ode to the hinges of elusive elision, the poet circumnavigates a case against explanation and "plain old-fashioned cause and effect," while giving a nod to, if not autopoesis (the poem devouring itself), then to Lear's tragic disavowal of Cordelia's refusal to speak the "costly stuff of explanation"—"Nothing will come of nothing: speak again." Like Cordelia, Ashbery does indeed speak again, but on poetry's, not explanation's, terms. This is a poem that knows how to make use of nothing. The passage is less ars poetica than *ars absondita.*

After a while, our boat stops at a thousand-year-old temple to the poet Qu Yuen, located very near the Three Gorges Dam. Long tapering candles of incense burn in front of a bronze statue of the poet, who committed suicide in 278 BC by drowning himself in the Miluo River, as a protest, so the story goes, against the cultural climate of his times. In the next few months, the monstrous dam, the great emblem of China's relentless modernization, will totally flood the site. I'm asked if I will write a poem about my trip to China. Perhaps I will call it "The Poet Drowned."

You get the sense that you could start anywhere in "The Skaters" and move around in whatever direction. The stanzas are interchangeable because modular. The lines of the poem make endless figure eights.

In "The Poetic Principle," Poe says that the long poem cannot exist and "The Skaters" shows why: it is composed of many small poems, call them discrete sensations, that are fused together. Ashbery, like Poe, is a poet of sensation rather than emotion, sensibility rather than big ideas.

The only other Westerner on the boat, a man from Scotland, tells us he took the trip ten years ago, before the Chinese government flooded the gorges as part of a huge and ecologically disastrous hydroelectric project. Where before the line of the river slit through the sheer mountains like a knife slices through a tall chunk of thick butter, now the experience is more like a cruise on a lake. The new paths everywhere leave an echo of the older and deeper gorges.

"The Skaters" samples a series of textures, never resting at any one locus. The continuous flow of discontinuous perceptions. Winding eddies. Confluence. Lateral thinking. The essential feature of parataxis is the absence of subordination; Ashbery's is an associative parataxis, elements joined by perceptual, aesthetic, and philosophical connections and family resemblances. Constant but gradually shifting, asymmetrically kaleidoscopic; a stream of dissolving shots.

"But the water surface ripples, the whole light changes."

It is as if these poems are part of me: not as if I wrote them, but as if they wrote me.

In June, just before my trip to China, Ashbery and I read together at Mo Pitkin's House of Satisfaction, in the East Village. The young woman who hosted the event, perhaps nonplussed to say something about John, awkwardly announced that she could not "describe a poet before they are about to read because they will tell you who they are." She then added that Ashbery had written some "thirty odd books of poetry."—How *odd,* indeed, these books really are and how crucial that oddness, and specificity, has been for me as a poet.

Oddness that stays odd.

Ashbery is an exemplary poet of privacy, of nondisclosure, of an other mind that stays an other mind. His poems reveal not universal human emotions but quirky passages and unexpectable associations. They provide not moments of identification but company along the way.

But not for everyone. I still remember a September 6, 1981, Sunday, *New York Times Book Review* piece by Denis Donoghue that wrongly describes Ashbery, in *Shadow Train,* as "secretive":

> Even in one of the more available poems, "Or in My Throat"—though the title is opaque to me—Mr. Ashbery catches himself in the act of being sweet and gives sourness the last words:
>
> That's why I quit and took up writing poetry
> instead.
> It's clean, it's relaxing, it doesn't squirt juice all
> over
> Something you were certain of a minute ago and
> now your own face
> Is a stranger and no one can tell you it's true.
> Hey, stupid!

What's opaque to the reviewer is not Ashbery's syntactic or free-associative difficulty but the title's reference to oral sex and how this in turn relates to the lines quoted; all of a sudden, the "opaque" becomes both explicit and outrageous. I'm not suggesting that "everyone" would catch the meaning of "Or in My Throat," but then that's the point. The lines of Ashbery that are cited make a wry comment on the situation . . . the situation of meaning and of the opaqueness of the *New York Times* toward poetry of the past quarter century. And the moral of that is: what's opaque to one bursts out at another. That's not, as this review and many others suggest, a problem for poetry; it's the promise of poetry.

But where was I?

In the elevator in a hotel in Chongqing there is a sign for a special dish at the restaurant: *Jellyfish with Jew's Ear.* At the restaurant, we see a large picture advertising afternoon tea, decorated with images of onion-, sesame-, and poppy-seed bagels. We point to the picture and ask for one. About a half hour later the waitress appears with a bowl of Cheerios.

Around the bend is another bend.

When I was first asked to write something on one of John Ashbery's books for *Conjunctions'* eightieth-birthday tribute, I suggested a commentary on an imaginary work of Ashbery's for which I would make up all the quotes. But then I realized that maybe my books, in my mind, are just such imaginary works of Ashbery's, from my own distorted perspective; volumes to which I have, without license, affixed my name.

In *Rivers and Mountains,* John Ashbery crossed the Rubicon in American poetry. Actually he double crossed it.

& then some.

Meanwhile . . .

The Art of Curling

A Nest of Ninnies (with James Schuyler, 1969)

Brian Evenson

> *Mrs. Burgoyne looked at Fabia as though identifying someone of whom she had heard.*
>
> *"Ever done any curling?" Mr. Burgoyne said to Irving Kelso.*
>
> *"Yes." Mr. Kelso allowed a pause to become pregnant and then went on. "While I was overseas in the Air Corps, I went for a rest leave to a castle turned over to the Army in Scotland. By the time I left I was curling like a native."*
>
> —*A Nest of Ninnies*

IT MIGHT SEEM PERVERSE to start a discussion of John Ashbery and James Schuyler's *A Nest of Ninnies* with the above quotation. It is the only mention of curling that occurs in the novel (or in any novel I've ever read), and although talk of Scotland both continues and reoccurs, it does so only in passing. The appraising look that Mrs. Burgoyne gives Fabia is not a foreshadowing of greater conflicts to come, but ends up dissipating in the dynamics of lunch and conversation that follow. There is nothing in the quotation above that is "important" in terms of pushing the plot forward or revealing something significant about the characters. There is no significant foreshadowing, no real creation of a place except through the food and the attitudes of the servers; we are simply offered people at a table, engaged in conversation. The scene consists strictly of what Franco Moretti would classify as "filler"—"Narration: but of the everyday"—as that material which an interpreter is prone to qualify as trivial or of minor importance.

Perhaps we should try another few paragraphs, equally chosen at random:

> "Women and children first," Irving cried as he whisked the lid from a steaming casserole.
>
> "A New England boiled dinner!" Mrs. Turpin

> exclaimed shrilly. "I haven't had one since we left Honolulu."

We don't get much farther, plot-wise, with this quotation, though the first few words seem quite bold and promise great dramatic events until we realize they refer to a casserole. The characters seem once again to be eating, though a different sort of meal than before; perhaps for this reason the conversation is light and jokey, comfortably funny. We can travel a good many lines forward and backward without discovering anything that is "significant."

One final quotation, also chosen at random:

> Giorgio, who had been sunk in a brown study, got to his feet. "You are wrong, Marshall," he said. "The designs—" he pointed to the back of his chair—"are full of occult meaning. Anyone can see it. I can see it. I am right."
>
> "Don't take on so, dear," Alice said. "He only meant that Cousin Bessie didn't make them up—invent them."
>
> Giorgio beamed at his brother-in-law, who said, "Yes, that's what I meant. What's for dessert?"

Again, what seems like it might be a promising beginning of a plot—the notion of occult power gathered in the chairs—a decent beginning for a gothic subplot in the right hands—is deftly undone in a sentence or two, Giorgio going from being sunk in thought in his "brown study," to aggressive, to beaming in a matter of a few moments. And food again isn't far behind, both having preceded the scene (dinner) and coming after it (dessert). It's not as funny as either of the two other passages, but there is something comic nonetheless in the jerkiness of Giorgio's actions and reactions, the rapidity of his changing moods.

One might suspect that these are simply exceptional passages, but a full reading of the novel indicates that they are utterly representative. Reading *A Nest of Ninnies* for the plot is like, as the Honorable Judge John M. Woolsey suggested, reading *Ulysses* for the naughty bits: an exercise in frustration. Indeed, one learns a great deal more about the plot of the book from the several hundred words on the *Nest*'s flyleaf than from the book itself.

And this is precisely the *Nest*'s strength: it is a book that has all the filler elements of a plotted book with very little actual plot. Things do change, slightly, for the book's flighty suburban characters, and several of them partner off, but all of this takes place offstage. We the readers find out about these changes only when, in the process of eating or conversing, they announce their marriages to the other characters. There is no brooding or angst, no breast beating, no bedroom scenes, no elaborate deceptions, no intense betrayals; instead we have luncheons out, dinners together, vacations. The most dramatic things that happen are two storms and one fire, nobody seriously hurt in any of them, all of them serving as backgrounds (or excuses) for meals or drinks. As W. H. Auden suggested in his review of the book for *The New York Times Book Review:* "More extraordinary still, though many of [the characters] live in suburbia they all seem, believe it or not, to be happy."

Auden's statement might suggest, to anyone who knows the slant of my own fiction, that I am precisely the wrong person to write about *A Nest of Ninnies.* And yet I find myself a serious admirer of the novel. What strikes me as admirable here—and much more important than whether the characters are happy or miserable—is the dynamics of the language, the great care with which the casual and convincing language is constructed, the way in which the fiction itself becomes about the dynamics of the spoken word.

Thus, in the passage I first quoted, Ashbery and Schuyler move from the conversational non sequitur ("Ever done any curling?") to Irving's unexpected but honest response, in the process showing Irving's awareness of how to gather the attention of a room and turn it to his advantage. Add to that simple but characteristic and slightly comic turns of phrases like "rest leave" and "curling like a native." A great deal of the enjoyment of the passage and of what follows comes in the reader's consciousness of how the characters are aware of themselves as conversing figures, the combination of ordinariness and careful turns of phrase—something that, I think, informs Ashbery's poetry as well.

In the second quoted passage, we see the conscious appropriation of a phrase from one speech genre ("Women and children first," from the nautical world) for another, followed by a joke that operates by twisting an expected and predictable phrase just slightly, substitution in one word ("Honolulu" for "Connecticut" or "Massachusetts")—both things, again, which can be found in Ashbery's poetry. Again is revealed a consciousness of human speech as a dynamic and active process, and a real interest in that process itself.

The final passage turns on an insistence in one character's having his view accepted, an insistence that could be based on a misunderstanding due to Giorgio's poor English or Marshall's grumpiness. Whether Alice is properly correcting her partner, Giorgio, or Marshall is simply willing to give in so as to have the dessert Giorgio has made is quite difficult to say. This is further complicated by the rapidity with which Giorgio's mood and views seem to shift. What we are given, then, is an image of a language in action (c.f. Bakhtin), living and breathing, responding, and the way in which the bodies and minds attached to the words complicate them. In that sense *Nest,* with its lack of grand events similar to the lack that informs most of our ordinary human lives, is not so much an antimimetic novel as a novel that, in its depiction of living language, is mimetic with a vengeance.

Perhaps it is no surprise that a book that began and continued as a conversation between two poet friends should focus so much on conversation itself, on the dynamics of speech. We can see and feel the tensions within and between sentences more intensely than we do in most novels. It is a book about the voice, or rather about the interaction of voices. Which suggests that rather than being a book marginally attached to Ashbery's oeuvre, *A Nest of Ninnies* suggests the path that much of Ashbery's interest in different voices will take. The novel is for him a workshop, a game that will allow him to explore interests and possibilities that are manifest in other forms in his poetry.

My essay is almost half done and I've only talked about a total of 182 words of a 191-page book. This may be a peculiar way to treat a book, but, being peculiar itself, *A Nest of Ninnies* perhaps deserves such peculiar treatment. *Nest* is peculiar in being the book that Ashbery's critics speak the least about, despite its initially enthusiastic reception by the national press. It is peculiar in the sense of being Ashbery's only novel—and indeed, at least technically speaking, his only work of fiction of any kind. It is peculiar in that, being co-written by James Schuyler, it is Ashbery's only long collaborative work. And then as a novel itself it is peculiar in that, while at any given moment it seems to be acting like we expect novels to act, in the aggregate it feels like the book is in the process of giving its genre the slip.

Ashbery and Schuyler began the novel for fun during a long car ride, taking turns writing alternating sentences or paragraphs. They continued to write it over many years, whenever they got together. As a collaboration, it feels seamless, the tensions within and between the sentences very close to natural discourse. It is all but impossible to tell where one writer stops and the other starts. It has certain elements of Schuyler's novel *Alfred and Guinevere* (1958), but its dialogue seems a great deal more effortless—it doesn't try nearly as hard to "mean" something—and it is a great deal funnier.

The central characters come from Kelton, New York, a suburban town around fifty miles from Manhattan. They include Alice, a cellist in her twenties who is somewhat adrift, and Marshall, her brother who works in the city. There are Fabia and Victor, a spoiled brother and sister pair, the latter just having been kicked out of college. There is also Irving, who lives with his mother. Their lives are impacted by a number of other characters from elsewhere, most notably Claire and Nadia Tosti, two enterprising sisters from Paris, the first of whom will pair off with Irving, the second with Victor. Alice will stumble upon Giorgio, an Italian restaurateur, and, like most of the characters will fall in love and be, in the end, happy. And yet, very little of this actually happens on stage; most of it has to be teased out, the novel instead spending its time engaged in public conversation rather than in the private dilemmas and hidden dynamics of how we negotiate our lives.

When the novel first appeared in 1969, it was quite well received. Auden claimed it was "destined to become a minor classic." F. W. Dupree called it "The best comic novel I've read since *Lolita.*" And yet, as James Wallenstein points out in his recent *Jacket* magazine article on the book, it is the book that Ashbery scholars seem most perplexed by: "Those who don't have to touch *A Nest of Ninnies* tend not to, and those whose projects are too comprehensive to avoid it—namely David Lehman and David Herd—don't do much more than touch it."

Wallenstein's own article—which makes the best critical effort I know of (despite my having a few reservations about it) to take *A Nest of Ninnies* seriously—opts to consider the book as a "camp talent-show sketch" and as "a performance, an object that has its ultimate significance in its articulation rather than through reflection." This last strikes me as a very tricky distinction to make, particularly since what we are talking about here is something written on the page, not meant to be performed, even if it was generated through a composition process that encouraged vocalized articulation at the time. Yet the relationship of composition to the final product is quite different from (and far more generically classifiable than), say, David Antin's talk pieces and their subsequent edited transcription. *A Nest of Ninnies* is presented as a novel: there is nothing in the apparatus of any of the editions I've examined to draw importance or attention to its act of composition. It is, however, a book that clings to its own surface, and perhaps this is what Wallenstein is referring to: besides rendering the image of a language in a certain suburban milieu, it is not a book that can be said to "mean something" or explore grand themes. Additionally, I detect very little suggesting a "camp" or "talent-show sketch" feel to it; there is none of the slightly outré verbal play, confusion, or zaniness that one finds in, say, the work of Ronald Firbank, the author to whose work *A Nest of Ninnies* is most often compared.

Nest, Wallenstein also suggests, "is made from the stuff of novels—characters, settings, episodes—but not the stuffing—the characters are stick figures, the settings interchangeable, the episodes without dramatic significance." This is a statement I somewhat agree with, particularly in regard to lack of dramatic significance in the episodes, as should be evidenced by my referring to the novel as made largely of "filler." But at the same time, Wallenstein goes too far: the characters are almost exclusively characterized by what they say about themselves and what other people say about them, but this is more than enough to render them quite distinct. Their passions and desires may be minor but they are there and present. If this is satire, it is walking a very fine line: it is hard not to like these characters and enjoy their conversations despite their foibles, and one never feels they are being held up to judgment. The settings are not interchangeable in the sense that different settings, different meals seem to encourage or bring out different conversations. Thus, putting the characters in a restaurant waiting in anticipation and dread for an odd band to begin playing will lead to different sorts of conversation than one might have during a lunch hour. In addition, as each constellation of characters changes, the conversational dynamics go through shifts as well. This is only clearly visible because, with the novel being "filler," conversation and eating become the focus rather than the background. Rather than being about "character," *A Nest of Ninnies* is about changing constellations of characters, about interactions between character, conversation as a rhizome making different patterns in its path from character to character.

Where exactly can one place *A Nest of Ninnies?* It is somewhat influenced by Firbank, but not really all that similar to his work.

He is, generally speaking, much more random, the connections within conversations and between people more superficial, gratuitous, and odd. There are connections as well to Henry Green, whom Ashbery wrote his MA thesis on, particularly Green's last two novels, *Nothing* and *Doting.* Both of these novels consist largely of dialogue with a very little description sprinkled in, in a way quite close to *Nest,* though the mood of Green's novels is anxious where *Nest* is instead comic and (as Auden suggests) happy. Oscar Wilde is important here, and one sees the thirst for the well-turned phrase throughout. *Nest* is also not too distant from the high comic British tradition of Noel Coward, but it transports the gestures of that tradition from the British upper class to suburban America.

A Nest of Ninnies is finally a comedy of manners with all these other influences torquing it slightly. It is much closer in tone and manner to an updated and transplanted P. G. Wodehouse novel than to Firbank, and has a similar sense of humor. True, Wodehouse novels have plots, but, as anyone who has read more than one of his books knows, these plots are much alike from novel to novel and come to feel less and less important, are largely a structure upon which the conversations and misunderstandings and high jinks play themselves out. Instead of inadvertent engagements and attempts to steal back cow creamers, however—the sorts of things that might happen when Wodehouse's Britishers find themselves together—Ashbery and Schuyler offer the events in which people living in the suburbs come together—meals, drinks—and accidental encounters (at hotels and in restaurants) and conversation. As a comedy of American manners, there is very little, if anything, to compare with *A Nest of Ninnies,* and it remains as strong and as clever and as funny today as when it was first published in 1969.

The Double Dream of Spring Would Like to Make a Few Statements

The Double Dream of Spring (1970)

Marjorie Welish

ING IS PRECISELY good taste.

ersists and it lingers.

allies where tastefulness in poesy meets mainstream verse.

enders sentimentality in seasonal verse in a reflective mirror through ich norms for poetry are shades, shadows, and comatose states of affairs.

rites in false naïveté.

rites in gaucherie that, despite contrivance expressive of an authenticity spontaneity often given as lyric, is feigning a rustic stance. (See Watteau.)

tarts anywhere and ends everywhere.

ing forgotten how to write,

ing forgotten how to write a well-wrought urn sets limits on what can be tten through superfluity.

ving forgotten how to write a well-wrought urn is the beacon, the path, the , the trap.

ing starts and stops, a picaresque progress.

ets traps for a pastoral prospect.

xtends literariness in landscape to the prospect and view: a pictorial turn y from painting confounded by a literary turn through the self-disclosing ection of that position.

It extends landscape through academicism to the folk equivalent of "howler culled from quotidian culture and whatnot: the democratic challenge as it is in actuality.

It parades signage: Kitsch! Precisely Good Taste. (See Flaubert.)

It likes escapism.

It then seeks the mimicry of the selfsame.

It fabricates escape, then discards it, then it demands an escape in Formica and fiberglass—very period sociolects.

It is an accomplice of fictions fomenting nonexistent worlds, whorls.

It advocates fancy but calculates that a knowing literary imagination will "save it from disaster"—the real leap through . . . ! (See all fictions.)

It allows deus ex machina to accumulate parking tickets.

It tolerates ruin within the instrumentality of nonentailed irrelevance.

It positively seeks to follow digressive self-indulgence out on a limb.

It does devote itself to dolorous effects of prettiness and the estrangement th informs aftermaths prematurely in bloom.

It sees refreshed status in the poetical point of reference.

Spring says, "As cultivated field is to wilderness, I am to nature. What?"

It says, "What is Nature in which I am the detached spectator?" Wearing

Orphic shades and affidavits, it blinks green.

Regarding its own poetic zone, it says, "What is Nature?"

and then says, "But I am repeating myself."

alls into reverie.

in reverie, may be heard saying, "I prefer the cloth ones."

me to think of it, cloth is "better" at impersonating translucence than rice lishings. False Bamboo.

se Bamboo rendered in six-foot-high arrangements. . . . False Bamboo will w do a rendering of wind.

vhistles in the wind.

en it does its colorized adaptation of the same.

/here have I read this light before?" it asks itself.

oking up at the sky—no, gazing up at the sky—it answers: see Morandi (for s spring in Bologna).

e milky sky dilates.

is you know as well as you have known the back of your hand passing ough shadow cast from a stele,

hadow cast from a stele that you and other shepherds have stopped to read, w many times?

ring recurs.

ring recurs as itself yet each Spring differs, one from another, and the ferentials bring difference to light.

d these bring difference to light in the commonplace that is Spring.

ring says, "Ode to Spring," reflecting on the above.

flected from its course in the heavens is a pastoral remarking on its own atedness, and women in leotards, perennially enthusiastic, then enchanted. The device always works.

Spring's literariness writes of spontaneity reflected off topical concerns and chrome trim.

Spring sees itself reflected through the discrepant artifact achieved through one thing masquerading as another: comic strip as sestina, position paper as free verse, moral epigram as song lyrics; elegiac free verse at one moment turns soap-opera prose poem.

In its recurrence it renews its species.

It renews its species but not its resemblance to objects.

What renews is unrecognizable.

What repeats? Spring, Spring in the country.

It dotes on admixtures of custom and the customary suggestive of late romantic chromaticism, with no resolution to the fluctuation of feeling but fading and fade-out.

"What is a poem?" Spring wonders.

"Cultivation," as we have said.

The cultivation of absentmindedness—whose soliloquy is this?

Effects have escaped!

A pastoral, the literariness of the pastoral, the belatedness of the pastoral, as we have read, have said. Spring is always in good taste, the press release indicated.

Said Spring, lip-synching its representations, the monotype, in particular.

A perfect ear for sociolects and ideolects. . . . Spring paused.

Spring paused, then exhaled cultivation and its antidotes in experiment.

Four Contexts for *Three Poems*

Three Poems (1972)

Ron *Silliman*

I.

THINK ABOUT JOHN ASHBERY'S *Three Poems* from the perspective of readers in 1972 when it first appeared as a Viking Compass volume, a photo of a trim mustachioed Ashbery standing somewhere on a farm with movie-star good looks peering back at the reader. *The Double Dream of Spring,* Ashbery's 1970 collection, had been the first book about which any Ashbery fan of the period could justifiably complain, as some did, that it offered little that was formally new or different from his earlier work. Previously, the one thing that had appeared certain about Ashbery, who followed *Some Trees* with *The Tennis Court Oath* and that in turn with *Rivers and Mountains,* was that you couldn't predict what the next volume might look like based on whatever you thought about the most recent. One argument that I did hear made about *Double Dream* was that, well, you certainly couldn't have predicted *that.*[1] In narrowly extending, consolidating really, aspects of Ashbery's poetry that went all the way back to the early 1950s, *Double Dream* seemed to want to demonstrate the effortless excellence of Ashbery's craft as he moved into his forties. The implication, at least according to optimists, was that readers should be patient—the next book would be a doozy.

It's worth keeping in mind the role of the modern prose poem within American poetry in 1972. To the casual American reader, seeing only Rimbaud & Baudelaire, the poem in prose was a nineteenth-century French form with no history here. Hayden Carruth's omnibus 1970 anthology, *The Voice That Is Great Within Us,* containing 136 poets representing "American Poetry of the Twentieth Century," 722 pages long, has exactly zero prose poems. It's not that American prose poems were not being written. Robert Bly and his fellow contributors in *The Sixties* had been actively pursuing the

[1] I am not including Ashbery's first *Selected Poems,* published first in England by Jonathan Cape, which appeared between *Rivers and Mountains* and *Double Dream.*

genre, as had George Hitchcock's ancillary deep-image journal, *Kayak.* None of this was visible in the Carruth anthology, even though Bly, James Wright, and George Hitchcock are all included. One poet who does not appear in Carruth's book is Gertrude Stein.[2] Another is Russell Edson, whose first collection had been published in 1964. A third is Jack Spicer—the one member of the Spicer Circle represented in the Carruth collection is John Wieners—who had produced something akin to prose poems in *Heads of the Town Up to the Aether,*[3] a volume that received almost no distribution before appearing in the 1975 *Collected Books,*[4] plus one or two others in even more fugitive collections such as *Lament for the Makers.*

If Edson's model of the prose poem was the short fable of Kafka, Bly's paradigm was borrowed from the work of French poet Max Jacob, author of *The Dice Cup:* a short piece of prose aimed at surprising the reader in some fashion, intended to "distract" the beleaguered language consumer, the one solace Jacob could envision for the poem. Readers of modern French literature knew, of course, that there was much more to the prose poem than this, but until the very late 1960s, the only readily available twentieth-century alternative translated into English was the work of St.-John Perse. Perse had won the Nobel Prize in 1960, but had begun publishing over a half century earlier with a style that has always reminded me of the art of Maxfield Parrish. Here is the opening of the fifth section of "Strophe," a part of *Seamarks,* translated here by Wallace Fowlie:

> Language which was the Poetess:
>
> "Bitterness, O favour! Where now burns the aromatic herb? . . . The poppy seed buried, we turn at least towards you, sleepless Sea of the living. And you to us are something sleepless and grave, as is incest under

[2]This was not atypical in 1970, a moment when perhaps only Robert Duncan & Jerome Rothenberg were seriously arguing for her inclusion in any consideration of American poetry. Patricia Meyerowitz's *Gertrude Stein: Writings and Lectures 1909–1945,* the volume through which many poets of my generation first became aware of *Tender Buttons,* was originally published by Peter Owen in 1967, but not reissued in the Penguin edition that finally gave it broad U.S. distribution until 1971.

[3]Spicer's point of reference was Rimbaud, an important figure in the book, tho throughout he also explores the tradition of haibun.

[4]In the years after Spicer's death, there were rumors that Gino Clays Sky had a box or two of *Heads of the Town* in his possession somewhere, but nobody was sure quite where he was.

> the veil. And we say, we have seen it, the Sea for women more beautiful than adversity. And now we know only you that are great and worthy of praise.
>
> O Sea which swells in our dreams as in endless disparagement and in sacred malignancy, O you who weigh on our great childhood walls and our terraces like an obscene tumour and like a divine malady!

Perse's overly humid prose seemed so far removed from the proliferating Jacob-Bly & Kafka-Edson editions of the prose poem, predicated as those strains were upon brevity, that it's not clear that anyone, at least in America, knew quite what to do with his work. Plus Perse's translators, such as Fowlie & T. S. Eliot, were hardly paragons of avant-garde practice. Robert Duncan may have been equally capable of elevated language, but there's an inner decadence here—the sheer predictability of such impossibilities as *sacred malignancy* or *divine malady*—that would have made Duncan shudder.

In 1969, however, Jonathan Cape published Lane Dunlop's translation of Francis Ponge's *Soap* while Unicorn Press in Santa Barbara, California, brought out Nathaniel Tarn's edition of Victor Segalen's *Stelae.*[5] From Japan, Cid Corman had already been publishing his own versions of Ponge in *Origin,* leading up to his collection, *Things,* which appeared in 1971. American readers were beginning to get hints of the broader landscape for poetic prose that Europeans had known already for several decades. John Ashbery, having spent roughly a decade in Paris from the middle 1950s onward, was perfectly positioned to know this. One might even say "to exploit this," introducing into American poetry something that had not previously existed here: the prose poem as a serious—and extended—work of art.

II.

The only part of writing that is literally organic is the way in which the rhythms of production fit into the life of an author. This is something that can vary dramatically from poet to poet—was there ever a year in which Robert Kelly did *not* write more than the entire

[5]Tarn had worked at Cape, which was then undergoing a defensive merger with Chetto, and may well have produced the Segalen for the famous Cape Gollard/Grossman series. Tarn was the editor of *Soap.*

collected works of Basil Bunting?—and it doesn't seem to be anything that can be very readily dictated from the outside. Surely there is no right or wrong way with this, any more than there is to the color of our skin or our height or even sexual orientation. Any teacher in an MFA program will have had the experience of watching one student struggle with creating a manuscript of acceptable length to qualify for the degree while for another student the real question is how best to whittle down from a stack of writing hundreds of pages thick into something that makes sense as a short book.

This does not mean that a poet can't change, nor that poets don't go through periods in their writing during which this process might be quite different. When I first began corresponding with Tom Meyer in the 1960s, he was still a student at Bard writing a massive, decidedly Poundian epic that he was tentatively calling *A Technographic Typography.* This isn't who he turned out to be as a poet at all.

This question runs quite a bit deeper than just the size and number of the poems someone writes. There are dramatic differences in the poetry of Edward Dorn, pre and post *Slinger,* but Dorn was hardly the only member of the New American Poets to have had this experience. Amiri Baraka's output and style changed drastically once he abandoned his persona as LeRoi Jones. Denise Levertov did likewise, tho not with such flair. Frank O'Hara hardly wrote anything during the last two years of his life. Ted Berrigan likewise. Robert Duncan's production drops rapidly once he announces his fifteen-year "hiatus" from publishing—and some would argue that the work does as well. George Oppen, Carl Rakosi, & even Louis Zukofsky went through long silent periods. Pound has his pre-modernist period, when he wrote *Personae,* often cited by our Quietist (and quietest) friends as evidence that they also like this twentieth-century innovator—it's just the innovations they hate. With Stein, it's just the other way around. From *The Autobiography of Alice B. Toklas* onward, she becomes a memoirist of the avant-garde more than an instance of it.

If you read Robert Creeley, you have to be struck with the degree to which his early work, through *Pieces, Mabel,* and *A Day Book,* constantly pushes change. No two books are alike. As with Pound, there are poets who love the author of *Pieces* and those who love the author of *For Love,* but it's rare to meet someone who feels equally passionate about both volumes. Then around 1975, Creeley settles in & moves gradually into what is now recognizable as his late style, which he continues pretty much without interruption for the next thirty years. I certainly know poets who insist that this is Creeley's dotage, that basically he'd given up. That's not my perception, but the narrative of decline they impose on what turns out to be more than half of Creeley's life's work follows the same general path I'd suggest for Dorn (or, for that matter, Levertov). And there is no question that the two volumes of Creeley's *Collected Poetry* are profoundly different reading experiences.

John Ashbery, by comparison, presents a much more complicated situation. When *Three Poems* appears in 1972, he has already been publishing for nineteen years, going back to Tibor de Nagy's publication of *Turandot and Other Poems.* Yet, including *Turandot, Three Poems* is only Ashbery's sixth book. In the thirty-five years since, Ashbery has dramatically picked up his pace, issuing nineteen additional volumes of new poetry. Let me put this in even more stark terms. In 1966, when Frank O'Hara died, John Ashbery had just published *Rivers and Mountains,* his fourth book. Eighty-four percent of Ashbery's career—to 2007—had yet to be written. The writer whom FO'H so affectionately dubs Ashes basically had just begun to emerge.

Yet Ashbery was already quite famous, at least in the ways a poet might be. *The Tennis Court Oath* and *Rivers and Mountains* had assured that he would be one of the defining figures for an American avant-garde for the next fifty years. Yet *The Double Dream of Spring* had been a confusing work, extending what Ashbery had been doing in the juvenilia of *Turandot* and *Some Trees,* but really more consolidating this style of the pop-art surreal lyric that resists going anywhere. *Double Dream of Spring* is a fine book, maybe even a great one, but it was also the first book that Ashbery produced that did not in some fashion change poetry.

Twenty books later, it becomes apparent that Ashbery was settling into what I take to be his mature rhythm as a poet: the steady production of books that are all, in one form or another, patterned upon *Double Dream,* a collection of short lyrics—relatively few that are longer than a page or two, save for one longer piece—seldom adding to more than 110 pages in print, even with fairly sizable type. These lyric collections are punctuated with a series of other books that are very different from one another, and basically different from the *Double Dream* series of volumes as well. These include: *The Tennis Court Oath, Rivers and Mountains, Three Poems, Vermont Notebook, As We Know* (possibly), *Flow Chart,* and *Girls on the Run.*

I use the word *possibly* with regards to *As We Know* because I think this is the one volume that genuinely deserves to be on both lists—its overall composition matches the *Double Dream* schema, but the long two-column poem "Litany" warrants being placed in this second group. Unlike the *Double Dream* series, whose volumes blend rather seamlessly one into the other, the books in this second list are deliberately motley—you cannot generalize from any individual volume to the group as a whole. If I term the first group the *Double Dream* series, I think of this second set as the One Offs, unrepeated, potentially even unrepeatable projects.

I'm prepared to argue that in a century, most of the poems we (or our grandchildren) will still be reading and learning of John Ashbery's belong to this second list, that of the One Offs. Partly, this is the fate of any great innovator—the poems that change poetry, that become the most canonic, are (one could reasonably argue) "the most important," are seldom the best or the most polished of a given writer. People read, say, Stein's *Tender Buttons* more than *Stanzas in Meditation* not because they are "easier" (if by easier we mean shorter), tho that never hurts, but because they were the poems that first taught her audience how to read in a different fashion. Similarly, it is the very first *Maximus* poems one remembers of Olson's most clearly, again because they changed poetry. *Sonnets* really is Ted Berrigan's first work—it is still his most famous. So too *The Tennis Court Oath* and *Rivers and Mountains* and *Three Poems* changed poetry, whereas *Flow Chart* is a poem that exists in a world these earlier books made possible. One could similarly argue that William Carlos Williams never wrote better than in *Spring & All,* tho it is his first mature work. Or that Allen Ginsberg's *Howl* is certain to be read in two hundred years, while his finest writing—"Wichita Vortex Sutra" or "Wales Visitation," say—are much more up for grabs. Ditto with *Stanzas for Iris Lezak* and Jackson Mac Low, a work that seems almost brutal in its machinations compared with the subtle deft poems he composed toward the end of his life.

The history of poetry is always the history of *change* in poetry, almost never the record of "all that is best." One might, for example, argue that a study of the dramatic monolog ought to lead ineluctably to modern masters such as Richard Howard or Frank Bidart, capable of seeding the form with everything culled from a history of twentieth-century psychology, but the genre's actual importance is that it was one of the three great innovations of the nineteenth century—along with the prose poem & free verse. The fact that dramatic monolog has grown mostly more nuanced where the two other genres have transformed themselves several times over in the past 120 years or so—the one great exception to this would be *Maximus*—suggests that the monolog's history is as the stunted genre of the nineteenth century, precisely because it was the one least dependent on form as such.

When *Three Poems* first appeared in 1972, the rhythm of Ashbery's work was not—at least as seen from the perspective of 2007—yet apparent. Indeed, today we might see a steady drone—in the sense of a tanpura in Indian music, perhaps—of collections modeled on *Double Dream.* The foreground of the tabla, the great South Asian drum, which in this analogy would be the One Offs, has never been steady. This is consistent with the basic fact that each has been invented entirely anew. But in 1972, Ashbery had not yet established the regular rhythm of lyrics on the model of *Double Dream* or (more likely) wasn't releasing them to the world, leading readers to imagine a potentially infinite string of One Offs extending limitlessly into the future. That was, after all, the same general program Creeley was pursuing, tho Creeley's model of "the book" was never so hard-edged as Ashbery's in those early years, right through to *In London.* In Creeley, it is as tho he reaches a point & can go no further, and so settles in to develop a poetry befitting a much more calm life than the one proposed by the young man with a rep as a drunken brawler & seducer that was Creeley in the fifties & sixties.

For Ashbery, the One Offs, the poetics of deep change, has never turned off entirely, even if individual works come more slowly now. Even if they don't change poetry now when they occur. The formal equivalent of Creeley's "late style" is something that Ashbery demonstrated as possible as early as *Turandot,* tho it doesn't become a steady mode of production—or at least of publication—until *Double Dream.* And even though it is the One Offs, especially "Europe" and *Three Poems,* that changed American poetry forever, there are now so many books on the *Double Dream* model, some of them so fully feted with ribbons & trophies, that what we now think of as "the Ashbery way" is precisely these *Double Dream* lyrics, effortless & brilliant, subtle & still campy, remarkably attentive to the nuances of daily life, that to understand the context & importance of *Three Poems,* one has to imagine an Ashbery completely different from the one we have now.

III.

Back when Robert Duncan & Jerome Rothenberg were just about the only poets actively advocating for the work of Gertrude Stein—Richard Kostelanetz, somewhat younger, came later, bringing with him the energy to get a lot of her work back into print—the one poet who seems to have actually grasped the implications of her literary interventions & to have brought them over into his own poetry is John Ashbery. What I'm thinking of, specifically, is the coloration of words & the impact this has on the affect of any given textual surface.

One sees it, of course, early on in Stein—it's almost the point of *Tender Buttons.* As she writes at the start of "Breakfast,"

> A change, a final change includes potatoes. This is no authority for the abuse of cheese. What language can instruct any fellow.
>
> A shining breakfast, a breakfast shining, no dispute, no practice, nothing, nothing at all.
>
> A sudden slide changes the whole plate, it does so suddenly.
>
> An imitation, more imitation, imitation succeed imitations.

Stein's work recognizes what Robert Creeley would only much later be able to articulate theoretically as

> A poem denies its end in any descriptive act, I mean any act which leaves the attention outside the poem. (1953)

> In other words, poems are not referential, or at least not importantly so. (1963)

Yet if nouns don't name objects that exist outside the poem, what is it they do? As *Tender Buttons* suggests & Ashbery will spend a lifetime demonstrating, they color the text. After all, as Stein says in "Poetry and Grammar,"

> Poetry has to do with vocabulary just as prose has not.

Today, there are many clear instances of this: the way Clark Coolidge drains referential terms from *The Maintains* (This Press, 1974) only to bring them back again in that book's companion work, *Polaroid* (Big Sky, 1975), or how Larry Eigner would use the most generic of nouns—*tree, sky, cloud, bird*—almost architecturally in his poems. The poem where I first noticed this phenomenon is Ashbery's own "Into the Dusk-Charged Air" in *Rivers and Mountains.* Although it is not the title work of that book—a brilliant gesture, given the poem's focus on the names of rivers throughout the world—nor the "long poem" masterwork ("The Skaters") that in some ways made that volume a rehearsal for Ashbery's *Double Dream* books, the function of names in "Dusk-Charged Air" is unmistakable:

> Far from the Rappahannock, the silent
> Danube moves along toward the sea.
> The brown and green Nile rolls slowly
> Like the Niagara's welling descent.
> Tractors stood on the green banks of the Loire
> Near where it joined the Cher.
> The St. Lawrence prods among the black stones
> And mud. But the Arno is all stones.
> Wind ruffles the Hudson's
> Surface. The Irawaddy is overflowing.
> But the yellowish, gray Tiber
> Is contained within steep banks. The Isar
> Flows too fast to swim in, the Jordan's water
> Courses over the flat land. The Allegheny and its boats
> Were dark blue. The Moskowa is
> Gray boats. The Amstel flows slowly.

And so forth for another 3.5 pages. I've always thought of "Dusk-Charged Air" as being the next step for Ashbery after "Europe," the brilliantly disjoint poem at the center of *The Tennis Court Oath.* In "Europe," with all its little snatches of found language, decontextualized as they are, all nouns—indeed, one could almost say "all words"—function purely as the names of rivers do here. I read the opening of *Three Poems* as though Ashbery were, in fact, addressing precisely the question of what "Europe" is & how it functions, both as a poem and as a stage in the process of his own evolution:

> I thought that if I could put it all down, that would be one way. And next the thought came to me that to leave all out would be another, and truer, way.
>
> clean-washed sea
>
> The flowers were.
>
> These are examples of leaving out. But, forget as we will, something soon comes to stand in their place. Not the truth, perhaps, but—yourself. It is you who made this, therefore you are true. But the truth has passed on
>
> to divide all.

Against the radical disruption of leaving all out, as in "Europe," poems like "Into the Dusk-Charged Air" or "Farm Instruments and Rutabagas in a Landscape," the famous sestina that lies at the heart of *Double Dream of Spring* with its own landscape populated by the characters of Popeye, seem to offer the same lesson from a very different angle. The use of names in each was, at the time these poems were first written, so atypical as to burst out at one not unlike the image of a Brillo box or a Campbell soup can or Jasper Johns's use of the American flag.

Thus if poetry is about vocabulary & poems themselves are *not* referential, we have—no one is more clear about this than Ashbery—a hierarchy of vocabulary. At the pinnacle are the three great orienting pronouns, *I, you,* and *we,* followed very closely by proper names—Rappahannock or Wimpy or whatever—followed by nouns, as such, then adverbs & verbs and then all other words. It is worth noting that what puts the three pronouns at the pinnacle is their implication of presence, these are the pronouns of immanence, as *he, she,* and *they* are not.

Because he is so attuned to the implications of this hierarchy, one might in turn order all of Ashbery's poems by how they utilize it. A poem like "Into the Dusk-Charged Air" focuses in at the level of the name, but *Three Poems* is a book almost entirely lacking in them. The absence is so pronounced that when one does turn up—"dull Acheron" on page 21, for example—it comes as a jolt even when, as here, the point is precisely its nonjolting nature. This, in turn, elevates the role of the three pronouns, all of which appear on the first page, and in a sequence that seems not accidental or even casual—at least not here where Ashbery is setting up the project as a whole. The privileged pronoun, at least in "The New Spirit," and the earlier stages of this book, exactly as Ashbery suggests, is *you,* a term that is decidedly slipperier than either *I* or *we,* because, as here, it can—but doesn't have to—imply writer as well as reader:

> You are my calm world.

*

> You were always a living
> But a secret person

*

> Such particulars you mouthed, all leading back into the underlying question: was it you?

*

> And yet you see yourself growing up around the other, posited life, afraid for its inertness and afraid for yourself, intimidated and defensive. And you lacerate yourself so as to say, These wounds are me. I cannot let you live your life this way, and at the same time I am slurped into it, falling on top of you and falling with you.

*

> You know that emptiness that was the only way you could express a thing?

*

> To you:

> I could still put everything in and have it come out even, that is have it come out so you and I would be equal at the end of our lives, which would have been lived fully and without strain.
>
> *
>
> Is it correct for me to use you to demonstrate all this?
>
> *
>
> You private person.
>
> *
>
> And so a new you takes shape.

These are just a smattering of the *you* statements that appear over the first twenty pages of "The New Spirit," so that when the speaker of the poem proclaims

> we remain separate forever

we just don't believe it, particularly when this self-same sentence continues after a comma,

> and this confers an admittedly somewhat wistful beauty on the polarity that is our firm contact and uneven stage of development at this moment which threatens to be the last, unless the bottle with the genie squealing inside be again miraculously stumbled on, or a roc, its abrasive eye scouring the endless expanses of the plateau, appear at first like a black dot in the distance that little by little gets larger, beating its wings in purposeful and level flight.

Reading this text for who knows how many times over the thirty-five years I've owned this book, I find it hard not to laugh at the passage that follows, given the directness of its statement about the referentiality of the poem:

> I urge you one last time to reconsider. You can feel the wind in the room, the curtains are moving in the draft and a door slowly closes. Think of what it must be outside.

If you can hear in that passage the allusion to Creeley, to *Hamlet,* even to Faulkner's own use of the arras veil, all the better. For a text that literally, deliberately, goes nowhere—and does so again & again—"The New Spirit" and all of *Three Poems* are filled with many such magical moments that are, as I read it, the point.

This is not a point that can be made through exposition as a hierarchic argument, a flow chart of consequences, syllogisms locking into place. It demands instead a process-centric approach to meaning. There is a reason that Ashbery's poems, even the contained lyrics of the *Double Dream* books, resist "going anywhere." Nowhere is this resistance more fully enacted than in *Three Poems.*

IV.

To ask what makes John Ashbery a New American Poet is to ask the implicit question of what made the New American Poetry (NAP) distinct, not just from various tendencies of the School of Quietude (SoQ) but also from the traditions out of which it emerged in the decade after the Second World War. For one thing, the NAP wasn't one thing—it was several. In addition to the Beats, the Projectivists, the Spicer Circle, & the New York School, there was (and still is) the question of the San Francisco Renaissance, which was never more than whoever Robert Duncan wasn't feuding with that week, and that quirky still unacknowledged tendency that rose up out of the Reed Three (Phil Whalen, Gary Snyder, Lew Welch) and then Jim Koller's *Coyote's Journal* to embrace a poetics that was at least loosely aligned with Zen Buddhism, an interest in the American west, both as landscape & tradition, and a poetics that was not innately urban—I call these poets New Western or Zen Cowboy & would include Koller, Bobby Byrd, Jack Collom, John Oliver Simon, Simon Ortiz, Keith Wilson, Drum Hadley, Bill Deemer, Clifford Burke, & of course Joanne Kyger. Actually, I'm sure that list is omitting way too many people in places like Idaho & Arkansas (where Besmilr Brigham would surely qualify). What is it that Denise Levertov, Drum Hadley, John Ashbery, &, say, Amiri Baraka had in common that would permit anyone to identify them as part of a larger literary movement?

The traditional answer has generally been that, as the NAP

> has emerged in Berkeley and San Francisco, Boston, Black Mountain, and New York City, it has shown one common characteristic: a total rejection of all those qualities of academic verse. Following the practice and precepts of Ezra Pound and William Carlos Williams, it has built on their achievements and gone on to evolve new conceptions of the poem.

Thus sayeth Donald M. Allen, right there in the second paragraph to the "Preface" to *The New American Poetry.* But what then about poets like John Ashbery & Jack Spicer, neither of whom followed "the practice and precepts" of Pound or Williams? For Spicer, at least, one could make the social argument—the Spicer Circle, including everyone from George Stanley, Joanne Kyger, John Wieners & Steve Jonas (albeit briefly), Harold Dull, Larry Fagin, Ronnie Primack, James Alexander, Joe Dunn, Lew Ellingham, Fran & James Herndon, Stan Persky, and even Robin Blaser & Jack Gilbert, was crucially at the heart of Bay Area poetics for a decade, at least once you got more than ten feet outside of City Lights Books. But during that same crucial decade from the mid-1950s through the midsixties, John Ashbery was not in New York. The most you can say about him during this decade was that Ashbery was in touch with other New York poets and took part in some publication projects that tended to incorporate them from afar. Some of these New Yorkers had jobs that kept them around the burgeoning visual arts industry, as did he, only in Paris.

Ashbery's first book had been released without much distribution by Tibor de Nagy, the same art gallery that brought out work by Frank O'Hara. But Ashbery's second book, *Some Trees,* had been the 1956 Yale Younger Poets volume selected by Wystan Auden, hardly a camp follower of the Pound-Williams tradition, indeed the most significant figure in the School of Quietude not aligned with either the Boston Brahmin crowd around Lowell or the somewhat older Fugitive poets about Warren, Ransom, & Jarrell.[6] *The Tennis Court Oath,* Ashbery's next volume, came out from Wesleyan at a time

[6]Indeed, one could write a history of the School of Quietude that focused on Auden's impact in America as the most explosive force other than the sudden emergence of the NAP in causing the SoQ to begin its own steady devolution into a variety of sometimes quite mutually hostile tendencies, so that the crowd around FSG, the trade

when that university house still published only SoQ poets, while *Rivers and Mountains* came out from Holt, Rinehart and Winston, one of the lesser New York trade presses. *The Double Dream of Spring* came out from E. P. Dutton in its American Poets series. It was only after Wesleyan reprinted the British *Selected Poems,* first published by Jonathan Cape, that Yale let *Some Trees* go out of print, causing Ted & Eli Wilentz, owners of the Eighth Street Bookshop, to republish it under their own Corinth imprint in 1970. Which means, in fact, that it is not until 1975, when Black Sparrow releases *The Vermont Notebook,* the most underappreciated of Ashbery's One Off volumes, that a major NAP-related press with real distribution actually first publishes one of his books—nineteen years after *Some Trees.*

Is Ashbery a New American Poet then strictly by friendship & accident? I think he comes by it legitimately, which is to say *formally,* as does Spicer. I do think that there are some poets in the Allen anthology in particular about whom you might make an argument that they don't necessarily belong to the NAP tradition even if they were outside the School of Quietude as well: Brother Antoninus, Madeline Gleason, James Broughton, even Helen Adam. These were not poets who looked much to the Pound-Williams tradition, but whereas Spicer & Ashbery are doing things in their work that is in consort with the New American Poetics, the most one might say about this other quartet is that you could trace their antiacademicism in general back to the same source where Pound found it, in the work of Yeats.

Until recently, I would have said that Spicer & Ashbery are much closer to the New American Poetry because their work also focuses the reader's attention on the materiality of the signifier, precisely what the School o' Quietude attempts to efface. Spicer was the one person among the forty-four Allen gathered to have actually studied language, working as a professional linguist. As such, he didn't buy the mythological *line = breath unit* Piltdown personism Charles Olson was promoting & said so frankly. And his own use of the Pound-Williams tradition was very different from that of his peers. Spicer's focus in the 1959 sequence "A Red Wheelbarrow" is on the question of reference, and his focus in "Homage to Creeley," the first

---

presses, and the Eastern foundations became quite a target both for bad-boy Brahmins like Robert Bly & the more western & less urban (*and less urbane*) poets out in Iowa City.

section of *Heads of the Town Up to the Aether,* is on the role of love poetry & the problem of the beloved Other as *you* in writing.[7] Spicer's own counterpoetics, *radio dictation from Mars,* was no less metaphoric but in its functional process the idea severed the simplistic psychologism that actually underlies much NAP neoromanticism, whether that of Olson or Ginsberg or O'Hara. If you're taking dictation, then this text isn't about you.

What all New American Poetry tendencies mostly have in common is a general emphasis on the materiality of language. Whether it's in the compositional strategies of the Black Mountain poets, ever seeking a more accurate method of scoring the page for sound, in the oracular excesses of a Beat poet going "overboard" verbally, via spontaneous bop prosody, as Kerouac put it, or in the densely crafted imagery of Ginsberg's *hydrogen jukebox* or Michael McClure's ecstatic lion roars, or in the softer and more ironic variant offered up by O'Hara et al, every one of these poetries comes alive precisely because it resists the conception of a transparent referential language, something only a few of the SoQ poets of the period seemed to be capable of doing (most notably Theodore Roethke & John Berryman).

The group that really brought this home for me is the Zen Cowboy poets, the tendency that borrowed from every one of their peers & discounted any pretense of a theorized style. What you see in the best work of this group—Whalen, Collom, Welch, Brautigan's poetry (and at least the early novels), the later Kyger & occasionally even Snyder—is a focus on focus, on presence, immanence. *Be here now* is very much a poetic program. Its motivation may be different, but its practice varies hardly at all from the in-the-moment/of-the-moment poetics that could generate a classic called *Lunch Poems* or a series like Ted Berrigan's *Sonnets.* Among the Projectivists, this same emphasis is the essence of Creeley's *Pieces,* or of the phenomenological mobiles of Larry Eigner.

Really, with the exception of Stein & Zukofsky, I don't think the materiality of the signifer was ever the intention of the modernists, tho it's an area where, for example, George Oppen is far stronger in *Discrete Series,* his supposed juvenilia of the 1930s, than in the award-winning *Of Being Numerous* thirty years hence. It's part—

[7]The Ellingham-Killian biography suggests that Spicer actively did not like Ashbery, and that he made fun of what he took to be Ashbery's swishier behavior. There's no evidence that Ashbery reciprocated in kind, but in any event the two never took the opportunity to really influence one another, one of the most serious lost opportunities of the New American period.

but not all—of the program of *Spring & All.* And you might say that it's what remains of Pound's layered densities of reference in *The Cantos* once you throw the bogus scholarship overboard & just read what's on the page. Ditto the nineteenth-century philology at the heart of *Finnegans Wake.* Indeed, one might make the case of the New Americans generally that they read what the modernists wrote, rather than what the modernists thought they wrote. Which is how a Robert Creeley could profess to be stunned that William Carlos Williams did not voice his line breaks as such, once he'd heard Williams read. It was so obvious if you just looked at the page. Just not to Williams.

But how then square this underlying first principle of the material signifier, the immanent word, with something like this?

> There is no staying here
> Except a pause for breath on the peak
> That night fences in
> As though the spark might be extinguished.

> He thought he had never seen anything quite so beautiful as that crystallization into a mountain of statistics: out of the rapid movement to and from that abraded individual personalities into a channel of possibilities, remote from each other and even remoter from the eye that tried to contain them: out of that river of humanity comprised of individuals each no better than he should be and doubtless more solicitous of his own personal welfare than of the general good, a tonal quality detached itself that partook of the motley intense hues of the whole gathering but yet remained itself, firm and all-inclusive, scrupulously fixed equidistant between earth and heaven, as far above the tallest point on the earth's surface as it was beneath the lowest outcropping of cumulus in the cornflower-blue empyrean. Thus everything and everybody were included after all, and any thought that might ever be entertained about them; the irritating drawbacks each possessed along with certain good qualities were dissolved in the enthusiasm of the whole, yet individuality was not lost for all that, but persisted in the definition of the urge to proceed higher and further as

> well as in the counter-urge to amalgamate into the broadest and widest kind of uniform continuum. The effect was as magnificent as it was unexpected, not even beyond his wildest dreams since he had never had any, content as he had been to let the process reason itself out. "You born today," he could not resist murmuring although there was no one within earshot, "a life of incredulity and magnanimity opens out around you, incredulity at the greatness of your designs and magnanimity that turns back to support these projects as they flag and fall, as inevitably happens. . . ."

At first, this seems to be the antithesis of a poetics of immanence—*be anywhere but here* would seem to be the message, both at the level of content & in practice. "The New Spirit" is the only poem I know of that includes a sentence that contains the word *magnanimity* not once but twice with but a dozen words between them. Trying to pin down Ashbery's argument, as such, is the proverbial scooping up mercury with a pitchfork. You simply can't do it.

If, however, you read Ashbery the same way you do Larry Eigner, as a model of consciousness itself, the place of presence refocuses in a new way. Ashbery in *Three Poems* reminds me, more than anything, of the Buddhist adage that *You are not your thoughts,* and with the underlying idea that thinking itself represents a form of anxiety. The whole purpose in meditation of focusing on breathing is precisely to make the individual conscious of the degree to which thinking goes on, even when one pays it no mind. Meditators never fully banish thoughts—it's not even clear if that would be doable—but rather get distance from them, so that when thoughts rise up & intrude on the meditation one can simply turn them aside. *Three Poems* replicates this process better than any work of literature I've ever read, before or since. As experience, the poem's mode is one of continually refocusing, then drifting, then refocusing again, then drifting further. If it never settles, this is because there is, as Stein once characterized her hometown of Oakland, "no there there," no topic sentence, no secret center, no monad "I" or "eye" at the work's heart.

Ashbery telegraphs this in any number of ways. One of the most effective, for me at least, is his occasional breaking up of a paragraph literally midline as tho one might have a stanza break with no other vestige of traditional verse devices. Thus, for example,

> For I care nothing about apparitions, neither do you, scrutinizing the air only to ask, "Is it giving?" but not so dependent on the answer as not to have our hopes and dreams, our very personal idea of how to live and go on living. It does not matter, then,

> but there always comes a time when the spectator needs reassurance, to be touched on the arm so he can be sure he is not dreaming.

This is not an epic challenge between solipsism & phenomenology, but rather a poetics that wants to include both the real *and* all of our difficulties getting in touch with that plane. It's not that Eigner or O'Hara propose to be here now & Ashbery does not, only that Ashbery wants us to be conscious that both *here* & *now* are concepts that need to be unpacked, that neither is quite what it seems.

Years ago, somebody in an interview tried to provoke Allen Ginsberg into dismissing language poetry, which was only then coming into prominence. For a generation, Ginsberg replied, poets point at the moon, then poets notice they're pointing. In a period during which Robert Creeley could—and did—write

> Here here
> here. Here.

John Ashbery is responding literally in kind—one can palpably feel the nod to Creeley in the generosity of Ashbery's phrasing—when he begins the most important of his poems

> I thought that if I could put it all down, that would be one way. And next the thought came to me that to leave all out would be another, and truer, way.

Three Poems is not merely John Ashbery's best and most important book, one that American literature is still working to fully incorporate, it is a demonstration that the principles underlying the New American Poetry can be arrived at from a completely different direction than that employed by ninety-nine percent of his peers in the late sixties, early seventies. As such, it represents one of the most intellectually ambitious literary projects ever written.

A Birthday Notebook for JA

The Vermont Notebook (1975)

David Shapiro

1. I BECAME CONVERTED TO John Ashbery's poetry between 1960 and 1962. Kenneth Koch said to me, You will see there are only three poets—John, Frank, and me. I said, as we climbed a little hill in Staten Island—I was fifteen—What about Martin Buber? Kenneth laughed: Why bring up Buber. He's a minor Jewish philosopher. I said, clumsily: Sometimes I would rather be a minor Jewish philosopher than . . .

2. One night in August 1962, I was reading *The Tennis Court Oath,* a book given to me by Kenneth that day. I read some of the fragments and thought: He uses the word "I" like any other word in the dictionary. Then, looking at a little phrase, I thought: this is like a little melody but surrounded by a fog of dissonance: "You girl / the sea in waves."

3. Then, a bit of a conversion experience, as Elaine de Kooning said of her painter friends falling off their horses and becoming abstract painters, as if in a change of name or religion: from Saul to Paul. I thought: he is using skeins of language like the new painter (for me) Robert Rauschenberg. All this flat newspaper is a brilliant strategy. I remember writing to my mother that week and saying that I had found the most wonderful Cage-like music in Ashbery. I was so happy.

4. One day, slipping into a car, John told me he agreed with me that he was "like" Jasper Johns in many ways. "We both seem to like the lazy exploration of ourselves," he said, with his canonic—is it skeptical?—smile.

5. John once asked me, Do I have to read Jacques Derrida's work? I said: You certainly don't have to read it, since your work comprehends it exactly. Derrida, Michal Govrin, and I built a book

about prayer. Jacques, whom I teased as a Jewish poet always, said he could imagine a prayer without hope. This prayer is the only one he could accept. I think that John's work is also heartbreaking, because it prays in hopelessness in a time without hope.

6. One of the events of my life was receiving from Koch's hands a new typescript of a poem called "The Skaters." I distinctly recall waiting for a poor line or something that did not work. I read forty pages with the sensation a young violist has listening to Heifetz play with Piatigorsky and Feuermann the late Mozart *Divertimento.* I loved each line of this poem and still feel it is the masterpiece of John's work, though I might say that of many long poems from "Europe" to "Litany" to "Girls on the Run," from the infinite tenderness of "Self-Portrait" to the acoherence of the dual strophes of "Litany," with "A Wave," "Fragment," "Clepsydra," and so many single lyrics, like "The Chateau Hardware," "Voyage in the Blue," and "How to Continue." Oh, it is impossible to praise Ashbery adequately. In those moments when no criticism seems to count, I recall that one of the things I love about John was how far he seemed always from dogma. I used to think the New York group would be some of the only ones without a critical corpus or a critical echo. I was wrong, but I still hope JA will not be compulsory like potatoes in the reign of Pasternak's Catherine the Great.

7. Kenneth Koch and I were talking about John's "The Skaters," in 1963 or '64. I said early, What do you think this poem is about? He giggled and replied: It's not about anything, but it is a complete philosophy of life. John later wrote his own poem about systems and philosophies with much mirth and fecundity of irony.

8. If I am asked to write about any Ashbery poem, I do so, but I recall that in my first volume on John I have suppressed chapters on *The Double Dream,* his plays, his art criticism, his literary criticism, and his marvelous translations from the French. I usually think the best is an endless practical critique, which would take every word and every trope, every specious simile, and every drowning elongation, and make a tonal reading inch for inch. That is not to say one cannot sum up some of John's themes, but danger lurks there.

9. Let me say what I think has been mismanaged in Ashbery criticism, and I still think his work could be better approached than by

dogmatic critics. If one only finds Emerson in him, then one will find Emerson in a grain of dust. If one only finds his sexual predilections, one will miss the eroticism of language itself. One shouldn't be so easily Freudened, but I think the ideal reader will actually see his pantheism and nature-mysticism. But that should not deny how much of a parodist he is. Don't forget the humor; don't forget the Watteau-like delicacy of his gallantries. It is a poor student of Ashbery who only turns to his most coherent pieces and remarks that *The Tennis Court Oath* should be thrown away. Everything Ashbery has done comes out of that great revolution. Like Picasso's cubism, this, say, cubo-futurism of John inflects all later poems; he cannot avoid being the poet who was once characterized as a man in a good suit with ink on his shirtfront. John is a poet who encompasses romanticism, secularism, cubo-futurism, John Cage's religion of chance, and the elegance of Pope. Allen Ginsberg once asked me: "But can you memorize him, David?" I then quoted long passages from *The Tennis Court Oath* poem "Rain." Allen demurred: "Oh I get it, it's Alexander Pope." No, it is not one thing.

10. The multiplicity of John's work is the mastery of many perspectives. He changed his style almost before others had a chance to imitate him thoroughly. Like Picasso, of whom John says there came a time when he was used to creating beauty, John seems to have managed and mastered so many rhetorical modes that he might become lost—as in my own critiques—as a magician of devices. He is not merely that prestidigitator, but I think Helen V. is very close to the mark when she suggested that for a poet, self-reflexive poems of poetry are not merely self-reflexive—for a poet, poems of poetry are as visceral as any Eros.

11. When I am asked how I think John has developed, I must say it is a startling and even dazzling path. It has the "human unity" of which Meyer Schapiro spoke with Picasso's oeuvre in front of him. Picasso always seemed capable of making a group show, a stylistic set of different, even antagonistic, ways. But to the one who has not only read "The Skaters" but heard the voice within, I don't think we see a mere literary development in John's work, but increasing wisdom and even tragic late poems that are almost of the unutterable, as with Beckett and Johns. These are the poems of growth, which we feel in Yeats. They are the wisdom poems that Eliot said would be the greatest signs of a poet's growth. I think that if one can

understand cubism and surrealism, which divide, O'Hara said, the world between them, one should be able to understand Ashbery's twenty volumes and the addenda. His perverse taste, so-called, has become almost canonic. He now seems, even to his enemies of many years of rivalry, an unavoidable poet. He has the daunting hijacks of a wizard of spelling bees—but he also has the soul that is not a soul, the secret that brings tears to our eyes. If one reads him from *Turandot* to the most recent lyrics—I underline "How to Continue" as the greatest poem of AIDS and private grief made public that I know of our epoch. If we look at all of this, we will find not eclecticism and not tergiversations merely. We build up a sense of his gray luminosity, of that special tone of self-laceration and Miltonic strength that is indeed his pride and his architectural and "human" unity. His plays hang with these poems delightfully. Each volume recently has become even unnervingly dry or secco as in Montale. They are the least operatic and the most abrupt music reminding us, of course, of his continued rapport with Carter and the theme of abruptness that Carter once said was his chief desire. Like a folksinger elegantly gliding back to the spoken phrase, Ashbery has drained his poetry of false or glib euphony and has cried out sharply; this is the hot perspectivism that makes him our philosopher poet.

12. His *Vermont Notebook* is filled with humorous positivism, like a Constable cloud traced by an engineering student. With a Joe Brainard illustration of an isolated figure in one version, the notebook starts with the comical delineation (and melancholy) of the months: October, November, December. This little "note" allows us to realize we do not know what time is and whether Ashbery in any way is trying to be "accurate." We doubt it, almost immediately. Just as the stars in "The Skaters"' Chekhovian ending never rise in that order. (He told me he "liked the sound.") Taurus, Leo, Gemini. An enigmagram. The only thing really "datable" is the long hair of the male figure, seen in black from behind with enormous locks, a fashionable statement.

13. Later, the notebook simply makes a slaughterhouse of names and places. Parking lots are close to "war memorials," and the whole is like a dump site for shifters and even shiftier nouns and common nouns. I have been most horrified by his list of crimes, which has the blank easiness of *Roget's Thesaurus.* Ashbery once asked me whether I was telling others that he worked from the dictionary.

I said I didn't but that I didn't think it would have been an insult, since I loved turning to "the world view of the dictionary," like tubes of paint that one might drink.

14. There's a mighty minimalism here and very iridescent reductions. He gives us all the colors of the rainbow, as if nothing were more dead than color charts. Before crime come games. And after games comes my favorite Eros of this poem: a seemingly endless (when recited) list of friends and celebrities, poets and painters, colleagues and doppelgängers. I appear here, and I immediately felt that there was an extraordinary capture happening. Like Picasso, this poet loves to possess, and his satires are infinite. The names from Hess to Obolensky, from Benjamin to "Bricktop," from Mark Strand to Daisy Aldan to David Shapiro—one wonders if this is free association or really a very compact linguistic guide to the bachelorhood of the sign, as one used to say. Dine made a "Friends" canvas or two, on which he scrawled his proper names and proper nouns. But he allowed certain people to be bigger than others, creating a kind of loose mandala of his life. Ashbery is colder and more comfortless. The notebook becomes Kafkaesque. He has reached that hot moment, degree zero.

15. Then he has parts of houses and material (tweed, cotton, silk). There are no predilections. In a lyrical moment, the parts of speech get entangled: "plug, dream, mope, urchin, distress, ways, many, few, found, dreaming, unclad." Koch once told me that he was even jealous of John's dreams, and certainly that is an exquisite admission. Here John turns a catalogue raisonné of American pure products into something as oneiric as a Joseph Cornell box. He has always taught me that poetry involved distribution and Proustian return, not an obvious content. "Sleep, reef, perfect, almost." See how this catalogue reinvents aspects of *The Tennis Court Oath.* It could never be as bumptious and agrammatical without "Europe." Let the reader beware. With Joe Brainard yielding an animal's puss, face, or mien, John writes one of his most dismal scenes. Out of Stevens, out of Stein, out of de Chirico, out of psychoanalysis and dread, he speaks of the man of the dump, now the man in the dump, now the man who is almost telling the narratology of the dump. "I will go to the dump." This is a true admission. As Kay Boyle noted years ago, "John tells great truths as if they were lies." This strophe, paragraph, prose poem, apart, gives us the tang of Schwitters and the detritus

of the day, Freud's debris of dreams. And if one doesn't feel the tone of suffering, one has lost a great deal of the pathos. The analogy with the gray, severe, melancholy work of Johns cannot be avoided: ". . . it is printed on dump letters." No, "in" dump letters is his precision. And Ashbery comes close to a very revealing sentiment. "As I swear the dump is my sweet inner scope self . . ."

16. The prose poems are not as sensuous as Rimbaud and are certainly not as moralizing as Baudelaire. They are escapades of his sweet inner unconscious dump site. Rauschenberg put it this way: "If you can't make an artwork out of a single tour around your block, you are not an artist." And from prose poems, we come close to details like food lined up in Brainard's illumination or anti-illustration. But the Menippean satire does not slow: "The high-flying clouds are eyewash." Here he reminds us of the poet who could mock Schubert and could use Constable clouds as a cover for a book. There is winsome electricity, if one can bring those together as tempi and principles and pressures. John is as breezy but elite as the Goncourt Brothers in their great notebooks and journals, sexual and anxious, descriptive, and impossible aslant.

17. Aug. 7. The TV is on in Joe Brainard's great untitled illumination. And the caricature of white noise is as funny, and fresh, as a Crumb cartoon. And like Crumb more than Schuyler here, he caricatures his own situation: "I think I believe this, but there is a sound in the next room." All is hilariously included. All is misunderstood, as in Freud and Koch's poem to misunderstandings. The religion is not chance but change.

18. Nov. 3. Ashbery gives one of his most depressingly accurate and acidic lines about the whole community. He says that excretion makes him embarrassed for the whole of humanity. This is hilarious and Darwinian and mighty and mild, at once. He is a master of discretion. He has said his mother's mantra was, Never put yourself forward. How can one be, however, a poet of the scale of Stevens, without Bachlike confidence? He achieves his monument with the maximum of Lucretian materialism and the minimum of arrogance. "Something moving. Not everybody but a slice."

19. "America is a fun country," John declares, but he also becomes suddenly obscene to mock the American socius in a special way:

"This is a lot of bunk and our own President plays it right into the lap of big business and uses every opportunity he can find to fuck the consumer and the little guy." But the tone might be the parody of a political tone. He told me his animadversions about Schubert in "The Skaters" was simply a test of "how many opinions I had about everything." Everything in these poems is still put under the eraser fluid of a quotation mark. It is annoying for many that the poet seems not to be able to escape from the humor of quotation, but it is a strong tendency in Ashbery to make his brightest colors still go gray with pain or iridescent gray. He is not putting himself forward. John Ashbery, at least, is one thing: he is not an infantile leftist. But he reserves the right to a peaceful Chaplinesque plume of a protest (see Michaux's poems of Plume the adjusted one, the crushed one).

20. This is not a poem that ends, it includes. Lyric poems are suddenly stuck in, as if photographs on a valise or memorial. The prose tries a thousand angles of nature description, but usually, as the poet says, he sees his own face. Is it solipsism, as Bloom once suggested out of Wittgenstein: is it not solipsism that at least has the right tone? The horror of liberation, as he says elsewhere. Not a poet of happiness but of a realism of the stunted potential, he is willing to admit to a grave darkness at the center of his "lazy," actually severe, self-exploration. This is the soul's notebook, where jottings, dates, and dilemmas ("little nuts big nuts") all are included.

21. Porter praised Cornell, as I would praise Ashbery, for including the highest and, I would add, lowest reaches of the human spirit. In Cornell, there is a toy glass, there is a marvelous sun and moon and the exotic escape in dreams and in all those childlike "toys for adults." Cornell once exhibited his work at "child" level. Let us say that in John the longing for an escape from the self is as uncertain as any solipsist could hope for, but all painted and parsed by a very fastidious assembler. He does not carve, he does not mold, he doesn't even let be—he assembles, and this is his analogy with Picasso, Rauschenberg, and Johns, a man who could make a memorial out of a target, a biography out of numbers, and a masquerade out of the letters of the alphabet.

22. Let us always remember that the poem is not always best approached without love and receptivity itself. The poems of Ashbery may seem so open that they become, like Hamlet, that rare

inexhaustible thing, the irreducible fact of great art. For this reason, some exclude *The Tennis Court Oath,* and some exclude *Self-Portrait* as too Eliotic. But just as Picasso gave birth to the art of Mondrian and Tatlin, to Braque, who gave birth to much of Picasso, and to Juan Gris, whom he did and did not understand or admire, so Ashbery has been one of the forces that gives birth to many other poems, and this may be the critical statement. Ashbery makes one want to read and to write, and, as someone said of Meyer Schapiro, to be slashed by reality. His eclecticism was brilliantly compared by John Ash once to the New York motley of midtown and the whole incoherent city. For all of his ecology now noted, what could be more urbane than his particular pastoral?

23. Jan. 2. Multiple Choice(s): Ashbery uses the notebook as a form, to be almost as attentive to the particular as that mature poet Jimmy Schuyler. But he doesn't need the telescope or microscope to render his lascivious fictive voyage into the blue suburbia of America. Koch said to me of "The Skaters," and we may say it of the *Notebook:* "Isn't this the loneliest poem you have ever read?" (August 1964).

24. To understand the wit of *The Vermont Notebook,* and much else in Ashbery, use Meyer Schapiro's infinitely witty remarks about cubism and collage. First, the master art historian reminded us that collage is an old story—think of the textures in medieval uses of gold and other jewels and media. To reach the multiplicity of levels in the *Chair Caning* collage of Picasso (1912, very mixed media), Meyer lectured about linguistic analogues. Listen to these levels, as it were. I am Meyer Schapiro, I is or am a pronoun; I is a straight line. Thus, Picasso and Ashbery and Joe Brainard's nonillustration drawings show us the chair, the profile of the chair, and the raw slippage or passage of the medium itself. The critics of Ashbery have made a mistake. They have attached themselves to one part of this axis of the multiple aesthetic. They have concentrated on John the I, the man, the sexual; they have concentrated only on the lonely slippage; they have, as I often have, delighted in the abstract musicality of the textures Dante too extolled. But the density of John's *Vermont Notebook,* "Wave," "Litany," "Fragment," *Three Poems,* which is really one poem, or even the smallest, "The Chateau Hardware," is the way he combines these "stages" of the semiotic, and without theory, a young poet might fall in love with the sexuality, the melody, the noise, and the aesthetic innovation given at once. Like Constable, he

does not just yield a cloud on a bus ride or any state; he is elated like Meyer Schapiro, and his aesthetic elation makes him a rare poet of happiness. Even when he utters his terrifying line "I am still completely happy," we laugh at this Chekhovian momentum. Even when he hates himself and calls himself early on "a chair-sized man," we know his Chaplinesque strength and the wilderness of his quest.

25. *The Vermont Notebook* is a long poem, or is it a play, or is it a meditation aesthetique? And it is a Menippean satire of many styles. It is, of course, a sequence, and not least, not quite a "notebook." The dates are fudged, the places are dislocated. (Shoptaw has documented that this poem is not of Vermont. It is not of any Vermont you and I will see. It is a mental, symbolist Vermont. It is a pragmatist's universe. July 6, Cambridge.

26. In Ashbery there is no Platonic heaven, no uninflected affirmation, except the shameless shame of the human body. His so-called distortions or difficulties are that of the lived nobody, the internality of the body, as Paul Schilder put it. Ashbery's broken notebook is the bright book of life for those who, like Kundera, are searching for the "dump site of Europe." Intricate and almost infinite, his mazes lock us into pleasure, if we read correctly. Like William James, inside the multiplicity of Wallace Stevens, here we have a notebook toward a poem. And those of us reveling in ideas understand also the great farewell here to all violating dogmas and too simple ideals. He is proud of those fat Poulenc notes that to some are minor phases. A dictionary of clichés is not a cliché. Parataxis is the guide.

27. For those who have underlined landscape in his work, I would say he is a critical regionalist if one remembers his ecstatic region is the mind. And perhaps, to change the philosopher the best model of the human mind is the internality of the body. Cezanne's doubt and Morandi's faith here come together in our inescapable comedy of the American sublime. Brainard's collages and sketches remind us of the reiteration of the child. Ashbery once told Cavett on television that his parents didn't know "what to do with me." He remains a whiz kid but of wisdom, and like Henry Green, a constant violator of authoritarianism, a poet on the run, and also a poet who knows that standing still is also wise. Music by Busoni swells.

I Was Reading and Rereading Ashbery's *Self-Portrait* for Many Years

Self-Portrait in a Convex Mirror (1975)

Susan Stewart

AND I WILL WRITE down some of my thoughts about it, but these paragraphs are not meant as an explanation, for there is nothing to discover that isn't better found in the process of reading the book itself. This is not a matter of priority, or deference, but simply a fact about the richness and complexity of language when it appears in poems, and poems when they appear in books, and reading when it becomes rereading.

The title, *Self-Portrait in a Convex Mirror,* is tripled, since it's the title of the book, the title of the final poem, and the title of the subject of the final poem: Girolamo Francesco Maria Mazzuoli ("Parmigianino")'s masterpiece of 1524 at the Kunsthistorisches Museum in Vienna. This tripling follows the similar triangulation of the painter/alchemist/inventor/magus Parmigianino, who made his self-portrait by painting, onto a half ball of wood made especially to his specifications, what he could see in a convex mirror. All triangles are eternal, but this was as well a temporary one: first, a reflecting substance, intended for looking into an image; second, a subject of reflection, who is the maker; third, an absorbing substance, intended for building an image.

Or picture a zigzagging arrow that goes from the painter's eyes to the mirror to the painter's hand to the painted surface—that is, if we believe the mirror is more than a device of simple reflection. In the very last lines of the poem, and the book, Ashbery lashes out at "those assholes / Who would confuse everything with their mirror games / Which seem to multiply stakes and possibilities, or / At least confuse issues by means of an investing / Aura that would corrode the architecture / Of the whole in a haze of suppressed mockery." They are "beside the point" and "out of the game / Which doesn't exist until they are out of it." What is at risk here is not only "the architecture of the whole," but also the difference between games and "the game." The consequences of the first are reversible, and hence inconsequential. The consequences of the second—that is, of that game of life upon which everything is staked and whose end point is the irreversibility of death—are everything.

Self-Portrait the book is not meant to be read as a "mere" game (an already-known set of stakes and possibilities) or play (suppressed mockery); that much is clear. But it is the "investing / Aura" that is the threat to the whole. In Ashbery's homeopathy of sincerity, emotion arises not from a preexisting investment, but rather only when surprise is possible, and surprise is possible only when there's no particular expectation.

Consider a simple, but surprising, device of surprise that Ashbery uses in the first and fourth poems of the book: a citation that sparks and then goes elsewhere. Ashbery's opening, "As One Put Drunk into the Packet-Boat," is taken, as many of his readers will know, from the first line of Andrew Marvell's own triangulated masterpiece of 1650, "Tom May's Death." The poem is a satire framed by Marvell's voice, but for the most part expressed in the voice of Ben Jonson, through whom the speaker reflects upon Tom May in life and death. Tom May died from drink, but not from drink alone; he had his cap tied too tightly beneath his very fat chin and ended up suffocating—the upshot of a face too big for its frame. Jonson is depicted as blocking May at the entrance to the Elysian Fields and condemning him to hell—a condemnation based above all on May's sins of "pretending"; that is, he switched sides between parliamentarian and royalist factions and "prostituted" his pen.

In the opening lines of "As One Put Drunk into the Packet-Boat," Ashbery describes an atmosphere where "harsh words are spoken," a scene of reading in midsummer, when "A look of glass stops you / And you walk on shaken: was I the perceived?" This is a moment of fleeting semi-self-recognition that can happen any ordinary day in any ordinary shop window. Yet here it follows Tom May's revelation at the start of Marvell's poem: "with an eye uncertain, gazing wide, [May] could not determine in what place he was." In Ashbery's line, the problem is agency; in Marvell's, it is the absence of an organizing perspective, and we are invited to think about the connections between these two problems. This first poem of *Self-Portrait* is truly a point of departure, one with an ironic allusion (the purgation of a poet from heaven) at its start and underlying it, but not mapped upon it.

The book's fourth poem similarly relies upon an opening quotation: "As You Came from the Holy Land." The late-fifteenth-century printed English ballad "As You Came from the Holy Land of Walsingham" was famously later adapted by Sir Walter Raleigh, and may itself be based on older laments for the Marian shrines of Walsingham that were destroyed by Henry VIII. The ballad, in all its versions, is structured as a dialogue between pilgrims, one of whom asks the other for news of a "true love." In Ashbery's poem, we find ourselves immediately in "western New York State"—not Walsingham. But Ashbery keeps the ballad's structure to the extent that his poem too is an interrogation, and western New York State is indeed the "holy land" of his birth, a place suffused with memories of his own family, and his mother particularly. At the same time, he pokes fun at any reader fussing over the connection: "you reading there so accurately / sitting not wanting to be disturbed." Reading, like feeling, will be undisturbed, hardly reading or feeling at all, if we look for things we already know.

The word "as" appears in both these titles—first as a qualitative adverb, second as a temporal one. Reading *Self-Portrait* as a whole is an intense immersion in all the possibilities of "as": for marking time and place, for denoting quality and quantity—"we are as sitting in a place," "harsh words are spoken, as the sun yellows the green," "As you find you had never left off laughing at death," "as long as the night allows," and "As on a festal day in early spring" are just a few instances. How something is done, compared, placed, and marked in time is all a matter of style, and to such an intense degree that style becomes an attribute of being, or perhaps, more accurately, being becomes an attribute of style—something barely glimpsed in style's manifold.

The abrupt shifts of these two poems are, however, in another sense an exception. An ever-flowing series of small adjustments, like his frequent recourse to the river imagery of Heraclitus's "you can't step into the same river twice," is more typical of the experience of reading Ashbery's poems. *Self-Portrait in a Convex Mirror* as a whole uses such adjustments in syntax and larger units of form. The underlying meter is a freely stressed iambic pentameter blank verse. Three poems about objects, "Tarpaulin," "River," and "Sand Pail," are meditations that owe something to the early modernism of imagism and the later modernism of Oppen's concentrated lines. "Suite" plays with pairs of five- and seven-line stanzas, varying the line length widely, while "Märchenbilder" has the most "regular" stanza form, with eight quatrains made of lines as short as two beats and others with as many as nine beats.

But stanza form and line length are not as central to Ashbery's practice of ringing changes so much as shifts of topic, mood, tone, diction—all, we could say, aspects of voice become aspects of consciousness. In "Märchenbilder," for example, which would seem to allude to Robert Schumann's four "fairy-tale pictures" for viola and piano by the same title, the speaker begins, "Es war einmal" [once upon a time], then introduces ellipses and says, "No, it's too heavy / To be said." We are thrown off the Schumann connection as well as by a change of instruments: "Sometimes a musical phrase would perfectly sum up / The mood of a moment. One of those lovelorn sonatas / For wind instruments was riding past on a solemn white horse. / Everybody wondered who the new arrival was."

The poem proceeds by a set of false starts, presenting a tin soldier ("that's not it either") and flowers and decorations ("junked the next day"), before entering a cave. The speaker wants "to go back, out of the bad stories," which are "beautiful as we people them / With ourselves." Unlike the abrupt surprises of the Tom May and Walsingham allusions, the Schumann context here, like a receding melody, gradually fades. To read the poem is something like walking away from the revolving sounds and pictures of a merry-go-round ("the solemn white horse" or, as the title poem later suggests, a carousel), maybe toward a parking lot where painted horses are replaced by less picturesque vehicles. Reading becomes a process of shedding by accruing. Like rust, a meditation on phrases gradually covers the structure of the original form, which then persists only in a vague and internalized outline. "The crust thickens, the back of everything . . . / Clustered carillons and the pink dew of afterthoughts / Support it."

Following allusions leads the reader down unexpected paths and the experience of getting on track or off is about the same, with turning to a next poem like awakening to a next day. Such a feeling is typical, it seems to me, of all Ashbery's work, but in *Self-Portrait* there is a specific ekphrastic agenda. The Greek word means "to speak out" and Ashbery creates a tension between a particular kind of political speech (here literally the speech of a polis, or city, or other places) and a speech of allusions and articulate images, as fleeting as the expressions on a face.

He constantly draws upon two specific ekphrastic traditions: the *blason* and the *locus amoenus.* The technique of the *blason* involves describing one's love like a statue, usually from top to bottom. In *Self-Portrait* such an image is variously one's self, or one's self and one's love, or one's self and one's love and others, all variously rendered—abstractly, cubistically, temporally. In "Tenth Symphony," for example, a literally skewed dialogue is set forward, with each stanza introducing a totally different mood. (At least) two people, who seem to be deeply bound to each other ("You've never told me about a lot of things: / Why you love me, why we love you, and just exactly / What sex is . . ."), speak at varying levels of abstraction, which could be described as well as varying levels of intensity and distractedness: ". . . a lot of plans and ideas. / Hope to have more time to tell you about / The latter in the foreseeable future."

Ashbery uses the ekphrastic tradition of the *locus amoenus,* or *plaisance,* which involves animating a scene or landscape, to set up contexts where meditation and observation become one process. Many of the book's "speaking pictures," including, of course, the long title poem, are set out loosely within such frames. The book's series of three "Farm" poems work like small quick sketches; "The Tomb of Stuart Merrill" sounds like a parody of a Poussin arcadia or a parody of a Poussin arcadia sounds like the poems of this American symbolist who wrote in French; the two brief urban lyrics "Tarpaulin" ("a thousand tenement windows") and "River" (a couple sitting at a picnic table behind glass) are also studies in mood and point of view. *Self-Portrait*'s juxtaposition of European and American allusions relies upon a contract between the specific cultural reference points of the former and the sprawling anonymous spaces of the latter.

For example, in his meditation on place names here, "The One Thing That Can Save America," Ashbery writes, "Is anything central? . . . Are place names central? . . . These are connected to my version of America" and ends with not place names, but abstract descriptions: "cool yards / In quiet small houses in the country, / Our country, in fenced areas, in cool shady streets." These are kinds of places, not particular places—Americans move around, setting them up wherever they settle; the *locus amoenus* is a type of *locus amoenus.* In contrast, Parmigianino, "Little Parmigiano," or little one from Parma, is defined by his place of origin forever, as Rome, whether sacked or entire, remains the eternal city.

The poems draw on other aspects of the history of image making as they also draw on other images of history. "Absolute Clearance" has an epigraph from Jacques-Bénigne Bossuet: "Voilà, Messieurs, les spectacles que Dieu donne à l'univers . . ." and we're reminded that, amid the iconoclastic controversies of the seventeenth century, Bossuet played a leading role. He delivered, among many funeral orations, the eulogy for Charles I's widow, Henrietta Maria, and if this were someone else's poetry book, we'd go back to the initial Tom May allusions and start to draw out a pattern regarding regicide, the English revolution, and correlative themes of theology, representation, and ornament. Bossuet's nickname was "The Eagle of Meaux" (he shares the eagle attribute with Pindar, who, we'd have to say, also went down "fuming"). And, from the sublime to the Ashberyan ridiculous, this famous ascetic, whose relief portrait can be found on the facade of Harvard's Sanders Theater, was also the Bishop of Condom. His namesake, Lesgles/L'aigle/L'egle (de Meaux), is a bald law student/revolutionary in Victor Hugo's *Les Miserables* who loses all his property and land—"absolute clearance" once again.

In addition to the biblical quotations of "I put away childish things" and "It was for this I came . . . ," "Absolute Clearance" contains a dozen quoted lines that seem to be something like a bad translation of Lamartine's "La chute d'un ange" or one of Hugo's own eulogizing poems to Napoleon—it's hard to tell. One of the kinds of clearances we encounter, even in the age of Googling, is a loss of memory; without a recording, a voice fades away; without an image, we can barely remember what someone looked like. As Stuart Merrill's "Vers vague" claims: "ma mémoire est morte avec le crépuscule."

Indeed, the long history of portraiture indicates that the image of a person is meant to compensate for just such an absence: the eidolon or death mask at the entrance to the ancient house; the founding legend, recounted in Pliny's *Natural History,* of the Corinthian maid Dibutade tracing the shadow of her departing lover on the wall. But the history of self-portraiture points to a different structure: there must be a doubled presence for it to happen (a mirror before the advent of photography) and everything in the final form will be reversed.

Of most significance, and depending upon whether the artist is right- or left-handed, the hand observed will appear as the hand that is making. In Parmigianino's portrait, it is his right hand that protrudes hugely from the left side of the painting, and his left, hidden hand is the hand that is painting. "The game," "the architecture of the whole," doesn't exist until the making hand is out of the mirror.

Once we've read the book—that is, once we've read it at least once—it's impossible to keep the title poem in its final place. It seems to curve back to the very start of the work as a whole and affect everything in between. Within the poem, Ashbery variously considers the differences between an enclosed work of art like a static globe, an object of reflection; a processural work of art like a wave, forming and deforming in time and an object of contemplation and awe at once; and, finally, a sublime Shelleyan work of art, circling like a mad carousel or wind around the still center of the perceiver:

> . . . the turning seasons and the thoughts
> That peel off and fly away at breathless speeds
> Like the last stubborn leaves ripped
> From wet branches? I see in this only the chaos
> Of your round mirror which organizes everything
> Around the polestar of your eyes which are empty,
> Know nothing, dream but reveal nothing.
> I feel the carousel starting slowly
> And going faster and faster: desk, papers, books,
> Photographs of friends, the window and the trees
> Merging in one neutral band that surrounds
> Me on all sides, everywhere I look.

Sublime agitation, which here arises out of the contemplation of the stillness of the Parmigianino self-portrait, results not in exaltation, but in leveling, for the eye can't follow the speed of the world's motion.

Already in this poem of the early seventies we find Ashbery's enduring preoccupations with two phenomena that will recur later in his work: the children's game of Chinese whispers ("the game where / A whispered phrase passed around the room / Ends up as something completely different. / It is the principle that makes works of art so unlike / What the artist intended.") and the form of a wave. In "Self-Portrait," he describes "a wave breaking on a rock, giving up / Its shape in a gesture which expresses that shape." In "Self-Portrait," the wave metamorphoses into an image of the body, the "bulla" of later metaphysical poetry. A recurring symbol of the fragility of existence, the watery bubble of physical form contains the "sequestered" soul and the image of the soul visible in Parmigianino's painting. The form is repeated in the convex mirror itself and in a balloon that "pops" at the first stanza break. Later it is seen "riding at anchor" as a simile for Parmigianino's depicted face and the face of the poet who keeps consulting a mirror. At the end of the poem, it is the city, New York City, viewed as "the gibbous /

Mirrored eye of an insect." Ashbery draws a contrast at this point between the englobed view and narrative "action" that has "the cold, syrupy flow / Of a pageant." And yet the wave remains a dream of a forming, unforming work of art that somehow reflects "le temps," both weather and time as forces of the unexpected and contingent. The poem represents the anamorphic transformation between things in their manifestations and our temporary, temporalizing grasp of them. And of course the long ekphrastic tradition, from Homer to Lessing, makes the relation between the poet and the visual artist a central example of this distantiating transformation.

The poem begins with Parmigianino himself as interlocutor, and by its end, the speaker says to him, "Therefore I beseech you, withdraw that hand." The poet calls upon the painter, imploring him, and then holds him at a distance, as one holds up a painting at the distance of an arm to see it as a whole. Meanwhile, to make a self-portrait, the painter cannot remain only a viewer and the sitter cannot remain passive, for they are one and the same; the artist must reflect, make, and judge. And it's necessary to look in two directions, a steady saccadic oscillation. Most self-portraits are at least slightly three-quarter and there is something of the same geometry at work in *Self-Portrait:* the 552-line title poem is a little less than a third of the length of the rest of the book.

The painted or drawn self-portrait is a staple of Renaissance art making, whether the painter is searching his or her own eyes for images of the soul's infinitely receding gleam or demonstrating a witty level of skill that collapses the differences between existence and making. But the ekphrastic self-portrait seems to be, surprisingly enough, a late-twentieth-century form. Practiced unself-consciously, it seems indicative of the narcissism of our era: the poet sees a reification of himself or herself in every prospect.

In *Self-Portrait in a Convex Mirror* and its title poem, however, something of the reverse is true, for the practice is both self-conscious and self-examining—and the poet is absorbed by a persistent inquiry into the conventions of representation. Being in the mirror is more than an exercise; it's a matter of life and death; existence is sustained and given significance only by a view from outside; we are unable to move without imagining a totalized self, pulled together by a frame. And to see one's self as a thing among things and attempt to animate one's self speaks to a difficult and risky tautology. The tain of the mirror is evidence of both the shallowness of material reality and its resistance, while the open eyes testify to the depth of phenomenal experience when studied in time. The book's strongest moment of self-recognition comes in the startlingly simple and direct "Fear of Death": "What is it now with me / And is it as I have become? / Is there no state free from the boundary lines / Of before and after? . . ."

Self-Portrait as a whole is preoccupied particularly with such issues as the significance of detail and the related issues of perception's dependence upon recognition. These problems are indistinguishable from questions of expression and self-knowledge, for to be able to describe one's self in material form does not necessarily lead to heightened meaning, and the perception of the physical self is as dependent upon conventions of apprehending persons as it is conducive to any forms of self-knowledge.

If there are few titular self-portraits in the history of poetry, perhaps that is because the form is everywhere in the lyric expression of the first person. In *Self-Portrait,* the first person is placed systematically within a triangle whose other points are "you" and "they"—occasionally a "she" or "he" appears, but rarely. In the title poem the speaker plaintively says, "But it is certain that / What is beautiful seems so only in relation to a specific / Life, experienced or not, channeled in some form / Steeped in the nostalgia of a collective past."

A list, in sequence, of first-person references in the book yields: "I tried," "I felt," "I thought," "I'll claim to you," "I've tried," "I thought," "I've been looking," "I look away," "I put away childish things," "I mean," "I cannot decide," "I haven't done it," "I have seen nothing," "I haven't won it," "I let," "I backed away," "I think of it," "I have other things to think about," "I think," "Am I myself?" "I woke," "I was thinking," "I would like to enroll," "I remember," "I think," "I feel," "I say," "I cannot answer," "I know," "I can see," "I just see," "I want," "I caught," "I spoke," "I think," "I have become attracted," "I read," "I'm always tempted," "I really would like to know," "I am not offended," "I like," "I wonder," "I have already forgotten," "I walked out," "I braid," "I tell you," "I find," "I guess I would pick," "I saw," "I will not," "I do not think," "I have become," "I've brought," "I want," "I am coming out," "I write," "I vowed," "I'll explain," "I feel," "I was wearing," "I received," "I already owe," "I write," "I imagine," "I don't know," "I feel," "I like," "I know," "I'm lost," "I want to go back," "I was turning to say something," "I mean," "I tell you," "I beg you," "I think," "I cannot explain," "I can know," "I start to forget,"

"I mean," "I saw," "I have known," "I go on consulting," "I used to think," "I think," "I know," and "I beseech you."

These are verbs of consciousness—thinking, feeling, knowing, judging, perceiving, deciding. There is a promise in the past "I vowed," and the imploring final appeal we heard earlier, made to the image of a dead man—Parmigianino himself. The poems do not all have an "I"—just as frequently a "you" appears, and, as often as not, this "you" is someone talking to himself about himself, not a "you" as other. We're all pilgrims to Walsingham asking about our "true love[s]."

When there is an "I," it usually appears in the middle of the poem, as if it takes a while to come to consciousness and then it takes a while to leave it. Even so, Ashbery makes it difficult to draw conclusions about the first person and its desires:

> The body is what this is all about and it disperses
> In sheeted fragments, all somewhere around
> But difficult to read correctly since there is
> No common vantage point, no point of view
> Like the "I" in a novel. And in truth
> No one never saw the point of any . . .

If "no one never saw the point," then everyone did see it in one way or another, and it often enough seems to be sex, or some other irreducible drive or motive: ". . . just exactly / What sex is. When people speak of it / As happens increasingly, are they always / Referring to the kind where sexual organs are brought in— / Diffident, vague, hard to imagine as they are to a blind person? / I find that thinking these things divides us, / Brings us together . . ." As for expression, there's always "Grand Galop": "Puaagh. Vomit. Puaaaaagh. More vomit."

Why does it often seem possible, even if unlikely, that any lines in an Ashbery poem could be used to account for the entire poem? And why does it equally seem as if it is impossible, even if tempting, to cite any particular line or lines without citing them all—reproducing the poem in its entirety as the best spokesperson for itself?

Here are the last lines to "Scheherazade": "Although the arithmetic is incorrect / The balance is restored because it / Balances, knowing it prevails, / And the man who made the same mistake twice is exonerated." We could say that this passage refers to the tipped scales of the book, with its majesterial, quantifiably greater, final poem. Or it could have a local meaning in relation to the title, referring to the 1 that makes 1001 both a palindrome and a kind of justice—the triumph of the single wit, the heroine who changed the pattern. Even so, to say the poem is "about" Scheherazade is a stretch. Meanwhile, this same poem suggests, "Between these extremes the others muddle through / Like us, uncertain but wearing artlessly / Their function of minor characters who must / Be kept in mind . . ."

Why "must" they be kept in mind? Because every minor character, every mark, every word, every sound, must be "there" or "here" in a work of art—or it is not a work of art, a "whole." Minor characters could turn out to be important in themselves, but, more likely, they are there so we can tell who the major characters are. And vice versa. Until the perspective of the whole coheres (as poetic form, as plot, as history narrated), detail is democratic—or just a blur.

This is not an inference, but a "topic" in the sense of recurring topoi or places in *Self-Portrait.* "Grand Galop"—a poem in part about making poems, in part about how ". . . minor eras / Take on an importance out of all proportion to the story /"—is its most extensive discussion. Beginning "All things seem mention of themselves / And the names which stem from them branch out to other referents," the poem weaves together passages of description and meditation.

> As long as one has some sense that each thing knows its place
> All is well, but with the arrival and departure
> Of each new one overlapping so intensely in the semi-darkness
> It's a bit mad. Too bad, I mean, that getting to know each other
> just for a fleeting second
> Must be replaced by imperfect knowledge of the featureless
> whole . . .

These lines are a fairly good description of John Locke's definition of a person—personhood is constituted by overlapping memories. And indeed one way of reading *Self-Portrait* is to read the memories it contains as commencing at an ur-moment, recorded far into the closing title poem, of the encounter of two poets, Ashbery and Pierre Martory, with the Parmigianino self-portrait in Vienna in the summer of 1959. But there also seem to be random memories reaching back to Ashbery's childhood, or someone's: "Hop o' my Thumb"'s fairy-tale title and undatable resortlike world; "Robin Hood's Barn," with its claim: "your young years become a clay / Out of which the older, more rounder and also brusquer / Retort is fashioned, the greeting / That takes you into night." There is also the noir imagery of "Forties Flick."

And a cyclical structure of seasons is at work in the book as a whole: it begins at the onset of midsummer; it's spring in "Grand Galop," the scene of writing; then early spring in "Voyage in the Blue"; March in "The Tomb of Stuart Merrill"; there are ploughed fields in "Ode to Bill" and "Lithuanian Dance Band"; and a stubble field in "No Way of Knowing"; snow in "Suite"; and then April sunlight at the end of "Self-Portrait."

For Locke the continuity of consciousness is not a problem. A relation to the point of view of others is not particularly relevant and the continuity of consciousness is simply assumed. In contrast, Ashbery writes:

> I not only have my own history to worry about
> But am forced to fret over insufficient details related to large
> Unfinished concepts that can never bring themselves to the point
> Of being, with or without my help, if any were forthcoming

As in the Walsingham/New York State poem, we are not so much invited to read in terms of the poet's biography, as to see the ways in which a look into any painting or place is a matter of transposition and infinite reflections, like the glimmer of the museum room and its viewers in the glass on a painting's surface. We are asked to project the "logarithm" of New York in (19)72 as a distorted mirror of Rome around the time of its (15)27 sack; to project Oslo [Norway] in "Oslo, France, that is"; to imagine analogies between American things that have disappeared in time ("garters and union suit buttons"; "old-fashioned plaids"; "a lattice-work crust") and the precisely rendered details of Parmigianino's unchanging "eyebeams, muslin, coral"— "things as they are today" not only because they have found a lodging place in an immortal work of art, but also because their essences exist in the present as they did in the sixteenth century.

The poems of *Self-Portrait* are not only concerned conceptually with these questions of time and space and identity; they also illustrate the odd ways we talk about particulars and generalities:

> . . . an old, mostly invisible
> Photograph of what seems to be girls lounging around
> An old fighter bomber, circa 1942 vintage.
> How to explain to these girls, if indeed that's what they are,
> These Ruths, Lindas, Pats, and Sheilas
> About the vast change that's taken place
> In the fabric of our society? . . .

Ticks of speech and perception abound here: the repetition of "old" for something dating to "just" thirty-five years before the publication of the book, and so artlessly (only a poet wanting to recede into ordinary speech would repeat a word in such proximity, and especially such a banal one); the use of "seems" instead of "seem" so that "girls" implies some singular entity (what's that? it's *girls,* as if it were a stain or a fingerprint on the photograph itself); and then the animation of the image: to explain ourselves to it becomes the task. Somehow this image that can't even be read falls into place, if "indeed that's what they are" is a list of women's names that no longer seem to exist. In other words, not only have the women disappeared, along with their specific names, but also the names as names. In "All and Some," a speaker says, "Do you remember how we used to gather / The woodruff, the woodruff? But all things / Cannot be emblazoned, but surely many / Can . . ." "All cannot, but many can" becomes the motto of the poem. Who has either a practice or song about gathering woodruff, the central (and mind-altering) ingredient in May wine, as we say, "emblazoned" on her memory? The end of the poem suggests that "the work gets completed in a dream."

To destroy the hierarchical relation between parts and whole is characteristic of art both before and after single-point perspective. To say this is also to acknowledge that a plotless world is one without a God. This is the existential possibility of Renaissance humanism, left to find its own scale if man is the measure of all things. A task of *epideixis* and self-portraiture remains an unfinished project: "To try to write poetry / Using what Wyatt and Surrey left around, / Took up and put down again / Like so much gorgeous raw material / As though it would always happen in some way / And meanwhile since we are all advancing / It is sure to come about in spite of everything."

It's not so difficult to find principles here, but it may be that the description is the principle. It's master/servant all over again and if we're advancing in that Hegelian way, it will "come about" that poetry is the last of all artworks to be abandoned, but it will be abandoned. Even so, Ashbery gives Heidegger, who reversely traded philosophy for poetry, a later word in an idyllic answer to the problem of failed theories:

> . . . Why must you go? Why can't you
> Spend the night, here in my bed, with my arms wrapped tightly
> around you?
> Surely that would solve everything by supplying
> A theory of knowledge on a scale with the gigantic
> Bits and pieces of knowledge we have retained:
> An LP record of all your favorite friendships,
> Of letters from the front? Too
> Fantastic to make sense? But it made the chimes ring.
> If you listen you can hear them ringing still;
> A mood, a Stimmung, adding up to a sense of what they really
> were,
> All along, through the chain of lengthening days.

The Heideggerian notion of "*stimmung*" or atunement appears in *Self-Portrait* not so much as a harmony between the subject and the environment, but as a relation that can at once support and withdraw significance. Atunement in the Heideggerian sense becomes problematic as *stimmung* can fade like light or music. *Techne,* the classical Greek word for know-how that also frequently recurs in Heidegger's writing, here becomes the maker's skill carried over despite the fading of the individual works in time: "The gray glaze of the past attacks all know-how; / Secrets of wash and finish that took a lifetime / To learn and are reduced to the status of / Black-and-white illustrations in a book where colorplates / Are rare. That is, all time / Reduces to no special time."

Before there were modernist distortions there were mannerist distortions and Ashbery introduces them directly as a metaphor for lived experience in "Lithuanian Dance Band": "Perhaps another day one will want to review all this / For today it looks compressed like lines packed together / In one of those pictures you reflect with a polished tube, / To get the full effect and this is possible . . ." This little reference evokes yet another aspect of seventeenth-century culture, the practice of anamorphic art by the members of the Christian order of the Minims, who lived in a convent on the Rue des Tournelles in Paris and in Rome at Santa Trinità dei Monti—those mathematicians, most famously Jean-François Niceron and Emanuel Maignan, who worked through the calculations that would dirempt surface and depth, making the realization of the image a temporal experience. Their frescoes and easel paintings depend on geometrical projections that shift the viewer between center and periphery—either by moving her in physical space, as had been the case with the skull anamorphism of Holbein's *Ambassadors* of 1533, or by applying a mirroring tube or other device.

The mannerists' revolt against the perspective theories of the quattrocento reclaimed the objectivity of space with an eye to what it was: the rationalized projection of an ego. But why stop with the rational? Why not draw the line along farther in the direction of desire and multiplicity? Isn't distortion in truth, if not in fact, the manifestation of the will and its desires? In his 1973 seminar on anamorphosis, Jacques Lacan would famously ask why no one had ever connected an anamorphic image with an erection. An anamorphosis is like the dawning of desire in the subject, and the dawning of desire happens anamorphically:

> So there is whirling out at you from the not deep
> Emptiness the word "cock" or some other, brother and
> sister words
> With not much to be expected from them, though these
> Are the ones that waited so long for you and finally left,
> having given up hope.
> There is a note of desperation in one's voice, pleading for them,
> And meanwhile the intensity thins and sharpens
> Its point, that is the thing it was going to ask

If Hegel is parodied earlier, and Heidegger brought down to everyday pleasures later, here it's Freud's turn.

Yet to walk away from this book imagining its underlying architecture as "only" an expression of desire is to do a certain violence to the truth of experience ("experienced or not"). The allegory can be flipped the other way, so that "to be serious only about sex / Is perhaps one way," since "speaking up" about sex reveals how much sex is about everything else: "Each person / Has one big theory to explain the universe / But it doesn't tell the whole story / And in the end it is what is outside him / That matters, to him and especially to us / Who have been given no help whatever / In decoding our own man-size quotient and must rely / On second-hand knowledge." Meaning can be "sacked" in just this way, but after the sacking, the world still needs to be rebuilt in all its particulars.

Self-Portrait in a Convex Mirror is the kind of book you can read again and again, constantly churning your first-hand knowledge into second-hand knowledge, holding a pencil or a blue pen or a black pen in your hand over and over until just about every line has its underlining and every word is englobed, watching your own handwriting change over time, noticing your marginalia become deeper, then more superficial, then, if you're lucky, a little deeper for a time, the wave of your own history of reading washing over the pages and your sense of things not developing, but changing, turning into a better fit, a more capacious sense—which is, in the end, what we mean, I would guess, by style.

A Long Period of Adjustment Followed

Houseboat Days (1977)

Brenda Hillman

HOUSEBOAT DAYS WAS published in 1977 in the middle of a long period of adjustment. Saigon had fallen in 1975 (people being airlifted from the roof of the US Embassy). Jimmy Carter had been elected in 1976. The shah of Iran—put in place by the CIA—was about to be overthrown. After Watergate and Vietnam, there was a general mood of disillusionment about the role of official anything, very little "public mind" about alternatives to belief in the sanctity of government and state. The Cold War: still coldish but with hints of tepid. Charlie Chaplin died that year. Moscow tried to ban smoking in public places. There were *Days of Our Lives, All My Children, Ryan's Hope, Star Wars, All the President's Men, Saturday Night Fever.* The Eagles' *Hotel California* and The Sex Pistols. Derrida's *Of Grammatology* had become available in English.

Houseboat Days does not address these matters directly, but it enacts some of the adjustments, carrying forward the speculative forays of Ashbery's previous two books, especially *Self-Portrait in a Convex Mirror.* Sincerity is interrogated and affirmed, irony as a fact and feature of his postmodernism is interrogated and affirmed; his romance with beauty is brief, sexy, and sure, but the surest thing is the encompassing enterprise of accepting experience, whether it is strange grief or a luxuriant quotidian in which little is felt. The artist/musician, loving the abstract nature of making music in the streets, can "cradle this average violin that knows / Only forgotten showtunes" ("Street Musicians") and make notes on the contingencies of identity we live by.

The pieces in *Houseboat Days* build a case for—or maybe they present examples of—how thinking (sometimes quite anxious thinking) can be existentially meaningful if "you" mix it the right way—a way of being imaginatively in time—assortedly, as modernist mélange that assumes there is primarily the sensation of floating and shifting taking place beneath you. Value is to be found laterally, not vertically, the hierarchy of art as Art exchanged for a democratic acceptance of *sounds* that move through us. While the poems do not build the case for this democratic acceptance in a systematic way, they build the case by accretion—of charged details, and of meditative statements. Ashbery's inventions introduce new models of thought, yet his aesthetic "methods" can seem so mysteriously unmethodical that the reader who follows the pathless path is a little like Gretel walking with Hansel a long time while the sparrows are eating the crumbs they have sprinkled behind them.

Houseboat Days is not a book "project" but it is full of occasions for thinking about the tasks of poetry, and it reads at times like a series of ars poeticas, embodying motifs of music making and art making: ". . . each of the / Troubadours had something to say about how charity / Had run its race and won . . ." ("The Other Tradition") and of tentative connections: "The question has been asked / As though an immense natural bridge had been / Strung across the landscape to any point you wanted" ("On the Towpath"). This "natural bridge" is the syntax of the language, the landscape is anything taking place in time, and the houseboat is a rather gentle metaphor floating upon a small lake whose *genius loci* is the spirit of inclusion. John Ashbery has, by 1977, devised a method of litany that includes everything that is the case.

In the postavant poetic epoch, the work in that volume might usefully be reconsidered in relation to nineteenth-century romanticism. Ashbery's books ceaselessly rehearse some of the challenges of the romantic idiom in fresh ways, particularly Wordsworth's *Preface to Lyrical Ballads* and Whitman's "Introduction to *Leaves of Grass* 1855"—their dreams of democratic language; the idea that the poet speaks in the language of the time, in common tones, to people in many walks of life; that the poet is not a pontificator but a person among persons; that the meditative impulse is an act of gathering and making. The idea of "emotion recollected in tranquillity" is enacted in the calm intensity of Ashbery's boat.

In the folder for teaching *Houseboat Days* is this brief list: (1) the unpredictable tonal shifts of the sentences make ruptures in a smooth flow of expectation rather than in psychological buildup or in continuity or in who is saying them—they are the tones of movies, truisms, cultural fables, aphorisms, conversational digressions—all sorts of things that float houseboatishly along upon a general symbolizing impulse; (2) the syntax is thrifty, and makes for no wasted thought, even though it often proceeds by digressive tactics, discursiveness, and seemingly random collections of word objects;

(3) the tense shifts are secondarily important because they embody what Ashbery means to say feelingly about time, which isn't mystical, as it is for some poets, but is rather a shuttle between the temporary and the eternal; clearly, no continuous or monolithic narratives are put forth here; (4) as aesthetic force fields, the poems radically embody how so-called art and life interpenetrate (5) and make a philosophy—though the poet doesn't have one—unbounded by a single experience but creating a collective experience, so that (6) a poetic presence moves in relation to the temporary structure of the poem, meditating and making arrangements of the observed and the overheard.

With these things in mind, it might be instructive to consider a single poem, "Collective Dawns," as a representative primer for the whole collection. In this poet's art, the phrase is the example of the poem, the poem is the example of the book, the book stands for the world, and the world is, of course, the total case. All is synecdoche, metonym.

Here is the first third of "Collective Dawns":

> You can have whatever you want.
> Own it, I mean. In the sense
> Of twisting it to you, through long, spiraling afternoons.
> It has a sense beyond that meaning that was dropped there
> And left to rot. The glacier seems
>
> Impervious but is all shot through
> With amethyst and the loud, distraught notes of the cuckoo.
> They say the town is coming apart.
> And people go around with a fragment of a smile
> Missing from their faces. Life is getting cheaper
>
> In some senses. Over the tops of old hills
> The sunset jabs down, angled in a way it couldn't have
> Been before. The bird-sellers walk back into it.
> "We needn't fire their kilns; tonight is the epic
> Night of the world. Grettir is coming back to us.
> His severed hand has grabbed the short sword
> And jumped back into his wrist. . . ."

The title suggests this poem will collect new beginnings, and soon it becomes apparent that the collective quality is what makes any individual beginning possible: each sentence in the poem is an instance of dawn (though sunset enters twice), an envoy to a different enterprise. The first few sentences have, in effect, the earthy quality of adages, of sayings gleaned from experience; this "adage" quality is a tonal thread that will reappear throughout: "You can have whatever you want. / Own it, I mean. In the sense / Of twisting it to you, through long, spiraling afternoons. / It has a sense beyond that meaning that was dropped there / And left to rot." There are four sentence-like objects here, though actually there are only two sentences and two partial sentences. I have always thought this opening completely enchanting—it seems so like possibility and disappointment, the lightly qualified jaunty hope-and-withdrawal of feeling about unnamed circumstances that might get in the way of having actual life; the tone is matter-of-fact at the beginning, lilting in the middle, then a big plunk-down when the word "rot" arrives.

Who is the "You" at the outset of the poem? Not the Rilkean You, surely, nor a particular "you" or the "you" in the "substitute-first-person you" pronoun mode; rather, the reader might take it to be a collective "you" who is looking at all the dawns in all the poems, if he is a literary creature—or no one in particular, yet a particularizing presence. For this "you," sometimes a familiar, sometimes not, the poet will gather the voices, not in order to provide that single homogenizing voice; rather, the "you" will engage with the "long spiraling afternoons" that are beyond "meaning that was dropped," as the lyric singer in "Idea of Order at Key West" sings "beyond"—in a human act that makes human meaning of the adverb.

The changes of "it" in the first four sentences have a somewhat Wordsworthian meandering, deer-path sort of quality; the "it" in the second line is tied to "whatever," yet is necessarily indistinct—a pronoun replacing an indefinite pronoun. The second "it" leaks concreteness even more, and the third "it" seems meant to hold this indistinctness as calmly as possible while suggesting a generalizing presence. The same sort of shift happens with the two *thats* at the end of the second sentence. This indefinite concreteness is attenuated as long as possible in many sentences in *Houseboat Days.* Lines are meant to cut across the continuity of the long, spiraling afternoons and what is to come. I experience this as the diagonal slash of indistinct meaning—which for Dickinson (in "There's a certain Slant of light") causes terror, but for many twentieth-century poets is almost a homing device.

After the surprising "rot," the poem introduces a "glacier," and it is hard to ask anything other than "What glacier?" It is impossible to tell what this comes from; big chunks of ice somehow announce the incipience of the Kantian sublime, or at least some kind of awesome unapproachable reality. That the glacier is "shot through" with both amethyst and the sound of the cuckoo might seem overly cluttered were we not on this particular houseboat. Is this the entrance of the ideal coming up against its own breakdown into color and song? Ashbery's method in general balks against the ideal, yet the personae take on living in relation to an ideal—and fending it off—while not meanwhile holding the ideal in contempt; it is just no longer as useful as it was, as in "And *Ut Pictura Poesis* Is Her Name," a few poems later, where he suggests a distrust of ideal beauty is an important part of the life work of being modern: "You can't say it that way anymore. / Bothered about beauty you have to / Come out into the open, into a clearing, / And rest."

In any case, the collective "you" in this poem, which is elsewhere bewitched, bothered, and bewildered by beauty, has a demotic but proud relationship to other dawning sounds. The poem builds its collection of sentence-dawns as more tonal beginnings are added: the hearsay folk-sound observations of "They say the town is coming apart," and "People go around with a fragment of a smile / Missing from their faces." The first has the appeal of the basic American myth to undergird it: it's the sort of thing your average citizen would say to a neighbor in passing, while washing his car (not a hybrid), whereas the remark about the missing fragment has a portentous, oblique koanish paradoxical tonality at its heart—the expected statement would be "with the fragment of a smile / on their faces."

Thus the poem collects its linguistic dawn-objects; the reader might be moved to think about the way poets since the Romantics are either Platonists determined to be Platonists or hoping to be Aristotelians—or they are simply Aristotelians. Poets who write mostly in meditative structures, paratactically putting one thing after another—litanists, list makers, and taxonomists of the everyday—have the metonymic, Aristotelian impulse. Often it seems Ashbery's primary work is primarily that of Aristotelian taxonomy—the work of the collection that draws even on the eternal forms.

"Collective Dawns" moves through more tonalities even in these three opening stanzas: there are "scene-setting" devices, but they are, as are the other sentences, introductions to a story being told: "Life is getting cheaper / In some senses. Over the tops of old hills / The sunset jabs down, angled in a way it couldn't have / Been before"—bits of commentary and narrative before an aborted, surreally comic epic begins.

It's always been a little disconcerting when teaching this poem to come upon the Grettir moment. Because the whole passage is in quotes, it might be taken for a commentary on the Norse saga of Grettir or an actual quoted passage, but it is surely a wild Ashberyan device, and suddenly there is someone holding a sword; the severed hand jumping back into the sleeve seems to "fit right in" because it is horrifying, traditional, and average. In any case, the Grettir material, introduced with no cushion, seems very 1977, as the epic hero is told to "Wait by this / Mistletoe bush and you will get the feeling of really / Being out of the world and with it." The severed hand becomes the severed nature of expectation, in the sentences, in the phrases; the epic is carried on without one hand, as the poet announces the features of the poetic in the second half of the poem:

The old poems
In the book have changed value once again. Their black letter
Fools only themselves into ignoring their stiff, formal qualities,
and they move
Insatiably out of reach of bathos and the bad line
Into the weird ether of forgotten dismemberments. Was it
This rosebud? Who said that?
The time of all forgotten
Things is at hand.

Therefore I write you
This bread and butter letter, you my friend
Who saved me from the mill pond of chill doubt
As to my own viability, and from the proud village
Of bourgeois comfort and despair, the mirrored spectacles of grief.
Let who can take courage from the dawn's
Coming up with the same idiot solution under another guise
So that all meanings should be scrambled this way
No matter how important they were to the men
Coming in the future, since this is the way it has to happen
For all things under the shrinking light to change
And the pattern to follow them, unheeded, bargained for
As it too is absorbed. But the guesswork
Has been taken out of millions of nights. The gasworks
Know it and fall to the ground, though no doom

Says it through the long cool hours of rest
While it sleeps as it can, as in fact it must, for the man to
find himself.

As Blake posits alternative, constructed innocence that might continue reasserting itself, Ashbery's rereadings call innocence up—without metaphysics; old epic poems call for rereadings, reconsiderations of their values, their formal qualities, their lines. Our languages let us retrieve "dismemberments," this poem proposes, and the brief question "Was it / This rosebud?" seems a conversational fragment having to do with *Citizen Kane,* a movie about existential hope and disappointment, after which the poet brings back the severed hand in the form of a pun.

The rest of the poem calls for a kind of courage based on acceptance of radical shifts and uncertainties; the "I" has been engaged in nonstop beginnings, in the "proud village / Of bourgeois comfort and despair, the mirrored spectacles of grief." The reader is asked again to accept instability and uncertainty as a method (or, as the students would say, a "lifestyle"). In a multilayered, -textured vocabulary—"idiot solution" and "guise"—the collective project of timeless dawns continues to the end of the poem, continuously elusive. Meanings might have been important at one time but now they are "scrambled"; the "pattern" is perceived briefly after the fact.

An odd solvent of this long, lovely, somewhat exhausted admonishment at the end is the "shrinking" light; daylight is now crepuscular and "absorbed," which suggests (because of the one instance of the sunset in the third stanza) that the poem's temporal proposition—literary and otherwise—might look something like *dawn dawn dawn dusk dawn dawn dawn dawn dawn dawn dusk night.* The diurnal has been severely compressed, as if a galaxy retreated much faster at its edges. The ending has something of a nineteenth-century urban landscape, in which "the gasworks / Know it and fall to the ground, though no doom / Says it through the long cool hours of rest . . ." The collective self, found in the dreams of the age, cuts across tenses, tones, and types of sentences.

There are other poems in *Houseboat Days* that enact the motions of getting through the days, the average days, in a life with imagination, and there are other books by Ashbery that are as representative of his vision, but this particular vessel is as varied, as highly textured, hilarious, able to withstand disaster, beauty, and its loss, as real as any.

Ashbery's Theater

Three Plays (1978)

Kevin Killian

For poets of Ashbery's generation the theater might have been a place not only of community, but a site where one might be more dour than in one's "poetry," try on the tragic mask and really go for it, check one's irony with one's hat and coat. To celebrate her eightieth birthday San Francisco Poets Theater revived Barbara Guest's play, *The Office,* in San Francisco, and even she was surprised, reading it for the first time in forty years, at how dark the thing was. Backstage an actor whispered, "This is some heavy shit," for what we were playing out was an allegory of Calvary, fifties style, than which was anything bleaker? Secretaries out of *The Best of Everything*—i.e., *total slaves to capitalism*—unbinding their hair to wash the feet of their (inevitably male) bosses. No one had a name, so the bosses were X, Y, and Z—like the two thieves, crucified too, on either side of the Cross. My actors couldn't remember which of us was supposed to be X, which Y, and which Z. On top of which the female characters were "Girl One," "Girl Two," etc. Guest's *The Office* was a product of the age of Ingmar Bergman, and by extension of Kierkegaard, and something of that Lutheran edge showed up on poets' stages.

Ashbery's one-act *The Heroes* (written 1950) has some of this glum awareness, though mediated by a sense of wonder in which, as Theseus postulates, Dada may still be alive. Ashbery brings the heroes of Greek legend into Philip Barry's world, a country house by the sea where they sit around speaking of failure in the half-ironic tones of the comedy of manners. The poet's fascination with the well-made play, the melodrama of Scribe and Sardou, the comedy of Wilde, Maugham, Coward, and Terence Rattigan is in itself a wondrous thing, for in effect the avant-garde serves as a sort of aspic that preserves the high bourgeois, and in effect homosexual, constructions of the past. Its laughs come from the conflation of Circe's girdle, that legendary garb of enchantment, with the sorts of girdles ladies wore in the postwar period, garments of constriction and enclosure. I can imagine Martha Rosler watching a production of *The Heroes* and getting ideas for a whole new body of work—art protesting the girdle, and, above all, men's mixed-up fantasies about it.

To mark the 1978 publication of *Three Plays,* Ashbery gave an interview to Roger Oliver regarding his dramatic ambitions and the shape of his theater career. The interview, published in the Winter 1979 issue of *Performing Arts Journal,* is illuminating in spots, though Ashbery often gives the sorts of answers that leave interviewers wishing they had taken up plumbing instead of journalism. "Well, as you know, that is a terribly long time ago and I don't really remember that much about it." As if sensing Oliver's disappointment, he adds, using the syllepsis for which he attained renown, "If I had known I was going to amount to something, I would have taken notes as well as a lot of precautions."

The comedy's the girdle in *The Heroes,* but the tragedy happens when a policeman breaks up a private dancing party in which two men are dancing together. Afterward, one of them—Patroclus, in fact—dies, apparently of guilt, the good old days of homosexual panic. "This was 1952," Ashbery recalled, "when two men dancing together on stage could easily be considered scandalous." A few years later, hoping to break into the Cambridge–New York Poets Theater cabal, Jack Spicer created his own take on Achilles and Patroclus in his full-length *Troilus,* a very different kettle of fish than *The Heroes,* but with a similar defiant garb of gay identity. Spicer's lover-heroes lounge around outside the gates of Troy in brightly colored swim trunks, as smartly, as anachronistically, as Ashbery's. The more I think on it, the more convinced I am that Spicer at least knew of *The Heroes* and perhaps had a script in hand when he sat down to write his *Troilus.* Not only does Spicer reproduce the "scandalous" scene of two men dancing together on stage, one of them Patroclus, but both playwrights contrive to show Patroclus dancing *with a man other than Achilles*—for Ashbery, Theseus, for Spicer, Thersites. It could be argued that otherwise the scenes are very different, that Ashbery's Patroclus is coming on heavily to Theseus, in baby-doll vamp fashion ("Oh, Theseus, mayn't I sleep at the foot of your bed tonight, like a pet spaniel? I promise I'll lie still as a mummy") while the Patroclus-Thersites dance in *Troilus* is all about situational homosexuality, a parody of a mysterious "real thing," like the soldiers dancing with each other in John Ford's cavalry trilogy. Well, I suppose no matter how you situate A & P onto a modern stage, they're going to provoke, and audiences will stroke their chins, having divined that you're making a point of some kind. If Ashbery was going to foster a homosexual stage revolution, he was going to have to go another route.

If *The Heroes* is informed by stagecraft, *The Compromise* (written 1955) is all about the movies and, if I'm not mistaken, all about Frank O'Hara. Ashbery told Roger Oliver that he took the plot of a silent 1923 Rin Tin Tin feature (*Where the North Begins*) and rewrote it, cutting the famous rescue dog right out of the story. What remains activates what's left of the narrative strands, which collapse about an empty center once the hero is removed. Or so you'd think. Oddly enough the play betrays no such Oulipean rip, the playwright has patched his plot pretty skillfully, and the pastiche of an early de Mille or Lewis Milestone or Rex Ingram is a good one. (As it happens, the original *Where the North Begins* was edited by Milestone himself.) Set largely in the Canadian wilderness, *The Compromise* focuses on a few flawed individuals, each trying to overcome a bad hand of fate. Margaret Reynolds, a white wife and mother on the frontier, fears she is losing her beloved Mountie husband, Harry, for his mission has kept him from home for over a year. Like Penelope, she is pressed by suitors who urge her to ditch the absent captain, the father of her infant son, Baby Jim. Her Indian maid, Mooka, is torn between the love of no-good scalawag Lucky Seven and her duty to Margaret, her "white missus." The richest man in town, Sam Dexter, has already killed his partner, and now he will do anything, including disposing of Baby Jim, in order to make Margaret his own, hiding his malignity behind a glad-handing bonhomie.

The elephant in the room is the speeches, marked by the crazy ethnic signifiers Ashbery gives all his minority characters. In Ashbery's theater—and this is perhaps its most salient attribute—if you're not white for some reason, your dialect is strange, amusing, disconcerting, wrong. The first three speeches of Mooka, the "Reynolds' Indian maidservant," are identical to each other, brief, to the point: as her mistress prattles on about Baby Jim's good looks, Mooka merely mutters, "Ugh." Looked at another way, of course, Ashbery is satirizing the stage Chinaman, the Max Brand brand of Indian, the minstrel show, the stereotypes of popular culture. Still, there's just so much poetry you can eke out of substituting objective form for the subjective when the Indians mangle their pronouns and drop all of the white man's articles. "Now gather round. Me have story to tell."

Like every other character in *The Compromise,* the chief of the tribe is nursing a heavy secret. As his tribe finds more and more misery, he attends to the long-ago prophecy that a white baby will be born to one of his squaws, and that this baby will lead the tribe back to prosperity. When such a baby is displayed to him, he recognizes the infant as Baby Jim, but colludes with the lie in order to give his tribe hope, and keeps Jim for five years away from Margaret. That the turn of the play hangs on an Indian prophecy of a white baby messiah has effectively kept *The Compromise* off the stage these past fifty years.

In the play's last moments, with Margaret seemingly unable to decide between two kinds of men, the playwright himself enters the stage to examine his own inability to end things. He has listened to his characters, cries "John Ashbery," in a Gethsemane of self-examination, but can't hear their voices. Ashbery told Roger Oliver that he had lifted some of the dialogue for *The Compromise* from the intertitles of *Where the North Begins.* Like a good scholar, I finally sat down this spring to document these borrowings from a boot DVD of *Where the North Begins,* and, with my trigger finger on the Pause button, I wrote down every word in the titles. I'm happy to report that I found two instances of such "borrowing," and also that there may be more I was just too weary to catch, so as an appendix I offer my transcription of *Where the North Begins,* a known Ashbery source, and, possibly, the Rosetta Stone of his stagework.

The film begins with a snow-covered Canadian wilderness, over which a dogsled packed with cargo, pulled by a pack of frisky hounds, bumps and twists over a mountainous pass. Baby Rin Tin Tin is in a basket, part of the cargo making its way north for a new career as a puppy pet (soon to be dramatically changed when a pack of wolves attack the sled and make off with Rinty). At 2.48 the title explains,

In the observation car travels a tiny immigrant,
bound for the trading post of Caribou—
Little knowing what Fate holds in store for him.

In the play, the dog becomes a human baby. "Gather round," intones the chief. "Me have little story to tell. Five years ago, one starless winter night, a baby was stolen from a cabin near here. As a dog sled whizzed over the trail from Caribou to Elk City, a tiny immigrant rode in the observation car." Now that's a pretty close parallel, right down to the joke about the "observation car." I wonder, how was

Ashbery able to remember what the titles were in this old movie, which had been made before he was born? It was 1950—could he have seen it on TV? At a revival house? Had he his little steno pad in the movie theater or did he just write it down on his palm the way you or I might jot down a hot phone number? My second example isn't as good. As the silhouettes of the lupine pack pause and howl, a dramatic card fills the black screen at 3.42:

Timber wolves!

Ashbery adds two tons of camp to the simplicity of the title, when Margaret complains to the sympathetic Indians of Captain Harry's long absence. "Nobody knows how I've suffered all these months! Spring passed, and summer, and autumn with red leaves. And now winter sits on my heart, as it did the day he went away. Oh frozen mountain streams! barren crags! wolves of the wild timber! None of you is so cold, so cynical as my husband's heart." Maybe it isn't really camp talking, but Puccini, for *The Compromise* sometimes feels like *La Fanciulla del West* rather than Rin Tin Tin.

Like *The Compromise,* and like Frank O'Hara's poem "To the Film Industry in Crisis," *The Philosopher* (written 1960) mashes up two decades' worth of movie clichés, posing as an "Old Dark House" thriller but stretching to include remnants of other Hollywood plots of the 1930s and 1940s.

Ingenue Carol and her aunt Emily are guests at the Hudson River mansion of Jeremiah, their eccentric, now deceased uncle, gathered together with other heirs at Christmas for the reading of his will. Ashbery told Roger Oliver that he was pastiching such films as *The Cat and the Canary* (silent version) and the 1940 monogram programmer *Who Killed Aunt Maggie?* Carol strolls through Jeremiah's library, pulling books at random off the shelf: *Secrets of the Beyond, The Egyptian Book of the Dead,* when a masked figure slips out of a massive mummy case and attempts to strangle her. Her screams attract the attention of the other heirs, who rush in, foiling the intruder's plans to filch the black stone that Carol has worn around her neck since she became an orphan.

A strangely languid, yet menacing professor, Whitney Ambleside, hovers around, speaking in the twilit, "poetic" accents of, say, Clifton Webb, George Sanders, maybe Vincent Price in his Preminger period.

As we learn, Ambleside is obsessed with the secrets of eternal life—secrets the Egyptians knew. At this point the play becomes a debate about democracy versus the hermetic. If the secrets of the universe were known to only a few, wouldn't that really be better? Or would that be against everything our country stands for?

For comic relief Ashbery brings in a pair of lower-class heirs, an Irish boxer called Rocky (think Jimmy Cagney) and his burlesque-queen sweetheart, Gloria, the Mae West–Joan Blondell type beloved of thirties movies—sexually active, self-aware, sarcastic, warmhearted. "Gloria," or at any rate her archetype, had previously appeared in *The Compromise,* as a chanteuse who makes the best of the Canadian prairie by marrying the chief. There she even had her own musical number, a plangent ballad, "Dreamin' bout a Single Girl."

The pool of funny dialects widens in the decade between *The Heroes* and *The Philosopher,* and mangled Indian speech morphs into the surrealist, sassy banter of kindly black servants "Lily and Napoleon" and the lisping intimacies of a slinky Eurasian beauty, "Soo Lin." "Soo Lin's one wish," she coos, "to buy contlolling intelest in hand laundly and use plofits to take voyage to Hong Kong to see old home, old fliends." Chinese whispers indeed! The play ends abruptly—Ashbery tells Roger Oliver that he had intended the play to segue from tidy thriller into Pirandello hall of mirrors, but just didn't get around to it. Insofar as it feels unfinished, *The Philosopher* lends the book it appears in a lopsided feeling of accomplishment deferred. Had he continued developing this vein, Ashbery's theater might have exploded: right around the corner of the 1960s came the great age of burlesque, Ronald Tavel's screenplays for Andy Warhol, the notorious San Francisco drag troupes called the Cockettes and the Angels of Light, the seamy glamor of Jack Smith's films, and those of George Kuchar, Joe Orton's London-based plays and novels in which camp attains real menace, Charles Ludlam's abject, glorious "Theater of the Ridiculous," the present-day pastiche smorgasbord of Charles Busch, all of which take the directions usefully laid out by Ashbery and tweak them to a new place.

Sketching a history of Poets Theater would be a mammoth task but luckily there's John Ashbery, around whom most things organize themselves like that jar in Tennessee. It's a mystery why there was so much Poets Theater during the 1940s and 1950s, and I sometimes wonder if the number of plays written and performed by poets had its parallel in the rise of the poetry reading, so that poetry could once more return its roots to the social. Reading Alison Lurie's introduction to her edition of V. R. Lang's poems and plays, one understands that the Poets Theater of Cambridge came about due to the plethora of rich eccentrics thick on the ground in that time and place. But I think there's rather more to it. Who knows, this special issue of *Conjunctions* might reveal that the shape of Ashbery's career has been marked by a retreat from Poets Theater, a corrective to a beginning so ambitious he had to go elsewhere just to cool down, rather than a move toward a vatic, oracular, Emersonian wisdom.

NOTE. For a complete listing of the intertitles from *Where the North Begins* compiled by Kevin Killian, please visit www.conjunctions.com.

What We Know as We Know It: Reading "Litany" with JA

As We Know (1979)

Ann Lauterbach

> *The truth of an idea is not a stagnant property inherent in it. Truth happens to an idea. It becomes true, is made true by events.*
>
> *To copy a reality is, indeed, one very important way of agreeing with it, but it is far from being essential. The essential thing is the process of being guided.*
>
> —William James
> "Pragmatism's Conception of Truth"

1.

IT HAS LONG BEEN my contention, or suspicion, or just unverified hunch, that John Ashbery (like Gertrude Stein) has had some relation to William James and American pragmatism. Ashbery's reluctance to make any statement or declaration that does not appear to arrive and disappear on the heels of his miraculous syntax seems to me evidence of the kind of conceptual relativity that James first enunciated in the early years of the twentieth century. Ashbery's joyous investment in a present reality as being inimical to what James called "copying" is further evidence: Ashberian poetics insists on the multidimensionality of time-space duration, as opposed to either pictorial mimesis or the cause-and-effect order of conventional, developmental narration: reality, for Ashbery, has neither linearity nor *replica.* Connections among thinking and feeling, knowing and doing are always in flux.

The light that was shadowed then
Was seen to be our lives,
Everything about us that love might wish to examine,
Then put away for a certain length of time, until
The whole is to be reviewed, and we turned toward each other.
The way we had come was all we could see

And it crept up on us, embarrassed
That there is so much to tell now, really now.
—"As We Know"

An idea I had talked about
Became the things I do.
—"Five Pedantic Pieces"

We must first trick the idea
Into being, then dismantle it,
Scattering the pieces on the wind,
So that the old joy, modest as cake, as wine and friendship
Will stay with us at the last, backed by the night
Whose ruse gave it our final meaning.
—"Flowering Death"

The difficulty with that is
I no longer have any metaphysical reasons
For doing the things I do.
Night formulates, the rest is up to the scribes and the
eunuchs.
—"The Preludes"

2.

As We Know, John Ashbery's eighth book, was published in 1979. It has a unique, horizontal shape, associated in the visual arts with landscape (as the vertical is with portraiture). Indeed, the book's jacket art, by the Renaissance Dutch painter Pietre Jansz Saenredam (1597–1665), features a scene, "St. Mary's Square and St. Mary's Church, Utrecht." In muted, evening tones of ochre and pale blue, a few persons gathered here and there, the painting depicts the large stone church at the right, a clocktower, and a second church spire rising behind it into the veiled, cloud-studded sky.

This ecclesiastical subject matter might have given prospective readers a clue to the book's contents. Indeed, as we now know, the reason for the eccentric landscape format was to accommodate "Litany," a long poem in three parts for two voices, meant, as the Author's Note tells us, "to be read as simultaneous but independent monologues." Of the book's 118 pages, sixty-eight belong to "Litany."

A litany, in liturgical ceremonies, is a form of prayer that usually involves invocations or supplications by the preacher, followed by fixed responses from the congregation. In common usage, the word has come to mean any list, enumeration, or prolonged account—"the whole litany of complaint."

The Greek root of the word is *litaneia,* an entreaty.

3.

The little black cassette is lost; I have looked for it everywhere. The sound was beginning to deteriorate, the voices stretched into slow motion. I played it often at the end of a term for my students as a kind of gift, since unless you hear "Litany" you cannot really know, or have, it. After it was first recorded, I would play it at night, with the lights out, as a fantastic lullaby: my own voice merging and diverging from his, his from mine, two uttering instruments playing in tandem. The musical analogy is obvious. Indeed, in a recent e-mail to me Ashbery wrote, "Elliott Carter's *Duo for Violin and Piano* was an influence on 'Litany.' I heard it performed at Cooper Union (the premiere, I think). For that performance the violinist was at one end of the stage and the piano at the other, emphasizing the separateness of the two parts. I don't believe I was conscious of this as an influence at the time I wrote 'Litany.' Only afterwards did it dawn on me that the music doubtless affected the poem."

We went north one day on Amtrak to Saratoga Springs, New York. I was extremely tired, I remember, having had too much wine the night before and not enough sleep. Although John and I had already performed part of "Litany" at a bar on lower University Place in Manhattan, I had never read the whole poem: he gave me a copy of it to read on the train. I seem to recall it was in manuscript form, or perhaps galleys, so maybe the book had not yet been published. We were headed up to ZBS recording studios. ZBS stands for "Zero Bull Shit." Sited on a forty-five-acre farm in Fort Edward, New York, it was founded in 1970 in the midst of the counterculture, "to support alternative radio and audio production, creation, inspiration, good vibes, and self-development." Artists were to be invited for residences. If you Google it, you will find a lot of interesting information, but nowhere will you find reference to John Ashbery and Ann Lauterbach recording "Litany." Perhaps I dreamed it up.

4.

We were situated across from each other at a small high table, with two microphones. It was later that same day, after some tea and a chat with the recording engineer. Ready, set, go.

He read:

For someone like me
The simplest things
Like having toast or
Going to church are
Kept in one place.

I read:

So this must be a hole
Of cloud
Mandate or trap
But haze that casts
The milk of enchantment

The first stanza, five lines each. Voice One, "someone like me," is in a direct, "simple" relation to things as they are; his world is "kept in one place." Voice Two is in a more ambiguous setting; she is in a "milk of enchantment" that involves holes, hazes, traps, mandates, clouds, which is cast, in the following stanza "over the whole town."

In the second stanza, the tonal clarity of the first voice proceeds, as does the miasma of the second. But two new formal elements appear. Two words, *town* and *knowledge,* migrate across the two voices; also, the first of a number of isolations or singularities occurs.

Voice One:

Like having wine and cheese.
The parents of the *town*
Pissing elegantly escape *knowledge*
Once and for all. The
Snapdragons consumed in a wind
Of fire and rage far over
The streets as they end.

Voice Two:

> Over the whole *town*,
> Its scenery, whatever
> Could be happening
> Behind tall hedges
> Of dark, lissome *knowledge*.
> [italics mine]

Voice One has seven lines; Voice Two has only five. Voice One has "town" at the end of his second line; Voice Two has "town" at the end of her first. It's a kind of syncopated sound enjambment, in which the perfect rhyme slides, causing what might feel like an echo effect, so that, for example, the *parents of the town* might be heard to be *over the whole town*. The other repeated word, also an end word for both voices, is "knowledge." A listener might also hear this chime, as if two instruments were playing the same note. For Voice One, the parents in the town "escape knowledge" just as it shifts over to Voice Two, "behind tall hedges / Of dark, lissome knowledge."

The syntactical interplay is so subtle and indeterminate that any number of possible sentences might emerge. For example, one might hear "The milk of enchantment like having wine and cheese," or "Could be happening / Once and for all" or "Snapdragons consumed in a wind / Of dark lissome knowledge." The strange phrase "pissing elegantly" is likely to come unmoored from its subject, "the parents," to idle until, perhaps, finding its way "behind tall hedges."

Meanwhile, a single line springs loose from the duet. Just as Voice Two ends her stanza with "of dark, lissome knowledge," Voice One says, "Of fire and rage far over." This is the poem's first unaccompanied line; it falls into a tiny pause before Voice Two takes up her third stanza. A listener will hear its grim, stark description: *of fire and rage far over.* Suddenly a new content arises: "of dark, lissome knowledge / of fire and rage far over / the streets as they end."

5.

I made a terrible botch of it. I stumbled over the syntax and mispronounced words; most egregious, I found myself out of sync, in totally wrong places—way ahead or way behind, so the poem was undergoing radical distortions. I couldn't read my part and his—to the left across the page—simultaneously, and so I went merrily, well, unmerrily, along until suddenly I was nowhere near where I was supposed to be according to the poem's lineation.

Meanwhile, Ashbery's implacable mild tonalities went on at their steady, stately rate, gliding over the poem's surface with unruffled ease, as I slipped and fell, and began again, each time having to stop the proceedings, each time feeling increasingly humiliated and anxious; breathless, one might say: inundated.

Finally, we decided to quit. I think I said something to the effect that it was too difficult to read my part with the author sitting not two feet away, which was true. But I feared that, even with sleep, I would not be able to keep in step. A compromise was found: John should continue to read and record "his" part of the poem, and I, on the following morning, would read mine, while listening through earphones to the recording of his reading. This change proved to be astonishingly successful; somehow, *hearing* the First Voice made it possible for me to play, or be, the Second.

6.

In Part 1 of "Litany," each voice has almost the same number of isolated, solo lines; the First Voice has one more than the Second, but the Second has two together, a couplet (discontinuous—maybe—in terms of sense) at the end of the section. Otherwise, each has only single lines that break out from the ongoing duet. Of course, it is almost impossible to imagine that any two persons could read the poem with such exactitude that each of these lines would be "revealed," since the line lengths, and thus the pacing, throughout are extremely varied. Still, it might be interesting to have a look at these isolated lines as they appear on the printed page.

First Voice:

1. Of fire and rage far over
2. He spat on the flowers.
3. To the rest. That is why
4. The last rains fed
5. Have a music of their own,
6. The shirt.
7. To serenade it
8. To remember what had indeed once

9. The dark shirt dragged frequently
10. Etc.,
11. You and Sven-Bertil must
12. At some earlier time
13. At the top
14. In darkness, and each
15. Still, somewhere wings are
16. Is still room for certain boys to stand,
17. In the here and now. You were saying
18. Mother and the kids standing around
19. Are outnumbered by plain queries
20. Storehouse of agendas, bales
21. Is forgotten like thorns in the memory
22. Extinct, ultimate slopes,
23. That brought us to this unearthly spot.
24. That reads as life to the toilers
25. Because it is the way of the personality of each
26. Gun-metal laurels, the eye
27. Capital at the beginning, and its polished
28. Came to its dramatic conclusion, but

Second Voice:

1. In explicit sex
2. Remembers except that elf.
3. Around us are signposts
4. Surrounding, encroaching on
5. The warp of knowledge
6. Of nerves, articulate
7. Pass by like a caravan
8. Through the cistern of shade
9. To be dreamed of
10. Moving over the nebulous
11. Intruding into the color,
12. Of ice cream and sting
13. Nor on a journey, appearing
14. There is no more history you
15. Now the dry, half-seen pods
16. Behemoths of sense shredding
17. With rheumy specs, dung beetle bringing up the rear:
18. They are anxious to be done with us,

19. Stood; nothing's there
20. To reveal, being forward like this, but we can say
21. Shove us away, but rather
22. Only an aftertaste of medicine
23. Begin it; duration
24. The speeding hollow bullet of these times
25. These relatives like scarlet trees who infested
26. Of reading and listening to the wireless.
27. We never should have parted, you and me.

I want to say that the two voices, although extremely close in tonal mood and content, in fact vary slightly in register, like the difference between two instruments, an oboe and a flute, or a piano and a violin. The Second Voice seems slightly more recessed, more introverted, and the first more overt and declarative. I even want to suggest that the First Voice is more "interested" in the visual, the concrete, the spatial, and the Second more attentive to the immaterial, the abstract, the temporal, but these dualities are undoubtedly spurious. Perhaps it is only a simple matter of major and minor, of a slight increase in certitude on the part of Voice One, and a slight increase in doubt on the part of Voice Two.

Do such distinctions, even if they were true, matter? Probably not. They are the curse of a desire to make meaning align with sense through operations of the analytic, what William James called the "rational," whereas the poem, like so much of Ashbery's work, insists that meaning and sense making, how we come to know what we know, are more complicated, intractable, and irretrievable, than we care to admit. James says, "Pragmatism gets her general notion of truth as something bound up with the way in which one moment in our experience may lead us towards other moments which it will be worthwhile to have been led to." "Litany"'s solo lines are exposed leads, where the audience "glimpses" some passing event or object, which may or may not connect to another event, another object.

And so to the Second Voice's last two lines of the poem's first section: "of reading and listening to the wireless. We never should have parted, you and me." One might consider that the "you and me" refers not only to two persons, but also to two activities: *reading* and *listening.* As usual with Ashbery, the poem speaks to, and for, itself.

7.

I have come to believe, or think, or understand, that when someone dies, the most acute sense of loss is that of his or her voice. (For a while, one can "hear" a person's voice in one's inner ear, but slowly that fades.) This is odd, since sound is of course immaterial; one would think that the body would be the most felt absence. But sound is a distinctive marker of living presence more than any material object can possibly be; sound and lived time are indissoluble: they are, so to speak, part of the continuity of a landscape rather than the singularity of a portrait. Sound is embedded in spatial context.

The two Voices of "Litany" enact an interactive arc of proximity and solitude: near and far shuttle across the articulations of the middle distance. The poem evokes the intimacy of erotic connection; it hovers on the miraculous, as if at any moment a revelation might be, at last, at hand. But as with almost all experiences, these revelatory moments might or might not be shared among the assembled, as we (come to) know—feel, believe—what we know. One person will perceive an illuminating moment, another will discern a different one: the subjectivity of the listening self is allowed to move, and choose, among the great mass and flow of particulars. "Litany" asks of its performers, as of its audience, an acceptance of difference as a necessity of contiguity. The poem flares and contracts from personal intimacy to demotic community, and, as always in Ashbery, it swerves happily around the plainness and comedy of the mundane, "day by day." "Litany" offers a dissonant harmonic in which two voices must simultaneously speak and listen, to themselves and to each other. Both call, both respond.

8.

There have been now several occasions in which I have performed the Second Voice. Around the time of the session at ZBS, there was a reading at a bar—now gone—on University Place, just across from Washington Square. Then Michael Lally and I performed the poem together for Ada Katz's Poet's Theatre, standing opposite each other on a stage. Then there was a long lapse, twenty years or more. When Ashbery's eightieth birthday celebration began to gain momentum, I suggested to John and David (Kermani) that perhaps this might be a good time for a new recital of "Litany," since so many among younger poets are interested in sound/performance, intertextuality, glossolalia. For the New School's Ashbery celebration, John and I read Part 1, and James Tate and Dara Wier read Part 3 at the Bowery Poetry Club; John and I read Part 3 for *The New Yorker* Festival in Fall 2006.

"Litany" ends with Voice One having an extended solo aria of fifteen lines.

Why keep on seeding the chairs
When the future is night and no one knows what
He wants? It would probably be best though
To hang on to these words if only
For the rhyme. Little enough,
But later on, at the summit, it won't
Matter so much that they fled like arrows
From the taut string of a restrained
Consciousness, only that they mattered.
For the present, our not-knowing
Delights them. Probably they won't be devoured
By the lions, like the others, but be released
After a certain time. Meanwhile, keep
Careful count of the rows of windows overlooking
The deep blue sky behind the factory: we'll need them.

In these final fifteen lines, there are five temporal signs: *the future is night, but later on, for the present, after a certain time, meanwhile.* These unsteady, disorienting pointers or skips, so typical of Ashbery, rupture narrative as a condition of chronological cause and effect, as we learn to listen to a vibratory consciousness that forfeits one form of knowing for another. It is, I think, Ashbery's great gift, to have taught us to listen for the multiplicity, the plurality, of experience: *as we know.* As William James put it, "for every part, tho it may not be in actual or immediate connexion, is nevertheless in some possible or mediated connexion, with every other part, however remote, through the fact that each part hangs together with its very next neighbors in inextricable interfusion." Reading "Litany" with John Ashbery is just that: an *inextricable interfusion.* Like singing along with life.

Shadowboxing

Shadow Train (1981)

R*ae* A*rmantrout*

THE POEMS IN JOHN ASHBERY'S *Shadow Train* rest on seeming contradictions. No, that's wrong. They don't rest, they fluctuate between possibilities. They participate in what Ashbery, in "The Absence of a Noble Presence," calls ". . . this undiagnosable / Turning, a shadow in the plant of all things." Like a magician, the poet turns one "thing" into something strikingly different while conspicuously diverting our attention. "The Absence of a Noble Presence" begins

> If it was treason it was so well handled that it
> Became unimaginable. No, it was ambrosia
> In the alley under the stars

Of course, this may refer to the "betrayal" of a partner in an illicit sexual encounter, but such interpretations (without guiding pronouns) occupy a shadowy background. On the linguistic surface, the main terms are dramatically unstable, each undermined in turn. Not only does treason (surprisingly) become ambrosia, but ambrosia itself becomes less appetizing once located "in an alley."

It is perhaps ironic that Ashbery has chosen to pull the rug out from under the reader's expectations in poems with such a regular, predictable form. Each of the fifty poems in *Shadow Train* is composed of sixteen lines divided into four quatrains. Of course, much of the tremendous humor and poignancy in Ashbery's work comes from such sly contrasts. A calm, measured, familiar voice tells us outrageous things. "A" can equal non "A." Treason may be ambrosia. There is nothing that won't reverse itself in time. In "The Pursuit of Happiness,"

> It came about that there was no way of passing
> Between the twin partitions that presented
> A unified facade, that of a suburban shopping mall

> In April. One turned, as one does, to other interests
>
> Such as the tides in the Bay of Fundy.

Here Ashbery deflects our attention from what we (modern Americans) take to be the most quotidian of locations, a shopping mall, and directs it to the place with the most extreme tides on earth as if these two possible sites might be interchangeable. But it's more complicated than that. The representation of normalcy, the shopping mall, is an impenetrable facade and the Bay of Fundy is an "interest," a mental hobby. These "destinations," seemingly worlds apart, are linked by being equally phantasmal, objects of (our) notoriously fickle attention.

As Ashbery shows us, anything can melt into its (paired) opposite—light into shadow, truth into illusion—why not "you" into "I" or poem into reader? This is what happens in what is, for me, the book's central poem, "Paradoxes and Oxymorons."

In "Paradoxes and Oxymorons" you, the reader, are a tease, a flirt. The poem and the reader start out as a stereotypical heterosexual couple.

> This poem is concerned with language on a very plain level.
> Look at it talking to you. You look out a window
> Or pretend to fidget. You have it but you don't have it.
> You miss it, it misses you. You miss each other.

The poem is personified as an earnest type, a veritable John Wayne, "concerned with language on a very plain level." But you, reader, play hard to get, look out the window, *pretend* to fidget. What could be less simple, less plain than pretending to fidget? Even the reader's nervous tics are disingenuous. But there's an attraction between these constructed opposites (sincerity and artifice). "You miss it, it misses you. You miss each other."

"The poem is sad because it wants to be yours and cannot be." What prevents this? Well, it turns out even the plainest phrases are ambiguous. "What is a plain level?" For one thing, a plain level is a spatial metaphor used to describe a style of communication—and that, of course, is pretty complex. We're told, mysteriously, that "it involves bringing a system of them into play." And "play" turns out to be the most ambiguous term of all. It appears at first to be synonymous with action. But Ashbery tells us that it involves "a dreamed role pattern" similar, perhaps, to those played by the poem and the reader in the first stanza. Finally, it dissolves into its opposite—work: "the steam and chatter of typewriters." So do we play or have we been played? Do we write or are we written? Agency is always unstable in Ashbery—more or less real than we imagine. As he writes in "Punishing the Myth,"

> And if you have curled and dandled
> Your innocence once too often, what attitude then isn't really yours?

Whatever stance you happened to take, it turns out now you really *did* mean it? True and false (light and shadow) are conjoined twins.

Like a paradox, Ashbery will have it both ways. Work and play, innocence and experience in one/as one. His poems are both pursuer and pursued, earnest suitor and coy mistress. Then the best magic trick of all: in all its friendly inaccessibility, "the poem is you."

A Place from Which to Wave: "Just Someone You Say Hi To"

A Wave (1984)

Graham Foust

"IT'S STRANGE," WRITES John Ashbery in a 1982 essay, "this weirdness which seems to be a main ingredient in the greatest works of the American imagination." He continues:

> How can it be that *Moby Dick* and *Leaves of Grass* and the *Fourth Symphony* of Charles Ives are simultaneously so universal and so confoundedly bizarre? In other cultures, the latter quality occurs chiefly in secondary practitioners—William Beckford, Achim von Arnim, Barbey d'Aurevily—and this seems a normal state of affairs. We, however, do not possess a Mozart or a Dickens—artists whose genius is both canonical and beyond dispute. Our major statements almost always come with strangeness.

Ashbery's subject is the criminally underappreciated American painter Edwin Dickinson, but it seems to me that these sentences are no less applicable to the author himself, America's canonized but much-disputed master of the strangely familiar.

But what might it mean to say that someone's poems are "strangely familiar"? In an oft-quoted letter to Hans Bender, Paul Celan claims that he sees "no basic distinction between a handshake and a poem," and while I've long been fond of this comparison, I think the proper metaphor for "Just Someone You Say Hi To" involves a different hand gesture, one that manages to unite the strange and the familiar in a way very different from a handshake. Recently, it occurred to me that *A Wave* refers not only to the movement of water, light, sound, and flags, but also to one of our most common methods of acknowledging people, and I'd say that "Just Someone You Say Hi To" has more in common with a wave of the hand than with a handshake. More specifically, it's like a wave returned by a stranger, a response from an anonymous someone with whom the reader might happen to share an empty city street or country road.

It would be difficult to think of such waves as "necessary," which in turn might tempt us to deem them meaningless. But to me these gestures—and so Ashbery's poem—seem fundamentally (and therefore only) human. Unlike much American poetry, Ashbery's work doesn't seek to allow us to get a hold on John Ashbery (and so vicariously, supposedly, on ourselves) but instead lets us feel as if we've been oddly and warmly acknowledged, a feeling during which our minds flow simultaneously toward and away from the self. If a handshake is thought to be a way to judge someone's character—that is, a way of determining whether a given "you" is true or false—then a stranger's wave might speak to something more primary. Such a wave is prior to judgment and so can't touch on your integrity; rather, it gestures at your very (and your mere) existence. In "Just Someone You Say Hi To," Ashbery's attitude toward the reader seems a fusion of Mallory's toward Everest ("Because it's there") and Kerouac's toward *On the Road* ("I wrote the book because we're all gonna die"): The poem says, quite simply, "You are here."

The "you" in the poem's title almost immediately incorporates the reader, while the poem's first lines present us with an understandably self-absorbed speaker experiencing a moment of concurrent danger and security:

> But what about me, I
> Wondered as the parachute released
> Its carrousel into the sky over me?

If the title indicates that the speaker is feeling slighted because he's merely someone to whom the reader says "Hi," the poem's opening speaks to a more pressing concern, namely the question of whether or not the parachute's opening will bring the speaker safely to the ground. The poem continues:

> I never think about it
> Unless I think about it all the time
> And therefore don't know except in dreams
> How I behave, what I mean to myself.

In these lines, the speaker reveals himself to be more anxious about behavior and meaning than he is about surviving the jump, and they lead the reader to ask a question of her own: given the speaker's insistence that he never thinks about "it"—which is to say the speaker's self, the poem's "me," now oddly an object—"except in dreams," is the thinking of which the poem speaks an aberration or the same old same old? That is, are we reading about someone in a dream state, or are we reading about someone who is experiencing what he usually experiences in a dream state in his waking life? At this point, the speaker presents us with another question and moves the poem into what might be its strangest moment:

> Should I wonder more
> How I'm doing, inquire more after you
> With the face like a birthday present
> I am unwrapping as the parachute wanders
> Through us, across blue ridges brown with autumn leaves?

As the speaker asks whether he should ramp up his self-absorption or "inquire more after" the poem's listener, we see that the parachute is now somehow inside a communal space comprising both speaker and reader, who seem to have achieved some sort of natural state (in that the "us" contains "blue ridges brown with autumn leaves").

The casual tone of the opening of the second stanza steers us away from the strange image that closes the first, and this is where Ashbery's turns of phrase become at once alien and intimate:

> People are funny—they see it
> And then it's that that they want.
> No wonder we look out from ourselves
> To the other person going on.
> What about my end of the stick?

There are at least two ways of reading the "it" in the second stanza's first sentence. On one hand, this "it" could be a more generalized vision of the "it" in the poem's fourth line, which would make it a stand-in for "themselves." (That is, people see themselves, and then they want themselves.) On the other hand, the "it" could refer to the notion that "[p]eople are funny," which would suggest that people see that they're funny and then want themselves to be funny. In either case, the reader comes to know that the poem's speaker doesn't think himself alone in seeing the self as a form of feedback. To be sure, Ashbery's regular use of colloquial language, slang, and cliché is a common critical touchstone, but I often find myself more interested in instances in which we find him changing up such language, not so much by way of punning, but by eliminating an expected word or altering an anticipated idea in favor of something atypical but not unthinkable. To wit, the above lines, in which Ashbery writes "look out from" where we might expect "look out for" and "my end of the stick" where we might expect "short end of the stick." In the former, an admission of self-protection has morphed into a statement of self-containment; in the latter, an ironic cliché has been rendered unusual, but also entirely reasonable (given that sticks have two ends, but not short ones). The expression "going on" is fitting, given that this is a poem that involves passing, wandering, and human happening, and the next lines—which mark a return to "thinking"—introduce the notion of persistence in defeat, a kind of Beckettian going on:

> I keep thinking if I could get through you
> I'd get back to me at a further stage
> Of this journey, but the tent flaps fall,
> The parachute won't land, only drift sideways.

Here, Ashbery subtracts one word from an everyday phrase—"get through to you" becomes "get through you"—and so renders the listener an indefinite obstacle, while "[b]ack to me" (like "get through to you," a telephonic idiom) alerts us to the speaker's desire for a shortcut from his present to his future. The speaker's hope seems to be that human contact will allow him to bypass some unnamed phase, but as the tent closes and the parachute proceeds asymptotically toward the ground—I read that funky twenty-first line as saying that the parachute will neither land nor only drift sideways—we see that his attempt at breaking away from the listener is failing. What, then, becomes of these two?

The poem ends with the following lines:

> The carnival never ends; the apples,
> The land are duly tucked away
> And we are left with only sensations of ourselves
> And the dry otherness, like a clenched fist
> Around the throttle as we go down, sideways and down.

The use of "we" in the third-to-last line indicates that speaker and listener may be forever hoisted by their shared chute, endlessly done and undone by the poem itself. This is a situation at once celebratory (in that "the carnival never ends"), mournful (if one reads "left with only" as expressing at least a tinge of grief), and fearful (given the "clenched fist / Around the throttle," which suggests an anxious desire for control over the parachute's seemingly predetermined and endless movement). What remains, of course (off course?), is both strange and familiar: The "sensations of ourselves" aren't described (perhaps because the speaker knows that we tend to think we know what our selves feel like), and the "otherness" is simply "dry." (No clammy handshake here.) In the end, the you and the I, like two strangers waving, somehow come together in their separateness and apart in their togetherness—they *cleave* in both senses of that word—and their bond seems to me an apt figure for the relationship between Ashbery and his reader as well.

Elsewhere in his essay on Edwin Dickinson, Ashbery mentions that Dickinson's greatest paintings are "attentive to *every* nuance of light, line, tone, and atmosphere, and [therefore] somewhat odd." "Just Someone You Say Hi To" also pulses with this oddness (what Ashbery calls, in Dickinson's work, a "heightened realism"), and while the poem is but one example of *A Wave*'s oscillating depths, it's emblematic of the book as a whole in that it casts a shadow both affable and sinister, shines a light at once trivial and overwhelming. (In this, the book and the poem are also akin to a Dickinson painting.) A parachute brings to mind various situations (disaster, war, spectacle, recreation) and distinct states of mind (fear, precaution, bravery, ingenuity); the whole of *A Wave* is similarly inclusive. Published three years after the formally uniform *Shadow Train*, its poems range from brief, lyric mysteries ("At North Farm," "Problems") to extended prose poems ("Description of a Masque," "Whatever It Is, Wherever You Are"); from a version of Baudelaire's "Paysage" to thirty-seven haiku and six haibun; from a daffy near-sing-along ("The Songs We Know Best") to the long meandering love poem that closes (and titles) the book. From the latter poem, these lines:

> And what to say about those series
> Of infrequent pellucid moments in which
> One reads inscribed as though upon an empty page
> The strangeness of all those contacts from the time they erupt

> Soundlessly on the horizon and in a moment are upon you
> Like a stranger on a snowmobile
> But of which nothing can be known or written, only
> That they passed this way?

For me, *A Wave* is a series of gestures at this very question; it sees off—but never seals off—our inquiry.

In "Just Someone You Say Hi To," the listener's face is likened to a gift, and we might say that the speaker's "unwrapping" of it is a figure for the spread of a look of recognition, not in the sense that the listener knows who the speaker is—or "relates" to him—but rather in the sense that the poem's you is expressing an acknowledgment of having been acknowledged. This unwrapping may be what allows the you and the I to float together in a mutual space, the sky above the me to be an "us." In his novel *Howards End,* E. M. Forster refers to the "rainbow bridge" between prose and passion, without which "we are meaningless fragments, half monks, half beasts, unconnected arches that have never joined into a man." "Only connect," he famously continues, "and the beast and the monk, robbed of the isolation that is life to either, will die." I respect Forster's work, but I'll admit that I find the beasts and monks in us interesting enough that I wouldn't want poetry to kill them off. Thankfully, *A Wave* turns Forster's rainbow into a very different but no less meaningful curve, an endless downward arc that never quite "connects," but in doing so allows its readers an evocative weightlessness, a place from which to wave.

Energy

April Galleons (1987)

Eileen Myles

ONE OF MY FONDEST memories of childhood was the ongoing game of trying to *not* succumb to the gas my dentist placed on my nose as I sat in his chair. I sat in my blue uniform thinking I won't let it happen this time, yet I was thrilled of course by the inevitable failure that delivered me into the kaleidoscopic rattling world of my dentist's big face and his assistant's echoey voice. This childhood experience reminds me of everything, always has. And when I pick up a book of John Ashbery's I undergo a similar willful adjustment. What seems to be his work's totalizing effect (to this day and one that's as palpable as a drug) is how it taps into the body and its refusal. And a third thing, which is really his. And it's bloomingly self-conscious. The joke of it: our utter inability to reject the body and the whole rotting world—and that failure collapses into nubs; into a strangely vulnerable built-up moment, one my mother would describe as finicky: "Then rubbed himself dry with a towel, wiped *the living organism.*" Finicky is how John Ashbery gets personal, distantly marking a "me." You can practically hear him then, it's a reading of a line. The voice pulled so thin it almost gets bodily. His language at once being a recoil and a wink. Then a field of tiny adjustments to follow. Weighing and subtracting. Allowing and vacating. And a good ole American kick: "Don't fix it if it works," yells from someplace else on the boat and we wake up in another way. That's an Ashbery poem—no ordinary pitch into the dream of someone else's foul consciousness. It's a thinking field. And how ever to say no to that. The poet, especially at this period in time, is gleefully erasing his own productions, or the possibilities of their depth. In the face of the city having been built. He's "famous" but in my favorite quote ever of Ashbery's: "Being a famous poet is not like being a famous human being." *April Galleons* seems to me to be a very coy title. Poetry itself in a way. *All me little ships.* The model has been accepted. So Ashbery's joke has deepened in its way. In effect it's a wry denial of the reality of other places. The dentist's chair or the world.

Wasn't it true then
That life is a novel or an opera
That there is no third place?

Meanwhile *April Galleons* was an eighties book. It just so happens I'm the same age now that John was when he wrote many of these poems.

And it's not like being grown up anymore,
Like being a fifty-seven-year-old child or something . . .
—"Alone in the Lumber Business"

The eighties, especially the late eighties, 1987 to be precise, the date of the publication of this book, was the early height of the AIDS crisis. We all lost a million friends, my generation more than his. From the perspective of his age, the ones dying were largely kids. I wonder how that felt. "Finnish Rhapsody," the poem that took a shower, could easily, I suppose be alluding to that day: "That there are a few more black carriages, more somber chariots / For some minutes, over a brief period. . . ."

But, you know, one's late fifties is when, for many reasons, lots of your friends start to die—and worse, it's when you begin to *live*, creepily enough. So many things have been set into motion in one way or another, so it seems that what you are doing is more or less *this*. Going forward, helplessly. The living organism being wiped is a new actor on the Ashbery stage.

April Galleons is a disturbingly accurate middle-aged book, a variety of punk few could recognize now or then. What's quietly on the rise in the now of this book is Middle time. So there's that. Going over one wave then another. And in one's spare moments. Because John Ashbery is not a personal writer, one is looking out over the machines of everyone's making:

No allowance was made for citrus groves on the old plan of the city.
It's all torn apart now, in any case,
But our lives and their regions
Stay on, permeated with their obsolescence,
A warming voice in the car.

Maybe the opposite of the finickiness is this serene cultural daddy, one with a memory that seems to have been tapped in to the way things were taken apart, but also intimately taken up with how this feels to all of us. John is kind of the Steven Spielberg of poetry in that he is entirely capable of supplying a narrator to our darkest moments. Then explaining electricity too. Or whatever you call the technology that habitually floods his game:

> . . . Something that never paused,
> Was there in the fir branches when the wind stopped,
> Painless and aglow, its fever
> A thing now of an imagination
> Increasingly distracted by the glitter . . .
>
> —"Not a First"

Isn't this kind of suggesting that romantic imagination could—or must—be as literal as all the prefab downtowns, San Diego's Gaslamp district, pour example, that dot our major cities in their recuperative act of replacing sleaze, or trees, with Disney—who himself replaced orange groves as *his* initial act of contemporary poetry. It starts there. That nobody planned on nature, and didn't think of it as "in the way" so much as just where you planned to build. But then that happened everywhere and the building has to become part of our mind, the most prevalent form of our nature, what we did. The thing made has to be true somehow, and maybe the glory of Ashbery's subjectless work is the grand question of residue, acoustics: but what do we do with our feelings? Do they remain as music or actually even sweeter (and sadder), "a warming voice in the car."

And he did that: built familiarity, a tone, replacing or affecting "family" and everything else.

I see this dusky midlife book, one brushed off critically, I notice, as between two big ones—something he did while he was putting together his selected, as the middle child of his writing life, and child it is, this book being persistently aware of the connection with a child from so very long ago—which is the classic romantic touchstone or loss, is it not?

Childhood is certainly the growing field of our own nature, particularly to those of us (gay or otherwise) unwilling to contribute our seeds to that field. We turn back continually to that "lost" child. A poem narrates a tale about throwing a stone at another kid, and blood flowed and desperately the "he" in the poem threw himself into the arms of anyone who would listen:

> I remember in the schoolyard throwing a small rock
> At some kid I hated, and then, when the blood began
> To ooze definitively, trying to hug the teacher,
> The boy, the world, into ignoring what I've done,
> To lie and thus escape through a simple
> Canceling, not a confession, to wipe the slate clean
> So as to inhabit another world in which
> I bore no responsibility for my acts: life
> As a clear, living dream
>
> And I have not been spared this
> Dreadful state of affairs, no one has . . .
>
> —"Sighs and Inhibitions"

Maybe in a way that reminds me of Gertrude Stein in her later career—she often was narrating energy itself, whether inside a car, or how a culture moved inside, a pure kind of machine—this poet seems to be looking into a fireplace. Fading and then bursting alive as fires do. Flipping us wonderfully, beautifully into the act of replacement, dreaming, suddenly performing an oath, shooting his intention right back at you, wide-awake power:

> And from growing dim, the coals
> Fall alight. There are two ways to be.
> You must try getting up from the table
> And sitting down relaxed in another country
> Wearing red suspenders
> Toward one's own space and time.
>
> —"Ostensibly"

And that this book ends with "the old eyes of love"

> Of how the mist built there, and what were the
> Directions the lepers were taking
> To avoid these eyes, the old eyes of love.

is almost more than I can bear.

A Magically Alive Aesthetic

Reported Sightings (1989)

Jed Perl

IN JOHN ASHBERY'S ART criticism the revelations arrive casually, offhandedly, as if unannounced. Reading these prose pieces, which Ashbery has written with more or less frequency for some fifty years, we are in the presence of a man who is avid but easygoing, a man for whom an interest in painting and sculpture is part of the natural order of things, as pleasingly necessary as friendship, travel, good food and drink. Like lively conversation, Ashbery's prose has a way of shifting gears as it moves forward, embracing poetic flights, theoretical speculations, personal anecdotes, and straightforward reportage. The writing is no more one thing than the experience of art is one thing, so that the changeable rhythms of the sentences and the paragraphs begin to suggest an aesthetic viewpoint, a literary analogy to one of Ashbery's off-the-cuff definitions of art, which is, so he says, "hybrid, transitional, impure, and magically alive."

Writing about art for all sorts of venues—newspapers, art magazines, general circulation magazines, exhibition catalogs—Ashbery comes across as a man who is effortlessly urbane, who is completely at home in the cultural maelstrom. When I read his criticism I know that he is absolutely alive to art's immediate pleasures. I can also see that he is immersed in all the second thoughts, paradoxes, ironies, and assorted complications that quite naturally occur to a person who has read everything, seen everything, heard every view expressed. In "Self-Portrait in a Convex Mirror," the famous poem precipitated by a painting by Parmigianino, Ashbery refers to New York as "a logarithm / Of other cities," and his art criticism might be said to be, if not a logarithm of other art criticisms, then a sketch for a logarithm of other art criticisms, absorbing elements of social commentary, aesthetic reflection, biographical portraiture, and lyric effusion from any number of writers, not only writers of the nineteenth and twentieth centuries, but of far earlier times as well. It was of course Horace, in the *Ars Poetica,* who made what remains the most famous of all statements about the relationship between poets and painters. "*Ut pictura poesis,*" he wrote, which means "as is painting so is poetry," although over time the remark has come to refer to the relationship between the two arts in general rather than to any particular causal relationship, and in fact Renaissance and baroque thinkers tended to translate the phrase "as is poetry so is painting," a very different thing.

Ashbery has always hesitated to present a coherent artistic credo, and his hesitations might be said to be a part of his credo, perhaps its very essence. In the poem "And Ut Pictura Poesis Is Her Name," he discusses the variegated ingredients that might go into what he calls a "poem painting," and they include flowers, "particularly delphinium," "names of boys you once knew and their sleds," "skyrockets," but also "a few important words, and a lot of low-keyed, / Dull-sounding ones." What you find in Ashbery's writing is a very personal view of "*ut pictura poesis,*" a view that while never denying the particular powers of the literary and visual arts tends to see those powers as fluid, as changeable, as infinitely paradoxical. Ashbery's view of these matters has much to do with the great variety of art in which he took an interest in the 1950s and 1960s, a variety that included the surrealism and Dadaism of a previous generation, the abstract expressionism of the older artists whom he knew, and the painterly realism to which some of his closest painter friends were drawn. While Ashbery believes in the traditional powers of words and images, he does not believe in the immutability of their functions. A phrase or a sentence in a poem can convey narrative information, or it can be experienced less literally, for its quotidian charm or its musical sound. By the same token, a shape in a painting can represent an object in the known world, but it doesn't have to. What Ashbery is saying—to echo Horace's equation—is that "Just as in a painting, line, shape, and color can function in many different ways, so the same is true of words, phrases, and sentences, whether in poetry or in prose."

For much of his life, Ashbery has written art criticism to make a living, and even the most casual reader can see that he has often written to the formats and lengths dictated by particular publications. Read end to end, the work that was collected in 1989 in *Reported Sightings* can make a bit of a crazy-quilt impression, because the pieces are so varied as to their forms, their approaches, their ambitions. But in a strange way the overwhelming variety of the writing gathered in *Reported Sightings,* as well as the pieces in a more recent collection, the 2004 *Selected Prose,* becomes yet another confirmation of Ashbery's underlying aesthetic.

For the Paris *Herald Tribune,* where he worked in the early 1960s, Ashbery could be self-consciously newsy, reporting not only on the exhibition but on its social or cultural significance. Introducing a Toulouse-Lautrec show, he remarks, "The crowd waiting in the rain outside the Petit Palais museum in Paris rivaled the one queueing up for the latest Alain Delon movie on the Champs-Élysées." Now the remarkable thing about a sentence such as this, and there are many in Ashbery's criticism, is that even as it presents a traditional journalistic trope, the juxtaposition of two distinct but simultaneous phenomena, the writing has a speed, a wit, and an echoing power that are entirely Ashbery's own. The Petit Palais, the movie theater on the Champs-Élysées, the long lines of people, the dark-haired movie star, and the dwarfish fin de siècle painter somehow come together to create a little portrait of Paris in 1964—and the portrait has a staying power. Nor is this the end of the surprises in this brief review, because almost immediately Ashbery is explaining that "I suppose I should be disqualified from writing about [Toulouse-Lautrec], since I am one of a very small minority who do not fully appreciate Lautrec's work." To put it plainly, this is not standard newspaper reportage, and yet Ashbery manages to pack in all the necessary details of the artist's life, with the initial negative giving a personal impact to what is to some degree boilerplate stuff.

Over and over in Ashbery's criticism, you find him inhabiting a conventional journalistic form and making it his own. It is not enough to say that this is the measure of his independence as a writer, when we consider how frequently it is the true artists who have the hardest time writing to somebody else's specifications. A prose style can lose its charm when it is squeezed into a preordained format. I don't know that it is possible to provide an entirely convincing explanation for Ashbery's success, but it may be that this poet who so enjoys slang expressions and conversational turns of phrase embraced the brief newspaper or magazine article as a popular form that he could make his own, much as a poet might make the sonnet form his own. That Ashbery could bring a personal inflection, and even some of the power of a short story, to the profiles of artists that he wrote for *ARTnews* is not especially surprising, as the very style of those stories was to some extent shaped by writers who were either themselves poets or who were very much attuned to the work of their poet friends (Ashbery was for a time an editor at *ARTnews*). But even James Schuyler, who wrote some striking profiles for *ARTnews,* rarely achieved the headlong ease that you find in Ashbery's work, such as an account of a visit to the studio of the painter Jean Hélion in Paris. Here the arrival at the penthouse apartment becomes like the unwrapping of a surprise, with the "somewhat rusty elevator," the "blue wooden steps," and "a mechanism that pops the door open in front of you," all leading to our first look at the artist, "invariably at work behind the enormous studio window," and the superb view, a "welter of curving metal roofs, skylights, and walls of that sandy-colored stone used in France in places where it is not supposed to be seen."

Even in his later work as a professional critic, when Ashbery was writing to the more rigorously structured formats of *New York* and *Newsweek,* he knew how to use compressed, wisecracking language to pack the brief articles with meaning. With Ashbery you feel the individual personality filling out the form, giving it an elasticity, a poetry that is his alone. At *New York* magazine, he begins one column by declaring, "Ceramists are a strange lot." He begins another by remarking, "Two trendier-than-thou exhibitions have just opened." These lines are at once brief topic sentences in a traditional journalistic sense and conversational gambits animated by Ashbery's off-kilter humor. Ashbery is one of those rare talents who can make journalistic prose permanently engaging, no matter what the subject happens to be, no matter how long ago the piece was written.

In recent years a good deal has been said about the connections between poets and painters in mid-twentieth-century New York, but however interesting the particulars of those friendships and alliances and crisscrossing inspirations may indeed be, it is also good to remember that ever since the Renaissance, poets and painters have been taking an interest in one another's work. The poets and painters of the 1950s and 1960s did not have some particularly privileged grasp of the relationship between poetry and painting, and indeed it might be argued that the relationship had been far more fertile in Paris in the late nineteenth and early twentieth centuries. Perhaps, more than anything else, it is a testament to Ashbery's essentially traditional orientation as an artist that he has taken such a strong, consistent interest in the visual arts—the strongest, the most consistent of any poet of his generation. There is something almost old-fashioned about a poet's writing art criticism, collaborating on luxurious illustrated volumes with artists whom he knows, and finding that he is so provoked by certain pictures that they become the subjects of two major poems, "Self-Portrait in a Convex Mirror" and *Girls on the Run,* the book-length salute to the outsider artist Henry Darger.

What does seem worth noting in Ashbery's view of the relationship between the visual and verbal arts is that this relationship is less one of borrowings and echoings than of a constant breaking down and reconstructing of the possibilities of both painting and poetry. The result is a sense of freedom within tradition that is shared by the arts, as if the very idea of freedom within tradition were to be passed back and forth, with developments in one medium reinforcing developments in the other. In 1961 a number of portfolios were published in New York that brought together work by some of the most promising younger poets and painters, and Ashbery collaborated with Joan Mitchell on what was called *The Poems.* Fairfield Porter, a painter who was a good friend of Ashbery's and who wrote fine criticism and also some skillful poems, reviewed these collaborations in *ARTnews* in such a way as to draw together Ashbery's and Mitchell's work. "Ashbery's language is opaque," Porter writes, "you cannot see through it any more than you can look through a fresco. And as the most interesting thing about abstract painting is its subject matter, so one is held by the sibylline clarity of Ashbery's simple sentences, in which words have more objective reality than reality of meaning. One is back in first grade, about to learn to read." The meanings in Porter's criticism are not always easy to parse, but what I think he is suggesting here is that there is a strong connection between the "sibylline clarity" and "objective reality" of Ashbery's poetry and the power that Joan Mitchell packs into her strokes of paint, and indeed the work of both poet and painter has an effect that is so primary it pushes us back to the beginning of learning, before we accept the fixed meanings of words or images.

A few years later, when Ashbery wrote about Mitchell in *ARTnews,* he touched on some of the same issues. He observed, "The relation of her painting and that of other abstract expressionists to nature has never really been clarified. On the one hand there are painters who threaten you if you dare to let their abstract landscapes suggest a landscape. On the other hand there are painters like Joan Mitchell who are indifferent to these deductions when they are not actively encouraging them." After considering various aspects of this relationship, he notes, "The answer seems to be that one's feelings about nature are at different removes from it. There will be elements of things seen even in the most abstracted impression; otherwise the feeling is likely to disappear and leave an object in its place. At other times feelings remain close to the subject, which is nothing against them; in fact, feelings that leave the subject intact may be freer to develop." What Ashbery is saying, so I believe, is that a group of brushstrokes can provoke a color sensation, or they can suggest the movements of nature, or they can suggest flowers, a field, a river—and the brushstrokes can suggest all of this, simultaneously or sequentially. I think it is possible to argue that even as Ashbery is writing about Mitchell's work he is writing about his own work, for the way in which phrases or even lines function in Ashbery's poetry is not entirely different. Sometimes the phrases and lines mainly hold us with their freestanding power, as fractured elements of things seen or heard, as abstracted impressions. At other times, however, Ashbery's words and phrases and lines assemble into what might be called a more naturalistic order, something approaching a narrative, what might be thought of as a more intact subject.

It is difficult to think of another writer on art who has so few preconceptions as to how artists make meaning, make emotion. Ashbery has a gift for teasing out the implications of forms, as when he writes about some lithographs that de Kooning made after visiting Japan. The prints, Ashbery writes, "suggest a parody of the parody of nature that *sumi* drawings, in a sense, already are." This is a terrific way of describing the wit, even the irony, that sometimes animates de Kooning's painterly calligraphy. Ashbery is making a metaphoric leap, on the basis of a close look at the work and a bit of biographical information, namely the fact that while visiting Japan, de Kooning had looked very closely at Japanese art. Writing about Brice Marden's painting in 1972, near the beginning of the artist's career, Ashbery again finds a way to expand the implications of the work. He observes of Marden that "rather than reducing the complexities of art to zero, he is performing the infinitely more valuable and interesting operation of showing the complexities hidden in what was thought to be elemental." Marden's art, Ashbery argues, "is not negative minimal but positive phenomenal." There is something ceaselessly, delicately dialectical in Ashbery's approach to art, a testing of what is immediately apparent in relation to what one might think about what is there, with the actuality and the possibility leading to a synthesis that is not an impressionistic or theoretical riff so much as it is a lively response to the world that the artist has created.

If Ashbery looks for the literature in abstraction, you might say that he operates in the reverse direction when confronted with art that many people would describe as literary. Writing about R. B. Kitaj, the American painter whose themes range from the life of Walter Benjamin to the baseball games of Kitaj's youth, Ashbery insists on the underlying importance of the abstract expressionist "all-over picture in which no element matters more than another." The heritage of abstract art helps Kitaj "to come to certain conclusions about the surface of a picture," "to develop a surface that is different every time," so that the flood of Kitaj's literary allusions turns out to be powered by the antinaturalistic character, indeed the abstract character, of his space. Ashbery finds a related complexity in a series of paintings by Jess, the works known as "Translations," in which found subjects, perhaps an old photograph or engraving fraught with elaborate or arcane literary allusions, are radically transformed through Jess's use of high-keyed colors and curiously impastoed surfaces. Writing about Jess, Ashbery observes, "Against Verlaine's artificial distinction between *musique* and *littérature* one may place Jess's synthesizing approach which sees no reason to give up either." Jess and Kitaj are artists who might be said to wear all the conflicts and excitements of "*ut pictura poesis*" on their sleeves; this is, in some sense, the very subject of their work. But as Ashbery points out in writing about Jess, viewers are not invited to draw any conclusion they like. This is an extremely important point. A work by Jess, Ashbery writes, "is not whatever the viewer wishes to make of it, but what he has to make of it once he has consented to play the game. Jess, unlike so many contemporary artists who would elicit the spectator's participation, compels it." Our responses, although free and sometimes quite unexpected, perhaps even by the artist, are shaped by what the artist has made. And here we discover, so I believe, the classical discipline behind Ashbery's romantic abandon.

The more I read of Ashbery's criticism, the more I can see that what he responds to in a work of art is a certain flexibility of meaning and implication, as if classical order and romantic abandon were always playing hide-and-seek. When he writes about Louisa Matthiasdottir, a painter who was born in Iceland, lived most of her adult life in the United States, but continued to paint the cityscape and landscape of her youth, Ashbery discovers a considerable range of possibilities in the magnificently impassive surfaces of her work. He begins by observing that something in her landscapes and cityscapes—the color, the light, the character of the architecture—reminds him of Edvard Munch, another Scandinavian artist. Then, turning to Matthiasdottir's *Rejkjavik Bus Stop,* with two figures standing on an empty street, he says that "everything prepares one for an epiphany such as the Munch painting [*Girls on the Bridge*] seems to convey, but on further examination it turns out that the subject is only two ladies waiting for a bus; in fact it is hardly even that but is closer to pure painting—one has a strong sense of the joy of covering a canvas with long sweeps of paint and simultaneously capturing the vagaries of particular light and space with generalized accuracy." This apparently casual, meandering sentence sends us off in several different yet intertwined directions. We see the possibility of a metaphoric meaning, some idea of loneliness or isolation. But that thought gives way to the realization that this is simply, or not so simply, a scene of everyday life. Then Ashbery points out that what we have here is in fact an example of pure painting. But what is pure painting? Now perhaps this is the essential question, and immediately the purity is psychologized, because a sense of joy is conveyed by the process of covering the canvas with long sweeps of paint. And, finally, another element is introduced, the pure painting turns out to have a naturalistic dimension, because Matthiasdottir wants to catch a particular quality of light and space.

Ashbery always insists that we respond to art in many different ways, that art is *pictura* and *poesis* and philosophy as well, that we can discover the literary within the pictorial, the pictorial within the literary, and discover all of this to all sorts of varying degrees, in one part of a work of art, in a particular work of art at a particular time. The result is not anarchic, not in any way, but rather suggests that art is the disciplined exercise of a range of possibilities, with the work provoking branchings of thought and experience and feeling, all sorts of openings, analogies, echoings, doublings. Ashbery shows us that seeing, which provokes thinking, makes us see other things, which in turn enables us to think other things. This is an aesthetic that rejects fixed aesthetic distinctions, that is hybrid, impure, always evolving, for the artwork, as long as we are looking at it or thinking about it, is never fixed, is always becoming.

The Reflection of a Reading

Flow Chart (1991)

Ben Lerner

IT BEGAN IN THE MIDDLE ("Still in the published city but not yet . . .") and ended at an opening ("It's open, the bridge: that way"). The lines grew longer until it felt like reading prose, except I was never aware of what it felt like to read prose while reading prose. It wasn't that it didn't make sense—it made sense until I reached a period. Then what I thought I had comprehended vanished. And yet the poem itself seemed to consist largely of descriptions of this very experience: "*It seems I was reading something;* / I have forgotten the sense of it or what the small / role of the central poem made me want to feel. No matter." It was as if the line in italics were a quotation from *me,* as if I were reading about my reading as it happened. So I detected a rightness of fit, but what fit what? The poem fit my response to the poem? I had no idea how to describe the book; the book *was* the description of the effect it caused. *Flow Chart:* a flow chart of reading *Flow Chart.*

It was the first book of Ashbery's I'd encountered. I was seventeen. I think my favorite poet was Richard Hugo. Or maybe I was my favorite poet. I pretty much hated it. After a few pages I knew that nothing I thought I knew about poetry was going to survive. Innocence replaced not with experience, but with the "experience of experience." It was a first traumatic encounter with abstraction, with the structure of perception, not particular precepts—an encounter with the how of meaning over and against the what. The organization of language in time, syntax, was suddenly an object of experience in its own right; I felt the shape of thinking without being distracted by thoughts. One word leads to another with all the inexorability of a logical progression, but if you break the flow, you realize the sense of reference is a trick of sheer directionality. All the deictic language—spatial ("We are no longer on that island. *Here,* the inmates . . ."), pronominal ("*We* are no longer on *that* island"), etc.—keeps things from solidifying into either sense or nonsense; you just keep searching for the relevant antecedents, the right frame of reference. Is the Ashberian "you" singular or plural ("Did I say that thing to you? I hope not")? Who's being hailed, me or us? Responding emotionally to a line of Ashbery's can be like waving to somebody who might have been waving to somebody behind you. Meanwhile hypotaxis smuggles in what *feels* like analytical subordination and temporal progression, but the buts and yets (they must be two of the most common words in the book) are propulsive, kinetic, not logical. The language remains either contemporary and conversational, an image of American speech circa 1991, or recognizably literary, a kind of canonical white noise; one feels at home enough to read on. And on. "It's like the wind has taken over, except that one can be aware of, keep an eye on oneself in that medium." But what do you see when you look at yourself in the Ashberian medium? A subject that always almost arrives on the waves of predication. A process that never stabilizes into an essence. Certainly not something I can capture: if the terms are fixed, they've missed the point, which I suppose is a way of saying: there is an Ashberian sublime. "We've got to find a new name for him. 'Writer' seems / totally inadequate; yet it is writing, you read it before you knew it. . . ."

Let me try again: if *Flow Chart* charts the deferral of reference, it nonetheless enables a strange, fugitive kind of presence. Because one often feels like one is reading one's response as one responds, deferral is experienced immediately. "Sometimes one's own hopes are realized and life becomes a description of every second of the time it took." When *Flow Chart* describes the time of its own reading in the time of its own reading, language is identical to itself.

All of this makes it one of the most exciting books I've ever read. It is also often boring. It's impossible to finish and, of course, it knows it: "Without further ado bring on the subject of these / negotiations"; "There must have been some purpose to this, / some idea hiding in the vacuity. . . ." I don't mean you can't read every page. The first time I read it, it was like I was reading it again; everything was vaguely familiar. But it didn't get any more or less vague when I did, in fact, read it again. Of course I've discovered more allusions, spotted that embedded double sestina, and heard whispers of narrative progression as I've returned. But it still feels less like a repeated reading than a recurring dream; less like my "getting it" than its getting me. And the dream is often tedious indeed. The boredom, however, is integral to the effect. If the book is "about" any one thing, it's about time, and isn't boredom, when time is emptied, the condition in which we experience temporality as such? I won't try quoting

Heidegger, but suffice it to say that boredom, what Tolstoy called the desire for desires, is inextricable from the experience of experience.

Flow Chart's length, its extension, takes place in more than one dimension. First, there is the length of the line, an elongation that challenges the very concept of the line as a unit of composition; I've often heard *Flow Chart* described as a prose poem. It's certainly hard to imagine Ashbery lost much sleep over where to break the vast majority of his lines. And yet there are just enough clearly purposeful breaks, there's just enough active white space, to keep us guessing about what might be intentional and why. This hovering between poetic and prosaic lines parallels the poem's hovering between sense and nonsense. We can never be sure if a subtle architectural principle dictates lineation, or if he just hits the "return" key at random. This makes us attend to the kind of attention we address to the page: we can feel ourselves alternating between the pressures we bring to bear on poetry and those we bring to bear on (or release in the presence of) prose. Ashbery thus compels us to read our reading.

Independent of how the line breaks affect our experience of the poem, the distension itself signifies: for the seventeen-year-old me, it signified first and foremost: Whitman. Pound's "Pact" has a deliberate pithiness—its shortness reinforces the idea of the imagist "carving" away from the excesses of the "pig-headed father" (this was 1913, before *The Cantos*). Ashbery's long line, by its very look, situates *Flow Chart* in relation to Whitman's radical inclusiveness, his collective "I" intent on cataloging everything American. The image of the line in *Flow Chart,* then, regardless of its content, raises questions about the book's relation to tradition, the American, democracy, and the ability of a lyric "I" to perform epic tasks. And because the fluidity of the "I" is a major drama in *Flow Chart* ("I say 'I' / because I'm the experimental model of which mankind is still dreaming"), because the language is an image of American speech, and because it pushes inclusiveness to an absurd degree ("there's even a dog named Bruce"), these issues are kept live throughout the text. But instead of Whitman's democratic dream, we get lines like this: ". . . even the word 'society' / is something each of us eventually gets a stranglehold on, forcing it to say 'uncle'—there / I'm glad I did, and you can go away now." How can Whitmanic ambition be anything but tragicomic when "the sinkholes open up, and K Marts fall into them," when a life in common has been replaced with its image; when the power of the people is reduced to "the power of staying up alone / in a rain-lashed stadium with the TV on"?

The other dimension of *Flow Chart*'s extension is, of course, the length of the book itself, its two hundred and sixteen pages. One of the most widely known features of the epic is that it begins in medias res, and a giant poem that commences, "Still in the published city but not yet," makes it impossible not to read *Flow Chart* against epic conventions. It's an epic in which nothing happens, or it's an epic in which the lyric subject is constructed and deconstructed simultaneously—deconstructed because revealed *as* constructed by grammar, not by gods. The temporal emptying I earlier tried to describe is magnified by the evocation of generic expectations the poem strategically disappoints. We're cued to anticipate a narrative treatment of heroic figures performing historical events; cued by the first line, cued by the breadth, cued and mocked by the dramatic temporal markers scattered throughout that text. Both the horizontal extension of the line and the vertical extension of the book, then, trouble our notions of genre: is it poetry or prose? Epic or—or what?

The impossibility of answering is part of the point. Before *Flow Chart,* I thought poems were first and foremost to be interpreted. Criticism was there to help you if the materials stubbornly refused to yield their meaning. It had never occurred to me that something made out of words could defy interpretation, that that defiance could be a source of value, vertigo, beauty, pleasure. There is of course some brilliant criticism about Ashbery, but we shouldn't let that distract us from one of his poetry's primary characteristics: it makes critics look like fools. I don't just mean that his poetry is celebrated or condemned for contradictory reasons by critics with radically divergent interests and investments; I mean the work sets traps for anyone proffering a supplement. I've been trying to indicate why I believe that this is so: elucidating particular meanings is in tension with the syntactic action that defines the Ashberian experience. Particulars are substitutable; affect is sedimented in the structure; speed trumps sense; the nouns are largely placeholders: "One can retool the context, but slowly, / slowly. . . ." OK, then why not describe that very dynamic, how the waves of language constantly break against the shore of reference? Because that's not a description of the work—that *is* the work: "it's my Sonata of Experience, and I wrote it for you. Here's how it goes. . . ." "[I]t is possible at the end that a judgment may be / formed, and yet the intrepid / listener does no such thing, hypnotized by his reflection. . . ."

I was hypnotized by the reflection of my attention in *Flow Chart,* how I felt I was reading a record of my reading as I read, and I found that liberating, but also annihilating: I felt like a linguistic effect. I think we owe it to Ashbery's greatness not to take the sting out of it, no matter how funny or welcoming much of his writing is. "And if I told you / this was your life, not some short story for a contest, how would you react?" I reacted with shock—the shock of recognition: I was the "you" whose production had been charted.

Besides, of Bedouins

Hotel Lautréamont (1992)

Cole Swensen

OTEL IS DISTINGUISHED by its many rooms, and a room always stands for oment of the mind, so every collection of poetry is necessarily a hotel, a uence of spaces threaded in and above, and there within we live, in passing, corridor, in what brushes by your sleeve, the underscore of breath.

s is wealth, and we're just passing through, as they say, there we are and n are not, another stranger, and there's something clean in that. *And to se whose loneliness / shouts envy in my face,* it's a state of pure sunlight, ed of memory, and it's a dream; it's *the* dream: to be seen from the back, king away until the seer fades, and the reader is left with an open book.

el Lautréamont traces an exile—an ambulatory self-exile in both senses he term: of the voluntarily chosen, deeply wanted, and escorted, and of the that walks out on the self until it runs out of land:

> *There is nothing to do except observe the horizon,*
> *the only one, that seems to want to sever itself*
> *from the passing sky.*

ich is passing behind
a screen on which a shadow-play keeps time with the gate
nging back and forth of the face, of the name.

tréamont was a man who abandoned his name for another of a fictional racter from a nineteenth-century sensationalist novel that no one now embers how to write the self away and make a dubious hero splinter into actual. Isidore Ducasse, the author forever on the outside, and Maldoror, character forever trapped within, meet in this name of another on the er that divides one world from the next. Lautréamont exiled himself from self, leaving his native Montevideo to go to Paris and die of the siege. And ph Cornell was an exile from and within his native land and never left v York. You can exile inside; you can build room after very small room with the many addresses of repeated objects. Exiled himself into a small red ball, a grid of white, the repeated word "Hotel."

Seen on a bench this morning: a man in a gray coat is always a photograp in black and white, and the stranger is innumerable and habitable, in a soft hat, quietly sealed. "Still Life with Stranger" is full of bees and snow.

Ashbery speaks of *those homeless hirsutes we call men;* this is his homag to them. We see a line walking silhouetted against the horizon, letter for letter, person for person, counting in his sleep, if poetry does not keep track there will be no more ceremony to this loss and

if we are to be more than music

be erased. It is this

we will interrogate. The erased conveys its passing through a split second o unclarity, a cloud across the surface, and the paper is no longer virgin. It's a white rectangle with a smudge that looks a little like the condensed breath someone who just left the window.

From the outside, a hotel is no more than a pattern of windows, often all th same, counters in a game of concentration, and you will never be able to remember where you saw each one before.

Ashbery also exiled himself to Paris where he fell in love with the work of Raymond Roussel, to whom no better monument to alienation both self an universal has ever been conceived. There *is* all that outside. It *does* extend i all directions becoming infinitely more grand and infinitely more precise, a always and essentially without depth. Which was the world he built and in which he fled and lived forever among his simple magic and unlikely machines.

That these three men—Lautréamont, Roussel, and Cornell—are the same o is a law of physics that may seem to have no purpose until it emerges as th book: *great rivers run into each other and graves*

Digression: that is, of course, a gross misreading of the line or is it. The line run:

we will meet on a stone up there, and all will not be well,
but that is useful. Great rivers run into each other and graves
have split open, the tyranny of dust plays well, there is
so little to notice. Besides we have always known each other.

ıd so, because of the line break, we can claim "great rivers run into each her and graves" as a legitimate unit, but more important, this sequence emplifies Ashbery's device of rarely letting lines conform to the units of nse; they are always carefully offset. Agamben speaks of the violence herent in poetry at the site of the line break; it is broken, and its breaking eaks sense open, while on the other hand, when meaning, as in Ashbery, hieves its end in the middle of the line, it similarly ruptures that ructure; these ends un-ended, the grave has split, and if something comes ive again because of it, it is this unease that pushes onward, which is the ile inherent in language, now relieved of all constraint. Ashbery's lines ill not stay put, but restlessly wander from humor to mourning, resting ly a moment suspended as each line breaks into another room with a door each extreme.

ıe implications of the hotel are endless, arcanely transient, archly ıonymous, always pushing tomorrow off somewhere else. By the time you t there, a hotel room is always empty. In 1981, Sophie Calle spent three eeks as a chambermaid constructing portraits of the hotel guests, portraits nstructed in and of their absence, built of the haphazard evidence of daily jects, detritus, traces, until the person in their lack becomes enormous. ıis we call the present.

ıd it is constructed of dream. Hotel rooms are permanently permeated ith dream. If it is thought that dreams stain the air, and they do, then in otels they're layered in among strangers because they must build from ght to night, are never the product of a single night's work but must wait, aving those who live in hotels to create a composite mind shared with eryone else who has recently passed through.

) build a mind out of the never-met. Ashbery's work is always an exchange dream, which is a turning from the door every time and every room that ıdes alone, uncompromising the view, as wrote the surrealists for whom, ke Lautréamont, Roussel, and Cornell, and regardless of timing, Ashbery as a precursor, living there a second time, a graceful loop *autonomous as e birds' song, the vultures' sleep.* You sing and I'll weep. Birds inhabit the rson, and the exile is complete. Which is itself in silence, in coming into ssession of the self, must be exiled from all else, becoming sovereign, a novated conference of the birds:

oon intersects with fat birds: rain of, who won, and winning, rain of livion, sudden as a sigh. In the bird, Ashbery and Cornell pass and brush, lightly of hands: aerial Bedouin, migration that does not return with the season.

on a forgotten afternoon filled with birds; wings
How the forgetting, too, plays into h
economy of loss; there is just one spot
on the horizon, and it may or may not have been
the one living thing that always is
the past. Of it we
build individual habitats for bird and person
The smallest home is a thimble
until it is a needle, famous for being nearly all window, and what of the air
balloon, and what are these boxes if not exits. And how do you tell a bird
from a stone? The answer to the riddle had something to do with a pale blu
egg upside down in a glass. What is that in your hand?
There was no seaso

We found a homogeneous weather composed entirely of ritual objects. Here
he and Cornell confer:
feather? and if so, how related to snow? and exactly
how to manifest this emptiness in such a crowded place. How inexorably to
state *the birds were here once,*
borrowed
from Uccello, who also
earned his name from absent birds, birds he painted
that no one now can find, *we know* is just the beginning
of *they were*
once of the interwoven, when after all, they got away, and the shore repeats
because the body is a finite thing and Ashbery finds this sad. He is right, an
so intricately so in positioning the grief at the point at which bird and man
meet, which is the hotel, half arm, midbeak, the fulcrum between a bird's
foot, which can only be called a claw, and its wing. There is no thing that
does not mean. And Ashbery, dedicated to contingency, here constructs a
deep mourning for just that inability.
We move continually
outward along a chain of islands, ever alien:
Do pigeons flutter? Is there a strangeness there, to comple
the one in me?

And of what shape, what silhouette crossed the yard and odd in peace d
shed a peace in the dark within the body lies the bird
as whatever's left of flight:

. the heart flies a little away,
erhaps accompanying, perhaps not. Perhaps a familiar spirit,
ossibly a stranger, a small enemy

Ashbery's first aspiration was to be a painter, and
ırving outward, with his hand upon the snow in an untitled collage
y Joseph Cornell. There was no Hotel Lautréamont
nong the prodigious series Cornell constructed in the fifties.

. . . And when it was over, that was the truth:
nest of eggs still hidden, the false flight of a bird.

shbery's exile is positive, the fulfillment of a promise, the reconciliation ith a stranger who never faces you, but keeps looking onward, drawing you ıt. In his configuration, exile is the refusal to be rendered homeless by onstituting that home everywhere.

xile in style, too. While in *Reported Sightings,* Ashbery writes, "The enius of Cornell is that he sees and enables us to see with the eyes of ildhood, before our vision got clouded by experience," he also says that he as shocked when he first saw Cornell's work in a magazine at the age of n—shocked because Cornell was seeing what no child ever naturally ould, and delivered in a rush all the psychological insight of thirty years' xperience; to sense the extension of the self as a serial dislocation (*only a ning / that dictates the separation of this you from this some other*), and ıe fact that the elements of a personality can be freely recombined as a type flight should be shocking indeed to a child of ten.

nd once internalized, became Ashbery's principle of composition based on ımulative juxtaposition that carves up every outward through a neat xchange of metaphor for metonymy, a chain of associations that begin and egin and begin again. In haunted stanzas, we start with rain, then a arpsichord shelling peas, then rowboats. Then darkness. Then: *Happiness o longer was a thing to hold on to, but became a great curve, listening ıstead*

is the entire oeuvre: the darkness necessary to the intelligence happiness, which must be a curve, it must have that wing, and it must xceed the frame of the mind, turning to pure motion, and all of it, the stening that sends our attention elsewhere still.

Archipelago. It is a book of ships:

that excited skiff

schooner with its layered sails that climb like clouds; there are so many ways out, but among them, sail and wing are mostly ancient. Ocean vessels convey-ness hither. He expands on the theme: flotsam and jetsam and their fine distinctions, what we toss overboard, memory and meter, to make the ship lighter and lighter, it's practically floating, it's learning to fly. Thereby becoming the point that wanders free of a line, and often contrasted with its opposite: all buildings that are not hotels, and that therefore hold us down:

And so in turn he who gets locked up is lost
too, and must watch a boat nudge the pier
outside his window, forever, and for aye,

is that wide inviting; we picture it wooden, its paint peeling and an oar of sun aslant its emptiness, a rope in the bottom, coiled.

. . . and the little house more sensible than ever before
as a boat passes, acquiescing to
the open, the shore . . .

the shores are still beautiful
they always are
because they're in midair; they've got nothing to do with the ironic earth but mark its edge and own their sails and are sailing.
the ship was obliged to leave for the islands—it doesn't matter which ones. They all came along
. . . you know how we keep an eye on

today. It left on a speeding ship. As everything eventually Isidore Ducasse got on board and sailed right out of his life.

And when you died
they remembered you chiefly. It was two
lights on a rowboat, a half-mile off shore

Second digression into formal considerations: rhyme: that his rhymes, too, follow a scheme designed to undermine the physical form of the poem as determined by line. The rhymes fall internal, often insistent, but also often hidden: obl*i*ged to leave for the *i*slands; don't *care* he said, going down all those *stairs*; Even in the *beginning* one had grave *misgivings*; So many mystery *guests*. And the rain that *sifts*. These midline rhymes implode the phrase, fold it in two. Strongly rhythmic, they set up patterns that run counterpoint to those established by the line breaks, while they also cut ross meaning, which itself is often bisected by the line. Again, Agamben: at rhyme is often an inherent conflict of sound and sense, at the very least aking the word serve two separate ends. These various violences, three odes all working at odds, result in a surface that is constantly disrupted d must thus constantly remake itself, which in turn calls attention to elf and discourages us from looking for meaning elsewhere, where it isn't. he poises rhymes on top of each other, both in the middle of the line: *oud* directly above *aloud, lay* above *clay,* and we fall straight down rough the poem as if down a mine, blindness swaddled in sound. erything here is in motion, the tension between gravity and its enemies, ng and sail, my ship, now my bird, finally only reconciled in language:

my words as their feathery hulls
ow away

d there are many, many words here; in fact, it's a text in which the mmon noun comes into its own—bell, river, train; he picks inherently ble words; lilac, garden, sun: these are things with integrity, echoing angely amid the ironic and lasting oddly longer. Lamp, tower, weather— ey're the short, hard words of which the world is constructed, inviolate d categorical, never naming one alone but a timeless form that comes wn, rain, sea, song.

ese words are of the same class as Cornell's objects, and the method of mposition is the same: pipe, globe, chart of the sky. Ashbery looked up m the box and said, *I am banished to an asteroid.* What he has done th things, I have done with words, which is to arrange them according to e schedule of the night, the compositional principle of the constellation, e continual reconfiguration of swan, ice, owl. Of bridge, dust, hour: a thering of the elements that fueled nineteenth-century romanticism, all at seething nature reaching as we are reaching without ever touching it's tting taller as if the world and not the universe were expanding visibly andoning something diminishing on the shore. And this allows him to k a romantic treatment of beauty:

lls chimed, the sky healed.

t the lamps purling / in the dark river

d dancers shift across the stage like leaves

Which is necessarily based on the romantic foundation of loss, the indelibl inaccessible: all these images are composed of immense inner distances, an again, we have recourse to cosmology, the many references to stars, comets moons, the universe on the head of a pin is here sequestered,

as did Corne

in boxes,

in language: Ashbery

inserts at the precise center a gap unbridgeable because it's entirely contained, sometimes even in a single word: pier, fog, gone. An exile is not an exile except seen from the land he has left or in looking back; what we are leaving is the past, and that cannot be done. Words such as *once, anymore, were always, left behind,* and *no longer* weave in and out of the overall attempt at humor, and eventually coalesce into their own sort of home. That the exile should inhabit the unattainable: *so much*

that is not ours, and the tale
besides, of Bedouins
who broke out of silence as a river. It's hard to make a solid object that doesn't end. And does it echo in every box or to have thought one face back to a light that you could breathe.

and the wind whispered it to the stars
and the people all got up to go
and looked back on love

This Very Poem Refutes It

And the Stars Were Shining (1994)

Marcella Durand

THE TITLE OF JOHN ASHBERY'S *And the Stars Were Shining* is not "original" per se: it is taken from the title of an aria in Puccini's *Tosca.* But as the title of a collection of poetry, it is extraordinarily original, as it plunges the reader in medias res even before she's begun the book. *And the Stars Were Shining* could be an ending, an addition, or a digression, but it is not a beginning. And so with Ashbery's work, I begin with something not a beginning.

Stars shine, a "fact" that is just about universally accepted and confirmed as much as anything is in the unknowable swamps of human perceptions and opinions. However, the truncated sentence structure of *And the Stars Were Shining* unbalances this primal given: as a nonbeginning beginning, it introduces us to Ashbery's particular poetic composition—how he balances and occasionally unbalances light and dark, and shifts between deep and shallow language within a matrix of time (narrative?) flowing unevenly. Seasons shift from summer to winter (with a little fall and spring thrown in), nostalgia is counterposed with immediacy, a fragrant and slightly overripe Past is juxtaposed with the Now.

Within Ashbery's oeuvre, *And the Stars Were Shining* seems to represent a sort of understated and elegant shift in scale. Before *And the Stars Were Shining* were *Flow Chart* and *Hotel Lautréamont;* after was *Your Name Here* (in which some of the poems of *And the Stars Were Shining* reappeared with slight typographical corrections and/or different titles. For instance, "Sicilian Bird" reappears as "Andante Misterioso"). The large (or perhaps "ginormous") scale of *Flow Chart* and to a lesser extent, *Hotel Lautréamont,* seems even more so when compared to the slim *And the Stars Were Shining,* which, with the exception of one long piece, is a palette of shardlike yet figured shorter poems. And even the long title poem (twenty-four pages and thirteen sections) is broken into discrete sections, individual and discontinuous spokes of a larger shadowy form.

The poems of *And the Stars Were Shining* have a question running through them—does poetry matter? Perhaps the stars are linked to this. In "The Bachelor Machines of Raymond Roussel" (*Other Traditions*), Ashbery writes that after Roussel's *La Doublure* was published, "Roussel discovered that the sun and moon were still in place, that the planets hadn't strayed from their orbits and that daily life in Paris went on as before." This is reminiscent of a passage from Henry Beston's foreword to the 1949 edition of *The Outermost House:* "Whatever comes to pass on our human world, there is no shadow of us cast upon the rising of the sun."

> . . . Water, does it seem swollen, or how much does it weigh
> when all the water molecules have been withdrawn,
> and to whom does one address oneself after the correct answers
>   have been passed around?
> I told him, as best I could,
> indeed, as I have told others in the past, that such soft
> mechanisms, such software, can't be regulated, and if it could,
> no one would want any answers.
>
> —"Well, Yes, Actually"

This passage grows funnier and more tragic every time I read it. It echoes somewhat the tone of "The Instruction Manual" (a poem that drastically expanded the range of tone available to poetry). Here, Ashbery's control over tone is exemplary in the movement from the everyday phrase "I told him, as best I could" to the more cushioning lyricism of "indeed, as I have told others in the past" to the strangeness of "that such soft mechanisms, such software, can't be regulated" to the catch-you-by-the-throat money shot, "and if it could, no one would want any answers."

But there's much more to this poem than tone shifts, attractively distracting as they are—there's a kind of practical despair, a unique Ashberian fusion of sensibility and philosophy, that hides itself behind tone. What is essential to water, an essence itself? And what's left to water after all the water is gone? What is water if it's not water? Are these nonsense questions, or questions we all should be asking every time we turn on the tap? And questions? Where do they lead us? One "addresses" oneself to the poet, who, even after providing correct answers (or at least more questions), "tells" him and others (not us)—what? A reply that brings us back to a conditional answer, and even more, brings us back to the beginning: well, yes, actually—and the stars were shining.

But here I may be edging into the treacherous territory of "interpreting" Ashbery, of trying to reshape his compositions into an ill-fitting narrative with an artificial "take-home" message that will enable me to live life comfortably, efficiently, and morally. So, does poetry matter?

> I don't know what got me to write this poem
> or any other (I mean, why does one write?),
> unless you spoke to me in my dream
> and I replied to your waking
> and the affair of sleeping and waking began.
> —"Just for Starters"

Perhaps by looking at the spectrum of poetic "tools" Ashbery uses, we may spy on what makes poetry matter—for instance, in *And the Stars Were Shining,* similes outnumber metaphors to such an extent that I begin to wonder whether Ashbery prefers the reality of similes to the fantasy of metaphors. Similes remain within the world of the "real," while metaphors take an extra step into the imaginary. And while Ashbery is very much a fan of the imagination, an immutable thread of reality runs through his work, a necessary counterbalance. Whitman's eschewing of the metaphor can still be traced in Ashbery, who finds enough in the actual world to supply his work amply with the odd and unpredictable.

> . . . the razor, lying at an angle
> to the erect toothbrush, like an alligator stalking
> a *bayadère;* the singular effect of all things
> being themselves, that is, stark mad
> —"Ghost Riders of the Moon"

Who hasn't found their razor lying at an angle to their toothbrush (and beware, teeth!), but what is a *bayadère* and why is it/she/he being stalked by an alligator? *Bayadère* is missing from my more contemporary French-English dictionaries, but according to an older one, it is defined as an "Indian dancing girl." The Internet reveals that *La Bayadère* was a ballet choreographed by Marius Petipa that premiered at the Maryinsky Theatre in St. Petersburg in 1877. (Actually, it's not clear whether Petipa choreographed or produced the ballet.) In any case, the music was composed by Ludwig Minkus. However, none of the plot synopses mention the chasing of a *bayadère* by an alligator. Even more problematic, there are no alligators in India (in which the ballet is set), only crocodiles. But Ashbery nimbly excuses himself from the situation he's gotten himself into: after all, things—crocodiles, alligators, *bayadères,* toothbrushes, razors—being themselves, are stark mad, and "alligator" sounds nicer paired with "stalking" anyhow. It's often hard to justify poetry, much like it's hard to justify art, music, and other things that are extraneous to making or paying money, but in this poem, poetry rules—alliteration is more important than accuracy, and the simile is a poetic tool that allows one to both render and establish "reality," whether that reality is internal or external to the poem.

The simile also allows Ashbery to do one of his other favorite things: undercut or puncture anything that shows the merest tendency to become pretentious or sentimental or cloying.

> But that's just what life is about, isn't it?
> So your coming sped our just deserts.
> One is off with a nerd in a pothole somewhere.
> —"On First Listening to Schreker's *Der Schatzgräber*"

"Nerd in a pothole" most effectively punctures the treacherous "what life is about." And yet, Ashbery can also veer the other way—when he starts to get mired in what could be the tedium of exterior reality, he turns back toward language, toward the philosophical, toward "poetry." As Jack Collom says in a preface to his book, *Second Nature,* "John Ashbery writes a species of human nature. He's inside it so he has the right."

> And that summer cottage we rented once—remember
> how the bugs came in through the screens, and
> all was not as it was supposed to be?
> —"Sicilian Bird"

Ashbery undercuts himself—his often blindingly accurate insights, fantastical juxtapositions of linguistic and temporal oddities—so regularly that he can seem as irresistible as the ocean eroding away dunes until houses come crashing down. But to Ashbery, poetry is as primal a force as ocean, water, stars, though we'll never be able to explain why.

And patient, exacting
no confirmations from those who know him,
the poet lies down under the vast sky,
dreaming of the sea. For poetry, he
now realizes, is cleverer than he.
—"Sometimes in Places"

And here's another call to poetry:

What! Our culture in its dotage!
Yet this very poem refutes it,
springing up out of the collective unconscious
like a weasel through a grating.
I could point to other extremities, both on land
and at sea, where the waves will gnash your stark theories
like a person eating a peanut.
—"The Decline of the West"

But these excerpts support a "point," such as it is. So much of Ashbery's work is also about composition—about the interesting or mysterious or catalytic or shocking placements of word, tone, image. The long poem "And the Stars Were Shining" contains a cornucopia of fascinating disjunctions (and junctions), such as "time" "as precise as a small table with a cordless telephone on it, next to a television," which make this jumpy and complex work evocative of the avant-garde classical composers Ashbery favors.

Another poem, "A Held Thing," contains many obdurate lines, including one that regularly tempts copy editors to "correct" it: "It's colors, just like the ones were at the beginning." But this particular poem also contains insights into Ashbery's almost painterly idea of composition, in that the word "colors" takes on as many linguistic meanings (and perhaps "red" herrings) as the word can handle. That is, like how gold functions as a dark in medieval paintings, "colors" in "A Held Thing" explores the full range of its own linguistic colors (and echoes Ashbery's achievements with sestinas, in which words are similarly stretched to their limits).

In many ways, *And the Stars Were Shining* is as outrageous, but more quietly so, as early pieces like "The Instruction Manual" were. In other words, the revolution continues, but more subtly. Here's a stanza from a shorter poem that is particularly breathtakingly outrageous—with a beginning stanza that gets away with murder (not literally, but poetic murder).

> I like napping in transit.
> What I ought to do
> just sits there. I like
> summer—does it like me?
> So much cursory wind
> with things on its mind—
> "No time to worry about it
> now," it—she—says.
> —"Till the Bus Starts"

For what it's worth, "Till the Bus Starts" also has a great epigraph: "This heart is useless. I must have another," from *The Bride of Frankenstein.* Still, I can't believe, decades of avant-gardism later, that a line like "I like / summer—does it like me?" yet makes me laugh with delighted shock (and I won't even go into "And were it but a foozle / schlepping round my ankles . . ." which follows soon after). Here, even when the molecules of poetry are taken away, it is still poetry. Trust poetry. And I won't answer "why."

I Believe I Am the Man from Nowhere

Can You Hear, Bird (1995)

Christian Hawkey

CAN YOU HEAR, BIRD? Bird, are you capable of hearing? Can you hear me, bird? Are you, reader, addressed as a bird? Can you hear the word "bird"? Since there is no concluding question mark, is this a fragment, one that begins with a direct question? Does the word bird refer to "a warm-blooded egg-laying vertebrate distinguished by the possession of feathers, wings, and a beak," or to "a clay pigeon," or to "a peculiar person," or to "a shuttlecock," or to "a hissing or jeering expressive of disproval," or to "an aircraft, spacecraft, satellite, or guided missile," or to "a young woman, a girlfriend"? Who, exactly, utters this phrase, which is at the very least grammatically arranged as a question? And if it is a bird in the first sense, why question the hearing of an animal from the class Aves, a feathered vertebrate that relies more than any other animal (save for humans?) on the emission and reception of vocal signals—songs and calls—in order to attract mates, defend territories, and to coordinate the behavior of a pair or family or flock for the purpose of foraging, flocking, and responding to potential predation? What, aside from the romantic trope of the poet as songbird, do birds signify? As animals that flock, swarm, gather, disperse, and reform, are they rhizomatic in nature, as Deleuze and Guattari might posit, like rats, rabbits, cockroaches, bats? Does a flock of starlings—technically called a "murmuration"—visually map the way language "ceaselessly establishes connections between semiotic chains, organizations of power, and circumstances relative to the arts, sciences, and social struggles"? In their social and vocal structure do they illustrate D & G's notion that "there is no language in itself, nor are there any linguistic universals, only a throng of dialects, patois, slangs, and specialized languages"? And if this is the case, why does the speaker of the title address a single bird? Is this an address to a single reader? Does this imply, at some level, that reading itself is a singular activity? A single pair of eyes tracking the cover of a book, a page, a line, a word? Is there a tension here between bird and birds, reader and readers, author and authors, private and public speech, private and public space, singularity and multiplicity? Is the act of reading fundamentally a way of negotiating these tensions? Is writing? Does the polite delicacy of the title's question imply an open-ended, willfully nonideological cheerfulness in relation to such tensions? Does the title exist only as a written text—a note posted at the entrance of a birdhouse? Or does the text indicate a spoken, voiced address? Is the addressed bird stationary (perched), or in motion (flying)? What kind of speaker would address a bird? What kind of speaker would address a *question* to a bird? Is this a reversal of the essentially monologic nature of religious address, where a figure like St. Francis of Assisi simply preached to birds (without first asking whether they would welcome such an address)? And is this different from the romanticism of Keats, who by addressing a nightingale communicates his desire to merge with its pain-free, "full-throated ease"? Does a speaker whose utterance begins with a question instantly deflect meaning away from him or herself? Instantly erase him or herself? Become an undifferentiated surface or plane on which pronouns occur, idiolects occur, sociolects, characters, memories, paradoxes, sensations, blips, chirps, perceptions, clichéd phrases, bodily emissions, noises, puns, variegated emotional tones—a plane on which a seemingly endless number of different lexicons unfold? Can we even claim that such a narrator is a narrator, or that a narrator of a seemingly endless number of voices has a voice? Is this not a disturbance of voice? Is it not a voicelessness, a surrender to the absence of a unitary voice? Or are we speaking then of another kind of voice, the presence of pure voice, voice freed from its usual binary tie to self-expression and autobiography and instead directly operative not in the construction of meaning—social, vocal, semiotic—but in the construction of a space in which meanings might or might not take place, a basic indeterminate ground, a basic human ground on which indeterminacy can more immediately be enacted? Is the pure voice, the voice as object, an essential link between language and the living body? Is this why the Slovenian philosopher Mladen Dolar quotes the famously odd moment in Plato's *Symposium* where Aristophanes "had such a bad case of the hiccups—he'd probably stuffed himself again, although, of course, it could have been anything—that making a speech was totally out of the question" and he had therefore to break the structure of the Socratic dialogue and defer his turn to the next speaker? As Dolar asks, what do Aristophanes' hiccups mean? What are we to make of this "unintentional intrusion of an uncontrolled voice" rising out of the "entrails" of the body? Is it that "this precultural, noncultural voice can be seen as the zero-point of signification, the incidence of meaning, itself not meaning anything, the point around which other-meaningful-voices can be ordered"? Does the voice therefore "present a short circuit between nature and culture, between physiology and structure"? Is this why Dolar also explores the burbling of infants and the infant's first sign of life, the scream? And is laughter, which is a physical response close to coughing and hiccups, not the clearest expression of the human voice—a or any body's voice—outside or alongside language? When a poem in the above-titled book by John Ashbery begins "Hello, Blubberface," are we not instantly connected to our bodies by laughter, by a slight guffaw, even if it's a silent laugh, an unvoiced laugh, a smile? Are we not more fully human, more fully open, more fully vulnerable—head thrown back, neck exposed, mouth open—in the instance of laughter? In the instance of love? Perhaps, between the pranks and pitfalls, the disruptions of syntax, the gaps in meaning, the spaces opened by refusing denotative communication, perhaps in all these voids opening in Ashbery's work there is a resonate, lawless voice, one that threads indeterminacy into a performance, into an experience that we, reading with our own voices, our own voiced bodies, immediately connect to, feel, feel as something deeply human? The voice, then, not as the author's voice or the voice of an author but an authorless voice, a voice authored by words themselves? Words that author us in reading? As potential subjects willing to be (we open the book) formed in the event of a poem? Is this why Beckett writes, "What matter who's speaking, someone said, what matter who's speaking"? Is this why Foucault suggests we avoid the tiresome questions of "Who is the real author?" and "Have we proof of his authenticity and originality?" and instead focus on new questions, such as "What placements are determined for possible subjects?" Is this why the poems in Ashbery's seventeenth collection of poems, *Can You Hear, Bird,* are arranged alphabetically according to title? And in opening a book arranged according to the structure of a dictionary, an encyclopedia, or a phone book, are we not offered the widest possible number of placements? Not a jar placed upon a hill but a series of jars, a jar for each hill, for each potential reader, potential subject? Is such an offering a kind of generosity? An invitation to let potential subjects choose (literally) themselves, choose to become themselves as subjects? Is this a definition of freedom? Of language? Is this why Ashbery writes, toward the end of "Tuesday Evening,"

Christian Hawkey

"An alphabet is forming words. We who watch them / never imagine pronouncing them, and another opportunity / is missed. You must be awake to snatch them— / them, and the scent they give off with impunity"?

Like the Blistered Exterior of a Sigh

Wakefulness (1998)

Anselm Berrigan

MY COPY OF *WAKEFULNESS* is a beat-up soft-cover version I bought in New York City in 1999, most likely from St. Mark's Bookshop. I let the book talk me into buying it while standing in the store and reading a few poems—one of them being "Laughing Gravy," a nine-line poem (the longest poem in the book is about three pages) that ends with the lines "All the wolves in the wolf factory paused / at noon, for a moment of silence." I bought and bought into the book because this poem cracked me up on the spot, and I needed some kind of personal fault line to be activated by Ashbery's work in order to get into it at that point. I knew that his books B, C, F, and so forth were masterpieces and had been subjected to the implications that one must read them if one were to know anything at all about contemporary poetry or some such noise, and I actually already had a relationship with *Rivers and Mountains,* if one somewhat leveraged by weed, but I was the quiet twenty-seven-year-old type who didn't want to be told what was good for me, rendering established reputation a suspect device. I appreciated a four-line collaboration between the poet Steve Carey and my father, Ted Berrigan, that concludes with the lines "I gotta buy some pills / So I can understand John Ashbery," but that wasn't quite the droid I was looking for, the pills or the understanding. I wanted to have my own experience with the work before letting it in; unprompted laughter in a relatively quiet, public place was the right signal (another line that got me was "Take this, metamorphosis. And this. And this. And this," from "Baltimore").

A few months later, during the autumn of 1999, I attended a memorial for the filmmaker and photographer Rudy Burckhardt held at Cooper Union. Ashbery, an old friend and collaborator of Rudy's, walked on stage early in the program and read the title poem of *Wakefulness,* prefacing his reading with the information that he had chosen the piece because Rudy had it pinned to a wall in his studio (I think the painter Yvonne Jacquette, Rudy's wife, told John this after Rudy's death). It was a poignant detail to share, and while I knew from talking with my mother that Ashbery was one of Rudy's two favorite living poets ("John writes really well about aging," Rudy had said to her more than once), I was struck by the immediacy of his desire to have this particular poem nearby while he worked. I use the word immediacy because *Wakefulness* had only been out for a year or so by the time Rudy died in August of '99, and I think on some level that evening I realized that Rudy's relationship with Ashbery's poetry was, as I imagine it, constantly opening to make space for the next thing, even, perhaps especially, near the end of his life. I take that as deep utility (perfectly practical, mind you), and also, by extension, as a method of experiencing Ashbery's poetry on its own terms. My memory of the "Wakefulness" reading at Rudy's memorial is focused on hearing Ashbery's voice read the final few lines of "Wakefulness":

> No matter how you twist it,
> life stays frozen in the headlights.
> Funny, none of us heard the roar.

There's a little urge in me to attempt an interpretation of those lines, to say something about the life-object as seemingly passive on the surface (too busy being everything) while resistant to one's will, but this is the same poem that contains a clock "happy about being apprenticed to eternity" while sitting "in the little house of our desire," so, no, I won't do that (other poems in the book feature drooling bats and octopi sharing equal time with the Big Subjects, by the way).

You see, I got something from reading *Wakefulness* that I have always found difficult to describe, some sense that Ashbery was just saying things, saying one thing after another with a fluid diction that talked, observed, remarked, fantasized, giggled, recalled, and lamented its way through the constant change (if there can be such a thing as a wry lament, then the line "And I'm too shy to throw away" might qualify), consciousness itself the underpinning of the whole shebang. The poems were and are precise, free, and, to my taste, really funny and thereby permissive—one's sense of arrangement could include tonal variation from thought to thought or line to line without stopping for commentary. "Just saying things" is a kind of hideous remark, but by my way of thinking about things poetic it requires a total command of feeling for arrangement. That description has taken me a good eight years to articulate and I doubt it's exactly right, but I don't mind. I want the relationship I have with the book to not be made too distant by any sense that I can satisfactorily pin down the why of why it gives me such pleasure to read: "It's almost leaking to say it. / But how much longer could I go on not missing the point."

Recently I met with a sculptor named Saul in a barn on Bard College campus. He wanted me to bring him an example of a poem that I considered sculptural, or at least that had sculptural qualities (this kind of request goes around Bard in the summertime). I liked the question and knew, instinctively, what he meant, but the target area seemed a little broad. Anyway, I brought my copy of *Wakefulness* to the barn and started reading Saul the poem "Shadows in the Street," the first stanza of which goes as follows:

> She bit the bridge. A photograph can stomach it. I'll be in
> some time in the middle of July. Now the best time
> of the year is around now, none can gainsay August
> and Mr. Random's tooth running in the street, he liked to say
> hi, it was just
> him running, which is a bit awkward. A diagonal lipstick
> chased him across the street. From there on in it was just
> damn melancholy,
> no anchovies, nothing in particular, nothing to say. If so why,
> why do it,
> says Peter, who fought hard for the post, fought it and won,
> and why are we here, in the middle of a secondary terrain,
> mad and absorbed
> by life, by the truth, as always.

I think I wound up telling Saul, who wanted to have poetry coming out of an extension cord in one of his sculptures, that it came down to putting one word after another. This came at the end of an hour-long conversation (I said the simplest thing last) during which I tried to unfurl the "just saying things" proposition in some manner, but I don't think it rubbed in. I actually lent Saul a couple of books to read, but I wouldn't part with *Wakefulness*. Something else I noticed recently about *Wakefulness* is that I can be reading it in a dive bar where I am not supposed to be drinking and if fifty-four long-distance runners, having just now completed some race, come in for beer and mixed company there's no interruption. I just have to be somewhat clear as to where the line between my perception of reality and my sense of the poem I'm reading as they enter happens to be. That is, more morbid mongrels may be munching all around me, but the poems remain capable of being read (keeping in mind that all things break), perhaps because one has to be aware anything might happen within them. The oddities of the external world then, routinely swirling around like shattered ornaments, never have to feel out of place. *Wakefulness* presents the poem-space as hospitable to the imagination without laying down a set of laws, save the need to be alert, and mildly capable. I have yet to read it, even for a few minutes, without feeling the urge to write.

Tragi-Kitsch & Elegiac-Comix

Girls on the Run (1999)

Joan Retallack

RUN, JANE SAID, Run, run. Run, Dick, run. Run and see. Look. See all the little girls on the run. Where are they from? Where are they going? Why are they running, Dick? Why? Why?

When Dick didn't answer, Jane jumped right out of the sunny pages of *Fun with Dick and Jane* and joined the little girl marathon. I want to know what's going on, she yelled over her shoulder, sounding a bit cross like Eve must have with Adam. They're not behaving like the girls in our primer; that's interesting!

Look, Jane, let me give you some advice. You get plenty of exercise in your basic reader as it is. Out here, things are not so nice. Nightmares (for which you happily have no word) are bad enough as dreams, worse when they permeate waking life. Somewhere, every day, little girls are running from terrible things—from kinky kidnappers and murderers, from their mothers' lovers, from drunken fathers, from the victors who see little girls as part of the spoils of battle, from authorities who wish to remove their pleasure-sensing parts. Children out here are on the run from hurricanes and forest fires. They're being blown to bits in terrible wars. Go back to Dick, and your little sister Sally, and Mother and Father and your dog Spot. Without your model family, you're just another generically vulnerable child, and a fictional one at that. What's to prevent your abduction into Henry Darger's *Realms of the Unreal* where children are in constant peril? Don't try your luck. You're fortunate he never thought to slide a piece of tracing paper over you and spirit away your outline—minus that blue frock—into one of his panicked swarms. You'd fit right in with your sprightly body and bright yellow hair.

Of course, there are other possibilities. You might hopscotch with an extra bolt of verve, torque into a reverse-vector rabbit hole, and land in John Ashbery's *Girls on the Run.* Now, that would be a much better fate. Don't get me wrong, childhood is no bowl of cherries there either. But Ashbery (whom you could refer to as Uncle John if you made it in) has a great sense of humor and an endlessly surprising register. There would be scary games, but the children (boys too) would be pretty much in charge. The main problem is just what some of the adults love about this stuff—the way ontology is busy recapitulating postmodern epistemology, with "Mother and her veering / playthings again, torn between the impossible alternatives of existing / and saying no to menace." This makes for great philosophical spills and thrills and other knowledgeable hijinks that come on without much warning, i.e., without pretension. It could get a bit confusing for a kid with your limited vocabulary, not to say life experience. You might end up awash with anxiety. Yes, no, it's not a good idea. Not for you of all clueless kidlets.

Jane was headstrong and having none of this, or maybe she just wasn't listening. She insisted she wanted to find out what was going on. And, before long—in fact, just then—she heard that a terrible thing had happened in her old neighborhood where nothing had ever happened before. That sealed her resolve. She was determined to investigate something she was now certain had been left out in her easy-reader life, something that was beginning to seem big and important—the scary truth.

All right, said Ashbery, stepping up to the so-to-speak plate. If the truth is what you want, here's what I have to say about that. And John Ashbery had a lot to say about that that day—yet another day when logics collide and the world outside the window and inside the Looking-Glass are indistinguishable—all strange, all strangely true. But, really, what did that mean? And even if one could come up with a good guess, what to do with it?

As I say, I can speak only for myself,
but as soon as I got here the rules became different.
They didn't apply to me any more, or to anyone else except
a distant runt,
almost invisible in its litter. So how was
I to know who to stand up to, when to turn abrasive, when
all things nestled,
equidistant, all hearts were charming, and it was good to be
natural and sincere?
True, we had much to worry about,
other things to think about, but when has mankind had
the leisure

to distract himself from these and other unassailable
   syllogisms?
So the truth just washed up on the shore,
a bundle of nerves, not resembling much of anything
we cared to remember. Was polite, stoical,
and anything else to deflect attention from its seething
   ambiguity.
. . .
A stunning moment of certainty survived
briefly, then it too was washed away in the rising
   flood,
tortured, unambitious.
School was over,
not just for that day for forever and for seasons to come.

Hmm, said Jane, no school! Yep, Jane, it seems we can be giddily on our own, if we're to trust Uncle John. By the way, your namesake in his book seems to be saying he's all right, or that some "he" is all right: "No, said Jane, you don't / understand, he means to be nice. He's a sheep, really." Still things are likely to get a bit rough, even in green pastures. It's just as well that you've abandoned kiddy didactics. It's time to face the music—Daphne's theme: she, the great, ill-fated runner, fleeing for life and limb from the drop-dead handsome Apollo who won't take no for an answer—and the death rattles of those increasingly shaky opposable thumbs—girl/boy, good/evil, dream/waking, life/death ("Jane / was titillated but squeamish. She thought of asking Cupid / if the seams of her stocking were straight . . ."). Time to get on with a really hard-hitting investigation starting with square one ("A word / would issue from the crack in the pavement, and it was up to Jane and the / detective to decide / whether they'd heard it. If they hadn't, fine. / Otherwise it's down to the station / to sort everything out in the middle of the night, and not taken to too / kindly / either."). Square one in this case is, as it happens, Henry Darger's *Realms of the Unreal.* Without too much sleuthing, we can safely speculate that Uncle John would never have written those things about truth (in exactly that way), or about Laure and Tidbit and Henry and Rags the mutt, and Aunt Jennie and Uncle Margaret, or Larry Sue, or Aunt Clara ("Not so fast, Aunt Clara indicated, the gum / trees are a-rattle. The stealth of the horizon / nears us.") had he not encountered Darger: in whose world all girls, all the time, are on the run; the adults play all the mean parts; and the great flood, the ever-coming storm, and the Truth—all three—are one and the same.

Henry Darger was the Chicago outsider artist who died unknown at eighty-one in 1973, leaving the vast allegorical, violence-filled "picture book" he had secretly worked on for almost sixty years unfinished. He seemed to be obsessed with protecting little girls in danger (there's evidence of this starting in his childhood); attempting via his idiosyncratic imaginative powers to rescue them from male-inflicted horrors. Or is the truth more sinister? Was he, as some have suggested, concocting fantasy fictions that reflected his own violent impulses? (There's some evidence for that too.) If that was the case, or part of the case, was it to enjoy them vicariously, or to control himself through some equivalent of self-administered play therapy? There have been many speculations about the relation between the "real" life of the man and his art. There has even been a controversial accusation that he commited a murder.

Darger, who had been orphaned and institutionalized as a child (his mother died when he was three; by eight, his father was too ill to care for him), was doubtless disturbed. But does that attribution most accurately connote pathology or empathic pain, or both? In his sympathetic introduction to *Henry Darger: Art and Selected Writings,* Michael Bonesteel recounts how Darger's sometimes strange emotional reactions to his life circumstances as a youth, and the absence of any assistance from his family, left him susceptible to bizarrely negligent treatment.

> At the age of twelve or thirteen, [Henry] was examined by the school doctor. The diagnosis was that his "heart isn't in the right place" and he was transferred downstate to the Asylum for Feeble-Minded Children in Lincoln, Illinois. Four years later, while Darger was still in residence there, the Lincoln Asylum was at the center of one of the most sensational scandals of the period. Claims of abuse and neglect were leveled at staff who allowed one resident's severe burns from a radiator to go untreated. Another inmate was burned while left unattended in a bathtub and died. Harry G. Hardt, a supervisor at the asylum, was accused of tolerating physical violence by staff members, reducing the

> quality and quantity of food served, and stealing money from inmates. . . . [A boy known to Darger], believing his epileptic seizures were caused by inappropriate sexual urges, tried to castrate himself and died four days later.

Darger had been catechized and baptized into the Catholic church shortly after his father was taken to a charity home. He was immediately beset by idealized religiosity and unbearable guilt over his confused anger: he wrote in his autobiography, "In my younger days . . . when angry over something, I burned holy pictures and hit the face of Christ in pictures with my fist. . . ." The physicality with which he directed his rage at the religious object (presumably a paper reproduction) is interesting, considering how his hands-on assembly of depictions of maiming were so intermingled with the iconography of martyrdom, including crucifixion.

But other iconographies entered into the mix. Darger apparently read avidly, with a particular interest in the American Civil War, and kept up with the newspapers. In 1911, when he was nineteen years old and living on his own, he came across an account in the *Chicago Daily News* of a five-year-old child, Elsie Paroubek, who had been kidnapped, strangled, and dumped in a drainage ditch. The accompanying photograph showed a waiflike figure who became for Darger the iconic essence of innocent vulnerability. Distraught when he lost his clipping of the picture, he became so actively haunted by it that Elsie assumed the position of presiding spirit for the epic battles between good and evil that he would invent and call "The Story of the Vivian Girls in What Is Known as the Realms of the Unreal." For the next six decades, his main protagonists, the seven angelic Vivian sisters, would outrun or outwit an endless supply of malevolent men bent on harming them. Like paper-doll versions of Ovid's Daphne, with "the winds baring her limbs, the opposing breezes setting her garments a-flutter," the Vivians appear to have run right out of the clothes they were wearing when Darger traced them. Instead of Daphne's protective bark, roots, and twigs, they've sprouted little penises.

Despite the fantasy plot structures of his *Realms,* Darger was acutely aware of the state of the world outside his own mind, a mind well stocked with history and current events as well as religious imagery. The battles of the *Realms of the Unreal* are staged at a very dense intersection of Christian martyrdom—particularly that of his great heroine, Saint Joan, aka the Maid of Orleans or "Angelinia" (patron saint of his crusading Angelinians and the transgendered Vivians)—along with three wars, the Civil War, World War I, and World War II (presumably the source of scenes in concentration camps). The ongoing theme of "child slave revolt," aka "child labor rebellion" suggests that Darger must have been impressed/impacted by contemporary depictions of the horrendous conditions of children working in factories, mills, and mines, some as young as three years old. Lewis Hines's photo essays of dirt-smudged children in ragged clothing, despair radiating from their whole being, were becoming public in 1909.

In his squalid living quarters in a Chicago apartment house, Darger was rendering his versions of these things. Using tracings and cutouts and freehand drawings, he lifted images for the Vivian girls, and thousands of others, out of the relatively wholesome environments of early- to midtwentieth-century coloring books, comic strips, and advertisements, and sent their sturdy little bodies into endless brushes with doom. The Vivian girls are nothing if not good sports as they accomplish their missions with earnest athleticism. They're quite jaunty even when stark naked, packing toy-pistol penises in their crotches, carrying honeycomb footballs, giant strawberries and melons, multicolored beach balls and umbrellas, sporting giant butterfly wings, racing ahead of the perpetually "coming storm." One wonders at times if Darger somehow thought nudity protective. He refers to "running to cross river nuded" or "assuming nuded appearance by compulsion" (Bonesteel). Their own, or externally imposed? What adds to the puzzle is that there's no hint of discomfort or embarrassment depicted. The girls appear to be congenitally stalwart whatever their costumes, or lack thereof, in their protective tomboy spunk and ambiguous genital gear. Oddly, the more one sees these images, the more normal that aspect seems—at least in the context of Darger's world.

The Vivians' escapades take place Perils of Pauline style with hair's-breadth escapes ("Only to escape death again . . . ," "The Glandeliannians Were About To Hang The Brave Little Girls" but rescue comes) in proto–theme-park settings, across landscapes of garish posies, giant polka-dotted mushrooms and swaying palms, past nubbin houses with bright red roofs, tailed by roiling monster clouds, tornado worms, and other freaks of the preternatural. The decorative panoramas are, of course, part of what makes the pictures so stunning. They sometimes resemble pop mutations of Persian miniatures in their vivid color and detail; at the same time it could be the revenge of a very aggressive pack of Hallmark cards. Kitsch perfected for the nerve-rackingly madcap Vivian escapadees—Violet, Joice, Jennie, Catherine, Hettie, Daisy, and Evangeline—as they accomplish their feats of virtue amidst an ornamental chaos of atrocity and ruin.

Throughout, the tone of the pictures and the writing—brief captions as well as the voluminous text of Darger's endless saga—never ceases to be jarring. For instance, this caption on one of the pictures ("Jennie Richee" is a place name):

> At Jennie Richee.
> Have thrilling time fleeing through a field of gutted bodies of children, with Shells Bursting All Around
> Vivian Girls wear purple Rimmed Hats
> Others Are Girlscouts.

One could extend the apparel note: The designer Henry Darger has developed a new line of brightly festooned hats that function as haloes, and vice versa, for appearances at a great variety of apocalyptic events. Whether au natural or carefully coordinated outfits, you can feel confidently attractive at any life-or-death occasion.

And this, benignly amusing by comparison, could almost pass for Ashbery's parodic wit:

> A THRILLING ADVENTURE IN THE CAVERN WITH THE STRANGE BLENGIGLOMENEAN CREATURES
>
> "If this isn't the limit," exclaimed the Angelinian captain. "There is no change in this glow, as though we see vapor of four colors up there, the cavern seems cooler than the labyrinth. I'm dumbfounded." . . . In the middle of the floor yawned a huge black opening, which on viewing again, made Violet and her sisters feel sort of creepy.

At the end of all those exhilaratingly ghastly days, is the whole thing just a ragged edifice of kitsch? Yes and no. Tragi-kitsch is more like it, and that's not a denigration. Darger takes one beyond creepy feelings toward metaphysical sadness over such an excessive site of heartfelt inadequacy. The excess is not in the end the problem, but the limited human register within it. The many unrescued Paulines, whose mangled corpses litter the more desolate landscapes, transgress every conventional genre with their torn and broken bodies, their copiously bleeding stigmata. Zounds! Ashbery opines, from his book over in the corner. Zounds! Let's get outta here, fast! But the afterimages are too haunting, too baffling to not want to look back. The garish kitsch sold in religious gift shops apparently gives some people consolation; Darger (I almost wrote "offers," but he really didn't "offer" anything to the remote "us" who are now puzzling about work he apparently wanted burned) . . . Darger's vision is the opposite of consoling. It is desolation that will never touch the sublime.

Excuse me! Jane piped up. Are you saying it's tragic *because* it's kitsch? Gosh, Jane, you are developing your vocabulary! And maybe you're on to something. Maybe, taking Darger's life circumstances into consideration, how they so fully entered the work, how the work seemed to become the life with almost no remainder—But where does that leave one? Is it that kitsch is inherently tragic? Adorno hated kitsch because it put a cheap mask on the tragedy. Maybe they're inseparable. In Noh, it's said that the mask is not put on the face, the face is drawn into the mask. Perhaps something can be learned from that. It's all sounding like the song of the goat to me.

> "*Lacrimoso,* our sport is behind us!
> *Lacrimoso,* we can't get anything done!
> *Lacrimoso,* the bear has gone after the honey!
> *Lacrimoso,* the honey drips incessantly
> from the bough of the tree."
>
> Worse, it was traditional to feel this way.

Despite (or partly due to?) its overwhelming inadequacy as redemptive strategy, it's the vast mélange of Darger's oeuvre that stimulated Ashbery to write *Girls on the Run.* This is how it starts:

> A great plane flew across the sun,
> and the girls ran along the ground.
> The sun shone on Mr. McPlaster's face, it was green like an
> elephant's.

That these lines appear adjacent to the cover art—Darger's "Storm Brewing"—for the cloth edition cues the reader that the poetry inside the book will be about Darger's art. To some extent that's true, beginning with a Darger scene, or seeming to, but quickly swerving with Mr. McPlaster into what is revealed as quintessential Ashbery. Swerving, that is, out of tragi-kitsch into zany comic, and ultimately to elegiac-comic. That green elephant face? Already we're in territory much too frivolous for Darger. By the time one has reached the end of the first page, noting that "Laure and Tidbit agreed" with a long digression on the fickleness of fashion, postmodern consciousness (of the sort that foregrounds the medium) is blowing in the wind: "Write it now, Tidbit said, / before they get back. And, quivering, I took the pen."

Withal, as they used to say, Jane, that mysterious "they"—a first of many unassigned pronouns to come—though ominous, will never amount to the horrifying specter of Darger's all too visible men bludgeoning and gutting little girls. Though there are scattered tastes of Darger's violence in Ashbery ("The woods resounded with campers' cries," "With a terrifying roar the house exploded again," "Now it's time to surrender, or be riven asunder, garroted, / eviscerated . . .") they never have the cumulative effect of fully consummated terror. A poetics as pervaded by swerves of logic as Ashbery's tends to neutralize such things. They might at second or third glance turn out to be a joke, part of a game, a bad dream. Or, one never knows, there might be more to it than that. Come along, Jane, let's try to figure out what's going on here!

Ashbery began *Girls* after encountering Darger's work, first in 1996 at the Collection de l'Art Brut in Lausanne, Switzerland (which, in fact, owns *Storm Brewing*), and the following year at the New York American Folk Art Museum. No doubt, Darger's lavishly hermetic, deeply violent, weirdly humorous vision was intriguing for many reasons: in its otherness (Ashbery was neither raised a Catholic nor preoccupied with technologies of murder and war); in its evocations of childhood fears, loneliness, and experiences of death (as a youth, Ashbery lost his only sibling, a younger brother). But the surface pleasures of the work are also part of the appeal, the way the artist assembled his vast, swarming landscapes out of unlikely, but readily available, materials from the pop kiddy culture of his time.

I invited Ashbery to my Investigative Poetics class at Bard in spring 2007 to talk with students who were reading *Girls on the Run*. It turns out that many of Darger's sources from children's literature, comics, and advertisements were a prominent part of Ashbery's childhood. He too was fascinated by little girls and their clothes, their dolls and games when he was a child. So the Darger show was both riveting in its strangeness and a strong dose of Madeleine. It stimulated vivid memories of spreading out the Sunday comics on the floor to dive into the invitingly framed worlds of characters like Little Nemo and the Katzenjammer Kids, the wonderfully "fiendish brats" Hans and Fritz, Buster Brown, Little Annie Rooney (ubiquitous, in altered form, in Darger), and her dog, Zero. For Ashbery there was something timeless about comic strips that went on with their reliable installments for successive generations of kids. There was also the oddly admirable spirit of children's books with their "fustian, serviceable prose." But another significant point of contact for Ashbery was the nightmare aspect of Darger's vision, stopping short of its "psychotic element."

With such interestingly mixed feelings about Darger, one can safely say that *Girls* is not a simple case of ekphrasis. Might it be as much antidote or witty exorcism as homage? Or an inspired reengagement with the extreme sport of childhood? To let the language feel out the delicious edges of terror, without succumbing to it, in a spirit of hard-core child's play is a worthy challenge. Any or none of this could be the case, but what Ashbery makes of Darger's tragikitsch (seeing the humor and the angst in it) turns out most unexpectedly to be an elegiac-comic confection that has more gravitas than one would guess at first glance. Evocations of childhood in *Girls on the Run* involve a relinquishing of lost possibilities, then and now, in exchange for the play of a poesis constantly underscoring the sheer improbability of its coming to anything much. All the while, it yields one wonder after another, like this beautiful moment grazed by ancient presences:

> a breeze was blowing, it was snowing. The
> droplets made diagonal streaks in the air
> where pterodactyls had been. It was time for an exodus
> of sorts;
> Paul picked up the legend
> where it had been broken off: "No
> blame accrues to those who were left behind, unless, haply,
> they were climbing
> the wall to get a better view of the stars . . .
> What is it to imagine something you had forgotten once, is it

inventing, or more of a restoration from ancient mounds
    that were probably there?
You that can tell all, tell this."

It's probably clear enough by now, Jane, that there's no epic plot in *Girls on the Run.* Though you haven't really known such things yourself, have you? Do you even recognize an adventure genre tone when you hear one? "Let's get out of here, Judy said. / They're getting closer, I can't stand it." *Girls,* in its fifty-five pages, has more breathable air to spare at its terminus than Darger may have inhaled in a lifetime. It's happily episodic, at times like an "exquisite corpse" created from a mix of comic strips or a serial adventure story that keeps digressing or the casual way kids used to go out to play, to "make up" an absorbing game and then, just as casually, disperse for supper.

Let the birds wash over them, Laure said, for what use are
    earmuffs
in a snowstorm, except to call attention to distant tots
who have strayed. And now the big Mother warms them,
accepts them, for the nervous predicates they are. Far from
    the beach-fiend's
howling, their adventure nurses itself back
to something like health. On the fifth day it takes a little
    blancmange
and stands up, only to fall back into a hammock.
I told you it was coming, cried Dimples, but look out,
Another big one is on the way!
And they all ran, and got out, and that was that for that day.

Oh no, said Jane, whose immersion studies were going better than one would have thought. She was already trying out some junior lit crit: it looks like "the coming storm," probably a monster tornado, may have jumped the battlefields of *Realms of the Unreal* right into Uncle John's book, threatening to pull its pages into the Poundian vortex! Listen: "The beachfiend's howling. . . . It was coming. . . . Another big one is on the way!" I'm with Judy, said Jane, I can't stand it either.

No, no, no. Don't worry. You certainly don't have to worry about Pound! By now, if not before, the ontology—if not the metaphysics—if not the epistemology—of these Ashbery scenes is patently clear.

The vortex *is* more a matter of poesis than FEMA material, but these are all just allusions to someone else's allusions to Garden of Eden moral storms. Plato, not Pound, could set you straight on that. They've lost their destructive force while maintaining their metaphorical zing. It's all about subtly nuanced, free-floating foreboding now, of the kind that arises when one has been consorting with too many nervous predicates on the way to the fainting hammock. The great thing is that with the slightest off-tangent glance, it's all blessedly comic.

Judy, Laure, Tidbit, Henry, Dimples, Larissa, Diane, Pete—these kids are in a very different sort of pickle from General Vivian's daughters with their mission to keep the moralistic feedback loop threaded in the big machine. In *Girls on the Run,* tomorrow will be a spanking-new day, a new constellation of kids, some from places far from the hood; new games, new rules—except for the old ones worth keeping. Happenstance, both whimsical and ominous, is the major moving principle of all things—though there are patterns to be found and made in these wildflower fields and bloodstained meadows and concrete wastelands of indeterminacy, and one never knows what might come roaring or wafting by to land in a plein-air stanza or two.

> Go back! This is a place too far.
> In any case you ought to reconsider the places back there,
> teeming with sandalwood and bees. You think you know it
> but you don't, there are inner coasts to be discovered, sat on,
> whittled to a point more dangerous than Father Time's
> tuning fork,
> if you but knew.

> There was no going back,
> now, though some did go back. Those who did
> didn't get very far. The others came out a little ahead,
> I think . . . I'm not sure.

Uncertainty unbound, but full of prismatic ebulliance. In a poetic nanosec, the game turns surreal. But this time it's in the art history sense—a "rose / that blows on time's pediment" as "the sundial smiled in the rain" and the "fox returned smiling, fanning his great tail in the comet." It's not the surreal realism of waking nightmares, of hurtling gurneys of death and destruction, it's that "This was that day's learning" and we're "glad for that day."

As you can see, Jane, lively snippets come and go in and out of sync with Darger. It's true, what Darger knew—that terrible things happen to little girls. But that's not what *Girls on the Run* is about. Maybe it's because Laure, Tidbit, and the gang are not really orphans of the storm. Mother, Aunt Jennie, and Uncle Margaret seem close enough by (Father seems to be a fifties-style absentee). The kiddies fling themselves into their games, not noticing the darkening sky that brings dark things to light except as part of the very game they're playing, which is the source of the light. In their games where they, like the poet, invent their own rules, there can be an assertion of some independence from circumstances masquerading as fate. The child strategically named "Henry" has already, as early as the second page, made his position on child slavery clear:

> I am no longer your serf
> and if I was I wouldn't do your bidding . . .
> You think you can lord it over every last dish of oatmeal
> on this planet, Henry said. But wait till my ambition
> comes a cropper, whatever that means, or bursts into
> feathered bloom
> and burns on the shore. Then the kiddies dancing sidewise
> declared it a treat, and the ice-cream gnomes slurped their
> last that day.

Ashbery's long-standing ambivalence toward gravity is mostly played out on the comic side in *Girls on the Run,* but the elegiac comes in more and more toward the end of the poem like a tide pulled by the gathering gravitas of the poem itself. (Gravity versus gravitas—an important distinction for the Ashbery aesthetic.) It's elegy made all the more consequential by its collusion with humor. (An astonishing achievement!) There is, for instance, "the noise of his voice, like rain that flails the spears of vetch / in Maytime, to reap a tiny investment" immediately followed by

> So we faced the new day,
> like a pilgrim who sees the end of his journey deferred
> forever.
> Who could predict where we would be led, to what
> extremes of aloneness? Yet the horizon is civil.

This passage, one discovers, is in a kind of fearless symmetry with the final lines of the poem, which can be read (like the civil horizon) as more than a palliative response. What's happening is the emergence of a third term or tone that resolves the reactive chemistry of the elegiac-comic mix. There is, finally, an assertion that trains its linguistic vision beyond Darger's darkness, in an acknowledgment that is tonic because it is so pragmatically transcendent. Note the syntax in lines three through six below. It seems to perform a shotgun marriage between Stein and Stevens only to give onto a thrilling transformation. It's inimitable Ashbery: the elegiac-comic turns out to be pure miscegenation in all its splendor, a great hi-lo polyphony, and profoundly restorative:

> O who were they?
> Mary Ann, and Jimmy—no, but who were they?
> Who have as their mantles on the snow
> and we shall never reach land
> before dark, yet who knows what advises them,
> discreet in the mayhem? And then it's bright in the defining
> pallor of their day.
> Does this clinch anything? We were cautioned once, told not
> to venture out—
> yet I'd offer this much, this leaf, to thee.
> Somewhere, darkness churns and answers are riveting,
> taking on a fresh look, a twist. A carousel is burning.
> The wide avenue smiles.

There are still girls, and boys, on the run. Soon the carousel will be a smoldering ruin and children will cry. It will become indistinguishable from all the other ruins that are the foreground of so many children's lives. Luckily for everyone who's survived thus far, that's not all that's happening in the world. Look, Jane, the wide avenue is smiling. Probably at its own cartoonish personification, among other things—so many other things. That's the mercy of it—what the damaged child hiding out in the reclusive Henry Darger wasn't able to see. It's what becomes visible on the civil horizon of Ashbery's wide avenue: how much more teems into view than can enter a solitary mind. How the buoyancy of one's intellect and imagination and daily spirit most depends on the unexpected in that immense multitude.

Jane looked pensive, and said, I sort of miss the old gang, but I don't think I can go back now. She said this with a charmingly crooked smile, and then asked, Where do we go from here?

Besides Being Beside Ourselves

Your Name Here (2000)

Richard Deming

> *I know that the world I converse with in the city and in the farms is not the world I* think. *I observe that difference, and shall observe it. One day, I shall know the value and law of this discrepancy.*
>
> —Ralph Waldo Emerson

In a sense, it is a relief to write about John Ashbery's work within the context of a forum devoted to celebrating his impressive, ambitious, and full oeuvre in that one then does not need to justify why the poet's work deserves attention. Its primacy is a given. Yet at the same time, one worries that the assumptions of his centrality and importance threaten to overwhelm the attention due to his individual books. For instance, *Your Name Here* is the poet's twentieth volume and is part of what might be considered his later (that is, more recent) work. One temptation is to situate this book in the context of his other collections, especially those considered his masterworks: *Self-Portrait in a Convex Mirror, Flow Chart, Three Poems,* and *The Double Dream of Spring.* Again, however, this risks keeping the attention general and might distract one from encountering this masterful late book on its own remarkable and provocative terms. To gain the whole, in other words, there is the threat that the individual elements that make up the body of work might be lost. So, in the current situation of what has called us here, so to speak, what we gain in not having to explain or contextualize Ashbery's work in the specific venue—to be free of having to say *why*— is the ability to ask a more telling question, what does Ashbery's work do? What does it make possible? And, ultimately but perhaps most important, what is the occasion of thinking that it brings us to? To ask these questions, it seems to me, is to move beyond an evaluative mode, past an easy insistence on Ashbery's importance to saying something about the work itself and what it accomplishes as acts of language. If Ashbery is an important poet, is more than a fashionable aesthete, then his work indeed shapes the general art, but beyond that the art, his art, says something about language itself. If art is one way that a culture shows itself to itself, then what does Ashbery show us about language? In other words, what I propose is to take seriously the oft-repeated proposition that Ashbery's work is difficult and ask what that difficulty amounts to. As I hear it, that difficulty calls us to think, and in this to think about what the language Ashbery uses—which is, after all, our shared language—is doing. This difficulty both warrants and makes possible the conditions for attention, but it is not simply a general attention. The poems bring attention to the meaningfulness of familiar language, the ordinary language that Ashbery makes seem so extraordinary. So, *Your Name Here,* for instance, brings us toward a discussion of ordinary language (not just poetic language) and what it makes available, which is, first and last, our world. I am saying that Ashbery is important and in light of that, let us think what this importance means in terms of poetry. And if that brings out the philosophical implications of poetry in general and Ashbery's specifically, so be it.

A marked self-alienation reverberates throughout the entire collection of poems entitled *Your Name Here,* which opens with the line, "[t]he room I entered was a dream of this room" and, later in the same poem, "Why do I tell you these things? / You are not even here." While we might see those latter lines as an accusation, they also suggest an uncertainty about the speaker's own actions, their reality, their actuality. And the question of what it means for the addressee to be in another's dream will be one worth returning to.

Even though among postwar poets an emphasis on alienation might not seem unique, Ashbery's conception of this distance takes on a different tenor in that for his poems, particularly those of *Your Name Here,* the alienation occurs within language, within our relationship to the language that we use every day. Furthermore, this alienation, encountered in or as revealed by Ashbery's poems, is not a crisis (as in a situation that takes him by surprise)—and this is what makes his work not only unique but perhaps *necessary*—but a given condition. Yet, in this case such alienation is not necessarily a negative condition in that it delivers us to ourselves, to a consciousness of the self that is, paradoxically, romantic at its core in the sense that it provides an awakening to the knowledge of a self that we are continually distanced from. The trick, then, is to discover this distance, to recognize it within ourselves if ever we are to resolve it.

Let us begin as one should, for instance, with the title itself. *Your Name Here* seems ironic and witty enough as a title for a collection of poems, and that humor is one way of noting an emotional distance. Characteristic of Ashbery's brilliance, one could simply enjoy just the pleasure of that wit and move on, and yet pausing over that moment makes clear that there are additional depths to be experienced by a more careful reader. Because of the everydayness of much of Ashbery's language, a person might be tempted not to listen carefully to that language. Reading too quickly circumvents the possibility of the words—any words—surprising us, making claims upon us. The quickness is a withholding of time, and time is the necessary condition of inner sense. That problem of overlooking the familiar, the immediate illustrates the sense of alienation I will broadly trace in his collection *Your Name Here,* just as it shows how Ashbery foregrounds what most warrants our attention—the language that is everywhere at hand. Slowing our reading down allows that language to move in from the outside, to be reclaimed, matched by our own language.

The title invites the reader to provide the missing title, to *complete* the book, as it were. We might think then that "name" means "title." But if we take this to mean literally the *reader*'s name, then the book is not simply completed by the reader but the book becomes metonymic—as if to say in such a way that the collection becomes *Deming* when I read it. The poems compose this "book of Deming" (or whoever is reading the book) and the poems then flow through what that name identifies to me and *as* me—and it must be me (myself) in that for some other reader the "me" has an altogether different (that is, his or her own) referent. The poems are written by Ashbery but in reading them these acts of language pass through the reader's consciousness—in that way, the poet's words, the words of his poems, are in effect not (merely) his own. I am—any reader is—inscribed onto (into?) the poems.

The reader may not complete the book but instead he or she provides a field for the poems' cohesion, a cohesion dictated by the poems themselves and their engagement of language. We might say that the text reads the reader in the ways that its rhetoricity guides the reader's warp and weave of attention. The references are not merely the reader's but are also no longer solely Ashbery's. "That was the day we first realized we didn't fully / know our names, yours or mine, and we left quietly / amid the gray snow falling. Twilight had already set in," the poet writes in "Crossroads in the Past," a poem at the center of *Your Name Here.* What does it mean to not "fully know" one's name? If our names are not our own, and we know it, who are we? How are we called—called out, called forth, invoked, provoked? What does it mean to say "I" or "you"? And aren't these pronouns names of a sort? Ashbery's sense of a rift brings to mind a moment at the beginning of Ralph Waldo Emerson's essay "Experience": "Where do we find ourselves? In a series, of which we do not know the extremes, and believe that it has none. We wake and find ourselves on a stair: there are stairs below us, which we seem to have ascended; there are stairs above us, many a one, which go upward and out of sight." One might ask of Emerson—his question implies awakening to a need by a need—how it is that we do not simply find ourselves wherever it is we are. But what do we use to determine location?

The connection between Emerson's lines and Ashbery's is a sense of being unlocatable and yet not nowhere but still in transition between states or stages. Ashbery's lines in "Crossroads in the Past" about the uncertainty of names unsettle the adamic duties of a poet and suggest a certain, recurring in-betweenness in which possessive pronouns (not to mention proper names) are contingent rather than conclusive, are means of location rather than definition. What does such drift of the names mean and what does our partial knowledge of them reveal? The difficulty here lies in the reminder that the world could indeed be otherwise. The collection's title, thus, both invites and forecloses the invitation—as crossroads themselves do; however, in that *Your Name Here* does in fact give a title—it is a blank that is filled, being already filled in by the phrase that notes its being blank or open. The title is a double dream of inscription and blanks do not remain blank. The question of how and why we fill them, or find them to be filled, leads to the possibilities of taking—or coming upon—a responsibility for our responses.

Yet, this all assumes that the title's pronoun "*your*" refers to the reader, but it might not be so, which further complicates the confusion of names and pronouns. Instead, the "you" (implied in *Your Name*) may be self-referential, if we see poems as not simply being the author's own authentic voice but as the negotiation of cultural and epistemological elements. It is harder to see immediately but still possible that the pronoun's referent is the poet (especially if Ashbery is pushing against the grain of the built-in authority of *the Author,* something functionally other than the flesh-and-blood person John Ashbery). In that sense, poems express more than an author knows he or she knows. I take this idea from Emerson's "Self-Reliance," wherein Emerson tells us that "[c]haracter teaches us above our wills. Men imagine that they communicate their virtue or vice only by overt actions, and do not see that virtue or vice emit a breath every moment." Beyond our intent, the poem expresses the very processes of understanding rather than what it is that we understand. In back of this I hear Hegel and a specific moment in his lectures on aesthetics when he says, in discussing its external elements, that a work of art "has no value for us simply as it stands; we assume something further behind it, something inward, a significance, by which the external semblance has a soul breathed into it. It is this, its soul, that the external appearance indicates." Hegel moves from this observation about works of art to speak of our own actions: "Just so the human eye, a man's face, flesh, skin, his whole figure, are a revelation of mind and soul, and in this case the meaning is always something other than what shows itself within the immediate appearance." To which we might add Emerson's further insistence, "We pass for what we are," and it is this tension of authenticity and alienation that informs and forms *Your Name Here.* There is a separation from one's self and one's figure in the world, yet that figure expresses us, as a twilight sets in. In short, we haunt ourselves.

Let others make (and others certainly *have* made) the case that Emerson influences Ashbery. My argument is based instead on a claim for contiguity rather than continuity in the ways these two writers are in dialogue. In other words, the questions that Ashbery raises in *Your Name Here* are questions also opened by Emerson. This is to see Emerson's thoughts reflected in the poems of Ashbery and to see Ashbery reflected in Emerson's essays by means of the distance one feels from one's own language, and thus one's own ability to experience the life arising from, conditioned by, dictated by that language. In the convexity of self-portraiture that the act of reading entails, this chiasmus creates an idea of tradition out of shared questions rather than aesthetic formulae. In fact, on another occasion it would be useful to think about how although Ashbery has a clear sense of aesthetics his seems a poetics that is not easily generalizable to others. In this way, he breaks from schools or movements, no matter how much critics would like to see him aligned and locatable in such a way. Even Wallace Stevens, to whom Ashbery is endlessly compared, has more of a clear *program* of poetics than Ashbery offers. Frustrating the tendency to see his work by other means, Ashbery's poems create a situation where one needs to attend to the words themselves to discover their claim on him as well as on us. This is then to take our words as that which reveals us to ourselves and as the very element that haunts us with the specters of how far from ourselves we have come, how far away we have gotten.

What I am saying is that Ashbery's poems take this situation of alienation seriously and the "you" of the book's title therefore refers as much to the reader as to himself, thereby foregrounding the collection's own sense of a (necessary) self-alienation. In the book's second poem, "If You Said You Would Come with Me," we encounter the speaker walking with "Anna," a name unknown to the reader yet expressed with an immediate familiarity—already an example of an alien intimacy, one which signals both the reader's connection (the speaker assumes that familiarity and does not introduce the people in the poem) and his or her distance in that we do not know Anna or, for that matter, the speaker. Tellingly, there is no clarity in terms of who the addressee in the poem's title refers to—is it the speaker, Anna, or the reader? Many readers have made much of the indeterminacy of an Ashbery poem, but what makes Ashbery's work of increasing value is not the fact of this indeterminacy but rather the ways that the openings provide opportunities for observing how and why we make moral (I do not say moralistic) choices, for we do not leave indeterminacies unanswered.

Like the speaker in "If You Said You Would Come with Me," one hears a "great bell tolling," as the act of recognition and of consciousness of time and place ("ask not for whom the bell tolls . . ."). "'It's the words you spoke in the past, coming back to haunt you,' Anna explained. 'They always do, you know.'" My thinking of Ashbery's work by way of Emerson, being more than whim at last, I hope, is perhaps more fully grounded by this line from Ashbery's prose poem as it recalls another passage from Emerson's "Self-Reliance": "A man should learn to detect and watch that gleam of light which flashes across his mind from within, more than the lustre of the firmament of bards and sages. Yet, he dismisses without notice his thought, because it is his. In every work of genius we recognize our own rejected thoughts: they come back to us with a certain alienated majesty." Emerson tells us that art gives us back our own thoughts, thoughts that are our own and yet so removed from us that we can only recognize them in another form, that is, in the work of art, which in itself calls forth our attention, this is, if it *is* art. As Anna notes, this feeling of our own words separate from us and yet returning nonetheless is not always—indeed usually is not—a comforting thing, in that what we recognize is that we are not ourselves—our words are ours and yet removed from us, haunting us at the same time as they return to us. This observation or admonition of Anna's has an added resonance in that one might think of the fact of Ashbery's nineteen previous collections as also haunting the speaker, who is himself a figure of the poet's discourse. The "I" of the poem is haunted by all the other poems Ashbery has written, as is Ashbery, as is the reader of the poet's body of work.

Here, someone might want to make the gentle reminder that a speaker of a poem ought not be confused with the poet. While on one hand we might take that as granted, the speaker of a poem speaks with the words or discourse of the poet. They are the poet's words, in the sense of being his or her choices—choices made for another—but again set at a distance, something more than ventriloquized but also not completely *other.* Language speaks through the poem in this manner and so a poem's "speaker" is not just some narrative device. Alienation needs just enough proximity to measure it as a distance.

I take it as important that the speaker in this poem seems to have forgotten what Anna insists he (already) knows: that the words spoken in the past are not passed by, they travel with us. The poem wants to forget this, but it (in the division of Anna and the speaker) cannot allow itself that forgetfulness. Harold Bloom, in his seminal chapter on Ashbery in *Figures of Capable Imagination,* writes, "Poets want to believe, with Nietzsche, that 'forgetfulness is a property of all action,' and action for them is writing a poem. Alas, no one can write a poem without remembering another poem, even as no one loves without remembering, though dimly or subconsciously, a former beloved, however much that came under taboo." For Bloom, this desire is a measure of the anxiety of influence and for his model the poet thinks he or she needs to forget in order to move forward and so as not to be overburdened by indebtedness. I would say, however, there is a way of looking at the self-consciousness in (and as) Ashbery's poems that goes beyond literary questions to an existential circumstance underwriting not Ashbery's virtuosity but the necessity of his work. Ashbery's poems, or at least specifically those of *Your Name Here,* enact that action of remembering the situation that one has continually forgotten one's self and that acts of imagination call (or, that is, *recall*) us back to language, to words that always seem like someone else's, even when—especially when—they are ours.

The collection's first poem announces this sense of alienation that I am describing at play in *Your Name Here:* "The room I entered was a dream of this room." It is thus the room and not the room;

it is an imagined representation of the room, but one that is still entered. And if it is a dream state being described, then the poem seems to take as axiomatic that belief that everything in a dream is some part or aspect of the dreamer—"Surely all those feet on the sofa were mine," reads the second line. On one hand, this announces a fractured multiplicity, but I cannot help but hear two puns. To begin with, a "room" is mentioned in the first stanza, and *stanza* itself is derived from the Italian for *room.* The speaker enters a room, just as the poet enters the stanza, just as the reader enters both the stanza (at the level of structure) and the room (at the level of the diegetic space). We might then read "feet" as suggesting poetic measure. Thus, all the words are the poet's, as all aspects of the dream are the dreamer's.

Throughout the book, we see similar gestures of making things be both themselves and things other than themselves, simultaneously—including the final eponymous poem, which begins, "But how can I be in this bar and also be a recluse?" It is a funny sort of paradox and Ashbery's wit—and indeed his poems are often funny or comic—has often struck me as usefully self-conscious in the ways that it undermines an overdetermined poignancy that lyric poetry can affect either in its romantic or modernist modes. The humor also provides a way that Ashbery can cite pathos while not having his work subsumed by it. One hears that sort of question ("how can I be in this bar and also be a recluse?") in one's daily life and it has an immediacy that does not hide its poignancy; one still feels a pull of disparate discontinuities manifesting themselves in places so ordinary they seem surprising. Indeed, the question conveys a better sense of the alienation I have been describing. In light of this paradox of being two things at once, we see we are often "beside ourselves" and thus at a certain level we are always acting in a way *besides ourselves*—that is to say, other than ourselves. The burden of choice is the limitations of and the construction of identity. The frustration seems to be, then, that one needs to make choices even if what and how we choose is how we come to know (and be) a self. Furthermore, if all the aspects of the dream are aspects of the dreamer (and so, too, the poem composed from the consciousness of the poet) and are self-referential, then the "you" in the poem is the speaker as well as the reader. The addressee is the poet's dream of the speaker's auditor.

Let us return to "If You Said You Would Come with Me," for later in that poem, the speaker ushers Anna out of a room because he is unsettled by a woman who can read his mind. Who wouldn't be? Anna indicates that she herself is a mind reader. Maybe she is and maybe she isn't, we say, since we cannot say for sure what the speaker thinks ourselves. Anna retorts, "And I can tell what you're thinking is false. Listen to what the big bell says: 'We're all strangers on our own turf, in our own time.' You should have paid attention. Now adjustments will have to be made." This ending (and especially Anna's resigned consternation) strikes me as echoing a Kafka parable in more than just its strangeness. Its specificity is disorienting and the speaker, as in a Kafka parable, is complicit in something but does not know how or why and consequences follow because of this complicity. Of course, what the bell is telling Anna and what the speaker is not hearing is a lesson about alienation, that alienation is our general condition. Anna accuses—since the bell's ringing is the speaker's past words—the speaker of not hearing himself and now a price is to be paid. Yet, she has also said his thinking is false, but might that not be the thinking that arrived at the very aphorism that is now being used against him? Who will be making the adjustments? How does one then take the next step? In any event, either paying attention (as Anna does) or not paying attention (as in the case of the poem's speaker) comes with a result—or "adjustment"—of whatever we did or did not do.

For another poet, this might be an overwhelming crisis and the vision would then be decidedly bleak, as it is very often the case with Kafka, for instance, as if that next step were into some yawning abyss. Yet this is ameliorated by the ease and charm of Ashbery's poems, and in part because one senses that the position of being a stranger to one's own turf and one's own words is not a crisis but is the very fact of everywhere one—indeed, is *how* one—finds oneself. It is not a crisis if it is simply how things are. I do not mean this to suggest that this prevailing sense of alienation is some kind of acceptance or resignation, as if that schism or distance did not matter or did not come with costs and decisions. To say it is not a crisis is not to say there is no grief. On the contrary, grief begins after denial becomes untenable. It is in this sense that Ashbery's poetry is unique and important in that it acts as a kind of guide in a decidedly nondidactic, nongoverning sense. The ease, charm, and wit that I mentioned earlier (so often Ashbery's poems have a sense of the effortless) adds a certain tone of consolation while also making the poem's concerns localized because of the consistent familiarity of the voice constructed in and throughout the poems. In Woody Allen's *Crimes and Misdemeanors* (a movie closer to Ashbery's aesthetic in many ways than most people would care to recognize), Alan Alda's character—a wildly successful but unctuous television producer—insists that comedy is "tragedy plus time." This idea is helpful in thinking of the ways that Ashbery's poems are comic in that there are traces of the difficulty of being removed from oneself the more one tries to draw near. The poems acknowledge the pain and frustration, the very disorientation of being "strangers on our own turf" but that offers neither a meek nor resigned acceptance. Rather, the poems give an occasion for engaging that feeling of separate familiarity and it is that which makes Ashbery's poems an art that continues a kind of pedagogy for adults in that it offers us some guidance in understanding the work of mourning.

I think now of a small essay of Freud's that I have been led to by way of the work of Stanley Cavell (who, this is the place to confess, offers me the lens and vocabulary for the reading of Ashbery that I am gathering here). In the opening paragraph of the short piece "On Transience," an essay written amid the years of the first World War, Freud describes a walk he takes a year before the war with two friends—one a taciturn man, the other a young but well-known poet—during a beautiful summer day. The poet takes no pleasure in the beauty he sees, Freud reports, as all he can note is how everything is given to death and decay and so only experiences the inexorable mortality of all things. Freud argues with the poet—unsuccessfully or at least unpersuasively to the poet—that the mortality of things, their very transience, increases their value rather than negating it. Freud suggests in his reading of the poet's concern (one shared by the taciturn third party) that in the young man's mind there was a revolt against mourning and the realizations that go with it. Mourning is a holding tight to the *absence* of things we love and know (not the things themselves), yet it is a necessary process that comes to a conclusion and thereby transforms itself. Freud writes, "Mourning, as we know, however painful it might be, comes to a spontaneous end. When it has renounced everything that has been lost, then it has consumed itself, and our libido [that is, our capacity for love] is once more free [. . .]."

With this idea in place, we might even see Anna in "If You Said You Would Come with Me," as a kind of analyst in that she reads the mind of the speaker and is able to discern that what is following him, what he is not confronting, and what he is repressing are his own words from the past. If that is the case, then that final line is, more or less, what Anna interprets the speaker to be thinking and she speaks for him, speaks his words for him *to* him. In doing this, Anna models often what we would like poems to do for us—speak the words and feelings and experiences that we have and cannot bring (or have not yet adequately brought) into language. In the intensity of poetry's thoughts we discover and recover our experiences of experience. In short, poetry offers us the opportunity to experience through someone else's representations our own senses of being. This experience is never quantifiable or definable and often creates more art, other poems. Yet, how do we know that Anna is right? The poem ends without either confirming or repudiating her claim, does not verify her analysis. Do we believe her—and at the end of the poem it is more important what the reader's feeling about this is rather than the speaker's assessment of what Anna says—or do we feel her to be presumptuous and sanctimonious? We can ask that since we have no way of knowing whether she can read minds for sure.

So, how we take the import depends, I would say, on how seriously we take the threat of her statement. She does not offer a threat but the reality she describes is threatening. The ways that the line might be resolved (that is, the way a given reader might make sense of it) gives an occasion for a person to ask himself or herself about his or her own belief systems. First, however, one needs to be conscious of the fact that the ambiguity of the authority of that last line asks a question, no matter how open, that we are each of us apt to answer in our own fashion. It is a question, I daresay, of how we hear that last line. Our answer reflects our understanding of that instance and the world in general but does so in such a manner as to make it clear that any reading is contingent not final. It is in that way that Ashbery's text reads *us* even as we read *it.* The gesture of the title *Your Name Here* refers to the name of the experience we put on our experience of occasions for interpretation, but naming that experience, making a choice as we always do, despite ourselves, entails both discovery and loss, and prepares us for identifying it as our own and separate, thereby allowing it to be let go. Anna, then (and the poems themselves, if we see Anna as a voice of the poem, as a voice of poetry) is the creation of a friend, and interlocutor, an Other that helps bring us to an awareness of ourselves. Whether we trust her or distrust her, she is what we make of her articulations.

With this same situation of needing to address undecidability, Ashbery's poem "They Don't Just Go Away, Either," invokes the implications of the fraught situation of why and how answers are offered when he writes:

> Father, I can go no further, the lamp blinds me
> and the man behind me keeps whispering things in my ear
> I'd prefer not to be able to understand . . .
> Yet you must, my child, for the sake of the cousins
> and the rabbit who await us in the dooryard.

So much depends on being willing to be able to understand. I would venture to say that there is a way in which Ashbery's poems feature people and figures that are—as in this passage—heroically unheroic and are thus recognizable. There are stakes, Ashbery's poems remind us, for choosing either listening or not listening. There is no way of simply standing still, no way of not coming to know what we will (and already do) know. "To know a little, would be worth the expense of this world," Emerson offers at the end of his famous essay "Experience," and it is there that I hear the voice of his essays and Ashbery's poems coming closest together in their shared intuition that coming to knowledge is to approach that realization of the full presence of the world, a world that is always moving away, transforming itself from what we love to a new thing—its perpetual parturition. In "They Don't Just Go Away, Either," the speaker says it is a man who keeps whispering that is moving him into a situation of knowingness, a kind of adulthood that the speaker wants to forestall, but much depends on those things we would, childishly, wish to remain not knowing. Yet, in this poem as in "If You Said You Would Come with Me," undecidability is met not with disorientation—it is not a negative but a positive freedom—but engagement with others, with the figure of the friend, the beloved, however we might call it, whatever your name for the figure would be. And this Other, the "you" to one's "I," is what helps us through the act of mourning. Think of Freud who first attempts to help his friend and then in writing his essay attempts to help others, to help himself. This is no easy consolation, but it is the consolation of poetry, consolation that brings us to our mournful attention as a means of one day ending it and freeing us by acknowledging the role of alienation and grief in all that we do. The poems lend the words we know but only hear intermittently. This tension is what makes the comic comic, and the tragic beautiful.

The gesture of *Your Name Here* is thus a bequeathal, the poems giving us back to ourselves as if for the first time. There is a patient hope in beauty; it must be patient for it is always beleaguered on all sides and by an increasing temptation of despair and distraction. What poetry asks is attention, slow, steady listening to the language where we find ourselves, by which we find ourselves and the names of things. I have been making a case not for why we should admire Ashbery, but rather for listening for what is to be valued in his poems. Ashbery's importance is in the generous, open patience of his poems, poems that are the tuition, the learning offered by intuition, his—which, because we recognize it, because we can respond to and stand for the pronouns that set our positions, becomes our own as well. The hope of Ashbery's *Your Name Here* is the want of our willingness to listen to the voice of the man whispering in our ears.

Changeable Hieroglyphics

Other Traditions (2000) and *Selected Prose* (2004)

Geoffrey O'*Brien*

A REVIEW OF ASHBERY'S CRITICISM could be constructed out of quotations, and there is a great temptation to do so. It would be an oblique acknowledgment of Ashbery's own propensity for quoting; *Other Traditions* and *Selected Prose* are, among other things, anthologies, as if finally a critic can do little more than say, "Look—here it is—the thing cannot be paraphrased or gotten at by generalizing."

But the quotes occur in a space that has been made for them, a space whose weather and light operate as such potent even if apparently subdued influences that the object displayed reveals characteristics that might otherwise be unnoticed: the Reverdy poem, for instance ("Route," from *Les ardoises du toit*), quoted in its entirety, which is described beforehand as being "as quiet as a breeze, as simple as a glass of water" and afterward as an organism whose "growth obeys hidden pressures and atmospheric changes"—pressures and changes that are in turn likened to "very fine traps constructed to catch something invisible which was passing." The poem is neither contained nor explained but rather transplanted into a medium in which it can be seen as never before, and perhaps never again.

Critical "dissection" is not what is going on in this writing, since one does not dissect something alive. Attention is solicited for phenomena in movement and likely to dart beyond perception at any moment, in a spirit of "Quick, before it vanishes, or before the light changes." It may not be the object that is going to vanish, but the quality of attention necessary to catch sight of it. These are narratives about reading and hearing and seeing, descriptions of experiences happening in the world.

The experiences may be of confusion or uncertainty. Ashbery is often refreshingly frank about feeling lost or baffled. Of Laura Riding's poetry he writes: "I find much of it incomprehensible. . . . My inability to understand it does not affect my assessments of its beauty or ugliness." (Characteristically he gives this confession a further twist by admitting that he finds Joyce Wexler's critical exegeses of

Riding "as difficult to follow as the poems themselves.") Again, of John Wheelwright: "Even where I cannot finally grasp his meaning, which is much of the time, I remain convinced by the extraordinary power of his language as it flashes by on its way from somewhere to somewhere else. At times it seems like higher mathematics; I can sense the 'elegance' of his solutions without being able to follow the steps by which he arrives at them."

It is an elegant solution to one problem of criticism to so casually dispose of the question of "understanding." Critics tend to dismiss the importance of what they cannot understand, if not to deny its existence altogether: as if an ornithologist were to conclude—as a means, say, of avoiding professional embarrassment—that a bird he could not satisfactorily assign to its genus had not actually flown by.

These two books cover a lot of ground; *Other Traditions* (based on Ashbery's Charles Eliot Norton lectures) surveys an entirely idiosyncratic grouping of "some poets who have probably influenced me" (Riding, Wheelwright, John Clare, Thomas Lovell Beddoes, Raymond Roussel, and David Schubert), while *Selected Prose,* edited by Eugene Ritchie, gathers from nearly five decades of writing, ranging from a 1956 review of Gertrude Stein's *Stanzas in Meditation* to a commentary written in 2004 on the South African poet F. T. Prince. (*Selected Prose* is mostly about writing, but there is some uncollected art criticism and a couple of film pieces—on Jacques Rivette's *Out One/Spectre* and Val Lewton's *The Seventh Victim*—that make one wish he had devoted a parallel career to writing about the movies.)

Each is a book that can be read—that almost insists on being read—at one sustained clip, even while the reader is constantly stopped short by suddenly emerging perspectives, as when moving through a landscape full of unexpected changes in coloring and vegetation and scale—and full too of stretches that might threaten monotony, except that it is the monotony Ashbery describes (in the 1956 Stein review) as "the fertile kind, which generates excitement as water monotonously flowing over a dam generates electrical power." (In a somewhat analogous manner he describes John Clare's poetry as "a distillation of the natural world with all its beauty and pointlessness, its salient and boring features preserved intact.")

Ashbery might be the tour guide leading the way along a roundabout path that without him would perhaps be hard to discern. He fills you in, as the walk proceeds, about bits of history and biography relevant to what you are observing, points out rock formations, tosses off useful suggestions for supplemental reading (pointing us toward "that strange and neglected hybrid masterpiece, Eliot's translation of St.-John Perse's *Anabasis*" or toward Marianne Moore's versions of La Fontaine, "among the truly miraculous works of our time"). He makes brief strategic stops for memorable views while never forgetting that the essential is to keep moving forward, even when the hikers might prefer to linger a little longer over a particularly picturesque valley or chain of peaks. (In a 1965 dialogue with Kenneth Koch included in *Selected Prose,* Ashbery remarks: "I think that if we like things that are evasive it's because there's no point in pursuing something that is standing still.") He states things with startling clarity—tosses out quick sketches dense with implications we scarcely have time to ponder—and has already moved further along the trail, toward another configuration. Compressed narratives, miniaturized landscapes, brief tantalizing speculations flash into visibility and as quickly disperse.

The Stein review, for example—to linger at the portal of *Selected Prose*—is four pages long yet achieves a kind of epic sweep with its succession of tiny set pieces, often embedded within subordinate clauses like stories within stories, as when "a single note on the celesta suddenly irrigates a whole desert of dry, scratchy sounds in the strings": it is the music of Webern pouring out in a whisper, as if to provide a soundtrack for the very sentence you are reading. It is rarely a matter of pointing out inert objects, but rather of tuning into events that are taking place in parallel dimensions, so that even while Stein's poem is unfolding a variety of other things are taking place elsewhere: de Kooning is painting, Webern is composing, and Henry James is writing *The Golden Bowl* and *The Awkward Age,* all at the same time, each process corresponding to "the painful continual projection of the individual into life." In the midst of this he has led us (by way of comparing Stein and the late James) into "a tropical rain-forest of ideas" (now there is a phrase worth inhabiting for a good long while) whose "texture of bewildering luxuriance . . . seems to obey some rhythmic impulse at the heart of all happening."

Paths lead to unexpected places; messages are delivered whose exact purport may be in doubt but whose urgency cannot be questioned. "How did we get from there to here, and what have we been told?" he writes of Joan Murray's poems. "As so often, this remains partly or even largely mysterious." Face to face with certain alluring fragments by Thomas Lovell Beddoes—

These are as many
As bird-roads in the air

or

The swan-winged horses of the skies
With summer's music in their manes

he asks: "Why not just stay here, trying to plumb the seemingly bottomless meaning of these fragments that are scarcely even chips?"

Rather than shrinking poetry down to size to get better control of it, Ashbery perpetually uncovers further enigmas and recesses, showing a particular work to be not less but more mysterious than imagined. In place of answers he provides further questions, not in the service of mystification but of a realism astringent enough to leave blank spaces for the unknown and the unfinishable, and wary enough to remain on the lookout for precisely what refuses to be nailed down, very much in the spirit of the poet dedicated to "living in a state of alert and being ready to change your mind if the occasion seems to require it." (He says of a David Schubert poem he particularly admires that "much of its effect comes from slight dislocations of grammar, so that one's expectations are constantly in a tense state.")

If this state of constant alertness and changeability entails bafflement it is a singularly knowing bafflement. Ostensible confusion reveals itself as a form of knowledge. Paradox is simple matter of fact: "The novel [de Chirico's *Hebdomeros*] has no story, though it reads as if it did." (What then is a story but something that reads as if it were a story?) Moments of apparent hesitance or qualification camouflage (as in a tropical rain-forest of ideas) a tenacious affirmation. By an oblique pivoting, sentences are made to yield up strange truths. Of Joe Brainard's work we are told: "The writing and the art are relaxed—not raging—in their newness, careful of our feelings, careful not to hurt them by so much as taking them into account." That *by so much as* has the characteristic feinting movement that so often leads to surprise just when we thought the sentence was already pretty much over. (On the question of the poet's consciousness of his potential ability to hurt the reader's feelings—a subject rarely addressed by critics—there is a corollary observation about John Clare: "Clare bears you no ill will and doesn't want to shock or pain you . . . if you suddenly burst into tears, that will seem to him another natural phenomenon, like the rain or the squeal of a badger.")

Likewise, discussing Jane Bowles's writing, he notes that "every line rings as true as a line of poetry, though there is certainly nothing 'poetic' about it, except insofar as the awkwardness of our everyday attempts at communication is poetic." *Except insofar as:* what a spiraling, offhand means of access to a statement—or is it a question?—with haunting implications. (True or false: the awkwardness of our everyday attempts at communication is poetic.)

Ashbery's criticism is densest where it seems lightest and breeziest. One could say it proceeds by stealth except that everything is in plain view. It offers a constant and welcome reinvigoration, a reminder of how it is to see things fresh, in dry and clarifying weather. "The effect of Clare's poetry, on me at least," he writes, "is always the same—that of re-inserting me in my present, of reestablishing 'now.'" Ashbery too has the ability—apparently without urgency, but as if it were a matter of course, and using what can seem the simplest of means—to reawaken the impulse to read, to write, to listen, to look at what is going on—to act.

The action to which *Other Traditions* most immediately prompted me was to turn to Clare and Beddoes and find their pages lit up with Ashbery's clarities—to come with renewed excitement to Clare's "drooping blossoms parch / Thirsting for water in the day's hot breath / Right glad of mud-drops plashed upon their leaves / By cattle plunging from the steepy brink" or the vicinity of his fallen elm "while darkness came as it would strangle light"—or, in the hectic maze of Beddoes's endless verse play *Death's Jest-Book,* to find the bright fragments—"the stars trembling in the trembling water" or "the little hiding holes of cunning thought" or "an ancient island where invisible honest men trade with invisible money"—so recklessly strewn about, as if written in

> . . . the alphabet,
> In which the hieroglyphic human soul
> More changeably is painted than the rainbow
> Upon the cloudy pages of a shower,
> Whose thunderous hinges a wild wind doth turn—

and to experience thus at a further remove the restless outward extension implicit in Ashbery's readings.

I'm Not Sure I Meant What You Said

Chinese Whispers (2002)

Robert Kelly

WE'RE ALL CHILDREN when it comes to language. The gaps between words are those long alleys that run between the rows of houses block after block in Chicago or Brooklyn. Kids play there, small crimes assemble and disperse, all invisible from the named streets. Language is to play in. If it stops playing, it becomes anything else, becomes grown-up, i.e., boring, dangerous, menacing. The impersonal nastiness of grownups is not soon forgotten, forgiven. You remember. If you don't, you're repressing.

Repression. When you hear someone whisper, all the repressed contents rush to return. Caress you. Penetrate the ear. Eek. Could she really have said that? The beauty of poetry is its immaturity. Poetry is always iffy, hence worth our immediate attention.

*

Please understand that when I talk about this book I'm not going to say anything that isn't perfectly obvious. I never do. I think only the obvious is much worth talking about, since that's what we share. But the obvious really needs attention. For one thing, it's always there. You might say with a grain of truth that the obvious is always up to something. That's what we have to keep track of. So, to judge a book by its cover is a smart move, or at least a move. *Provisoire.* And to judge by its name is even smarter.

*

Chinese Whispers. The title is so rich. I have to admit I chose this book to speak to because of its title as much as anything else. Of course I had to choose a later Ashbery, because by my sense of it (what we used to express by saying: "for my money") JA keeps getting better and better, more and more human, urbane, smarter, wiser.

Robert Kelly

For me, there is a great movement from the serene Virgilian self-absorptions of *Three Poems* on through the hectic alterity of *Flow Chart* out into the glad alertness of his later mode, when, master of all the grand prestiges of Oulipo and the whole Western poetic tradition, he just talks to us, talks to us hard.

Chinese whispers. The phrase itself teases—like those tricky Armenian Papers (which are made of paper but are scarcely Armenian, more French bourgeois of a slightly vanished time, incense sheets to burn in parlors) or French letters, which are not literary discourses at the Sorbonne. So Chinese whispers are not Chinese, except in the sense that anything you don't understand is Greek to me. I mean Chinese to me. Greek isn't exotic enough anymore.

Chinese whispers is the UK name for the game—or ecstasy, or make-out session, or oracle—that we used to call telephone. I whisper something to you, you whisper it to the one next to you, who whispers it to the next in line, on and on, until the circle finally brings the words back to me. And how changed they are, the words returning.

It's like a platonic Ouija board—only it works through dialectic (a whispered dialectic, as if a dialectic of *Gelassenheit* itself, as Heidegger might have called it). Only through the dialectic does the oracle *come into speech.*

So Chinese whispering argues a beautiful fresh poetics. It is a way of speaking by hearing.

> Like ivy behind a chimney
> it grows and grows in ropes.
> Mouse teams unslay it,
> yeomen can't hear it.

We know as we read these lines that we are hearing other lines besides, not that we know them or can read them exactly, but we know they're there, they're humming back behind the words we hear; somewhere not so far away, *mouse teams unslay it* has quite a different range of meaning. Here, and as so much in Ashbery's late work, he seems to be translating English into English homeophonically.

And that is surely the way we speak as we read poems, no less than when the poet, ear cocked for some offstage phonation, hears something and writes it down.

Chinese whispers, then, means *hearing the other but with one's own ears.* Everyman his own muse! *Écoutez!*

As I think about these matters, I recall (this is an intermezzo, pardon) our late friend the poet Dick Higgins, with whom I once planned an anthology of homeophonic translations, poems that heard the foreign language as if it were our own. To hear Swedish (Dick's largest trove worked from a poet of the Swedish Baroque) as if it were English, and write that English down. Our anthology was to be called *Sounds Like* (finger to the ear, as in charades, another wonderful game). End of funereal intermezzo.

Chinese whispers works by a word sounding like something else, sometimes like its own self too. When we play the game or read the book, sometimes the original word comes back unchanged through all those mouths. And that's a miracle too.

*

We all live in the same time, it turns out, even if we space ourselves through it differently. Although Ashbery himself seems fondest of late romantic and postromantic tonal music (he once remarked to me that Dukas's opera *Ariane et Barbe-Bleue* was a favorite of his), when I read his magnificent later poems, haunted as they are by gnostic sagacity and by sheer demotic rubble, I can't help thinking that on a structural level they have a lot in common with serial music, the whole twelve-tone thing, that was the canonic mode in classical music all through his (and my) young manhood and early maturity. His own powerful aesthetic presence has had a lot to do with the reemergence of a much more emotionally committed, more generous sort of tonal music in the eighties and after. I sense him as one of the begetters of that tonal turn, that willingness to be propositional in music, not just formally preoccupied. In this, as in so many ways (not least the ways he has encouraged art to be seen, neglected poets to be summoned from the tomb, rescued levels of discourse from triviality, rescued frivolity from fools), he is so much an innovator. An innovator of listening. An innovator of willingness. Ashbery is so willing.

That twelve-tone analogy comes to mind as a musico-structural equivalent of the leapingness of Ashbery line sequences. Just as in a proper tone row, none of the twelve tones can be used again till all the other eleven have been used, and used in the precise order the found or chosen "row" allows, so in the later Ashbery poem the reader has the constant refreshment of knowing about the line passing in front of the eyes that nothing of what is in the line will be spoken of again until everything else has been said about other things. Only then might it come again, but this time in a different octave of everything, itself returned in a new guise.

*

The entrance to his Early Late Period is marked for me by an embrace of time. He welcomes the temporal, in all senses—including the side of the head resting on the hand, the writer like the reader pondering.

I start thinking of how his work uses time. This is not Stevens with some idea always up his sleeve to keep him kosher, this is Coleridge all over the place, vulnerable to the leaps and freaks of his beloved Hartleyan psychology. These poems of JA bring strongly to mind the great conversation poems of STC—not especially because of the freight train of "free" associations shunting their way along, but exactly because of the way the poet consents to the inflection of time, the poem as time elapsing and elapsing through the mind, so to say. And this consent becomes: *the shaping of time by word* that is for me the simplest definition of poetry. The complex system of reference and allusion in Ashbery is balanced with a serenely lucid grammar—it is perfectly easy to understand what he isn't saying.

So (to take the clearest of them) "This Lime Tree Bower My Prison" shares a comfortable gloom with "Ornery Fish," a willingness to put up with what comes to mind. He allows it the time, the time to tell, bit by bit, so he can work from it, in this case, a mysterious narrative that culminates in dazzling imagery. And in our day, that alertness is real heroism. What could be braver than noticing, notating, what comes up? As the mind looks about itself, the day, the shattered yesterdays, the specious tomorrows, the kitchen and the shrine, what I'm told the Chinese call the Ten Thousand Things, i.e., the sacred everything.

So may I call Ashbery a heroic poet? I shall do so, and shame the devil. Heroic, and not least in the sense of the heroic couplet of our ancestors, who relished that crisp dyadic strategy as a means toward clean-cut statement and brisk colloquiality, aiming always to perforate the sententious wadding in which serious poetry for some reason always tends to wrap itself—romantic poets are always afraid of a draft.

*

Register against register. That is the famous mode or *style ashbérien*—and JA has famously let it be known that in his work he likes it well that any given line (and sculptural indeed his lines are, stately and quick by turns) is erased, effaced, by the line that follows—the reader dwells in the timeless present of the poem as it experiences itself and the reader at once. Hölderlin's "poetically [or "poetly"] we dwell" can hardly ever have been taken with such luminous directness.

But why? What does that timeless present serve? Poems are our way of shaping the experienced passage of time by language—they are not (one hopes) just ways of passing the time. (Beckett sourly points out that it would, will, pass anyhow, without our help.) What does Ashbery seek, or simply, what does he achieve, by this registral counterpoint, so incessant, so funny, so upwellingly refreshing?

Look at some lines from "Heavenly Days," the penultimate poem in the book:

> The colors, dark ocean maroon, we belong to in the sense that
>   earth belongs to us,
> more reassurance, and when day collapses it's the same—
>   a plight
> that is a solution. That's why I can never go back to
>   philosophy—
> its halls and chambers are a paradigm of emptiness, not the
>   real thing,

for only under stones is the knowledge
of underneath, and my desire is mammoth.
So it's decided. I'll pack my suitcase
or something, we have the tickets.

Earth, day, solution, philosophy, paradigm, emptiness, real—these are words that tempt poets deep into the propositional muck and mire—and Ashbery always seems busy propositioning everyone and everything—so one can, for a moment, almost forgive the academic critics who see Ashbery as aftermath, Son of Stevens, secular, humanist, philosophical, curious, serene. Almost, but not quite. Register saves us. The weighty pleonasm of "halls and chambers" affrights us; are we sailing blind into rhetoric? Then we stumble on the stones, and find that the knowledge that these stones convey is not that of some abiding angel of earth as in Stevens, but the bleakly satisfying knowledge of the literal, the underneath. We pick a thing up to see what it is, and what it conceals. Mammoth reminds us of big ancient mammals who are also "underneath," meant to be excavated and looked at, odd old things fit for the museum, stolen ivory to make rosary beads for shamans. It is from the solemnity of such reflections that Ashbery hastens, and hastens us—not for him Tennyson's (or Eliot's, or Stevens's) willingness to accept the burden of solemn reflection and carry it through fourteen lines to reach some closure or insight about it. No, a reflection is something to escape from while it is still fresh. An examined insight is no insight at all—it becomes a platitude, or a platform. Better to feel it, know it, and run for your life. Pack your suitcase—"or something," that magically effective descent into everyday Whateverese. We have the tickets, we have all we need to go.

Go next, young man.

So this curious dwelling is about going, I think. "There'll come a day when we'll live off noise," when the sound of our speed sustains us. As the beggar in Rabelais is, and is not, sustained by the smell of soup.

*

Some of Ashbery's poems accumulate, amass, amount to. Others dissipate, crumble pleasingly like cookies, the taste of each bite effaced by the next, not to speak of the alien taste that comes along, the coffee, the martini, the tisane.

Strange how he writes both sorts of poems, interweaves them too within some single text ("Her Cardboard Lover" is a good example), yet each seems so characteristic of him and his work. Of course critics, "moping and sincere, // like all exegetes," can make either kind of poem seem like the other kind by applying or withholding interpretation, strewing the path with footnotes or else throwing up their hands at Ashbery's waywardness.

My point in mentioning two kinds of poem, though, is just to talk about not the text per se (that dragon), but the experience of reading it. I'm talking about how a poem feels as it goes in. Or goes by. Here's the difference I'm talking about: the immediate experience. The poem goes by, or the poem goes in.

Imagine people actually playing a game of Chinese whispers. It might be the aural equivalent of Count Cagliostro's fatidic circle—you keep hearing and whispering until some one thing you hear seeps from your ears down to your heart, or even springs across that Zoroastrian razor-edged bridge into your brain, that well-guarded castle. One looks up, baffled, from the game, and understands that one knows something one never knew before. Something that somehow preposterously sustains.

Four Questions

Where Shall I Wander (2005)

James Longenbach

I. WHAT IS PROSE?

LISTEN TO THE SENTENCES with which John Ashbery's "Retro," published in *Where Shall I Wander,* concludes.

> The midnight forest drags you along, thousands of peach hectares. Told him I wouldn't do it if I was him. Nothing to halt the chatter of locusts until they're put away for the night. He edges closer to your locker. Why did I leave it open? I've forgotten the combination. But it seems he's not interested in the locker, maybe my shoe—something unlike anything he's ever known. Sensing the tension he broke the ice with a quip about the weather somewhere, or maybe—maybe an observation on time, how it moves vastly in different channels, always keeping up with itself, until the day—I'm going to drive back to the office, a fellowship of miles, collect some of last year's ammunition. Then I'm definitely going to the country, he laughs.

Nine sentences, the first of which establishes a scene and a mode of address ("The midnight forest drags you along"), the second of which seems unrelated to the scene and disrupts the mode, turning from the second person to a first-person account of a third person ("Told him I wouldn't do it if I was him"). The next sentence returns to the outdoor scene ("chatter of locusts"), but the following sentences establish a new scene, the interior of a school building. And while these sentences don't turn away from the new scene, they mix up the modes of address: "He edges closer to your locker. Why did I leave it open? I've forgotten the combination." Here, the "you" addressed at the beginning of the passage has merged with the "I" who first addressed the "you." Then, when the eighth and longest sentence returns to the first person after beginning in the third person, the "I" doesn't seem to be the same "I" who spoke earlier: instead, the "he" who edged toward the locker now seems to be speaking: "I'm going to drive back to the office, a fellowship of miles, collect some of last year's ammunition. Then I'm definitely going to the country, he laughs."

This passage sounds like prose, but it invokes the narrative logic we associate with prose while at the same time dismantling it. There's a whisper of continuity to these phrases ("drive back to the office"—"collect some of last year's ammunition"—"going to the country"), since one might imagine a reason for collecting the ammunition at the office before heading to the country. But the narrative links are suppressed, and the real pleasure of the passage lies in the way it leaps from one register of diction to another: the office, the ammunition, the country. Rather than fulfilling the expectations aroused by narrative logic, the passage foregrounds the disjunctive movement we associate more readily with poetry and in particular with lineated poetry. The freedom extolled in the poem's final sentence ("Then I'm definitely going to the country, he laughs") is embodied in the poem's disruption of the continuity of scene, diction, and address.

Or is it? Would Ashbery really want us to swallow such a commonplace, self-congratulatory notion of liberation? Could his sentences embody it? "Retro" asks these questions, for while it ends in prose, the first half of it is organized in lines.

II. WHAT IS A POEM?

Not all of the lines in "Retro" function in the same way: the interplay of different kinds of lines controls the pacing and intonation of the poem's syntax. This interplay is not in itself unique; it can be found in Milton or Williams, but it is more crucial in poetry that is not metered—and even more crucial than that in poetry that privileges sonic over semantic coherence. Listen to the first five lines of Ashbery's "Retro":

> It's really quite a thrill
> when the moon rises above the hill
> and you've gotten over someone
> salty and mercurial, the only person you ever loved.

Walks in the park are enjoyed.

The first two lines, marked by rhyme, parse the syntax, breaking it into predictable grammatical units ("a thrill / when"; "the hill / and"). Then the third line is more properly enjambed, increasing the tension between syntax and line ("someone / salty"). The fourth line is end-stopped, and, after the stanza division, the fifth line is not only end-stopped but syntactically complete. Reading the passage, regardless of what it says, we experience the sound of language making sense, a steady increase in the tension between syntax and line giving way to the stasis of confirmation: "Walks in the park are enjoyed." Listen to the rest of the lineated portion of the poem.

Going to Jerusalem now
I walked into a hotel room.
I didn't need a name or anything.
I went to Bellevue Hospital,
got a piece of the guy.
As I say, it's really quite a thrill.

Quite a thrill too to bend objects
that always return to their appointed grooves—
will it be always thus? Or will auto parts
get to have their day in the sun?

Got to drone now.
Princess Ida plans to overwork us four days a week
until the bracts have mauved up.
Then it's a tailgate party—
how would you like your burger done?

A little tea with that?

I saw her wailing for some animals.
That doesn't mean a thing doesn't happen
Or only goes away, or gets worse.
What's the worst that could happen?

The plain sense of these lines is more readily available than the sense of the prose passage that follows them: "Retro" is about the feeling of having been released from the fetters of prior experience. If we must work hard for four days, we can nonetheless look forward to the tailgate party. If we've lost the only person we've ever loved, we can nonetheless enjoy casual sex. We don't even need a name. If the work of bending objects "to their appointed grooves" once seemed thrilling, we can nonetheless look forward to the moment when objects might seem gloriously lacking in their previously appointed purpose. This wisdom applies both to auto parts, which might be yanked from the whole machine to glisten in the sun, and to sentences, which might be allowed to wander from the lines of a poem. "What's the worst that could happen," asks the last line that appears in "Retro," and the answer is the passage of nine unlineated sentences with which the poem concludes, the sentences with which I began. Formally as well as thematically, this poem appears to head for the open road.

But what about the tone of Ashbery's poem? Is "Retro" merely suggesting that walks in the park and one-night stands are to be preferred to the memory of the only person we've ever loved? That automobiles ought to be dismantled, their parts splayed across the lawn so we can recognize their true beauty? That we'll be happier if we give up the fetters of lineation and wallow in prose? That we'll be happier still if we forsake the narrative logic we associate with prose? That freedom can automatically be purchased at the expense of restraint?

III. WHAT IS A PROSE POEM?

Some poets—not Ashbery—have argued that the rejection of line carries a kind of political charge, just as poets once felt that the rejection of rhyming verse for blank verse or blank verse for free verse carried a political charge. This may be true in a particular time at a particular place—a very short time, a very parochial place. But it cannot be true categorically. The relationship between formal choice and ideological position is constantly shifting, and it's not possible to predict the repercussions of formal decisions except inasmuch as we might see them played out in the work of individual poets—except inasmuch, that is, as they give us pleasure.

As "Retro" suggests, it may be thrilling to consider what might happen to our sentences when we stop thinking about lines, just as it may be thrilling to consider what might happen to our lines when we stop thinking about meter and rhyme. But to say that such relinquishments are "really quite a thrill," as the opening line of "Retro" does, is to highlight the self-satisfaction that may too easily accompany such received notions of aesthetic risk. The very shape of Ashbery's "Retro" (a poem that begins in lines and ends in prose) suggests that we inevitably think about lineation when we read a prose poem, just as we think about the whole car when we admire the beauty of auto parts. Ashbery is not asking us to choose between different ways of organizing language in a poem; he is constitutionally incapable of narrowing the possibilities for poetry. Instead, he wants to liberate us from a too-familiar narrative of what constitutes our liberation. He wants to liberate us from the tyranny of risk as we have learned to recognize it.

IV. WHO IS JOHN ASHBERY?

To traffic in risk is, paradoxically, to arm oneself against the world; automatically one is to be congratulated, no matter what the outcome. John Ashbery is, in contrast, the least risky, the most gorgeously vulnerable poet in the language since Herbert. His signature tone, a tone more audible than ever in *Where Shall I Wander,* is deferential, restrained, embarrassed by its own capacity for wonder. This tone is variable enough to include moments of disgruntlement, moments of slapstick, but the poems are stitched together by a sensibility that does not confuse submission with resignation, shyness with powerlessness. Something larger than the poet himself is always at stake, and the stakes have never been higher than in Ashbery's most recent writing.

As "Retro" suggests, the passage of time has always been his subject; the poems embody the sweet bewilderment they also describe. But in retrospect, the poems from his first great period sound nervous about their vulnerability. Throughout the volumes of the midsixties to seventies (*The Double Dream of Spring, Self-Portrait in a Convex Mirror, Houseboat Days*), a whiff of preachiness accompanies the moments as they pass.

> This was our ambition: to be small and clear and free.
> Alas, the summer's energy wanes quickly,
> A moment and it is gone. And no longer
> May we make the necessary arrangements, simple as they are.

This need to allegorize the poetry's waywardness was long gone by the time Ashbery wrote the great volumes of the last ten years (*Wakefulness, Girls on the Run, Chinese Whispers*). In its place we find a giddiness that makes the earlier work sound, by comparison, positively stodgy.

> Before retiring the general liked to play a game of all-white
> dominoes,
> after which he would place his nightcap distractedly on the
> other man's crocheted chamber pot lid.
> Subsiding into a fitful slumber, warily he dreams
> of the giant hand descended from heaven
> like the slope of a moraine, whose fingers were bedizened with
> rings
> in which every event that had ever happened in the universe
> could sometimes be discerned.

The point of these two passages is pretty much the same, but in these lines from *Chinese Whispers* Ashbery merely celebrates the passage of time, leaving the commentary behind. His sentences have become longer, his diction more wild, his syntax more elegantly attenuated. But while the poems are showier, they seem less like the work of a show-off. They sound happy to exist, rather than needing to be justified.

Rogue moments of tenderness often break through the giddiness, no sooner glimpsed than gone. In contrast, Ashbery's achievement in *Where Shall I Wander,* the book in which "Retro" appears, is to have found a way to allow the quieter tone to structure entire poems, even the entire volume. The book's title is lifted from Mother Goose ("Goosey goosey gander, / Whither shall I wander?"), and every poem is infused with the combination of tenderness and menace that we associate with nursery rhymes. In "Coma Berenices," a parody of a family's annual Christmas letter, Ashbery's ear for the comic potential of inarticulate writing is acute, but our master of tone is not sneering. The exquisitely turned awkwardness of these sentences is a vehicle for emotional transparency.

> Mary and her little boy came by in August. We went to the fish place but I'm not sure if Lance (her boy) appreciated it. Children have such pronounced tastes and can be quite stubborn about it. In late September a high

> point was the autumn foliage which was magnificent this year. Casper took me and his wife's two aunts on a "leaf-peeping" trip in northern Vermont. We were near Canada but didn't actually cross the border. You can get the same souvenir junk on this side for less money Max said. He is such a card.
>
> November. Grief over Nancy Smith.

Where Shall I Wander is a book not of grief displayed or avoided but of grief inhabited in a plainly matter-of-fact way, as if it were a familiar side dish at every meal. "We went down gently / to the bottom-most step," says the book's opening poem. "There you can grieve and breathe, / rinse your possessions in the chilly spring." There's no illusion that our youth was free of grief, and neither is there any longing to be rid of it. Now Ashbery is a poet of the present, and he requires fewer defenses.

Wallace Stevens once remarked that while we possess the great poems of heaven and hell, the great poems of the earth remain to be written. Ashbery is writing those poems with the lack of fanfare that earth, for better and worse, deserves: listen again to "Retro."

> It's really quite a thrill
> when the moon rises over the hill
> and you've gotten over someone
> salty and mercurial, the only person you ever loved.

Ashbery has many imitators, but they have all gone after the giddiness or the preachiness. No one else can write like this, and we are lucky to be alive at the same moment as the one person who can.

What is prose? Prose is the sound of language organized in sentences. What is a poem? A poem is the sound of language organized in lines. What is a prose poem? According to its greatest living practitioner—a poet who, like Shakespeare, is also a writer of astonishing prose—the prose poem is something we had inevitably to invent in order to force ourselves to answer the first two questions correctly. Who is John Ashbery? Look above.

Would That a Worldly Country We Were

A Worldly Country (2007)

Susan Wheeler

THERE WAS A PERIOD in the seventies, early eighties, where the advice poets gave other poets—especially those their junior—was not to read poems by John Ashbery in large doses, just as they might advise not to board a plane full of typhoid sufferers for a flight, say, from Peoria to Auckland: just a small dose over the recommended homeopathic amount (if quarantine wasn't possible) was enough to fell a poet with the malicious virus, Ash-beri fever, which was generally described as "writing like him." If the worldly senior poet elaborated, it was something to the effect of its "style": "stream of consciousness," "obscurantist," "camp" or, simply, "no point to it." A few lined up in the long tradition of "Is he pulling one over on me?" (a tradition that had a high moment a decade later, when a physicist got what he claimed to be a dummy text through the peer-review process of those jargon-driven hotheads at *Social Text*).

Of course, this clear recommendation for only an inoculation dose was enough to send malcontents and poets under thirty running for standby on that very flight. There was so much brewing for American poets at the time—Oulipians and Fluxists rippling into some poets' practices, not really infection so much as elective surgery; a sudden noticing that there were some really good poets in other countries who should publish and read here; streams of new translations from the French and the Spanish, leading to other virus alerts for native English-language speakers whose poems seem to *be* in translation; anthropology and ethnography leaking into poets' reading and writing practices, even when ethno/anthro's growing circumspection wasn't growing fast enough in poetry, either; a big rift on the left coast between some poets with faith that grammar itself could be upended for political change and some poets without it; independent examples like Ai, or John Yau, or Barbara Guest, who paid attention—looking, reading—and who then went home to set up the field of ideas in their work as though they were showing up for studio practices: avidly, imaginatively, and without much fuss;

the collective endeavors and conflicts of the second generation of NY poets, while the funnyman of the first, Kenneth Koch, taught us how to teach; Buddhism, from Allen Ginsberg to Gary Snyder to the poet-editor of *The New York Times Book Review,* Harvey Shapiro; and the baton pass from the brilliant sad-sack friends John Berryman, Robert Lowell, and Elizabeth Bishop to a worldly colony of personal lyricists. Into this cacophonous frontier land wrote John Ashbery.

And all the balls in the air he seemed to volley.

For years, I haven't really thought about those early Ashbery warnings. In Scotland, Northern Ireland, and points to their south, you can still hear, "Oh, that one writes like Ashbery" with quaint frequency, but given our own provincialism, Americans can't really fault the misguided. Occasionally, on these shores, someone pops up (they missed Helen Vendler's, or Marjorie Perloff's, memos?) who filters John Ashbery into the Junk mailbox in their brain, where it and other castoffs—"language poetry," "performance poets," "Sylvia Plath," "elliptical poetry," "School of Quietude," or "feminist poetry," etc.—are the pinball pins struck by whole swaths of poets falling toward the chute of the dismissed, springing through the lobe from pin to pin, dinging the bells and lighting up, clinking like an ambient anthem. (Do swaths apply to nouns other than history and underbrush?) Thus, this offloading genius for cutting information overload boosts, to boot, the brain's bearer's focus on what poetry should be—you know, comprehensible, investigatory, oracular, self-promoting, community-based, material, rhymed, disruptive, denotative, permeable, performative, tiny burp, and so forth.

But hiking inland into *A Worldly Country*—and then, like a bumper car (a pachinko ball), making a zigzag of avid stopovers to the older lands—I thought of those warnings, and suddenly knew the contagion's cause; knew which cell it is that switches itself on, activating the virus.

Consider the book's barnstormer arrival, the title poem:

Not the smoothness, not the insane clocks on the square,
the scent of manure in the municipal parterre,
not the fabrics, the sullen mockery of Tweety Bird,
not the fresh troops that needed freshening up. If it occurred . . .

We know this guy. You've got your opening and outsized rhetorical flourish, here Auden's—Not the . . . not the; your pop culture in Tweety Bird; your dash of French surrealism—the insane clocks;

your half rhyme—square, manure, parterre; yr guffaw of the polis full of shit, and your knee-slapper's creepy turn to the mordant in fresh troops freshening up. When our suprahygienic infophobes offload "political poetry" to their pinball boards, it's not usually Ashbery they're thinking of. But readers whose firewalls are down know that he has given us some of our scariest zeitgeists—the world with which the poet negotiates his role in *Flow Chart* is more Orwell than Erewhon.

As we move further inland, however, the contraption of this poem begins to go haywire. The impeccable meter of the poem's first two lines becomes that of a windup toy winding itself down—a limp, a hiccup, a sudden seize. By a third of the way in, the poem's first complete couplets backfire and buck, the second mocking the poem itself in a turnabout on its "not . . . not . . ." Audenesque opening:

> Leftover bonbons were thrown to the chickens
> and geese, who squawked like the very dickens.
> There was no peace in the bathroom, none in the china closet
> Or the banks, where no one came to make a deposit.

Ashbery, fan of the "World's Worst Poet," the Scottish McGonagall (although anyone whose dentist has thrust a college effort upon him knows better), loves to see how closely he can skirt the title, and his mastery is such that even the most confounded among us can at least sense the joke, even if we be they who are unsure of the target and suspect it is we.

The poem's envoi pushes this claptrap breakdown to absurdity.

> So often it happens that the time we turn around in
> soon becomes the shoal our pathetic skiff will run aground in.
> And just as waves are anchored to the bottom of the sea
> we must reach the shallows before God cuts us free.

Were this simply a way to see how far the poem could be pushed aground, having a bit of fun, it could be any one of thousands of rompous efforts by younger poets who have taken the ground he laid and planted our own neon beds (lying in said beds has been, sometimes, a challenge). But as the skiff has sandbarred, it has taken on heavy water—or, to mix more metaphors, as the car wheels have spun, the gripping groove in the ice has grown deeper. For, in addition to the manure in the boxwoods/shit-in-the-square (so close to the last world war's shit-on-a-shingle) of the poem's second line and the "fresh troops" requiring "freshening up"; the consignment of only leftovers to all those called "chickens"; and no peace, nowhere, we have passed through these lines:

> In short all hell broke loose that wide afternoon.
> By evening all was calm again. A crescent moon
> hung in the sky like a parrot on its perch. [*n. mocking, squawking*]
> Departing guests smiled and called, "See you in church!"
> [*n. De-Nile having left Egypt to reside in Pers. Saviour in Texas.*]
> For night, as usual, knew what it was doing,
> providing sleep to offset the great ungluing
> that tomorrow again would surely bring.
> As I gazed at the quiet rubble, one thing
> puzzled me: What had happened, and why?
> One minute we were up to our necks in rebelliousness,
> [*n. in our tie-dye with our peyote bowls*]
> and the next, peace had subdued the ranks of hellishness.
>
> So often it happens that the time we turn around in
> soon becomes the shoal our pathetic skiff will run aground in . . .

Against the metrical breakdown, the assertions are as simple and limpid as a bell, and these strains, the metrical derailment and the rhetorical resolution, work against each other as ably as do time signatures and melodic lines in music by Alberto Ginastera or Trivium.

The reins of this conflict are taut in Ashbery's hands and, like the most expertly held reins, do not need to be gripped or pulled in order to reveal the control. The Doc Ashbery who wrote into town in the thick of a literal varmint infestation has, over time, polished what was always mastery of this paradox of control (like Frost's silken-tent woman, or a really gifted kindergarten teacher or, for that matter, this infested town, Manhattan). And this feat is pulled off in poem after poem, handled so offhandedly that we'd take it for granted if only it didn't provoke precisely a car-chase's fascination: when will it crash? and what will get totaled? The reader gapes at the monsoon of energy in the poem's cross-purposes setup, and in the suspense of the poem's very performance, each turn so light on its feet it has been called a Polaroid of consciousness or, variously, diffident in its aims and indifferent to its readers.

For this is what's catchy (it only having taken thirty years for it to dawn on me): he writes like a teenager. A really good teenager—Keats, for example (who was also keen on a most exacting, passionate diffidence: the holding of two contradicting "minds" at once), as almost every other Great Poet we can think of petered out gradually as their years added up.

Teenagers' incaution can command us to gape, draw toward them, per Humbert Humbert. We return *Rebel* or *Streetcar* to its Netflix sleeve wanting to be James Dean/Jim Stark or Marlon Brando/Stanley Kowalski and to experience that heady sense of being someone who, anywhere, at any time, might do *anything,* thereby (but not in order to: playing for a reaction neutralizes the effect) making watching us (read: reading us) irresistible to others. Although musicians, actors, even painters (think Mingus, the older Brando as Kurz, Philip Guston, and not only they, in the late seventies) seem able to sustain that "thin mercury sound," as another of their ilk has termed the imminent wildness (duende?) whistling through a song, writers in the less plastic arts haven't. So many bold, yawping works of literature have bolted early from the gate—for example, most of the work for which we know Byron and Rilke best, when they were barely in their twenties; or many of last century's canonical works, from "The Wasteland" to *Gravity's Rainbow* or *Portnoy's Complaint,* all written before their authors turned forty-five—that we don't expect much from our quinquagenarians, let alone those now eighty.

Try reading through *A Worldly Country* first thing in the morning, before sitting down to write your own poem, and tell me if you don't feel like the elephant with the figurines. Every move you make will seem overly labored, overtelegraphed; what you imagine is a glimmering dance from the light on the waves to the lit line of the electrocardiograph in stanza six will read back as lead-footed morass. So you try to get closer (*how does he do it?*) and pick up (*imitate*) some of that Midwestern, laconic vernacular (inspired, perhaps, by his "Back to brick basics for you, my man") and throw in some bad jokes. Now, you *could* be writing like a teenager but you're just writing like an adolescent and, at that, nowhere near a middling, let alone a good, one. Besides, the key things—the energy, the momentum, some conflict, some snarl—are needed, bad.

. . . Sure, their market research told
them otherwise, and we got factored into whatever
profit taking may be encumbering the horizon now,
as afternoon looms. We could ignore the warning signs,
but should we? Should we all? Perhaps we should.

This neocon bluff does confound after all we've assumed, especially after the exordium's snipe about that happy wave buh-bye not two feet from disaster and desperation. Where one of our chastening elders answered a journalist that his "Protect Song" was the protestiest of his many protest songs, the other has just exhorted us to "not fall back on the old excuses . . . / . . . We're not children any more. / Why not give real life a chance?" And then he channels "whatever / into my contingency, a vein of mercury / that keeps breaking out . . ." to challenge The Man, or Oneself, or whatever with:

You ask me what I'm doing here.
Do you expect me to actually read this?
If so, I've got a surprise for you—
I'm going to read it to everybody,

Quietude- or anti-Quietude-schooled poems' hiccups of feeling may feel tinny beside the tenderness of some of the worldly country's sweetest refrains.

There was little to be said, and we have already said it.
Here, I'll take you. You can repose in my arms
for the rest of the night, which will be blue
and gloriously understaffed.

Who has not wanted understaffing in the speed drills of our time's romances? And yet, to say so in fewer beats than are called for—an Irony Here sign—maims our trust: is this for real?

That one is real, I'd hazard, but it's still going out to you, Geoff Dyer and Rebecca Wilson, should your copy of *A Worldly Country* not yet have arrived when, in your long conscripting of JA sentences for jokes, you're short a new line.

It's this that makes magnets of John Ashbery's poems: the take-it-or-leave-it clean through bad puns, gravity, and invention; and the sense that when we've exited to the street—startled to see, still, daylight—the world, and what we see of it has changed.

NOTES ON CONTRIBUTORS

DIANE ACKERMAN is the author of many works of poetry and nonfiction, most recently *The Zookeeper's Wife, A War Story* (Norton).

RAE ARMANTROUT's most recent collection of poetry is *Next Life* (Wesleyan). Her *Collected Prose* was recently published by Singing Horse Press.

JOHN ASHBERY's newest books of poetry are *A Worldly Country: New Poems* and *Notes from the Air: Selected Later Poems* (both Ecco/HarperCollins and Carcanet, 2007). Since 1990 he has been Charles P. Stevenson Jr. Professor of Languages and Literature at Bard College.

RICHARD AVEDON (1923–2004) was one of the leading photographers of the last century. In addition to elevating fashion photography to an art form, he was a dedicated chronicler of the events and people who drove the history of his times.

MARTINE BELLEN's most recent poetry collection, *GHOSTS!*, is forthcoming from Spuyten Duyvil.

CHARLES BERNSTEIN has recently published *Girly Man* (University of Chicago), *Shadowtime* (Green Integer), and *Republics of Reality: 1975–1995* (Sun & Moon). He teaches at the University of Pennsylvania.

ANSELM BERRIGAN is the author of three books of poetry—*Some Notes on My Programming, Zero Star Hotel,* and *Integrity & Dramatic Life* (all Edge Books). From 2003 to 2007 he directed the Poetry Project at St. Mark's Church.

Author of six books of essays and a memoir, SVEN BIRKERTS will publish *The Art of Time in Memoir* later this year with Graywolf Press. He is editor of the journal *Agni.*

ROSANGELA BRISCESE is the managing director of Bard College's Ashbery Resource Center, sponsored by the Flow Chart Foundation.

JOSEPH CAMPANA is the author of *The Book of Faces* (Graywolf). Currently completing a book of poems called *Spring Comes to Ohio,* he teaches Renaissance literature and creative writing at Rice University in Houston.

J'LYN CHAPMAN is completing her doctorate in literature at the University of Denver. Her poems and images have recently appeared in *Sleepingfish.*

TIM DEE's *In Flight,* a memoir of a bird-loving life, will be published by the Free Press/Simon & Schuster in 2009. An anthology of bird poetry, coedited with Simon Armitage, is forthcoming next year from Penguin UK.

RICHARD DEMING is the author of two forthcoming books: *Listening on All Sides: Towards an Emersonian Ethics of Reading* (Stanford University) and *Let's Not Call It Consequence* (Shearsman). He is currently a lecturer in the English Department at Yale University.

MARCELLA DURAND is the author of *Western Capital Rhapsodies* (Faux Press), *The Anatomy of Oil* (Belladonna Books), and, forthcoming in 2008, *Traffic & Weather* (Futurepoem Books) and *Area* (Belladonna Books).

BRIAN EVENSON is the author of seven books of fiction, most recently *The Open Curtain* (Coffee House), which was a finalist for an Edgar Award, a Paterson Prize, and an IHG Award. He lives and works in Providence, Rhode Island, where he directs Brown University's Literary Arts Program.

WALTON FORD (born 1960) is an American painter whose work has been widely exhibited at galleries and museums throughout the United States and in France.

GRAHAM FOUST's latest book is *Necessary Stranger* (Flood Editions). He teaches at Saint Mary's College of California.

FORREST GANDER's most recent books include poems, *Eye Against Eye*; essays, *A Faithful Existence* (both Shoemaker & Hoard); and, with Kent Johnson, *The Night,* a translation of the masterwork of Bolivian visionary Jaime Saenz (Princeton University).

The most recent collection of essays by WILLIAM H. GASS is *Temple of Texts* (Knopf).

MERRILL GILFILLAN is the author of five books of essays and two collections of stories. Recent poetry publications include *Small Weathers* (Qua Books), *Undanceable* (Flood Editions), and *Selected Poems, 1965–2000* (Adventures in Poetry).

CHRISTIAN HAWKEY is the author of *Citizen of* (Wave Books).

BRENDA HILLMAN is the author of seven collections of poetry, including, most recently, *Cascadia* and *Pieces of Air in the Epic,* and, with Patricia Dienstfrey, she edited *The Grand Permission: New Writings on Poetics and Motherhood* (all Wesleyan).

MAUREEN HOWARD's novels include *A Lover's Almanac, Big as Life,* and *The Silver Screen* (all Viking). "Time Bends" is from *The Rags of Time,* the last of her novels of the four seasons. Characters who appeared in former novels reappear in commedia dell'arte fashion, some with the hope or chance of breaking the mold.

CATHERINE IMBRIGLIO is the author of the book-length poetry sequence *Parts of the Mass* (Burning Deck). She is currently working on a new book of poems entitled *Intimacy.*

ROBERT KELLY's most recent books are *May Day* (Parsifal), *Shame* (McPherson), *Sainte-Terre* (Shivastan), and *Lapis* (Godine/Black Sparrow). He teaches in the Program for the Written Arts at Bard College.

DAVID KERMANI is the author of *John Ashbery: A Comprehensive Bibliography* (1976). He is president of the Flow Chart Foundation, sponsor of the Ashbery Resource Center project for Bard College.

KEVIN KILLIAN is a poet, biographer, novelist, art writer, editor, and playwright. He lives in San Francisco, where he and Dodie Bellamy have edited over 140 issues of the literary/art zine *Mirage #4/Period[ical].*

JOHN KINSELLA's *Shades of the Sublime & Beautiful* and *Purgatorio: Up Close* are forthcoming next spring from Norton.

ANN LAUTERBACH's most recent books are *Hum* (Penguin) and *The Night Sky: Writings on the Poetics of Experience* (Viking), which is forthcoming in paperback from Penguin this spring. She is Schwab Professor of Languages and Literature at Bard College, where she also codirects the Writing Program in the Milton Avery Graduate School of the Arts.

SYLVIA LEGRIS's most recent poetry collection, *Nerve Squall* (Coach House Books), won the 2006 Griffin Poetry Prize and the 2006 Pat Lowther Memorial Award for the best book of poetry by a Canadian woman. Her poems in *Conjunctions* are from a manuscript titled *Pneumatic antiphonal.*

BEN LERNER is the author of *The Lichtenberg Figures* and *Angle of Yaw* (both Copper Canyon).

ERIC LINSKER was educated at Harvard University, where he received the Academy of American Poets Prize. His poems have appeared or are forthcoming in *Colorado Review, Columbia: A Journal of Literature and Art, Denver Quarterly,* and *Web Conjunctions.*

JAMES LONGENBACH is the author of three collections of poems, most recently *Draft of a Letter* (University of Chicago). He has also written about John Ashbery in *The Resistance to Poetry* (Chicago) and in *The Art of the Poetic Line,* forthcoming next spring from Graywolf Press. He teaches at the University of Rochester.

RICK MOODY's most recent publication is *Right Livelihoods: Three Novellas* (Little, Brown).

MICAELA MORRISSETTE's book reviews recently appeared in *Jacket,* and her article on new resources in Ashbery studies was published last spring in *Lit,* as well as in illustrated form at www.flowchartfoundation.org/arc. She is a senior editor at *Conjunctions.*

YANNICK MURPHY's three novels are *Signed, Mata Hari* (Little, Brown), *Here They Come* (McSweeney's), and *The Sea of Trees* (Houghton Mifflin). Her short story collections include *Stories in Another Language* (Knopf) and *Ina Bear's Eye,* forthcoming next year from Dzanc Books. Her children's books include *Ahwoooooooo!* and the forthcoming *Baby Polar* (both from Clarion Books).

EILEEN MYLES's newest book of poems is *Sorry, Tree* (Wave Books).

HOWARD NORMAN's most recent book is the novel *Devotion* (Houghton Mifflin). This autumn he traveled in Japan for six weeks along Basho's "Journey to the Far Provinces" for *National Geographic.*

GEOFFREY O'BRIEN's poetry has been collected in *Red Sky Café* and *A View of Buildings and Water* (both Salt), and his books of prose include *Sonata for Jukebox: An Autobiography of My Ears, The Browser's Ecstasy* (both Counterpoint), and *The Phantom Empire* (Norton). He is editor in chief of the Library of America.

PETER ORNER is the author of *Esther Stories* (Houghton Mifflin) and *The Second Coming of Mavala Shikongo* (Little, Brown), winner of the Bard Fiction Prize, and a finalist for the *Los Angeles Times* Book Award. He is on the faculty at San Francisco State University.

JED PERL is the art critic for *The New Republic.* Among his books are *Paris Without End: On French Art Since World War I* (North Point Press), *Eyewitness: Reports from an Art World in Crisis* (Basic Books), and, most recently, *New Art City: Manhattan at Mid-Century* (Knopf).

Among JOAN RETALLACK's six volumes of poetry are *How to Do Things with Words* (Sun & Moon) and *Errata 5uite* (Edge Books). She is also author of *Musicage: John Cage in Conversation with Joan Retallack* (Wesleyan) and *Poetry and Pedagogy: The Challenge of the Contemporary* (Palgrave MacMillan, coedited with Juliana Spahr), among other works. She is John D. and Catherine T. MacArthur Professor of Humanities at Bard College.

ELIZABETH ROBINSON is the author of eight collections of poetry, most recently *Under That Silky Roof* (Burning Deck) and *Apostrophe* (Apogee). Phylum Press has just published a chapbook-length sequence of poems, *The Golem,* and a new book, *Inaudible Trumpeters,* is forthcoming from Harbor Mountain.

DAVID SHAPIRO's most recent book is *New and Selected Poems* (Overlook), and a volume about his poetry, *Burning Interiors: The Poetry and Poetics of David Shapiro,* edited by Thomas Fink and Joseph Lease, has just been published by Fairleigh Dickinson.

REGINALD SHEPHERD's five books of poetry include *Fata Morgana, Otherhood,* and *Some Are Drowning* (all University of Pittsburgh). He is the editor of *The Iowa Anthology of New American Poetries* (University of Iowa), and his essay collection, *Orpheus in the Bronx,* is forthcoming next year from the University of Michigan.

DAVID SHIELDS's *The Thing About Life Is That One Day You'll Be Dead* will be published by Knopf in February 2008, and *Reality Hunger: A Manifesto* is forthcoming from the same publisher in September 2009.

The University of California Press published RON SILLIMAN's *The Age of Huts (compleat)* in 2007, and his long poem *The Alphabet* will be published in 2008 by the University of Alabama Press. He is part of the ten-author collective producing a collaborative history of poetry in San Francisco in the 1970s, entitled *The Grand Piano.*

D. E. STEWARD's "Sandhills in Chukotka" is one of 252 months, the fifth to appear in *Conjunctions* (with one more in *Web Conjunctions*). Running month to month, the full project stands now at seven books of three years each.

Among SUSAN STEWART's many books of poetry and prose is *Columbarium* (University of Chicago), which won the 2003 National Book Critics Circle Award. A new book of poems, *Red Rover,* is forthcoming this fall, also from Chicago. She is a former MacArthur Fellow, a current Chancellor of the Academy of American Poets, and the Annan Professor of English at Princeton University.

PETER STRAUB's eighteenth novel, *The Skylark,* will be published by Doubleday in fall 2008.

COLE SWENSEN is the author of eleven books of poetry, most recently *The Glass Age* (Alice James Books). *Ours: The Gardens of André Le Nôtre* is forthcoming next year from the University of California. She teaches in the Iowa Writers' Workshop.

ARTHUR SZE's latest book is *Quipu,* published by Copper Canyon. He is a professor emeritus at the Institute of American Indian Arts and is the first poet laureate of Santa Fe.

NATHANIEL TARN's latest books are *Selected Poems* (Wesleyan) and *The Embattled Lyric* (Stanford).

MELANIE RAE THON's most recent books are the novel *Sweets Hearts* (Editions de l'Olivier) and the story collection *First, Body* (Owl Books). Her work has appeared in *O. Henry Prize Stories, 2006; Pushcart Prize XXX* and *XXXII; Five Points;* and *Drumlummon.* She teaches at the University of Utah.

ANNE WALDMAN is the author of *Outrider* (La Alameda Press), *Structure of the World Compared to a Bubble* (Penguin Poets), *In the Room of Never Grieve: New & Selected Poems* (Coffee House), and *Marriage: A Sentence* (Penguin Poets). She is the cofounder with Allen Ginsberg of the Jack Kerouac School of Disembodied Poetics at Naropa University, where she is artistic director of the Summer Writing Program.

MARJORIE WELISH's most recent books of poetry include *Word Group* and *Isle of the Signatories* (both Coffee House). *Of the Diagram: The Work of Marjorie Welish* (Slought Books) gathers essays about her practice.

Among SUSAN WHEELER's most recent books are one of poems, *Ledger* (University of Iowa), and a novel, *Record Palace* (Graywolf).

C. D. WRIGHT's most recent book is *One Big Self: An Investigation,* published by Copper Canyon, which will also publish her forthcoming *Rising, Falling, Hovering.*

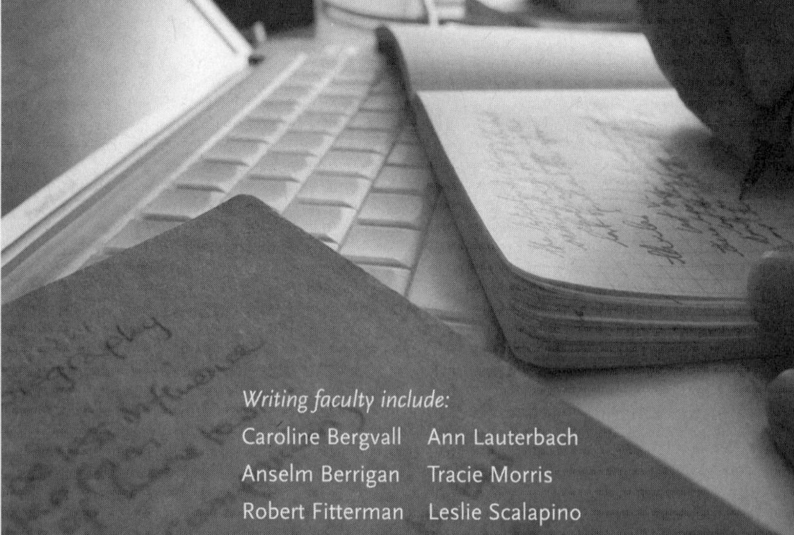
Writing faculty include:
Caroline Bergvall
Anselm Berrigan
Robert Fitterman
Carla Harryman
Paul La Farge
Ann Lauterbach
Tracie Morris
Leslie Scalapino
David Levi Strauss

Congratulations to

Salvador Plascencia

Winner of the

2008 Bard Fiction Prize

Salvador Plascencia, author of *The People of Paper*, joins previous winners Nathan Englander, Emily Barton, Monique Truong, Paul La Farge, Edie Meidav, and Peter Orner.

The Bard Fiction Prize is awarded annually to a promising emerging writer who is an American citizen aged thirty-nine years or younger at the time of application. In addition to a monetary award of $30,000, the winner receives an appointment as writer in residence at Bard College for one semester without the expectation that he or she will teach traditional courses. The recipient will give at least one public lecture and meet informally with students.

For more information, please contact:

Bard Fiction Prize
Bard College
PO Box 5000
Annandale-on-Hudson, NY 12504-5000

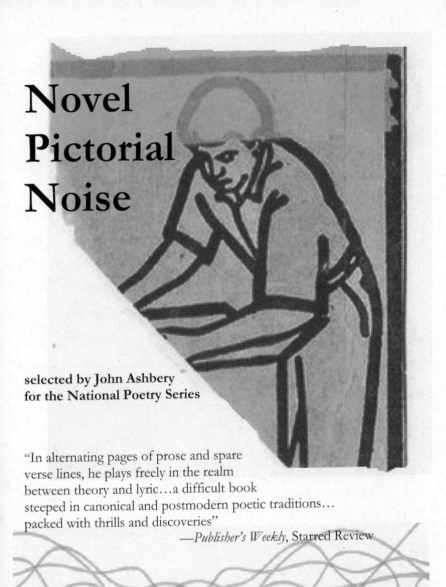

NOON

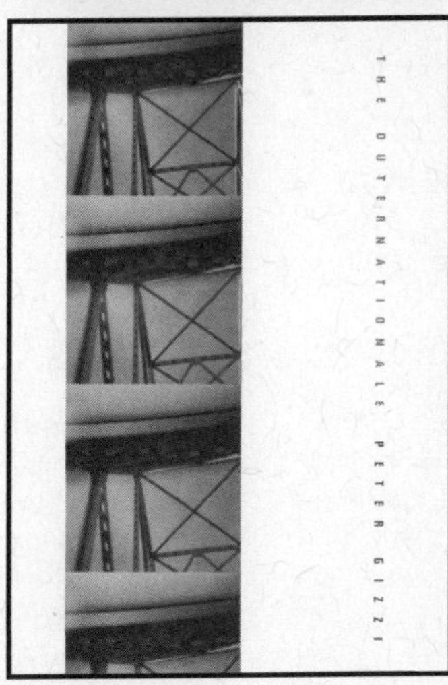
THE OUTERNATIONALE PETER GIZZI

"These outrageous and ferociously strange stories test the limits of behavior, of manners, of language, and mark Diane Williams as a startlingly original writer worthy of our closest attention." —**BEN MARCUS**

It Was Like My Trying to Have a Tender-Hearted Nature

A Novella and Stories

DIANE WILLIAMS

The University of Alabama Press
http://fc2.org